the PAINS of IMPRISONMENT

edited by

Robert Johnson
Hans Toch

Foreword by **Christopher S. Dunn**

WAVELAND PRESS, INC.
Prospect Heights, Illinois

For information about this book, write or call:
Waveland Press, Inc.
P.O. Box 400
Prospect Heights, Illinois 60070
(312) 634-0081

1988 reissued by Waveland Press, Inc.

ISBN 0-88133-369-7

Printed in the United States of America

7 6 5 4 3 2

Contents

To the memory of
Michael J. Hindelang

Foreword

Today's prisons are increasingly perceived as instruments of retribution. That being so, why be concerned with the pains of imprisonment and the programs that can ameliorate these difficulties?

Briefly stated, there are three related reasons for maintaining a humanitarian focus in corrections today, in spite of the prevailing punishment philosophy. These are:

(1) Only the continued application of social science perspectives (of the kind presented in this volume) produces crucial knowledge about the human effects, impacts, and harms of punishment.

(2) These harms must be revealed and understood because correctional practice is (rightly) constrained to be constitutionally responsible, thereby requiring the state to prevent certain harms to prisoners or to provide certain services for prisoners.

(3) The prevention of these harms or the provision of these services are not "do nothing" activities designed to fill a void left by the putative demise of rehabilitation, but instead are facilitated by and benefit from the knowledge, skills, and continuing involvement of mental health perspectives and workers.

If nothing else, the chapters in this volume collectively present a new and qualitatively different awareness and recognition of the effects of living and working in correctional institutions. The pictures of daily pain, deprivation, and suffering traced in this book are different from those revealed by the lenses of narrow disciplines concerned with corrections, such as sociology, organizational behavior, public administration, social work, or even traditional clinical psychology and psychiatry. As in the case of the blindfolded men describing the elephant, the part revealed depends upon the part observed, and segmental perspectives—as important to the whole picture as they are—are simply wanting in regard to concepts and tools that can fully describe and document the harms of imprisonment.

That being so, the question arises: Upon what must more comprehensive lenses focus attention? Relatedly, why is that still important? If the principal aim of corrections is punishment, the pictures presented in this volume represent information about the experience of punishment, including all its demands, struggles, pains, sufferings, coping and adjustment processes, breakdowns—summarized simply, all its *human* effects and consequences.

What is the rationale and need for such knowledge? Although the argument has been that no utilitarian rationale is required for adopting a retributive penal philosophy (that is, punishment need not be pursued because it deters or prevents crime), there is nevertheless a responsibility to know and understand the effects and consequences of punishment. That in part is what it means not to throw away the key. Precisely because our correctional policies and practices are accountable to some more fundamental principles, we have the responsibility to know the effects and consequences of whatever specific policy or practice is adopted.

First and foremost among these principles is the Eighth Amendment proscription against "cruel and unusual" punishment and its evolving criteria of whether the punishment in question is: (1) so barbarous as to shock the conscience; (2) grossly disproportionate to the offense; or (3) unnecessary and wanton infliction of pain. Despite the mentally unhealthy impacts of the conditions and processes described in this book, it is physically harmful conditions that have been most commonly encompassed within "cruel and unusual" as practices adjudged to remain outside "civilized standards of decency." Nevertheless, courts have recognized a number of conditions within correctional institutions that, if present, have serious mental health consequences *and* fall within the scope of the criteria for "cruel and unusual." They are: (1) negligent protection or abuse of personal safety; (2) dangerous and debilitating overall conditions of confinement; and (3) denial of access to medical or mental health care. Of these, two—the protection of personal safety and the overall conditions of confinement—indirectly involve major mental health problems such as pervasive fear and chronic anxiety; the third requires the provision of mental health services given identification of serious and treatable mental illness. Thus, despite a retribution policy for corrections, mental health problems and services are validly related to the constitutionally responsible practice of corrections.

Of course, it is not argued *a fortiori* that mental health services are constitutionally required in prisons for rehabilitation or to treat daily coping failures and adjustment problems. Apparently, only serious mental disease or life-threatening emergencies (such as psychotic breakdowns, self-mutilation, attempted suicide) *require* psychological or psychiatric service. However, in failing to act more comprehensively in view of the many problems and crises portrayed in this book, a first principle of intervention that should be adopted by all human service workers or screened for in their selection is violated: *primum non nocere*—first, do no harm. The value of this first principle of medical intervention was first recognized for criminal justice and corrections by

Silberman (in *Criminal Violence, Criminal Justice*), in its labeling or "schools for crime" sense: It can be argued that prisons and punishments cause more crime than they prevent or deter. I suggest that the relevance of that principle for this book's discussions of fear, stress, flawed coping and adjustment, and the role of mental health services is more limited but nonetheless important. I suggest that *to do no harm means to ameliorate human suffering and prevent personal breakdown.*

The rationale for a continued mental health role in corrections is that "an ounce of prevention is worth a pound of cure." Psychiatric disorders and psychological harm are inevitable aspects of correctional practice under today's conditions and for the foreseeable future. This volume documents in detail these unavoidable consequences of punishment, and in so doing provides the only available means for identifying likely victims, for understanding their vulnerabilities and problems, and for marshaling human resources (the only available resources) to combat stress and its harms.

Limited mental health resources must be directed equally at preventing stress and breakdown and at providing required treatment. Specifically, this means tackling the tough issues of reducing fears for personal safety, learning to cope with environmental deprivations, and providing relevant treatment for severely disordered offenders.

—*Christopher S. Dunn, Ph.D.*
Center for Studies of Crime and Delinquency
National Institute of Mental Health
U.S. Department of Health and Human Services

Preface

Rehabilitation used to be a respectable and even popular goal of prisons, but one doesn't hear much about it these days. Today, we seek to inflict a just measure of psychological pain or discomfort upon offenders, and let the matter of punishment go at that. This approach has appeal because it seems direct and to the point. Incarceration is necessarily painful, and indeed prisons have come to be virtually synonymous with punishment in the modern mind. But achieving just punishment in the prison is a deceptively difficult task. This will be clear to our readers, we trust, after even a cursory reading of this reissued anthology of essays on the pains of prison life.

One difficulty with the search for a just measure of pain in prison is that it is impossible to distribute the pains of imprisonment in any systematic or rational way. Some of the pressures of life in prison are both unintended and, under present conditions, largely uncontrolled. Crowding and victimization, including the sometimes ferocious violence of riots, are salient examples (see Part I). Other pains of confinement vary as functions of time and setting, or are determined in large measure by the personal susceptibilities of different offenders (see Parts II & III).

From the point of view of justice, these variations in suffering are inherently arbitrary because they are unrelated to the culpability of individual offenders. What is worse, such variations can be flagrantly unjust. Pretrial detainees, for example, though presumed innocent, often live in the bleakest penal environments and have the highest rates of suicide. Too often, hardened offenders with long records of violence do the easiest time in the most accommodating prison milieus, while callously exploiting their weaker but more deserving peers. That some prison staff countenance or even contribute to such abuses simply makes matters worse.

Arbitrary and unjust prison conditions are the bane of the correctional administrator's existence. They undermine the moral order of the prison, which is premised at least in part on a rough notion of defensible punishment. These conditions also make for instability and unrest. As a practical matter, then, the goal of punishment in prison often amounts to a quest for humaneness. The aim is to mitigate the pains of prison life, in the hope that we can maintain a decent order behind bars and do no harm to those we incarcerate. Accordingly, prison administrators worry less about punishing prisoners and more about sheltering them from indifference or abuse. This volume is responsive to such concerns. It makes a contribution to the modest though important goal of running humane prisons, for its purpose is quite explicitly to consider how we might better understand and ameliorate the inevitable pains of imprisonment.

Humane prisons seek to punish but not to harm offenders. They serve retribution rather than revenge, and this is a distinctively *civilized* undertaking. Humane prisons are also potentially *civilizing* because they allow prisoners to learn from their suffering. Inmates of humane prisons serve hard but potentially constructive time. Therein may live the roots of just punishment in prison.

As Plato long ago made clear, a just punishment must always hold out to the offender the prospect of moral education and, hence, personal reform. The person subjected to punishment should emerge, in Plato's words, "a better man, or failing that, less of a wretch" (Laws, 854d). Plato's point was that punishment should mete out redeeming pain, not debilitating harm. If prisons are to be settings of just punishment, then the pains wrought by imprisonment must be kept within humane limits and must be, moreover, incentives to personal reform. Interventions that address this more ambitious correctional agenda are examined in Parts IV & V of this book.

The pains of imprisonment can be a stimulus to self-scrutiny and an occasion for personal reform. The challenge is to arrange our correctional resources to promote growth through adversity. That challenge, though daunting, is one worth taking up. To the extent that this anthology moves us a step closer to achieving that goal, it will have served a fruitful purpose.

Robert Johnson
The American University
1988

CHAPTER 1

Introduction

ROBERT JOHNSON and HANS TOCH

One of the striking things about prisons is that we make no bones about the fact that we intend them to be uncomfortable. This feature is implied by two of prisons' most popular goals, punishment and deterrence, and it is a fond desideratum in the public's view of prisons. It is also a fact that has been sanctioned (one is tempted to say "sanctified") by the courts. In a recent ruling, the Supreme Court held that "to the extent that (prison) conditions are restrictive and even harsh, they are part of the penalty that criminal offenders must pay for their offenses against society" (Rhodes v. Chapman, 101 S. Ct. 2392, 1981). The Court's majority not only concluded that "the Constitution does not mandate comfortable prisons," but that "prisons . . . which house persons convicted of serious crimes, *cannot be free of discomfort*" (p. 2400; emphasis added).

Lines get drawn around definitions of appropriate and inappropriate discomfort. Such line drawing can be wild and ludicrous, as when depressing fortresses are classed as "country clubs," and it can be fateful and serious, as when courts decide (as they frequently have) that individual prisons, or whole prison systems, are unfit for habitation (Rhodes v. Chapman, p. 2404, n 2).

Some line drawing reflects emotions and sentiments, such as vengefulness and compassion. One senses the former feeling in conversations frequently overheard at lunch counters or taverns about inmates-in-general or those inmates involved in recent publicized offenses. The public's threshold for pains to which it would like to see inmates subjected is clearly high. Elsewhere, as among prison critics (see, for example, Alper, 1974; Nagel, 1973; American Friends Service Committee, 1971; Shaw, 1946), the accepted threshold is low enough to exclude most, if not all, prisons. Such emphases are often nonrational, but never always so because they rest partly on well-considered premises. The critic sees the inmate as a human being who happens to be in prison because he or she is disadvantaged and discriminated against. The public sees the inmate as a Doer of Foul Deeds (most likely to resume doing foul deeds) who has demonstrated consistent callousness and abrogated claims to compassion.

Judgments of this kind are *on the average* irreconcilable; however, *when focused on individual inmates* they sometimes converge. Some offenders generate fear and revulsion; others are pitiful enough (very young, old, harmless) to preclude disinhibition of anyone's empathy. Inmates range from those whose humanity is salient to those who strike us as unregenerate. The better we get to know individuals, the less easily they fit into preordained stereotypes.

Our sentiments about what is appropriate prison discomfort relate partly to our views of habitability, or about minimally acceptable quality of life. There are settings—rat-infested dungeons, for example—that few of us would countenance, and others—white-collar prison camps replete with tennis courts—that most of us would deem excessive luxury. Again, as we get to know individual prisons, they (like inmates) are less easily stereotyped.

Our sentiments also relate to our view of prison goals. The problem of goals is always confounded by the question, "Whose goals?" A judge has one end in mind when sentencing someone; the warden in whose institution the convict serves time has other objectives. The convict's incarceration and the way he or she experiences it are more intimately affected by some "purposes of prison" than they are by others.

The public sees prisons as a way to (1) get offenders off the streets, and (2) teach them a lesson. The first goal is that of exile or incapacitation; the second is mostly retribution, with a dash of hope for reform or rehabilitation. Judges typically see themselves in the business of fairly and equitably dispensing punishment; they emphasize *fairness* of punishment rather than any bloodthirsty punitive aim. Other extramural consumers of prisons—police, prosecutors, and legislators—may hope they can deter would-be criminals through prisons that are inhospitable enough to neutralize temptation. The same logic applies (decreasingly) to criminals who experience prisons and are loath to return to them.

In the past, prison administrators sometimes saw themselves as in the punishment business, but no corrections official today defends such a goal. To create pain is not what administrators do intentionally. Pure punishment is a real goal only in a prison where staff serve as in-house judges in disciplinary actions against violators of rules. The principal aims, ends, or goals of wardens are different. Wardens must store inmates. They must feed, clothe and protect inmates, must offer them vocational and recreational activities, must provide educational, medical, and mental health services, must permit access to mail, visits, and libraries (including law libraries), and must furnish basic amenities. The goal of wardens and other officials is to deploy their staff and resources to service inmates to the extent budgetary constraints permit. The *bottom line* is storage. Whatever the prison does, it must retain and restrain inmates. Other bottom-line goals are maintenance (keeping the prison running) and security (preventing riots and minimizing violence and in-house crime). Beyond these aims are program-related concerns such as education and training. The goals are to help inmates remedy deficits or improve themselves (rehabilitation) and to enhance the inmates' chances of "making it" after release (reintegration). Pain and stress are the undesired ingredients of prison life the official must live with. As constraints (such as crowding) increase the harshness of imprisonment, *ameliorating stress* becomes a new and salient goal. Unsurprisingly, many officials come to join prisoners, civil rights groups, and federal judges in the shared desire to modulate the impact of runaway retributive aims.

Punishment is an aim that requires that all inmates experience discomfort in prison. Punishment presupposes pain that is graduated to be commensurate with the prisoner's offense. The neatest formula assumes a constant level of discomfort, with time of incarceration (length of sentence) equaling the sum of discomfort (von Hirsch, 1976). Deterrence seeks "diminishing returns" for crime; discomfort must be higher (but only *just* higher) than gains derived from offenses (van den Haag, 1975). The deterrence of would-be offenders is pegged on *anticipated* rewards and *feared* discomfort. The crime recruit's impression of prison must be unfavorable enough for him or her to desist from incipient criminality (he or she must be "scared straight").

There are other aims that do not oppose inmate distress, but seek to limit and channel it. Reformation of inmates presupposes some limit setting and favors deployment of constructive (as opposed to disabling) anxiety. Reintegration requires transferability of prison experience to free-world experience, which is not possible where sharp disjunctures exist between the environment where one learns and the world where one lives. In reintegration we test the offender's capacity to cope. Stress that overtaxes coping capacity reduces coping skills and resources, and is counterproductive.

No aim of prison—including retributive punishment—is served by arbitrary, gratuitous, ill-distributed distress. Nor is any aim served by distress that is experienced by vulnerable men and women but not by tough, strong, and resilient ones. To inflict discomfort in service of a goal, but only *equitably* and *up to a point*, implies that stress and adjustment can be measured and orchestrated. Unfortunately, this is often untrue. To be sure, gathering and assessing facts about stress are easy in extreme cases. We can agree, for instance, that food must sustain life, or that it must be prepared in sanitary ways. We can also agree that suicides should not be generated, or that inmates should not be driven insane. Factual questions can then be asked—questions that can be answered with facts, such as facts about the incidence of beri beri, the prevalence of cockroaches, or the number (and types) of inmate fatalities and breakdowns.

But this enterprise is difficult to conduct dispassionately when stress and its consequences are less obvious or dramatic, as is often the case in prison. Where reasonable people can disagree about the nature and import of stress, biases can determine the facts we accept and the way we assess them. Some prison critics may assert that solitary confinement destroys the mind. They may base such assertions on vignettes from inmate autobiographies and on data from experiments that show disorienting effects of sensory deprivation. Others may derive reassurance from simulated segregation studies, and may question the representativeness of inmate accounts and the generalizability of laboratory findings (Suedfeld, 1980). Such battles are of necessity inconclusive, but they are waged because there is a great deal at stake. Science is a hard game to play where policy implications are immediate and where we are concerned about the consequences of our findings.

Scientifically accurate answers about prison stress may be hard to come by, but correctives to flagrantly misguided inquiries exist. Some that are most relevant to us include: (1) centering on the *promotion of humaneness* as a desideratum, a policy implication that remains relevant irrespective of our other values; (2) a commitment to *science as exploration*, the assumption that no matter how much we *think* we know, Plato's dictum "I know nothing" is the best starting point; (3) reserving policy questions for *last*, rather than garnering and viewing data with one eye on their deployment; (4) staying close to the phenomena being explored, attuned to their concreteness and uniqueness; (5) differentiating recommendations we base on *immediate* data from those that are more remotely derived; (6) accommodating complexity, recognizing that (a) it always precludes certitude because of variables that confound (or may confound), and (b) it always yields action implications that are multifaceted and differentiable.

Our book is not the final word on how science should be deployed to assess and ameliorate prison discomfort. Neither is it the first to frame the problem of prison stress in relation to prisoner adjustment. Our work has antecedents in a line of research and scholarship aimed at understanding the undesirable impacts of prison and improving the conditions of prison life.

An obvious debt is owed to Gresham Sykes. Over a quarter of a century ago, Sykes eloquently described the pains of imprisonment that afflicted prisoners and the various social roles and mores that guided their adjustment efforts. As Sykes (1966, p. 79) saw it, five basic deprivations—of liberty, goods and services, heterosexual relations, autonomy, and personal security—together dealt a "profound hurt" that went to "the very foundations of the prisoner's being." The prisoner thus wounded sought and found a modicum of support from his peers, and tried to take refuge behind a facade of calculated equanimity in the face of stress. He somctimes played one or more convict roles, such as merchant, gorilla, or tough, and advertised himself as cold, hard, and unfeeling—in a word, manly. His prison offered few programs, be they vocational, educational, or psychiatric, and little correction. His guards were custodians who trafficked with the convict elite to ensure compliance from the multitude of nondescript and powerless inmates over which they uneasily rode herd. Authority born of staff collusion with prisoners proved unstable, as the prisoner elite invariably sought to extend its power at the expense of its keepers' corrupted virtue. Periodic disturbances and occasional riots emerged as fixed costs of running confinement institutions. Recidivism rates were high.

Much of Sykes's work applies to today's prisons. Deprivations remain basic and painful, some convicts play stylized subcultural roles, and guards sometimes compromise principles to maintain order. Prisons still explode in senseless violence. Too many felons still find their way back to prison.

But prisons have changed, for better and for worse. Until recently, inmates saw their fate improved in a number of ways, ranging from increments in privileges to an expanded spectrum of program options. Veteran inmates returning to prison might be pleased (and often were) by proliferating developments such as staffed law libraries, expanded visiting privileges, reduced censorship, self-help groups, and grievance procedures; they might be surprised (though not necessarily pleased) by a more loose, more relaxed, less structured and regimented climate. Though changes have been described as incremental and inconsequential rather than qualitative (Murton, 1976; Orland, 1975), the direction of such changes was positive.

Today's prisons, however, are in recession. Due to converging trends, such as increases in the rates and absolute numbers of sentenced offenders and reduced growth of correctional budgets, prison overcrowding has become an endemic condition. The population of state prisons has increased by an average of 7.5 percent per annum, and prison construction has far from kept pace with this trend. Our returning inmates today are likely to be shocked rather than pleased. Their jails or detention facilities will be more congested and dismal than during prior confinement. Their classification on entering prison will be an empty, cursory gesture, since few relevant placements will be possible. Increasingly, their lives will be circumscribed by idleness and fear.

As prisons changed, we changed with them. Most relevantly, our conceptions of stress and adjustment have become more finely delineated. Our authors have shown that the pains of confinement commence in jails, and may be most acute for many inmates at that juncture of their confinement (Gibbs, 1975). We know also that the appearance of solidarity among captives masks a regimen of manipulation, exploitation, and violence (Bowker, 1980). We know, too, that crowded prisons are not just incommodious settings, but volatile milieus in which life and adjustment become tenuous (Paulus et al., 1978). Riots, we have learned from hard experience, are both organizational crises and personal tragedies, the origins and consequences of which extend beyond short-lived accommodations of power forged by some guards and inmates (Martinson, 1972). Rehabilitation programs, whatever their intrinsic merits, are all too often squandered in environments where the struggle for personal survival relegates long-term planned change to a low priority.

Yet, however widespread certain stresses may be, it has become increasingly obvious that the pains of imprisonment and the suffering of individual prisoners are not uniform or constant. Prisons possess diverse ecologies and house diverse populations; transactions of prisoners and prison environments make for a complex mosaic of stress and adaptation (Toch, 1977). Prisons provide varying degrees of privacy from irritants such as noise or crowding, safety from insult or attack, structure and consistency of procedures, support services that facilitate self-improvement, feedback or emotional support, activity to fill time, and freedom from circumscription of one's autonomy (Toch, 1977). Different personal needs shared by prisoners, in turn, produce different perceptions of prison environments and different reactions to imprisonment. One man's (or woman's) meat can indeed be another's poison; pressing problems for some are tangential or irrelevant to others. The safe harbor for the frightened prisoner may be an occasion of oppressive boredom for the savvy convict, who worries more about intrusive guards than about predatory inmates.

Differential reactions to confinement are associated with differences in prior socialization, in confinement conditions, or both. Black prisoners, for example, especially those who originate in inner-city slums, often find that their socialization equips them reasonably well to adjust to the deprivations and depredations of prison life (Carroll, 1974; Johnson, 1976). White prisoners, particularly rural, middle-class, or otherwise sheltered types, are more likely to be unprepared to assimilate the personal failure that marks imprisonment or to withstand violence-toned prison games (Johnson, 1976). Female inmates tend to experience problems relating to dependency that are different from the dominant concerns of male prisoners, who generally are more preoccupied with personal safety or autonomy (Fox, 1975). Younger inmates live in a prison world characterized by exaggerated concern for peer acceptance and a marked preoccupation with toughness; the more naive youths are notably susceptible to coercion by their peers and hence to problems and crises that reflect panic-inspired declarations of personal bankruptcy (Bartollas et al., 1976). Mentally ill and insecure offenders carry with them a substrate of emotional susceptibility that produces widespread vulnerability to prison pressure (Toch, 1975). Long-term prisoners, whatever their personal backgrounds or predispositions, must husband the social and psychological resources needed to endure lengthy confinement in settings geared to the needs of short-term convicts (Flanagan, 1982). Parolees, however long or short their term of confinement, must withstand a series of transition pressures before a civilian life can be reestablished (Glaser, 1964; Irwin, 1970). Finally, condemned prisoners, for whom a life sentence is a reprieve and parole a distant dream, must carve out an existence in the barren world of death row, a repository for people seen and treated as if they were more dead than alive (Johnson, 1981).

Living in prison has never been easy, and this holds true whether we are talking about the ostensibly hardened convict or the tender novice. The task of adjustment is made more difficult by the fact that simple survival or endurance is not enough. Prisoners must cope with prison life in *competent* and *socially constructive* ways if the experience of imprisonment is not to add to recurring problems of alienation and marginality. This means that problems must be met head on and resolved, however imperfectly; that conflict resolution, however incomplete, must occur without resort to deception, exploitation, or violence; and that an effort, however tentative, must be made to empathize with and assist others who are in need (Toch, 1975). Too often, however, the prisoner is confronted by a hostile or indifferent prison environment in which denial of personal problems and manipulation of others are primary ingredients of interpersonal life. The result is that the prison's survivors become tougher, more pugnacious, and less able to feel for themselves or others, while its nonsurvivors become weaker, more susceptible, and less able to control their lives. Tragically, this destructive process sometimes occurs in the presence of peers and authorities who choose to "do their own time" and ignore the suffering and inhumanity that surround them.

Correctional work must begin with humaneness if it is to break this cycle of predator and prey and address the day-to-day problems that confront our captives. Humaneness, in turn, requires sensitivity to diverse and varying individual predispositions and needs. Humane prison environments must be resilient environments—settings orchestrated by line and managerial staff to meet the adjustment needs of prisoners. Such environments can provide a viable context for adaptation and, ultimately, rehabilitation (Johnson & Price, 1981); they can ensure that the prisoner is not "engaged full-time in a fight for his survival" (Seymour, 1977, p. 205), but can instead direct his attention to the substantial challenge of rebuilding his life.

Stress is an important feature of prison life, and indeed may be the central feature of prison life as it is experienced by prisoners themselves. Stress can contaminate programs, undermine adjustment efforts, and leave a residue of bitterness and resentment among inmates. It can make the prison a destructive and debilitating institution; to ignore stress is to relegate prisons to the business of warehousing spoiled (and spoiling) human resources. Stress must be controlled if prisons are to become environments in which the work of corrections, in any sense of the word, can take place.

In this book we variously address the nature, import, and reduction of prison stress. Throughout, stress is studied as it impinges on men and women who populate prisons. Stress is examined in terms of widely shared difficulties related to overcrowding, victimization, and riots, and as it relates to the specific adjustment problems and crises of specific groups of prisoners, whether these unfold as a function of time (as in the case of pretrial detainees, long-term prisoners, condemned prisoners, and parolees) or as a function of preexisting susceptibilities (as with adolescents, minorities, women, and the mentally ill). Interventions that must be considered include the provision of meaningful classification and treatment, development of formal and informal environmental sanctuaries to shelter stressed prisoners, expansion of roles for line correctional personnel, and the use of management strategies that enhance the human and environmental resources of the prison. We close with an epilogue that examines the requisites of a decent and humane prison, "the kind of prison that we, as American inheritors of a magnanimous tradition, should be willing to maintain."

REFERENCES

Alper, B. S. *Prisons inside-out: Alternatives in correctional reform.* Cambridge, MA: Ballinger, 1974.

American Friends Service Committee. *Struggle for justice.* New York: Hill & Wang, 1971.

Bartollas, C., Miller, S., & Dinitz, S. *Juvenile victimization: The institutional paradox.* New York: Halstead, 1976.

Bowker, L. *Prison victimization.* New York: Elsevier, 1980.

Carroll, L. *Hacks, blacks and cons.* Lexington, MA: D. C. Heath, 1974.

Flanagan, T. Correctional policy and the long-term prisoner. *Crime and Delinquency,* 1982, 28(1), 82-95.

Fox, J. Women in crisis. In H. Toch, *Men in crisis: Human breakdowns in prison,* Chicago: Aldine, 1975.

Gibbs, J. J. Jailing and stress. In H. Toch, *Men in crisis: Human breakdowns in prison.* Chicago: Aldine, 1975.

Glaser, D. *The effectiveness of a prison and parole system.* Indianapolis: Bobbs-Merrill, 1964.

Irwin, J. *The felon.* Englewood Cliffs, NJ: Prentice-Hall, 1970.

Johnson, R. *Culture and crisis in confinement.* Lexington, MA: D. C. Heath, 1976.

Johnson, R. *Condemned to die: Life under sentence of death.* New York: Elsevier, 1981.

Johnson, R., & Price, S. The complete correctional officer: Human service and the human environment of prison. *Criminal Justice and Behavior,* 1981, 8(3), 343-373.

Martinson, R. Collective behavior at Attica. *Federal Probation,* 1972, 36(September), 3-7.

Murton, T. O. *The dilemma of prison reform.* New York: Holt, Rinehart & Winston, 1976.

Nagel, W. G. *The new red barn: A critical look at the modern American prison.* New York: Walker & Company, 1973.

Orland, L. *Prisons: Houses of darkness.* New York: Free Press, 1975.

Paulus, P. B., McCain, G., & Cox, V. C. Death rates, psychiatric commitments, blood pressure, and perceived crowding as a function of institutional crowding. *Environmental Psychology and Nonverbal Behavior,* 1978, 3(2), 107-116.

Seymour, J. Niches in prison. In H. Toch, *Living in prison: The ecology of survival.* New York: Free Press, 1977.

Shaw, G. B. *The crime of imprisonment.* New York: Philosophical Library, 1946.

Suedfeld, P. *Restricted environmental stimulation: Research and clinical applications.* New York: John Wiley, 1980.

Sykes, G. *The society of captives.* New York: Atheneum, 1966.

Toch, H. *Men in crisis: Human breakdowns in prison.* Chicago: Aldine, 1975.

Toch, H. *Living in prison: The ecology of survival.* New York: Free Press, 1977.

van den Haag, E. *Punishing criminals: Concerning a very old and painful question.* New York: Basic Books, 1975.

von Hirsch, A. *Doing justice: The choice of punishments.* New York: Hill & Wang, 1976.

PART I

Prison Stress

CHAPTER 2

Studying and Reducing Stress

HANS TOCH

If Gresham Sykes wanted to impress contemporary social scientists, he would retitle his subject[1] (and our book) "the stresses of imprisonment." Among others, McGrath (1970a, p. 1) points out that "stress happens to be an 'in' term" these days. McGrath cites a textbook on motivation that concludes that stress "has all but preempted a field previously shared by a number of other concepts" and that students of a problem such as imprisonment "substituted the word stress for it and continued in [the] same line of investigation" (Cofer & Appley, 1964, p. 449). He speculates that one of the attractions of stress research is its claim to practicality. "The study of stress," McGrath (1970a, p. 2) notes, "seems, on the face of it, to be directly applicable to some of the most pressing problems of the social order, and to offer a route to understanding, if not eliminating, these problems."

Given some fashionable definitions of stress (see below) and some meaningful ways of studying phenomena thus defined, the link between "understanding" and "eliminating problems" can be direct. Persons who have recently undergone stress can benefit from interviews in which they are asked to recount their experiences. This phenomenon was first uncovered by Freud, who showed us that our ability to cope with adversity can be improved by rehashing our past coping failures. To put the matter more psychoanalytically, verbally reliving our hurts can be regenerative. The reason for this paradox has to do with the power of undigested traumatic experience (live pain) to magnify perceptions of threat and to charge them with inherited panic. When we rehearse a sequence of events that produced a traumatic juncture in our lives, we can place our hurt into perspective, and we can keep leftover distress and self-doubt from haunting us. With an intervening cooling-off period, we can assimilate facts that previously were too painful to digest or to face. Not surprisingly, "psychiatric first aid" that is administered to stressed persons resembles sensitive stress research interviews. As Janis (1969, p. 72) points out, "Many psychotherapists who treat traumatized persons see their job as that of helping each person to do the amount of working through the trauma that is needed for him to regain his basic sense of self-confidence." "Working through" is what a good interview subject must do.

Research can also provide stressed persons with some momentary social support. Sarason (1980, p. 84) points out that when we are in trouble we need "people on whom we can rely, people who let us know that they care about, value and love us." A research interview that includes a salient component of caring and that communicates honest concern for a traumatized interviewee can thus be therapeutic.[2] It can be an encounter that has "stress-buffering value." This fact is one that is "consistent with the emphasis Rogerian therapists have for years placed on the importance of unconditional positive regard" (Sarason, 1980, p. 85).

A more obvious link between stress research and practice lies in the use of experiential data—such as data about life in prison—to help persons (inmates) who must face predictable stress experiences and do not know what to expect or how to react. Janis (1969, p. 102) reviews a large number of related experimental studies, from which he concludes that "if a normal person is given accurate prior warning of impending pain and discomfort, together with sufficient reassurances so that fear does not mount to a very high level, he will be less likely to develop acute emotional disturbances than a person who is not warned."

Data about unavoidable prison deprivations, either fairly widely shared deprivations or those specific to inmate groups, could shape modules of an orientation program for inexperienced new inmates. Such a program would resemble a three-step sequence of the sort described by Janis (1969). The first step in such a sequence would be "to give (the inmate) realistic information" (Janis, 1969, p. 196). The term "realistic" charts a middle course between reassurance and alarm. It does not paralyze by magnifying future danger (announcing, "What crowding means is that you'll sit in your cell going stir crazy" or "Chances are some guys will try to rape you soon as you step in the gate"), but it forewarns of probable or to-be-expected threats (for example, "Decent programs nowadays have long waiting lists" and "Some guys will threaten you and they'll make advances to you"). Anxiety at orientation is desirable; in its absence, the inmate will be "unmotivated to do the work of worrying or to plan preparatory actions for dealing with subsequent crisis" (Janis, 1969, p. 196).

As we shall see later on, stress is disabling for people who are overanxious or who are underanxious and overconfident. One must reduce feelings of invulnerability, but one must "counteract feelings of helplessness, hopelessness and demoralization" (Janis, 1969, p. 196). One does both by exploring the person's view of options and of resources for coping. One could ask the inmate, for example, "Do you have hobbies or could you develop some?" or "What do you do when some guy threatens you on the street?" Research data permit one to explore solutions used by others to cope with problems, in the form of statements such as "Lots of guys have used up cell time with correspondence courses" or "Booty bandits don't bother fellas who've made a couple of friends" or "Guards can transfer you if you tell 'em someone is after you."

The final step of inoculation is "to encourage the person to work out his own way of reassuring himself and his own plans for protecting himself" (Janis, 1969, p. 196). This step benefits less from data, but research may bear on the viability of the perspectives and strategies the stress candidate explores.

Another use of stress research is as *action* research, or (in Kurt Lewin's term) as "research-in-action." This means that those directly affected by stress situations can be mobilized to gather facts and—with or without social science assistance—to work through the implications of facts they have collected.

> For example, correctional officers could be convoked to consider consequences of overcrowding and ways of ameliorating such consequences. The group could consider such topics as "arranging placement to minimize congestion," "lowering tension in the prison," "helping stressed inmates," "helping stressed staff," "rearranging resources to enhance programs," "filling idle time," "locating low-risk inmates," and "maintaining security in congested prisons" [Toch & Grant, 1982].

Where prison units experience high levels of victimization, data could be collected in predetermined violence "hot spots" and could be reviewed by their staff and/or inmates:

> Staff and inmate groups can be run separately or together, charged with documenting the reasons for violence patterns, or asked to recommend policy changes to neutralize violence patterns. This must obviously be done with the understanding that documented and practical suggestions will be implemented [Toch, 1978, p. 24].

The point is that research—or at least data that help us understand sources of stress—can be collected and deployed to neutralize prevalent stressors, to ameliorate stress they produce, or both.

STRESS CONCEPTS RELEVANT TO OUR UNDERSTANDING OF PAINS OF IMPRISONMENT

The dictionary defines a "stress" as a "constraining force or influence." This view coincides with the use of the concept in engineering to describe the engineers' maltreatment of physical objects to produce "strain" in them and ultimately cause them to break. In contemporary psychological theories (such as those summarized by McGrath, 1970b), the stimulus-centered definition corresponds to the first stage of a hypothesized stress process or stress transaction. The "constraint or influence" is the demand, load, input, stressor, press, stress situation, or environmental force that is the occasion, precondition, or requisite to stress. Sykes's prison "deprivations" qualify as stressors; they describe features of the prison environment (such as separation from loved ones) that "deprive"—that is, adversely affect—inmates. The phrase "adversely affect" assumes that the deprivation involves commodities that have been present (excluding men who have led a solitary existence in rooming houses) and were valued. Depriving a person of commodities that have not been an asset to him or her (such as nagging, demanding, conflict-generating relatives) is not a demand or stressor.

Demands are divided into those that tax us by demanding more than we can deliver (stimulus overload) or by insufficiently challenging our interests and capacities (underload). Prison demands combine underload and overload. The press of other inmates can be an overload, and enforced inactivity an underload (Toch, 1977). Prison demands occur as onslaughts (such as a menacing cell mate with a knife) or as cumulative wear and tear (noisy tier mates). Janis (1969, p. 71) points out that low-grade chronic demands can translate into acute demands because "the relentless accumulation of stresses day after day lowers the person's stress tolerance to the point where he begins to react to every minor stress as though it were a serious threat." Prisons are also classed with dramatic demands (such as "loss of limb, slum existence," and the like) under the generic heading "life stresses" (McGrath, 1970b, p. 10).

A second stage of stress is defined as the "*reception* (recognition, cognitive appraisal, perception, acceptance)" of a stressor (McGrath, 1970b, p. 15), or its "*subjective demand* (or 'strain,' or 'personal definition')" (p. 16). Sykes's deprivation of autonomy, for example, means that inmates at some level (conscious or unconscious) see prison staff as intrusively controlling their fate or circumscribing their decisions. Given specialized past experiences—such as a transfer into a low-custody prison from a high-custody prison—deprivation of autonomy could become a nondemand; alternate experiences—such as overpermissive upbringing—could increase the salience of autonomy restrictions.

The reception process not only refers to whether or not stressors are perceived, but also describes the *meanings* assigned to the stressors (their "definition") by the perceiver. The situation must be perceived as noxious. Noxiousness converts a neutral or ambiguous scenario (inmate population density) into a stressful situation (a crowded prison). The inmates' definition of the situation also refers to the quality of the demand (undesirable connotations of crowdedness) that is salient and irritating to them. Crowding is thus experienced—given density—when people are "forced to participate, even passively, in an unwanted experience" (Cohen, 1980, p. 174), when their surrounding exercises "control over both their social and physical environments by dictating where and with whom they interact" (p. 175), and when control is seen as arbitrary. Such meanings define the nature of stress. Crowding then translates into deprivation of autonomy (arbitrary assignment), privacy (unwanted social contacts), and freedom (circumscribed movement); it also makes one feel unsafe and restricts one's activities and program options (see Chapter 3, this volume).

The third stage of stress is one McGrath (1970b) calls "responses." It covers very diverse grounds, as does Sykes's phrase "pains of imprisonment." One connotation of response is that of feelings (discomfort, fear, anxiety, rage, sense of impotence) that most of us think of when we think of stress. Sykes's deprivations presume "pains" such as loneliness, shame, and rage. More complex feelings are the experienced injuries to self-esteem ("I'm treated like a child, held in contempt, disrespected, arbitrarily degraded") that Sykes postulates. Responses also include physiological reactions (high blood pressure, ulcers) and indicators of psychosocial malfunction (alcoholism) beloved by stress researchers.

Responses are defined to include behavioral reactions. These must be read to comprise reactions such as those used by inmates (retreating, exploding, emulating a favored version of John Wayne, making home brew, attempting suicide, writing writs, and so on) to deal with stress. Two problems follow: One is that stress includes a fourth stage, "the consequences of response," which covers behavior *composites* such as Sykes's "society of captives." It becomes hard to draw a line between behavior as response (the inmates' individual efforts to salvage their self-esteem) and as the consequence of response (the sum of inmate efforts that salvages collective self-esteem). A more serious difficulty is that "response" becomes an overloaded concept, comprising the impacts of perceived demand (such as resentment at being "harassed"), the reaction to impact (refusing to take a shower and telling an officer to "shove" his nightstick), and the purposes of the reaction (salvaging wounded self-esteem, demonstrating manhood, reacting to sensed impotence, suppressing depression, anxiety, or rage).

Feedback loops are characteristic of stress reactions in life (McGrath, 1970b, p. 17). They also complicate matters. The "consequence" of the rebellious inmate's response may include (1) being forcibly restrained and (2) being confined to disciplinary segregation. These consequences in turn increase feelings of stress (confirmed impotence, helpless rage, panic) and reactions to them (tearing up the segregation cell). Such responses have their own consequences (classification of the inmate as disturbed and recalcitrant, segregation in an observation cell), which again increase felt stress and stress-produced conduct. Other consequences of responses (such as inmate explosions) are demands for others (guards faced with explosive inmates). Such stress transactions can recycle (short-tempered guards can increase inmate deprivation of autonomy), and escalations can occur on a collective scale (see Chapter 5, this volume).

To accommodate conceptual complexity, full-blooded stress paradigms center on the stress response stage and differentiate among response elements. Some paradigms highlight personal feelings of distress and the role they play in stressed people's lives. Others center on people's efforts to deal with stressors, and with the success and failure of their efforts. These two categories of response are critically related; if one attends to one's feelings of distress, one interferes with one's ability to neutralize or to address sources of stress in the environment.[3] Put differently, defending against distress reduces the stressed person's capacity to cope constructively (Mechanic, 1978).

STRESS AND PROBLEM SOLVING

Freud has shown us that our everyday behavior can be better understood once we understand more extreme or abnormal behavior. The reverse also holds. The line between stress and life in general is at best somewhat tenuous. Stressed persons are persons who experience crises, and nonstressed persons are persons with problems. The difference matters. Crises are problems that upset us because they seem insoluble or almost impossible to solve (Toch, 1975). The common ground between "soluble" and "insoluble" challenges helps us to understand how we can transmute crises into problems. This point is noted by White (1974, p. 49), who writes:

> It may well be that in stressful situations things happen that have no counterpart in easier circumstances, but some of what happens is likely to come straight from the repertoire that is common to all adaptive behavior. There is a sense in which all behavior can be considered an attempt at adaptation. Even in the smoothest and easiest of times behavior will not be adequate in a purely mechanical or habitual way. Every day raises its little problems: what clothes to put on, how to plan a timesaving and step-saving series of errands, how to schedule the hours to get through the day's work, how to manage the cranky child, appease the short-tempered tradesman, and bring the long-winded acquaintance to the end of his communication. It is not advisable to tell a group of college students that they have no problems, nothing to cope with, during the happy and uneventful junior year. They will quickly tell you what it takes to get through that golden year, and as you listen to the frustrations, bewilderments, and sorrows as well as the triumphs and joys you will have a hard time conceptualizing it all as well-adapted reflexes or smoothly running habits. Life is tough, they will tell you, in case you have forgotten; life is a never-ending challenge. Every step of the way demands the solution of problems and every step must therefore be novel and creative, even the putting together of words and sentences to make you understand what it is like to cope with being a college junior.

One of White's inferences (similar to our earlier discussion) is that knowledge of adaptive strategies, secured through research, helps us to help people in crisis. He points out that "there are many influences today that make us reluctant to tell people what to do. Partly, no doubt, it is the effect of the contemporary culture that has become so extravagantly negative to anything that smacks of direction and authority. . . . But partly, I think, the trouble is that we do not know what to say. Knowing so much about the ways in which common sense, realism, inventiveness, and courage can be spoiled, we have dismissed them rather than studying how they still work. Herein lies the importance of the study of strategies of adaptation" (White, 1974, p. 68).

A model that relates adaptation or problem solving to stress is one described by Howard and Scott (1965). These authors distinguish among helpful and unhelpful responses to problems. A helpful response is an *assertive* response, "in which the organism meets the problem directly and attempts a solution" (Howard & Scott, 1965, p. 147). In a response of this kind, we mobilize whatever resources we have in an effort to solve a problem. When we run into obstacles, we explore alternative solutions. Such a response may not actually solve our problem, but it has a chance of doing so. This is not true of *divergent* responses, "in which the organism diverts his energies and resources away from confronting the problem" (Howard & Scott, 1965, p. 147). The most frequent divergent response is to withdraw—to deny our problem or to retreat from it. Another such response is one of blind aggression against sources of frustration (those "responsible" for the problem) or bizarre panic-induced reactions. Equally unhelpful is an *inert* response, which consists of not responding at all.

Howard and Scott (1965) maintain that when problems are mastered, more than the solution has been gained, because our chances for successful future problem solving are enhanced. However, if the problem is not solved because our assertive responses fail or because dysfunctional responses have been used, the result we can expect is stress. Stress translates into tension, which reduces our problem-solving capabilities. Tension uses up energy and resources, and demands discharge. Where people are under tension, the situation can be ameliorated by providing "culturally sanctioned" mechanisms for tension release (Howard & Scott, 1965, p. 150). But if such mechanisms are not provided, "deviant (in the sense of socially disapproved) techniques will be resorted to." This occurs at a price: "These latter responses are likely to compound the individual's problems . . . by inducing social sanctions and producing further threats to his self-image" (p. 150).

Howard and Scott's message to prison administrators would *not* be for them to arrange for tension-releasing mechanisms (home brew, perhaps? boxing rings?) for their stressed inmates. Howard and Scott (1965, p. 151) point out that "even under the best circumstances, relief from tension is likely to be temporary, and if the tension-releasing activities are of a nature to compound problems, the tension-tension-release cycle may become a spiral involving increasing stress." The real solution is to reinforce the use of assertive responses, with particular attention to providing inmates with problem-solving resources. Such resources are usually human or social resources. After all, "the sociocultural environment has a double significance for the study of stress. First, it confronts each individual with ready-made problems, and second, it offers mechanisms by which problems may be solved" (p. 158).

We again infer that problems become crises—even escalating crises—if stress-induced or tension-releasing behavior occurs in lieu of problem-solving behavior. A less obvious theme is the need for resources ("supports") that stressed persons can mobilize so as to convert their crises into soluble problems.

THE SOCIAL CONTEXT OF STRESS

Sudden stress often causes people to withdraw. For a time, the stressed person builds a "shell" around his or her wounds that makes him or her refractory to help from others (Toch, 1975). This reaction to shock is part of the "working through" process to which Janis (1969) refers. It is a temporary reaction, however, and it does not preclude *some* helpful contact of a quiet, nonintrusive kind.

Given time, most stressed persons need and want assistance with problems of coping. Mechanic (1978, p. 140) observed graduate students who were badly traumatized by impending examinations, and he tells us that

> as stress increased, the student sought support from other students, friends, wives, faculty, the investigator, and sometimes anyone present. Faculty, wives and other students were quite liberal in giving support, and some students would identify very strongly with the source of support.... As examinations drew near even isolated students sought support from those around them. Some of the students under considerable stress started talking to almost anyone about examinations; it did not take much to get them talking on the topic. At times they would talk to strangers about their feelings and then feel embarrassed because they had said too much. Interpersonal support, however, continued to be a constant source of reassurance.

Search for support can be a sterile, rewarding, or damaging experience. Students who encounter even more stressed students can have their anxiety escalated or their fears "confirmed." An overcheerful, overconfident peer (or someone obviously better prepared) can increase a student's sense of inadequacy. Wallowing in self-conscious panic can be paralyzing, but indifferent responses can make one feel eccentric, rejected, or ashamed of one's concerns.

The most helpful support is task-oriented support. This is help that facilitates the addressing of one's problem, such as through reassurance, information, and the reinforcement of assertive behavior. Study groups, groups that facilitate preparation and review of notes, proved critical to Mechanic's students, as did faculty with helpful hints.

Janis (1969, pp. 92-93) points out that "in times of danger most people have a heightened need for social reassurance"; such need comprises "(1) the need to evaluate one's own feelings and emotional symptoms by comparing them with those displayed by others and (2) the need to obtain reassurances from being in the presence of others who will be supportive because they are in a similar predicament." Given such needs, it is clear that "not all companions will be equally desirable" (p. 103). People who are as anxious as oneself, or more anxious than one already is, can aggravate one's anxiety. The most "supportive" role is one that helps one to extricate oneself from wallowing in distress and that permits one to act constructively. In Janis's (1969, p. 103) words:

> If the group's norms concerning appropriate ways of dealing with the danger are based on sound information and realistic judgments, each individual who joins in the group discussions will become more ready to adopt some new reassuring beliefs and to adhere to the recommended precautionary measures, which can reduce his chances of becoming overwhelmed by feelings of helplessness.

Current usage of the term "support group" often misses the point that uncontrolled gripe sessions can backfire. For instance, if "burnt out" workers are induced to pool their discontent, they can emerge with an increased sense of alienation and confirmed feelings of impotence. Such results are debilitating because they discourage addressing sources of stress in the work place (Toch & Grant, 1982). It is not helpful to know that "others are in the same boat" if one believes the boat is sinking. Support means to legitimate feelings, but never as an end in itself. The task of coping includes diagnosis of occasions for stress and a review of options for ameliorating stressors.

To be sure, coping is impeded where we *lack* anxiety because an illusion of nonstress can be shattered easily. A study by Janis (1969, p. 96) of patients subjected to serious operations showed that

> these patients were constantly cheerful and optimistic about the impending operation. They denied feeling worried, slept well, and were able to read, listen to the radio, and socialize without any observable signs of emotional tension. They appeared to have unrealistic expectations of *almost complete invulnerability*. After the operation, however, they became acutely preoccupied with their vulnerability and were *more likely than others to display anger and resentment toward the staff*. Most of them complained bitterly about being mistreated and sometimes became so negativistic that they tried to refuse even routine postoperative treatments.

The best copers in the hospital situation were patients who suffered *constructive* levels of anxiety or "moderate fear." Janis (1969, p. 96) points out that

> these patients were occasionally worried and tense about specific features of the impending operation, such as the anesthesia. They asked for and received realistic information about what was going to happen to them from the hospital staff. They were able to be reassured, to engage in distracting activities, and to remain outwardly calm during most, though not every minute, of the day before the operation. They felt *somewhat vulnerable*, but their concerns were focused on realistic threats. After the operation they *were much less likely than others to display any emotional disturbance.*

Stress-related programs (training experiences, workshops) may seek to produce optimal anxiety levels through sequences that first enhance feelings and then temper them. This can be done by subjecting people to sensitization sessions ("Charley says he takes his life in his hands every day he works as a guard," "My wife says I gnash my teeth in my sleep," and so on) and then teaching them to relax ("You must make your mind a blank and breathe deeply").[4] Participants often find such orchestrating of catharsis and decompression exhilarating. Whether the experiences are also helpful hinges on their diagnostic validity and prognostic value. Validity is reduced where stress becomes an exculpatory gambit ("I drink because I hate my job," "I beat my wife because they don't let me discipline inmates," and so on) and utility hinges on the program's willingness to explore response options (such as "I can enrich my own job by relating to inmates") as opposed to denying them (for example, "The commissioner wants us to be hacks").

"Stress workshops" and other such experiences reduce feelings of resourcelessness. Even if crises defy solution or resolution, the knowledge of group membership and responsibility to others can facilitate the weathering of crises. Sarason (1980, p. 81) points out that

> a major contribution to prisoners' survival was ability to stay together with some members of their families or remain in contact with some of their prewar peers. Strong identification with ethnic or national groups proved quite supportive. Maintenance of self-esteem, a sense of human dignity and group belonging, and the belief that one was being useful all contributed to survival in both physical and psychological terms.

Prisoners with strong outside ties have an edge in facing pains of imprisonment, and community ties are essential to humane management of prisons. The creation of *in*-prison support is another essential, but this challenge is hard to operationalize. Sykes (1958) makes two critical points about this difficulty. One is that (among male inmates, at least) a prevalent norm prizes "doing your own time"; it places a taboo on admitting one's feelings and sharing them with others. Stoicism is valued, and expressions of fear are equated with stigmatized "weakness." The second point relates to the inmates' advertised distance from staff. We know that even where a majority privately prize support from prison staff, they view this desire as idiosyncratic and the perspective as unusual (Wheeler, 1961).

The norms cited by Sykes offer resistances to (1) peer support and (2) staff support, respectively. As a step to support-creation, such resistances must be faced and worked through. The task is a very hard one, but not impossible. Subcultural norms have been neutralized in treatment-oriented institutions (Street et al., 1966) and in therapeutic communities in prison (Toch, 1980). The climate in such settings often includes a staff-client culture that prizes exploring problems and inventing solutions. Such a culture not only avoids the usual inmate code, but it sometimes systematically reverses the polarities of its norms (Vorrath & Brendthro, 1974). In more usual prisons, there are niches for stressed inmates (see Chapter 16) that soften or suspend antisupport norms. Some of these niches also facilitate coping behavior, but most make do with allowing inmates to survive.

STRESS MANAGEMENT AND REHABILITATION

Sarason (1980, p. 74) writes that "stress follows a call for action when one's capabilities are perceived as falling short of the needed personal resources." For a situation to be a stressor, it must (1) represent a sharp break with past experience that is (2) unwelcome and that (3) cannot be addressed by means of one's customary coping strategies. Prisons would *not* be stressful for inmates whose lives have been spent successfully in prisonlike institutions. Such inmates (state-raised youths) can find the free world stressful but, for them, the prison is familiar (Irwin, 1970).

We know that stress in any given situation varies across people in the situation. We expect stress to vary with—among other things—(1) the disjuncture between past experience and the challenges one faces now, (2) the extent to which the disjuncture is traumatizing, and (3) the ability of the person to invent new solutions to new problems. Such differences are individual, but as averages they are found in groups. For instance, with everything held constant, we expect inmates who are not familiar with their prison peers (for instance, middle-class inmates) to have difficulty in prisons. We similarly expect persons with demonstrated lack of resilience (such as chronic mental patients) to have adjustment problems. Other differences are more complex because they relate to specific aspects of past experience (such as past levels of privacy, autonomy, and the like) and corresponding features of the stress environment. Such disjunctures, and the problems they produce, are explored later in this book.

Our present concern is with the question: Can we help stressed persons—such as inmates and guards—to cope with prison stress and to master the stressors of concern to them? More crucially, can we help inmates and/or guards to *profit* from stress, and to emerge more resilient and capable? In summarizing work related to crisis management, Janis (1969, p. 198) concludes that

> the central theme is that any instance of bereavement, separation, failure or suffering can be a turning point in the person's life, resulting either in emotional breakdown and sustained personality damage or a marked improvement in personality functioning. . . . Crises are viewed as rare occasions when the person faces serious threats, losses, and demands that are near the limits of his resources for coping. But if the person solves adequately the difficult problems confronting him, his sense of self-confidence is greatly increased, and he may be able to overcome other difficulties that had been interfering with his adjustment in the past.

Or, one might add, that might face the person in the *future*. If we help people to cope with stress we help them to cope with life, and vice versa. Many statements express the relationship that makes these syllogisms hold. The following observations all have a bearing:

(1) Past successes and failures in dealing with life situations enhance or reduce our capacity to respond to stress and to master stress-related problems.
(2) Our successes and failures reflect our level of coping skills and the confidence we have in our coping skills. The latter variable is our self-confidence or "self-esteem."
(3) Successes in coping cement our coping skills and build our self-esteem—the confidence we have in our coping skills.
(4) Being disabled by stress reduces our self-esteem and our future capacity to cope.
(5) Mastering stress enhances our self-esteem and our future capacity to cope.
(6) Limited coping skills and low self-esteem tend to be self-perpetuating; so are successful coping skills and high self-esteem.
(7) Interventions that help people cope with stress help to break the failure/low-self-esteem cycle.

These sorts of statements make up a "model" that is implicit in much of the stress literature. To the extent that this model is valid, it makes it difficult to argue that we can engage in stress amelioration without being involved in rehabilitating people (inmates) or in developing them (staff).

Competence and self-esteem are related because self-esteem translates into sense of competence. The converse also holds. If we have low self-esteem we distrust our abilities and shy away from tests of competence. If we somehow try and fail, our "incompetence" is confirmed and our self-esteem is in question. The relationship is highlighted by White (1974, p. 61), who writes:

> One thing that must be enhanced if possible, and desperately maintained if necessary, is the level of self-esteem. In part this shows itself as a struggle to keep intact a satisfactory self-picture, in part as attempts to preserve a sense of competence, an inner assurance that one can do the things necessary for a satisfactory life. Wide are the ramifications of keeping up one's self-esteem. Almost any situation that is not completely familiar, even discussing the day's news, can touch off internal questions like, "What sort of impression am I making?" "How well am I dealing with this?" "What kind of a person am I showing myself to be?" When self-esteem is tender or when the situation is strongly challenging, such questions, even if only vaguely felt, can lead to anxiety, shame, or guilt with their threat of further disorganization. No adaptive strategy that is careless of the level of self-esteem is likely to be any good. We certainly regard it as rare, unusually mature, and uncommonly heroic when after an unfortunate happening that diminishes his importance or shows him to be wrong, a person quietly lowers his estimate of himself without making excuses or seeking to lodge the blame elsewhere.

Compromised self-esteem calls for defensive reactions—personal moves designed to cement or to restore self-esteem. These moves often fall short or backfire. Where competence is not used by a person as the criterion of his or her worth, "toughness" or violence may take its place as a criterion (Toch, 1969). But violence invites retaliation, which leads to escalation of difficulties and to compounded stress. Self-esteem problems create tension and motivate nonassertive responses. Stotland (1975, p. 3) notes this in a discussion of police stress, in which he points out that

> the person with lower self-esteem not only has to attempt to solve the frustrating problem with which he is faced, but must also prevent any further loss of self-esteem. The latter task sometimes gets to be more important than the problem-oriented one, and the low self-esteem person defends himself by hostility, withdrawal, excessive assertiveness in the use of power, insults to others, etc. As the threat increases his anxiety, his

> thinking may become more rigidified and his solution of the problems at hand become less effective. On the other hand, the high self-esteem person is less diverted by a need to protect his self-esteem and can work more directly on the problem at hand. He approaches it with more confidence because his past experience has shown him that he can and does solve problems sufficiently effectively. He can act directly on the problems, and has little need to withdraw from them.

Stotland's (1975) prescriptions for stressed police officers—which apply to stressed guards as well—center on the creation of organizational supports for officer opportunities to demonstrate their competence. Such opportunities include the chance for increased participation in the running of the police organization (French, 1975) and the expansion of job attributes that are "professional" and prized by consumers. In the case of guards and police officers, these attributes expand human service contacts with clients (see Chapter 17, this volume) rather than "cops and robbers" interactions that invite resentment (Toch, 1976).

Convicted felons have many reasons to question their own coping competence, and they are reminded of this fact by their presence in prison. Some inmates, to be sure, make heroic efforts to blame others (police, courts, racism, and so on) for their fate. But destructive prison behavior—including violence and victimization—is compensatory, and attacks the esteem of victims to bolster that of aggressors (see Chapter 4).

Where assertive esteem-boosting opportunities are available to inmates, they are usually responded to. Inmates become eagerly involved in Christmas drives for toy repair—especially for orphanages. They seek atonement through drug testing. They fight fires, write poems, and enter art exhibits. Such activities are prized because they fill time and sometimes earn money, but also because they are approved vehicles for making a social contribution and demonstrating worth.

Sykes's point (and that of Goffman, 1961) is that prisons degrade inmates and assault their self-esteem. This means that inmates must cope where we negate their coping competence. The assault must be tempered for the enterprise to succeed.

Since prison is stressful, coping means solving prison problems. This (as in the case of guards) suggests that some inmates must be invited to address management issues. There are limits to this strategy because even managers must accept external constraints—but one can argue that it is better to go down coping than to vegetate or regress into recycling rage.

A NOTE ON STRESS RESEARCH

Studies of stress in "real life" take one of two popular forms. The first is "positivistic" and resembles the research model of the physical sciences. The design is correlational and straddles the stress experience. It tries to trace consequences of stress (such as sick calls, disciplinary reports, blood pressure readings, fatalities in prison) to stressors or stressor attributes (such as density rates or types of housing). Where correlations are found, stress is inferred, and the "black box" of stress is filled in with plausible inferences. For instance:

> Urban areas often exhibit a higher prevalence of a particular condition (e.g., hypertension) than rural areas. A frequent interpretation of this phenomenon is to assume that stress is associated with the development of hypertension, and then to reason that stress is associated more with urban than with rural living. It is not difficult to make a convincing argument and to conclude tautologically that stress increases hypertension. Example: more hypertension in the city. More stress in the city; evidence: overcrowding, noise, greater competition, etc. Therefore: more stress, more hypertension.

However,

> the trouble with this kind of reasoning is that it is often just as easy to "prove" the opposite. Example: "We found a mistake in our data. Actually the prevalence of hypertension is higher in rural than in urban areas." Evidence: great social isolation in the country, anxiety brought about by the lack of medical care facilities, lack of anonymity and privacy, and the punitive nature of gossip and social control. Only a lack of an imagination limits the extent to which social conditions found to be associated with a disorder can be interpreted as being stressful [Levine & Scotch, 1970, pp. 4-5].

Another problem with positivistic research is that it is unresponsive to human uniqueness and, at worst, defines it away. This feature is noted by McGrath (1970c, p. 49), who points out that

> for research in which stress is defined solely in terms of situation, individual differences . . . represent error variance—to be prevented by sampling and design, eliminated by statistical control, or neutralized by large samples. For research in which stress is defined solely in response terms, the problem is largely bypassed. By definition, individuals who

react in certain ways (those measured) *were* stressed, and individuals who did not react in those ways *were not* stressed, even though both sets were exposed to the same stressing conditions and even though the latter group may have exhibited stress reactions in other ways not tapped by the study's measures.

A different strategy is typified by most of the work exemplified in this book. It centers on the *experience* of being exposed to a stressor, and on the reactions to this experience. The approach is called "transactional" (Lazarus, 1966) because it examines stress at impact, where the (stressing) environment and the (stressed) person meet.[5] The approach accommodates interpersonal differences (Pa copes with S1; Pb falls apart; Pc explodes) and intrapersonal differences (Pa copes with S1 but falls apart in S2).[6] The approach has other virtues: (1) It corrects for our bias by seeing the stressor from the participant's vantage point, rather than ours; (2) it is sensitive to nuances that a stressor inventory would miss; (3) it documents dynamics of responses based on the stressed person's review of his or her purposes, perceptions, motives, and feelings; (4) it traces coping as well as noncoping; (5) it tracks the process over time, including stress-response-stress cycles; (6) it accommodates the context of stress, including the role played by social support; and (7) it provides a full-blooded perspective of stress, which invites empathy as well as understanding. Not least of all, the approach—as noted at the inception of this chapter—moves easily, directly, and neatly from research to reform. Given the obvious hurt of prison pains, the most plausible argument for this research approach is the potential it offers for amelioration through insight.

A POSTSCRIPT ON PERSPECTIVE

This book assumes the continued existence of prisons. It must assume congested, undersupplied, and undermanned prisons, human warehouses with a junglelike underworld. Such institutions (as we shall note in Chapter 19) are indefensible.

Then why stipulate them? Are we gilding the lily on the corpse of civilized society? Do we compromise with evil when we talk of "coping," "adaptation," "amelioration" in prisons? There are two justifications for prison work: One is that as inmates must cope, society must cope. While prisons exist it does no good to cry without effect in the wilderness of unresponsive public opinion. Assertive responding means doing what we can with as much effect as possible. This holds for inmates, guards, managers, and those who can help inmates, guards, and managers. (It also holds for advisors of legislators and judges who may have impact elsewhere on the system.)

The second issue is existential. Prisons are not an abstraction. They are a painful, tangible reality for some 360,000 American inmates, their thousands of keepers, and countless persons who live and work in prisons elsewhere in the world. These fellow humans are stressed now, and must be helped to survive. Though prisons be adjudged evil, human survival must be good. There are those—Frankl (1962) and Bettelheim (1960), for example—who surmounted the unspeakable evil of Nazi death camps. Such victories are monuments to human resilience. They are worth studying and emulating. Inmates too can conquer evil (ours and theirs) and they must do so if the race—with its cruelty to itself—is to survive.

NOTES

1. "The Pains of Imprisonment" is the title of Chapter 4 of Sykes's *The Society of Captives* (1958). The book is our bible, and the chapter is its centerpiece.

2. Sarason (1980, p. 89) specifically points out that "finding even one warm and attentive listener often works wonders."

3. The way Sarason (1980, p. 74) phrases this issue is that "the most adaptive response to stress is a task orientation that directs a person's attention to the task at hand rather than to emotional reactions. Recent work has shown the adaptive value of being able to set aside temporarily one's strong emotions in order to deal with the problematic situation." Anxiety that interferes with adaptation is often labeled "neurotic anxiety," though the phrase is less popular today than it was in Freud's day.

4. A less ritualistic way of defusing stress-generated anxiety is to systematically deploy humor. Humor tends to be relaxing and disinhibiting, and it redefines stressors to make them less threatening. Humor is prevalent in trenches and other chronic stress settings as a stress-reducing gambit; it is also prized as an attribute of leaders in stress situations (Dixon, 1980).

5. Lazarus and Launier (1978, p. 288) point out that the word "transaction" is necessary because "threat cannot be described in terms of person or environment alone, but must be defined by both. For example, a person may be threatened because the external demand seems very taxing and the resources for managing it weak, or the threat may arise from a weak demand that nevertheless appears stronger than the available resources for managing it. Both sides of the equation are necessary to the appraised relationship, meaning that threat depends on the 'balance of power between the demands and the resources.'"

6. Such data are essential to humane classification of inmates. Persons can be grouped or matched based on compatible stress susceptibilities. Flagrant inmate mismatches (such as between aggressors and victims and between active and privacy-oriented inmates) can be avoided through use of data (Toch, 1977).

REFERENCES

Bettelheim, B. *The informed heart.* New York: Free Press, 1960.

Cofer, C. N., & Appley, M. H. *Motivation: Theory and research.* New York: John Wiley, 1964.

Cohen, S. Cognitive processes as determinants of environmental stressors. In I. G. Sarason & C. D. Speilberger (Eds.), *Stress and anxiety* (Vol. 7). Washington, DC: Hemisphere, 1980.

Dixon, N. F. Humor: A cognitive alternative to stress? In I. G. Sarason & C. D. Spielberger (Eds.), *Stress and anxiety* (Vol. 7). Washington, DC: Hemisphere, 1980.

Frankl, V. E. *Man's search for meaning.* New York: Simon & Schuster, 1962.

French, J.R.P. A comparative look at stress and strain in policemen. In W. H. Kroes & J. J. Hurrell (Eds.), *Job stress and the police officer: Identifying stress reduction techniques.* Washington, DC: Government Printing Office, 1975.

Goffman, E. *Asylums: Essays on the social situation of mental patients and other inmates.* Garden City, NY: Doubleday, 1961.

Howard, A., & Scott, R. A. A proposed framework for the analysis of stress in the human organism. *Behavioral Science*, 1965, 10, 141-160.

Irwin, J. *The felon.* Englewood Cliffs, NJ: Prentice-Hall, 1970.

Janis, I. L. *Stress and frustration.* New York: Harcourt Brace Jovanovich, 1969.

Lazarus, R. S. *Psychological stress and the coping process.* New York: McGraw-Hill, 1966.

Lazarus, R. S., & Launier, R. Stress-related transactions between person and environment. In L. A. Pervin & M. Lewis (Eds.), *Perspectives in interactional psychology.* New York: Plenum, 1978.

Levine, S., & Scotch, N. A. *Social stress.* Chicago: Aldine, 1970.

McGrath, J. E. Introduction. In J. E. McGrath (Ed.), *Social and psychological factors in stress.* New York: Holt, Rinehart & Winston, 1970. (a)

McGrath, J. E. A conceptual formulation for research on stress. In J. E. McGrath (Ed.), *Social and psychological factors in stress.* New York: Holt, Rinehart & Winston, 1970. (b)

McGrath, J. E. Major methodological issues. In J. E. McGrath (Ed.), *Social and psychological factors in stress.* New York: Holt, Rinehart & Winston, 1970. (c)

Mechanic, D. *Students under stress: A study in the social psychology of adaptation.* Madison: University of Wisconsin Press, 1978.

Sarason, I. G. Life stress, self-preoccupation, and social supports. In I. G. Sarason & C. D. Spielberger (Eds.), *Stress and anxiety* (Vol. 7). Washington, DC: Hemisphere, 1980.

Stotland, E. Self-esteem and stress in police work. In W. H. Kroes & J. J. Hurrell (Eds.), *Job stress and the police officer: Identifying stress reduction techniques.* Washington, DC: Government Printing Office, 1975.

Street, D., Vinter, R., & Perrow, C. *Organization for treatment.* New York: Free Press, 1966.

Sykes, G. M. *The society of captives: A study of a maximum security prison.* Princeton, NJ: Princeton University Press, 1958.

Toch, H. *Violent men: An inquiry into the psychology of violence.* Chicago: Aldine, 1969.

Toch, H. *Men in crisis: Human breakdowns in prison.* Chicago: Aldine, 1975.

Toch, H. *Peacekeeping: Police, prisons and violence.* Lexington, MA: D. C. Heath, 1976.

Toch, H. *Living in prison: The ecology of survival.* New York: Free Press, 1977.

Toch, H. Social climate and prison violence. *Federal Probation*, 1978, 42, 21-25.

Toch, H. (Ed.). *Therapeutic communities in corrections*. New York: Praeger, 1980.

Toch, H., & Grant, J. D. *Reforming human services: Change through participation*. Beverly Hills, CA: Sage, 1982.

Vorrath, H. H., & Brendthro, L. K. *Positive peer culture*. Chicago: Aldine, 1974.

Wheeler, S. Socialization in correctional communities. *American Sociological Review*, 1961, 26, 697-712.

White, R. W. Strategies of adaptation: An attempt at systematic description. In G. V. Coelho, D. A. Hamburg, & J. E. Adams (Eds.), *Coping and adaptation*. New York: Basic Books, 1974.

CHAPTER 3

Crowding and Confinement

DALE E. SMITH

The single most critical issue confronting corrections today is the sheer number of individuals confined in our nation's prisons and jails. In state after state and county after county, the volume of prisoners has increased to such a degree that what were once considered "rated capacities" are milestones long passed, left only to mark some earlier period's standard of adequacy. In their place are found capacities ranging anywhere from "in excess of . . . " to capacities poignantly characterized as simply "at crisis." The reality of these exorbitant levels is depicted in facility after facility, where institutional attempts to "make do" have become the norm. These "make do" norms include the double-bunking of single cells, the converting of warehouses into dorms, the erecting of trailers and tents in recreation fields and prison yards, and the assigning of inmates to mattresses on the floor. Evidenced by the prevalence of these attempts, it would appear that many institutions have approached, if not surpassed, the point at which they can adequately provide for the basic human needs of shelter and housing.

Support for this assertion can readily be found in the numbers themselves. In 1961, the number of sentenced prisoners confined in state and federal facilities at year's end was 220,149, a figure that remained unexceeded for the next 13 years. By 1975, this figure rose to 242,750, or an increase of 11.1 percent over the preceding year. The latest figures available for 1981 place the number of prisoners held in state and federal facilities at 369,009. Thus in a 6-year period the number of prisoners confined in our nation's prisons has increased by 52 percent, a rate of increase unmatched in any other time period during the past 55 years for which such statistics are available (U.S. Department of Justice, 1982).

A similar increase can also be found in the rate at which offenders are incarcerated relative to the population at large. In 1961, the incarceration rate was 120.8 per 100,000 residents, a rate that steadily decreased over the next 11 years to a level of 94.6 per 100,000 residents in 1972. By 1974, the number of inmates confined relative to the general population was 103.6 per 100,000 residents. Paralleling the unprecedented growth in the prison population since that time, the incarceration rate for 1981 was placed at 154 per 100,000 residents. This represents a relative increase of 49 percent over the past 7 years and a 63 percent increase over the past 9 years (U.S. Department of Justice, 1982).

The significance of these numbers can best be understood in light of the resources available within our prisons and jails. These resources may be viewed in terms of tangible features such as size of housing units, frequency of programs offered, or number of staff employed, as well as in terms of more subjective commodities such as amount of privacy afforded, degree of support extended, or level of structure provided. Taken in total or alone, these resources serve as a standard by which the impact of a given institutional population may be judged. Thus, to the degree that assessments of institutional populations can be made relative to the resources provided, the impact of such "numbers of inmates" can be more clearly shown.

A series of findings recently reported by Mullen and Smith (1980) vividly portrays the importance of such "resource relative" assessments. Concerned with the adequacy of institutional attempts to meet the needs of those confined, Mullen and Smith sought to evaluate the extent to which institutional populations that are found in both prisons and jails exceeded spatial capacities and therefore constituted crowding. Aware of the limitations of institutionally generated capacity ratings as measures of spatial adequacy, Mullen and Smith based their assessment on guidelines developed by various standard-setting bodies such as the Commission on Accreditation for Corrections and the U.S. Department of Justice. The results of their analyses border on the dramatic. Using the recommended standard of 60 square feet of floor space per inmate within both dormitories and cells, Mullen and Smith estimated the capacity of our nation's prisons and jails during 1978 to be 256,500, a figure well below the 441,800 inmates confined for that year. By combining this standard with the recommended standard of single-occupant units, Mullen and Smith were able to derive a measure of crowding as assessed by the degree to which inmates were housed in units with one or more others with less than 60 square feet per inmate. Based upon this measure, these researchers estimated that 46 percent of the inmates confined in 1978 were housed under crowded conditions, that is, in high-density, multiple-occupancy units. The extremity of these conditions varied from state to state, with some states housing in excess of two-thirds of their prisoners under crowded conditions.

The relevance of Mullen and Smith's figures for prisons and jails today can only be assumed. Given the unprecedented rise in the prison population over the past four years, however, it would be difficult to imagine conditions having changed, except in the sense of having worsened. Thus the extent to which crowding must be regarded as a major concern within corrections seems difficult to refute. Moreover, the degree to which institutional resources have been stretched beyond the point at which inmate needs can be adequately met does not seem at issue. It is, instead, the human consequences of these numbers that form the crowding issue, for it is in the outcomes associated with such numbers that the gravity of this problem is realized.

CONSEQUENCES OF CROWDING

Though recently brought to focus by the surge in prison populations, concern over crowding has long been shared by administrators and reformers alike. In fact, throughout the history of corrections, charges of crowding have been raised in claims of institutional inadequacy and in support of correctional change. Such assertions can be found in the writings of corrections' earliest critics, individuals such as John Howard and Benjamin Rush, as well as in the policy statements of twentieth-century reform groups, such as those issued by the Wickersham Commission (1931) and, more recently, the National Advisory Commission on Criminal Justice Standards and Goals (1973). Implicit in these assertions is a general perception of crowding as one of several factors contributing to the undesirability of institutional conditions. This can be seen in the frequency with which words such as "crowding," "vermin," and "filth" have been linked together in describing the deplorable conditions found in prisons and jails since their inception.

Much as the conditions of confinement have been collectively deplored, it has been the totality of these conditions that has been seen as affecting those confined. Whether expressed in terms of "spiritual demise," "moral debasement," or "psychological deterioration," the consequences of these conditions have not been linked to crowding per se, but instead have been attributed to the destructiveness of prison conditions as a whole. Illustrations of this prevail throughout the reform literature of the past as well as in many of the judicial decisions of the present. Included among such decisions are those of Holt v. Sarver (1969) and Pugh v. Locke (1976), wherein the totality of conditions found within the Arkansas and Alabama penal systems, respectively, were judged to be in violation of the Eighth Amendment's prohibition against cruel and unusual punishment. Among the conditions cited in these rulings were massive overcrowding, unsanitary living quarters, insufficient medical services, the absence of recreational and work opportunities, and inadequate staffing. The implications of such a stance for the consequences of crowding may not be that clear, however. As demonstrated in the recent actions taken in Bell v. Wolfish (1978) and Rhodes v. Chapman (1981), crowding, in the absence of other substandard conditions, may be judged as not in itself detrimental to those imprisoned.

A somewhat clearer picture of the impact of crowding unfolds from a review of the research conducted on the consequences of prison density. Much like the larger body of literature of which it is a part, this research has sought to demonstrate a link between the amount of space afforded per person and various measures of personal and institutional strain. Included among these measures have been such indicators as blood pressure levels, illness complaints, disciplinary infractions, and recidivism rates. These phenomena have been linked with institutional density in one of two ways. First, several researchers have correlated impact measures with the levels of density found within and across correctional environments. Megargee (1977), in an investigation of a single facility over a three-year period, found density levels to be correlated with rates of disciplinary infractions such that the greater the number of inmates confined per space available, the greater the number of infractions committed per inmate. This relationship between density and institutional misconduct has also been found by Nacci et al. (1977) as well as by Jan (1980). Other indices associated with increased levels of density have been reported by Paulus et al. (1978, 1981). These include an increased rate of mortality for inmates over 45 years of age and an increased rate of psychiatric commitments and suicides for inmates as a whole. One other factor with which institutional density has been linked is inmate recidivism. Support for this relation has been offered by Farrington and Nuttall (1980), who found reconviction rates to be higher for facilities that were more densely populated.

The impact of prison density has also been examined by comparing inmates housed in living units of differing sizes and numbers. D'Atri (1975), in a comparison of inmates housed in dormitories versus those housed in either one-person or two-person cells, found inmates housed in the more socially dense conditions to exhibit more elevated blood pressures. Similarly, Paulus et al. (1978) have reported finding inmates housed in six-person cells to exhibit higher blood pressures than those housed in either two- or three-person cells. Other comparisons indicate that inmates housed in dormitories versus those housed in single- and two-person cells exhibit a greater rate of illness complaints (McCain et al., 1976) and a greater sensitivity to crowding (Paulus et al., 1975).

Thus it would at first appear that the consequences of prison crowding are highly detrimental. Support for such a conclusion seems obvious in the findings themselves, for among the outcomes that have been associated with increased density are found behaviors that can only be considered as damaging to the individual's emotional and physical well-being. However, upon closer inspection of the findings several inconsistencies arise. These inconsistencies, in turn, cast doubt on the conclusiveness of these findings for all correctional environments. For instance, while Megargee (1977) obtained a positive relationship between density and disciplinary infractions, Nacci et al. (1977) found such a relationship to exist only among institutions housing younger populations. However, when Nacci et al. considered infractions in a more inclusive sense, much like the manner employed by Megargee, no such pattern emerged, in that a positive relationship was obtained only with two of four types of facilities surveyed, those housing younger inmates and those housing older inmates. Similarly, Jan (1980), in an investigation of several facilities, found density levels to be correlated with inmate assaults in two of four environments, one of which housed younger males and the other of which housed older males. Moreover, when Jan considered indices such as number of assaults on employees and number of inmates held in disciplinary confinement, the relationship between density and misconduct diminished. To perhaps cloud these findings further, Paulus et al. (1978) have reported death rates due to external causes—that is, violence, poisoning, and accidents—to be higher during periods of lower population levels for inmates 45 years of age or less. Finally, in an investigation of inmates detained within a jail setting, Bonta and Nanckivell (1980) found population size and frequency of institutional misconduct to be unrelated.

In accounting for these inconsistencies, several limitations may be noted. For one, questions may be raised concerning the use of institutional records. These records, though providing a readily accessible source of data, have long been criticized for the inconsistency with which they are maintained and the infrequency with which incidents are reported. Similarly, questions can be raised concerning the phenomena that such recorded incidents actually describe. For instance, it could be argued that an incident such as a "psychiatric commitment" is as much an indicator of administrative willingness to transfer an inmate to another system as it is an indicator of emotional strain. And finally, limitations arise regarding the use of density as a measure of crowding. An illustration of this can be found in the work of Bonta and Nanckivell (1980), who found the population size of a local jail to be unrelated to the number of infractions committed by those detained. It seems important to note, however, that the population levels that Bonta and

Nanckivell considered fell below the rated capacity of the facility they examined. It would appear then that to the degree that density levels fall short of institutional capacities, the extent to which such levels can be conceived as crowding may be debated.

Beyond these limitations, the inconsistencies that have been cited reflect a basic weakness common to many studies conducted in the field. This weakness arises from a failure to control for other factors that, though falling outside the scope of study, may affect the findings that are obtained. This failure most often reflects the nature of the methods employed. In fact, it is a common tenet of social research that as one departs from the structure of the lab, the ability to control for the multitude of factors that exist in the situation being studied is diminished. However, in regard to the research on prison density, this failure reflects as much a simplicity in thought as it does a restriction in methods. This can be seen in the major premise upon which this research has been founded, which is that crowding itself is stress producing. This is so in spite of findings suggesting that the impact of density differs across institutions and offender types. Moreover, such a premise has remained in spite of the inconsistencies encountered by those who have sought to link crowding and pathology among the general population. Thus it would appear that a more elaborate model of crowding is needed, one that attempts to incorporate the findings on the impact of crowding both within the correctional environment and among the general population.

A MODEL OF CROWDING

The theoretical basis for the research on crowding can be traced to the work of Calhoun (1962). This work marks what many would consider the initial exploration of the impact of increased density within a scientific context. To examine the impact of density, Calhoun set about to create an environment inhabited by a population far surpassing its resources. He accomplished this by overbreeding a colony of laboratory rats to the point where their numbers greatly exceeded those normally found for this species. The consequences he found this environment to produce set the stage for the research on crowding that has since appeared. Specifically, Calhoun observed this environment to produce behaviors indicative of extreme social disorganization. Included among such behaviors were increases in aggression, homosexuality, and mortality as well as decreases in the caring for oneself and the young. It is on the basis of these findings that the link between crowding and pathology has been assumed.

Research on the impact of density among humans has failed to yield consequences as grave as those observed by Calhoun. In fact, as revealed in a review of the literature in this area, it appears that density may not always be an aversive experience for humans. This has been demonstrated in study upon study, wherein the results reported by one investigator have failed to be replicated by another. This lack of replication can be illustrated by the research on urban density. Continuing in the tradition established by the social disorganizationists of the early 1900s, various researchers have attempted to correlate increased levels of urban density with the increased frequency of crime, mental disorder, mortality, and so on found in the center city. Much like the research on prison density, these investigations have revealed a pattern of inconsistency, with some reporting a positive relationship among these factors (Galle et al., 1972; Marsella et al., 1970) and others reporting the absence of any relationship at all (Michelson, 1970; Schmitt, 1963; Schwartz & Mintz, 1963). A similar state of affairs may be found in the research on the effects of density within laboratory settings. For example, it appears that density has little, if any, effect on emotional states (Freedman et al., 1972; Ross et al., 1973) task performance (Freedman et al., 1971; Rawls et al., 1972), or aggression (Hutt & Vaizey, 1966; Loo, 1973; McGrew, 1970).

In the face of this apparent absence of effect, a series of studies has emerged in which the impact of density has been shown to be mediated by various other factors. This mediation may occur in one of two ways. First, certain factors may serve to lessen the impact of density, such that it appears as if there are few consequences of being exposed to these conditions. Alternatively, these factors may act to heighten the impact of density, as exhibited in behaviors indicative of extreme personal and social strain. Among the factors that have been identified as mediating the consequences of density are the perception of personal control (Sherrod, 1974; Langer & Saegert, 1977), the social structure of the group (Freedman, 1975; Baum et al., 1975), the type of activity performed (Desor, 1972), and the physical environment itself (Griffitt & Veitch, 1971; Worchel & Teddlie, 1976). As suggested by this research, it is not density in and of itself that is stress producing, but instead, it is density in combination with other factors that creates an environment of strain.

This notion of density as mediated by contextual factors has provided a basis from which more elaborate conceptualizations of crowding have been derived. Among such conceptualizations is a model of crowding proposed by Epstein (1981). Adopting a goal attainment framework, Epstein premises his model on a view of the environment as resource limited. To Epstein, such a view is integral since it implies that any increase in population can make the attainment of one's goals more difficult. These goals may take the form of physical activities. material possessions, or interpersonal relations. Regardless of their form, these goals can become more difficult to achieve as more individuals must compete for the same amount of resources. It is in this sense that limitations imposed by increased populations pose a threat to the individual's well-being. In order to cope with such a threat, the individual may elect to seek the support of others in facilitating the distribution of resources, or may simply choose to act on his or her own volition. To the degree that the group is supportive and to the degree that the individual perceives an ability to control external events, the stresses posed by increased numbers will be experienced less severely. Thus it is the orientation of the group and the individual's sense of personal control that, according to Epstein, mediate the consequences of crowding.

The advantage of Epstein's model is that it provides a framework from which the consequences of crowding may be viewed within specific environmental contexts. Moreover, through such a model it becomes clear why the link between crowding and strain cannot be assumed to exist within all environments, and why discrepancies have been obtained in previous attempts to correlate crowding and pathology across different settings.

CROWDING AND CONFINEMENT

The model proposed by Epstein (1981) is in many ways similar in concept to images that have appeared in depictions of the prison environment. This similarity can be found in what many have recognized to be among the more salient features of incarceration, that is, the absence of personal control that institutional life imposes and the weakening of social support that such a condition fosters. However, more than mere descriptions, these features have been conceived as serving an integral role in the socialization of those confined, as illustrated by the work of Sykes (1958).

Among deprivations termed by Sykes the "pains of imprisonment" was the absence of autonomy that resulted from the restrictions imposed upon the inmate's daily routine. To Sykes, it was the nature of these impositions—the enforced respect and deference, the finality of authoritarian decisions, and the demands for conduct deemed by others to be in one's best interest—that threatened the inmate most, for in this absence of control a sense of helplessness arose. Consistent with this depiction, the inmate was seen by Sykes as having to cope with the threats that such deprivations invoked. For many, this was attained by adopting the inmate code, for in this code was found a means by which to reject one's captors and, by so doing, to bolster one's self-esteem. Coupled with this rejection was the inmates' perception of toughness, as epitomized by one who could take care of oneself and didn't show any weakness. This image was further reflected in the social system which emerged, that of a society wherein those who were stronger and more cunning controlled what few commodities existed, and those who were weaker were left to fend for themselves.

Though the image of the confinement has since been modified, the deprivations incurred in prison have continued to be recognized as contributing to the social structures found among those confined. It is the nature of the perceived contribution that has changed. Whereas in the past such deprivations were held to be the sole cause of these structures, such deprivations are now seen as serving to intensify and heighten those social structures that may already exist. Nonetheless, the implications of such an intensification may be as devastating. Illustrations of this may be found in the recent depictions offered by Jacobs (1977) and Irwin (1980), both of whom have described the inmate society of today as dominated by violent gangs and cliques.

It is within this context of the deprivations imposed and the social structures that exist that the consequences of crowding may be more fully understood. Conforming to be model developed by Epstein, the correctional environment has long been characterized by its limited resources. In fact, among the deprivations cited by Sykes was the impoverishment of living an existence of only the barest necessities. While for many inmates institutional life has improved, the barrenness of many facilities still remains, whether in the limited availability of amenities or comforts or in the limited opportunities for work, programs, or activities. Thus for many the reality of confinement is a reality of limitations. It is within these limitations that the inmate must carve out an existence such that those needs judged to be important are satisfied as well as possible. For many, this may mean having to settle for a less than ideal solution, due simply to the necessity of compromise that results from the limitations imposed by institutional life. Even so, for those who achieve such a solution it may be highly valued, for the individual's needs are at least partially being met.

Faced with an increase in the number of inmates confined, the demands placed upon an institution's resources must naturally increase. Much like the resources themselves, these demands are not experienced equally among all confined. Instead, these demands are experienced in proportion to the magnitude with which the individual's pattern of attaining his or her needs is disrupted. To the extent to which the demands of others fall outside the realm of one's need attainment patterns, the presence of increased numbers will be of little consequence. However, to the degree that the demands of others interfere in the individual's attainment of his or her needs, the consequences of increased numbers may be quite severe. These consequences inhere from the threats that spiraling demands pose, for essential to a sense of well-being is the attainment of that which is deemed to be important.

Turning to the model developed by Epstein, the consequences that increased demands impose may be mediated by the social support that exists and the degree of control that is experienced among those who are threatened. As depicted by Sykes, Irwin, and others, the correctional environment is a world often devoid of either. This can be seen in their descriptions of an adaptive style ("doing one's time") wherein the mode of survival is to take care of oneself, often in total disregard of the needs and requisites of others. It is within this world that the individual is left to cope with the burdens of crowding. However, these coping efforts may be hampered by the very nature of confinement, the essence of which is embodied in externally imposed regulations and routine. The outcome of such impositions in an existence wherein the opportunity to control one's destiny, if not one's being, may often appear beyond reach. This, then, is the environment of corrections, a world of nonsupport and limited control. Moreover, this is the environment in which the individual must attempt to maintain those need attainment patterns disrupted by the demands of crowding.

Left on his or her own to cope with these demands, the individual must struggle to seek out those few solutions that appear to be most readily available. The nature of this struggle has recently been examined in an investigation conducted by the author (Smith, 1982). Unlike much of the research that has appeared on prison density, this study sought to assess the impact of crowding as constructed from the perceptions and experiences of individuals forced to reside within crowded conditions. The setting in which the investigation was conducted was a small, rural facility, the population of which was four times that of its original intended capacity. The degree of crowding was reflected in the space afforded to each inmate, which for cells and common areas combined was a mere 16 square feet. The extremity of this crowding was further revealed in the average length of time prisoners spent outside their housing unit, which comprised only one-half hour per week. Consistent with the facility's function of detainment, many of its population were held within such conditions for periods of several months, with a few held as long as one year.

The consequences of exposure to these extreme conditions were vividly evident. These consequences were revealed in the patterns of responses that emerged. Within some inmates, a heightened level of assertiveness was manifested, characterized by an increased readiness for aggression and displays of force. Many of these individuals reported becoming more quick tempered and described incidents wherein an inmate would "explode" into an aggressive outburst over the slightest provocation. For example, several inmates reported having been witnesses to, as well as participants in, fights over a cup of coffee, a piece of leftover food, or simply where one happened to be standing. The explosiveness of such incidents is illustrated by an incident in which an inmate whose rage over not receiving his medication was unleased in his stabbing another inmate several times with a pencil. For others, an opposite effect emerged, one that could be characterized as passive in nature. The behaviors exhibited by these more passive individuals included those typical of avoidance and withdrawal. For instance, many of these individuals reported spending virtually all of their time in their cells, in hopes of staying as removed from others as possible. Others expressed an unwillingness to fight back, even if their personal belongings, and in some cases their safety, were threatened. And finally, several individuals expressed perhaps the ultimate effect of submission, that of being overwhelmed with a sense of no longer caring, or of giving up.

Though consistent with the findings on the impact of prison density, the form of these responses cannot be attributed solely to crowding. Indeed, these behaviors are similar in nature to those patterns of dominance and submission that have been observed among inmates since the writings of Clemmer (1940). It is in the extremity of these responses, however, that the consequences of crowding are to be found. Much like the extreme levels of crowding that existed in the setting examined, the intensity of these responses far exceeded those found in facilities of similar function and design. This is underscored by the relatively short lengths of stay of those who were detained within this facility. Yet in spite of the limited duration of exposure, the responses that were observed parallel those found in the most extreme of prison conditions, conditions to which individuals are exposed for years. Thus it is not the dominance or the submission that crowding creates; it is, instead, the intensification of such personal responses that crowding produces. This was expressed by several of the respondents themselves, who saw individuals who tended toward aggression being forced, due to crowding, to be more aggressive, and individuals who tended toward submission being forced, due to crowding, to be more passive. Other respondents spoke of this effect as "bringing out the worst in an individual" or "bringing out the extremes in one's personality." A similar notion has been suggested by Clements (1979), who described the stresses imposed by crowding as demanding of the individual more exaggerated ways of coping.

The heightening of responses was evident not only in personal strategies of coping, but in the inmate social structure as well. Similar in form to descriptions of the inmate society in general, the social structure found within this setting was characterized by a hierarchy in which those who were stronger and more powerful dominated those who were smaller and weaker. The form of this domination varied from the hoarding and stockpiling of those few commodities that existed to the stealing and robbing of the belongings of others. Regardless of the form, the means by which this domination was induced remained the same, that of physical harm or psychological intimidation. This domination was depicted by the inmates themselves as a society wherein the fit survived, while the weak were left to fend for themselves through whatever form of refuge could be found. Coupled with this mode of survival was a heightened level of concern for self-preservation. This was conveyed in admonitions common to the inmate code in general, such as "Only worry about yourself" and "Don't interfere in the affairs of others." However, much like the heightened levels of dominance and submission that emerged, these concerns were of a greatly magnified proportion.

In sum, the consequences noted in this study are similar in nature to those behaviors that have characterized the correctional environment for quite some time. Nonetheless, the same cannot be said of the severity of these responses, for relative to facilities of similar function and design, these behaviors were of a much more extreme level. Thus it would appear from these findings that the consequences of crowding are to be found in the intensification of behaviors common to this environment.

Turning once again to the model developed by Epstein (1981), the severity of the consequences of crowding should be a function of the degree of social support and personal control afforded by the environment in which increased density occurs. Thus responses of the magnitude of those reported here are congruent with the limitations of control and the absence of support common to corrections at its worst. This may not, however, solely account for the nature of these responses.

Instead, it is in the socialization of those who experience such conditions that the nature of these consequences may be understood.

IMPLICATIONS FOR REFORM

Though institutional populations have continued to rise, few alternatives have been sought to counteract the consequences that such increased numbers produce. Instead, correctional policy seems guided by a belief that the problems posed by crowding will be solved when more facilities are built. The prevalence of this belief can be seen in the current surge in prison construction. As revealed in a recent survey (Hunzeker, 1982), 44 of 48 states as well as the District of Columbia and the Federal Bureau of Prisons are actively engaged in efforts to enlarge institutional capacities by either expanding existing structures or building new ones. Support for such a policy has also appeared in the recommendations offered by the Attorney General's Task Force on Violent Crime (1981), which advocated the expansion of institutional capacities as a means to combat the increase in violent offenders. The fruits of such a policy, however, may be long in coming. Resistance arises from the financial burdens that such a commitment entails, for, as recent estimates have indicated, the cost of institutional construction is roughly $50,000 per cell. Using the recommended standard of single-occupancy housing as a guide, this cost would translate into an overall cost of approximately $12.5 million per 250-person facility constructed. Multiplied many times over, the expense required to increase institutional capacities to a level equal to the increase in institutional populations may well be in the billions of dollars. This is a cost that, even during the best of economic conditions, would be difficult to bear. Thus it would appear that for many institutions the current reality of too little space for individuals confined will be a reality for some time to come.

Despite the fervor with which institutional expansion is now being advocated, the implications of such a policy for alleviating the consequences of crowding cannot be automatically assumed. As has been suggested by the present analysis, the consequences of crowding reflect as much the conditions common to incarceration as they do the demands imposed by crowding itself. Consistent with this analysis, a solution that seeks to alleviate the spatial inadequacies invoked by crowding may serve only to lessen the severity of adaptive responses without modifying their nature. Moreover, to advocate a policy of increasing institutional capacities as the only solution to crowding is to obscure other factors that contribute to the problems associated with increased numbers. Included among such factors are the limitation of resources, the denial of personal control, and the weakening of social support that institutional life imposes. Thus to seek a modification in these factors may be as integral a solution to the problems posed by crowding as is a policy of increased institutional capacities.

Institutional resources may vary both in quantity and in kind. At a more basic level, these resources may be conceived as the "goods and services" provided to those who are confined. These may range from the personal possessions allowed to the food, clothing, and medical attention all inmates are provided. Spatially, these resources may be seen in such terms as the type of housing unit to which an inmate is assigned and the number of individuals with whom such housing must be shared. In addition to such goods and services, these resources may be conceived as the opportunities that institutional life affords. Such opportunities may take the form of meaningful job assignments, relevant program placements, and activities of a varied nature. The significance of these resources inheres in the avenues that are available for the satisfaction of the individual's personal needs.

In a sense, these need satisfaction patterns serve as a mechanism by which the individual is able to cope with the deprivations of confinement. To the degree that these patterns can be maintained under conditions of crowding, the impact of increased numbers may be lessened successfully. The likelihood of this is diminished, however, by the nature of the environment in which the individual is most often confined, an environment in which inadequacies are compounded by the lethargy with which alternatives are attempted. This can be illustrated by the responses that have ensued in light of the demands posed by crowding. Except with respect to the most basic of necessities, such as food, clothing, and shelter, rarely have such increased demands been met with increased resources. Instead, many institutions attempt to make do with the resources they have. The result is often a reduction in the number of goods, services, and opportunities available per individual confined. More than merely providing the individual with less, these reductions serve to weaken the means by which the person has come to survive the deprivations of confinement; they may thereby indirectly promote victimization and violence, including collective violence (see Chapters 4 and 5). However, to the degree that increases in institutional populations can be matched by increases in the resources institutional life provides, the demands of crowding may be reduced.

Implicit in such an expansion of institutional resources is an enhanced capacity to choose among those resources provided. This opportunity may be conceived as one of increasing personal control. Consonant with the definition of control is an ability to determine for oneself those events to which one will be exposed. It is important to recognize, however, that the expansion of institutional resources may not in itself result in a greater sense of control. For such an opportunity to be realized, the provision of resources must be coupled with the increased freedom to choose among them.

The significance of personal control has been demonstrated in studies wherein the presentation of stimuli such as excessive noise (Glass & Singer, 1972) and density (Sherrod, 1974; Langer & Saegert, 1977) has been shown to be mediated by the perceived ability to regulate their exposure. The implications of these studies can be found in attempts to modify the correctional environment so as to promote within the individual a greater sense of control. An example of such an attempt is to allow the individual access to his or her living quarters through a commonly accepted means, such as a key to a door. Similarly, other modifications may take the form of allowing the individual to regulate the temperature, ventilation, and lighting within his or her housing assignment. Much as the resources of the institution include aspects other than its physical structure, the opportunity for mediating the effects of crowding may inhere in those other resources that are provided. For example, opportunities for choice may be enhanced to the degree that individuals are free to choose among the services, programs, and activities offered by the institution. Other opportunities may arise from the options allowed in the selection of food, clothing, and personal items. It must, however, be realized that opportunities for control may be limited by the existing resources. This is in fact the reality of many institutions today, for with the increasing numbers who are being imprisoned there are few institutions with resources that have not been exceeded by the demands of those they confine. Nonetheless, to the degree that scarce resources can be freely chosen, the opportunities for control exist, as do the means to ameliorate the problems produced by crowding.

To summarize, the demands imposed by crowding may be alleviated by means other than increasing institutional capacities alone. Specifically, through a policy of resource enrichment coupled with a widening in the opportunities for personal control, the consequences that have been associated with crowding may be diminished. The implications of such a policy, of course, go beyond the mitigation of crowding, for in adopting such a policy the structure of the inmate society may itself be altered. The inmate society has long been characterized by its competition for survival and its hierarchy of domination. It is in the mitigation of these struggles and resolutions that the potential of a policy of increased resources and increased control arises. To the degree that institutional resources can be expanded, the incentive to compete may be reduced. Similarly, to the extent that opportunities for control are more widely available, the need to dominate others may be lessened. This is not to suggest that the motivations for competition and dominance will no longer exist, for there are many goods and services that individuals desire and the institution must deny. Even so, the potential of the present policy must be considered in light of the alternatives it provides for those who desire a less depriving existence and a greater opportunity for control. It is perhaps for these individuals that the adoption of such a policy may result in a social structure in which competition and dominance are replaced by cooperation and support. Interestingly, it is through such a society that the stress imposed by crowding may be further lessened.

REFERENCES

Attorney General's Task Force on Violent Crime. *Phase I recommendations*. Washington, DC: U.S. Department of Justice, 1981.

Baum, A., Harpin, R.E., & Valins, S. The role of group phenomena in the experience of crowding. *Environment and Behavior,* 1975, 7, 185-198.

Bell v. Wolfish, 99 S. Ct. 76, 1978.

Bonta, J. L., & Nanckivell, G. Institutional misconducts and anxiety levels among jailed inmates. *Criminal Justice and Behavior,* 1980, 7(2), 203-214.

Calhoun, J. B. Population density and social pathology. *Scientific American,* 1962, 206, 139-148.

Clements, C. B. Crowded prisons: A review of psychological and environmental effects. *Law and Human Behavior,* 1979, 3(3), 217-225.

Clemmer, D. *The prison community*. New York: Holt, Rinehart & Winston, 1940.

D'Atri, D. A. Psychophysiological responses to crowding. *Environment and Behavior,* 1975, 7, 237-252.

Desor, J. A. Toward a psychological theory of crowding. *Journal of Personality and Social Psychologycal,* 1972, 21, 79-83.

Epstein, Y. M. Crowding stress and human behavior. *Journal of Social Issues,* 1981, 37(1), 126-144.

Farrington, D. P., & Nuttall, C. P. Prison size, overcrowding, prison violence, and recidivism. *Journal of Criminal Justice,* 1980, 8, 221-231.

Freedman, J. L. *Crowding and behavior.* San Francisco: Freeman, 1975.

Freedman, J. L., Klevansky, S., & Ehrlich, P. The effect of crowding on human task performance. *Journal of Applied Social Psychology,* 1971, 1, 7-25.

Freedman, J. L., Levy, A. S., Buchanan, R. W., & Price, J. Crowding and human aggressiveness. *Journal of Experimental Social Psychology,* 1972, 8, 528-548.

Galle, O. R., Gove, W. R., & McPherson, J. B. Population density and pathology: What are the relationships for man? *Science,* 1972, 176, 23-30.

Glass, D., & Singer, J. *Urban stress: Experiments on noise and social stressors*. New York: Academic, 1972.
Griffitt, W., & Veitch, R. Hot and crowded: Influences of population density and temperature on interpersonal affective behavior. *Journal of Personality and Social Psychology*, 1971, 17, 92-98.
Holt v. Sarver, 300 F. Supp. 825, E.D. Ark., 1969.
Hunzeker, D. Constitution and overcrowding. *Corrections Compendium*, 1982, 6(9), 1-7.
Hutt, C., & Vaizey, J. J. Differential effects of group density on social behavior. *Nature*, 1966, 209, 1371-1372.
Irwin, J. *Prisons in turmoil*. Boston: Little, Brown, 1980.
Jacobs, J. B. *Stateville: The penitentiary in mass society*. Chicago: University of Chicago Press, 1977.
Jan, L. Overcrowding and inmate behavior: Some preliminary findings. *Criminal Justice and Behavior*, 1980, 7(3), 293-301.
Langer, E. J., & Saegert, S. Crowding and cognitive control. *Journal of Personality and Social Psychology*, 1977, 35, 175-182.
Loo, C. M. The effect of spatial density on the social behavior of children. *Journal of Applied Social Psychology*, 1973, 2(4), 372-381.
McCain, G., Cox, V. C., & Paulus, P. B. The relationship between illness complaints and degree of crowding in a prison environment. *Environment and Behavior*, 1976, 8(2), 283-290.
McGrew, P. L. Social and spatial density effects on spacing behavior in preschool children. *Journal of Child Psychology and Psychiatry*, 1970, 11, 197-205.
Marsella, A. J., Escudero, M., & Gordon, P. The effects of dwelling density on mental disorders in Filipino men. *Journal of Health and Social Behavior*, 1970, 11(4), 288-294.
Megargee, E. I. The association of population density, reduced space, and uncomfortable temperatures with misconduct in a prison community. *American Journal of Community Psychology*, 1977, 5(3), 289-298.
Michelson, W. *Man and his urban environment: A sociological approach*. Reading, MA: Addison-Wesley, 1970.
Mullen, J., & Smith, B. *American prisons and jails, volume III: Conditions and costs of confinement*. Washington, DC: Government Printing Office, 1980.
Nacci, P. L., Teitelbaum, H. E., & Prather, J. Population density and inmate misconduct rates in the federal prison system. *Federal Probation*, 1977, 6, 26-31.
National Advisory Commission on Criminal Justice Standards and Goals. *Corrections*. Washington, DC: Government Printing Office, 1973.
Paulus, P. B., Cox, V., McCain, G., & Chandler, J. Some effects of crowding in a prison environment. *Journal of Applied Social Psychology*, 1975, 5(1), 86-91.
Paulus, P. B., McCain, G., & Cox, V. C. Death rates, psychiatric commitments, blood pressure, and perceived crowding as a function of institutional crowding. *Environmental Psychology and Nonverbal Behavior*, 1978, 3(2), 107-116.
Paulus, P. B., McCain, G., & Cox, V. Prison standards: Some pertinent data on crowding. *Federal Probation*, 1981, 4, 48-54.
Pugh v. Locke, 406 F. Supp, 318, M.D. Ala., 1976.
Rawls, J. R., Trego, R. E., McGaffey, C. N., & Rawls, D. J. Personal space as a predictor of performance under close working conditions. *Journal of Social Psychology*, 1972, 86(2), 261-267.
Rhodes v. Chapman 101 S. Ct. 49, 1981.
Ross, M., Layton, B., Erickson, B., & Schopler, J. Affect, facial regard, and reactions to crowding. *Journal of Personality and Social Psychology*, 1973, 28(1), 69-76.

Schmitt, R. C. Implications of density in Hong Kong. *Journal of the American Institute of Planners,* 1963, 24(3), 210-217.

Schwartz, D. T., & Mintz, N. L. Ecology and psychoses among Italians in 27 Boston communities. *Social Problems,* 1963, 19(4), 371-375.

Sherrod, D. R. Crowding, perceived control and behavioral after effects. *Journal of Applied Social Psychology,* 1974, 4, 171-186.

Smith, D. E. *Crowding and corrections: Coping with high density confinement.* Article in preparation, 1982.

Sykes, G. M. *The society of captives: A study of a maximum security prison.* Princeton, NJ: Princeton University Press, 1958.

U.S. Department of Justice, Bureau of Justice Statistics. Statistics supplied in reply to personal request, May 1982.

Wickersham Commission (National Commission on Law Observance and Enforcement). *Report no. 12: The cost of crime.* Washington, DC: Author, 1931.

Worchel, D., & Teddlie, C. The experience of crowding: A two factor theory. *Journal of Personality and Social Psychology,* 1976, 34, 30-40.

CHAPTER 4

Victimizers and Victims in American Correctional Institutions

LEE H. BOWKER

In his classic study, *The Society of Captives*, Gresham Sykes (1966) identified loss of security as one of the pains of imprisonment. He found that prisoners suffered because of having to live in intimate contact with other prisoners whom they believed to be dangerous. The force of this observation is brought home by the fact that Sykes found that fully three-fourths of the prisoners he studied played predatory social roles: 10 percent of them specialized in the use of violence (as in the "tough" and the "gorilla" roles); 30 percent subjected others to manipulations (as in the "merchant" role); and 35 percent used both violence and manipulations to victimize their fellow prisoners. We must conclude, as Sykes did, that exploitation is a central element in prison life.

TYPES OF PRISON VICTIMIZATION

Prison victimization is effectively shielded from public knowledge by security practices that block easy communication with the outside world, as well as by prisoner norms that favor hiding the evidence of all criminal acts by prisoners from the authorities and the public alike. The only victimizing incidents that are likely to overcome these communication barriers are those associated with homicides and riots. As a result, there is a common impression that victimization in correctional institutions is limited to fighting, with perhaps an occasional homosexual rape for leavening. This impression is fundamentally in error, and the remainder of this section is designed to give readers a grasp of the comprehensiveness and pervasiveness of prison victimization. There are four general types of prison victimization: physical, psychological, economic, and social (Bowker, 1979).

Physical Victimization

Physical victimization includes assault, homicide, and homosexual rape. Reports by Jones (1976), Astrachan (1975), Park (1976), Grasewicz (1977), Fuller et al. (1977), Sylvester et al. (1977), and others show that physical victimization is a relatively common occurrence in correctional institutions. Although there are substantial differences among the various estimates of victimization levels, nobody seriously puts forth a claim that assault is an insignificant aspect of prison life.

The prison environment combines a number of different factors into what amounts to a controlled war. These factors include: (1) inadequate supervision by staff members, (2) architectural designs that promote rather than inhibit victimization, (3) the easy availability of deadly weapons, (4) the housing of violence-prone prisoners in close proximity to relatively defenseless victims, and (5) a generally high level of tension produced by the close quarters and multiple, crosscutting conflicts among both individuals and groups of prisoners. To these factors, we must add feedback systems through which prisoners feel the need to take revenge for real or imagined slights or past victimizations, the interrelationships among types of victimization, and the moral and administrative confusion that occurs when the aggressor becomes the victim within a single incident (as has been described by Lockwood, 1980).

No assault is completely without risk. There is always the possibility that the victim will win in a fair fight, or that the victim's friends or relatives might be in a position to exact revenge at some future time. In view of the risk, and assuming a modicum of rational control over behavior, we must ask why prisoners choose to assault one another. The first reason is the desire to achieve higher status in the prison society, since violent prisoners generally have higher status than nonviolent prisoners. One way to move up in the status hierarchy is therefore to defeat someone who is ranked above you, thus winning a higher place on the ladder and a better reputation. A closely related second reason is that victories in the field of battle reassure the winners of their competence as human beings in the face of the passivity enforced by institutional regulations. This is particularly important for prisoners whose masculinity is threatened by the conditions of confinement.

Defense through offense is the third reason for engaging in prison violence. Prisoners who achieve notoriety as fighters are much less likely to be attacked than those who appear to fear overt conflict. It is not necessary to engage in fights constantly in order to maintain a fierce enough reputation to deter potential victimizers. Several well-chosen events early in a prison career, if properly milked, can protect a prisoner throughout an extensive period of incarceration.

Tension release cannot be ignored as a reinforcer for prison violence. It can be cathartic to beat someone up, even at expense of modest injuries to oneself. As tensions build to intolerable proportions, the attractiveness of a "good fight" multiplies. This psychological reward is also a powerful reinforcer for prison rape, which provides the aggressor with sexual release without the time and effort of a courtship.

Two final reasons for engaging in prison violence are economic gain and "the gate." Violence or the threat of violence can net the aggressor canteen items, appliances, prison scrip or U.S. currency, cigarettes, drugs, a more desirable social setting, and less obvious resources such as a "willing" sexual partner who wishes to avoid becoming a rape victim. The judicious use of violence can guarantee the aggressor a favorably located cell, preferred cell partners, access to the best recreational facilities and rehabilitative programs, and membership in a high-status prisoner friendship group or gang. "The gate" refers to the possibility that prison administrators will opt to recommend an early release (or at least not a late one) for prisoners who continually stir up trouble, but who do so in such a way that there is never enough evidence available to punish them. Another manipulation designed to shorten the distance to the gate is to deliberately accumulate a number of disciplinary citations for fights early in one's prison career, and then to maintain a clean record so that administrators and parole board members will think that one has reformed and release one as soon as possible. One advantage of flat time sentences is that the utility of these manipulations is diminished.

Prison rape includes all forced sex acts, not just anal intercourse. Although much more common in male institutions, force is not unknown in women's prisons, and there is apparently much variation in rape rates among institutions. Few prisons have a rape rate comparable to the virtual epidemic in the Philadelphia prison system reported by Davis (1968), but even where the objective incidence is low the fear of rape often pervades prisoner life. The racial imbalance in rape victimization statistics (black aggressor, white victim) reminds us that another benefit of victimizing others is to use aggression to demonstrate racial superiority.

Rape victims, like the victims of other forms of prison violence, are not randomly distributed in prison populations. Victims tend to be white, small, young, middle class (or at least not ghetto residents), disproportionately convicted of sex crimes against children or relatively minor property crimes, socially isolated, cooperative with the administration ("rats" and "snitches"), and lacking in mental toughness and street survival skills. As long as judges insist on incarcerating these offenders and correctional systems continue to house them together with hardened, predatory offenders, prison physical victimization rates will remain high. From the viewpoint of the aggressors, incarceration simply means switching from victimizing the weak and defenseless on the street to victimizing weak and defenseless fellow prisoners.

Psychological Victimization

Psychological victimization is much more common than physical victimization in prisons. Most of its manifestations are legal under prison regulations, and some of its victims never even realize that they have been made fools of. Much psychological victimization consists of verbal manipulations—subtle distortions of reality and outright lies that trick victims into giving up sex, material goods, or other desired commodities without a fight. Other manipulations involve minor alterations of the social structure or physical environment. Victims may be "set up" by having their friends moved to other cell blocks, thus leaving them socially isolated, and may be agitated by having their possessions continually moved around or their mail withheld. A good example of this involved a psychotic male prisoner who moved from a protected environment to one in which he could easily be victimized simply because he found a nut (as in nuts and bolts) sitting outside his cell and concluded that his fellow prisoners were insulting him by signaling to him that he was nuts.

Since toughness and high status in prison are maintained more through reputation than action, prisoners are always in danger of having their reputations eroded through the rumor mill. It is easy to weaken the position of prisoners who are not firmly situated in the prisoner subculture by planting rumors that they are homosexuals, "snitches," or "baby rapists."

Another vulnerability that can be turned into an opportunity for psychological victimization is the tenuousness of relations between prisoners and relatives or lovers in the free society. With visits restricted and letters infrequent, most prisoners have no way of being sure that their spouses are still faithful, their children well, and their property safe. Rumors about unfaithfulness, illness, and other problems among loved ones invariably throw prisoners into a state of extreme agitation. Agitated prisoners are distracted from their accustomed defensive posture, and so are easily victimized. They leave their cells unlocked (inviting burglary), fail to use care in their movements about the institution (increasing their vulnerability to rape), and are more easily talked into participating in risky schemes involving the smuggling of contraband.

In general, psychological victimization provides the same benefits to the successful aggressor as physical victimization, but it differs from assaultive behavior in that it is much less risky and it gives somewhat less of a boost to the social status of the aggressor. It also requires a considerable amount of "street sophistication" about human behavior and is unlikely to provide the same degree of tension release as physical victimization.

Economic Victimization

One of the components of prisoner subcultures is a sub rosa economic system that operates illegally right under the noses of correctional officers and is the setting for many of the same forms of economic victimization that are common in the free society. Bowker (1980) has developed a typology of economic victimization that identifies eight analytically distinct forms: (1) loan sharking, (2) gambling frauds, (3) pricing violations, (4) theft, (5) robbery, (6) protection rackets, (7) deliberate misrepresentation of products, and (8) nondelivery of products. In practice, two or more of these forms are often integrated into complex victimization schemes. Only theft and robbery are typical street crimes. The other forms of economic victimization have a closer resemblance to the free-world activities of organized crime and "legitimate" business.

Money is always tight in prison, which forces prisoners to pay high interest rates on both money and goods. Inexperienced prisoners may borrow money without realizing the magnitude of the interest rate until they attempt to pay back the loan. Part of the loan-sharking system is that interest rates escalate when payments are not made on time, so that the level of indebtedness quickly rises beyond the prisoner's ability to pay. The victim may then have to perform sexual or other illegal services in lieu of payment, or may be assaulted (or even murdered) as an example for other delinquent debtors.

Prison gambling is only safe when it is conducted among friends. Fraud is always a possibility in gambling operations, whether with cards, dice, or betting pools. As with other forms of victimization, inexperienced "fish" are the preferred victims. Gambling frauds and loan sharking are often combined in a single operation, backed up with the threat of violence.

Systematic overcharging is an accepted business practice in the free society. At some point this practice becomes a pricing violation and is defined as victimizing. Demand exceeds supply by such a wide margin in prison that sellers are able to charge extremely high prices and to protect their profit margins by price fixing and market manipulation. In price fixing, the suppliers of a desired commodity (such as psychoactive drugs) agree on an unrealistically high price so that no prisoners can obtain the items at a more reasonable price. Market manipulation reduces the competition among sellers by forcing some out of business through violence or "snitch kites" that expose competitors' activities to the prison administration.

Theft is the stealing of prisoners' goods in their absence, while robbery involves a face-to-face confrontation and at least a threat of violence. Protection rackets provide a guarantee of freedom from harassment in return for regular payments of goods, money, or services in prison, just as they do on the streets. A subtype of protection racket is the blackmail scheme in which prisoners pay for protection against having their reputations (instead of their bodies) damaged.

The deliberate misrepresentation of products occurs when prisoners "hype" their products or otherwise portray them as better than they in fact are. Rat poison instead of LSD, marijuana that is half tobacco, and pornography that turns out to be uninspiring are examples of this form of economic victimization. It is only a short step from misrepresentation to "burning" customers by taking their money and then inventing a rationale to explain why it has become impossible to deliver the goods.

Economic crimes that are most efficiently carried out by organized crime in the free world also require group support within the prison if they are to be most fully and profitably developed. The takeover of the sub rosa economic system in many prisons by gangs in the late 1960s and early 1970s has heightened the level of economic victimization at the same time that it has routinized and rationalized it. No individual entrepreneur, no matter how strong and crafty, can hold out against an organized prisoner gang (Jacobs, 1977).

Social Victimization

To the extent that prisoners are victimized because of their membership in an identifiable social category or group, they are experiencing social victimization. It is difficult to determine whether a single incident falls into this category of victimization, but if we aggregate individual incidents and see them against the background of group conflicts, prejudice, and discrimination in the prisoner subculture, patterns may emerge that can be labeled as social victimization. When blacks systematically victimize whites, or when "baby rapers" are forced to fear for their lives throughout their prison careers, this composite is social victimization. Social victimization took on new meaning in the late

1960s when prisoner gangs, formed on the basis of neighborhood, race, or ethnicity, began to vie for the control of prisoner subcultures in major industrial states from New York to California. Hundreds of prisoners were assaulted or murdered during the gang conflicts in these states for no reason other than that they held membership in rival gangs.

EFFECTS OF PRISONER VICTIMIZATION

A general effect of victimization in any setting is that it curbs the victim's freedom to act. A person who has been victimized may no longer have the money to choose an attractive vacation or may have to give up the pleasures of daily life while spending time in the hospital. Psychological curbs on freedom may be more limiting than physical curbs for many victims. Some victims become afraid to frequent certain areas of town, to engage in dangerous activities, or even to leave their houses, in a kind of induced agoraphobia. Prisoners have, by definition, lost most of their freedom as punishment for their crimes. Through prisoner subcultures, they construct new social worlds in which they can regain some measure of psychological (if not physical) freedom. This final dollop of freedom is what is attenuated by prison victimization. It is not uncommon for recently victimized prisoners to miss meals, resign from their favorite clubs, skip recreation periods, or ask to be placed in segregation in order to reduce the chances of additional victimization.

Other major effects of prison victimization include feelings of helplessness and depression, economic hardship, physical injury, disruption of social relationships, damaged self-image, possible self-destructive acts such as self-mutilation and suicide, adoption of increasingly antisocial values, lowered social status, psychosomatic diseases, increased difficulties in adjusting to life after release, and possibly even an increased risk of recidivism. These are essentially the same consequences as the effects of victimization in the free society; however, there are several differences worth noting. The first of these is that prisoners already face a series of crises in adapting to prison life and then in readapting to freedom while avoiding recidivism (see Chapter 9, this volume). These crises make psychological survival precarious for many prisoners, and victimization can be what forces some individuals over the brink into serious difficulty (see Johnson, 1976; Toch, 1975, 1977a, for examples of these crises). The other difference is that most (but by no means all) free peole can ecologically isolate themselves from aggressors through relocation, target hardening, and modified habits. In contrast, prisoners cannot escape from their aggressors. Even being locked in solitary confinement is not perfect protection from the possibility of continued victimization, and few prison administrators are willing to authorize protective confinement for all prisoners who need it, or to continue it indefinitely. When the victim is forced back into the general population his or her victimizers are still there, and often must be faced under conditions of inconsistent and inadequate custodial supervision.

INTERVENTIONS

Once victimized, a prisoner should have access to a wide range of medical and psychological support services. These include medical treatment by qualified physicians, psychiatric examinations, individual psychotherapy, group counseling, and self-help groups. Steps should also be taken to protect the victim from the possibility of further mistreatment. It is unfortunate that there is scarcely a handful of maximum security prisons in which these activities occur, or where they could possibly occur under current funding limitations. For this reason, greater benefits are to be expected from preventive measures than from treatment after victimization has taken place.

The listing of preventive measures is a dangerous activity, for the linkages between all sorts of prison problems and victimization soon lead into what amounts to no more than a catalogue of the deficiencies of correctional institutions. Keeping this danger in mind, I have constructed a short list of preventive measures derived from the following assumptions:

- (A1) Prison administrators could reduce victimization if they had better data at hand on its frequency and distribution.
- (A2) Prison administrators could reduce victimization if they had increased resources.
- (A3) Prison victimization is inversely related to the proportion of potential aggressors' social relations that are humanistically oriented (involving caring and valuing human life).
- (A4) Prison victimization is inversely related to the degree of normalization of prison life (normalization with respect to working-class life in the free society).
- (A5) Prison victimization is directly proportional to the presence of easy victims in the prisoner population.
- (A6) Prison victimization could be reduced if prisoners were rewarded for nonvictimizing behavior.

This chapter concludes with a representative list of thirteen interventive strategies designed to reduce prison victimization. The assumptions to which each strategy relates are given in parentheses.

Victimization Data Systems (A1)

Prisons typically process incidents as they arise and then file them under the names of the aggressors. This case management system is completely individualistic in nature, so it never builds a body of knowledge about historical trends, relationships between the characteristics of victims and aggressors, and the ecological distribution of victimization within the institution or correctional system. The implementation of a victimization data system in each institution would make it possible for administrators to allocate resources rationally to combat the problem, and a systemwide victimization data system (which is already in place in states such as Wisconsin and California) would allow system administrators to allocate resources to the institutions experiencing the highest victimization rates.

Minor Structural and Utilization Changes (A2)

Victimization rates are high in those areas of prisons that are not constantly open to the view of staff members. An analysis of victimization patterns identifies these areas, which can then be modified without a great expenditure of funds in most cases. A covered walkway can have the roof removed so that tower guards can have an open view of everything that happens there. A cul-de-sac in a hallway that does not lend itself to staff observation can be walled off or can be monitored with a remote television camera. When physical modifications are too expensive, utilization patterns can be modified. For example, a recreation area can be closed during hours when there is inadequate supervision and prisoners can be locked *out* of their cells when there is not sufficient staff to supervise the cell block and the day use areas simultaneously.

The Correctional Ombudsman (A1, A2, A4)

The correctional ombudsman was proposed as a way of reducing prison violence by Hans Toch in his book, *Police, Prisons, and the Problem of Violence* (1977a). Toch holds that ombudsmen who consistently demonstrate integrity in their dealings with prisoners and staff can solve some of the tension-producing prison problems that often lead to violence. In addition, ombudsmen serve as a channel of information from prisoners to administrators, short-circuiting the usual route through custody staff members. The information thus gained can be used to focus resources on conditions and situations that appear to be most conducive to victimization.

Classification by Victimization Potential (A5)

Prison researchers rarely report an altercation between two strong, high-status prisoners. Most violence proceeds from the strong to the weak, and this lineup appears even more strikingly in nonviolent forms of victimization. An obvious strategy suggested by this observation is to remove the weak from the presence of the strong through a careful classification process. Violent prisoners should not generally be housed together with nonviolent prisoners, and prisoners with a lower-class background of street survival should not be mixed with those from more sedate, middle- or working-class backgrounds. Male prisoners who are effeminate or slight of build require special protection from the minute they are jailed to their release from institutional supervision.

Increased Security (A2)

One reason for the high level of prison violence is the surprisingly lackadaisical attitude toward security that exists in many correctional institutions. Inadequate security assures that there will be an abundance of contraband to fight over and more than enough weapons to fight with. Drugs smuggled into the prison are a major source of prisoner disputes that lead to violence, and weapons smuggled into living areas from prison industries guarantee that knives, or even more deadly weapons, will always be available.

Facilitating Visiting (A3, A4)

The more visits prisoners have with their loved ones, or with other law-abiding citizens who display caring attitudes toward them, the less likely they are to victimize their fellow prisoners. The chain of facilitating conditions for visiting begins with arranging child care and transportation to and from the institution (remembering that many prisons are located far from the population centers from which most of their prisoners are drawn), and also includes the improvement of visiting facilities at the institution and the framing of liberal regulations to meet the visiting capabilities of friends and relatives having a wide variety of scheduling needs. An example of flexible scheduling is the willingness of the institution to permit unusually long visiting periods for relatives who live far away or have such difficult work schedules that they can travel to the institution only infrequently.

Conjugal Visits (A3, A4, A6)

Family visits in tasteful surroundings permit prisoners to become reacquainted with their spouses and children for periods as long as 24 to 48 hours, scheduled as frequently as once a month. Although sexual behavior obviously can occur during these visits, the emphasis is on family social relations rather than on sexual relations. Since prisoners in punitive detention would be unavailable for conjugal visits, there is a deterrent effect in operating an extensive conjugal visiting program. More subtly, but not less importantly, these visits have a humanizing effect. Prisoners looking forward to conjugal visits are less subject to the antisocial influences of the prisoner subculture.

Normalizing Prison Industries (A4, A6)

One of the paradoxes of imprisonment is that the economic deprivation accompanying it increases the incentives for prison victimization and simultaneously reduces the incentives for refraining from victimizing others. It increases victimization incentives by widening the gap between the prisoners' accustomed standards of living and their everyday experiences. At the same time, it reduces the incentives for refraining from victimizing others in that prisoners who earn no more than several dollars a day have little to lose if they are placed in solitary confinement as punishment for their predatory activities. By widening the gap between legitimate earnings and potential illegal gains, legislators and prison administrators increase victimization rates. The paradox is thus that policies intended to deter crime in the long run actually increase crime in the short run. Reversal of this situation requires that prisoners be paid at least the minimum wage, preferably the same as their labor would be worth in the free society. This reform will shift the balance of incentives to favor law-abiding behavior instead of victimization.

More Therapeutic Roles for Correctional Officers (A3)

It is impossible to humanize correctional environments unless we modify the roles and job descriptions of correctional officers to give them responsibilities for the personal growth and development of the prisoners (see Chapters 17 and 18). In essence, this means eliminating the purely custodial role of the prison guard, except in the observation towers. It does not, however, necessarily require officers with college degrees. In-service training can prepare officers for a lifetime of therapeutic service delivery to prisoners. Caring staff members can influence prisoners to be less predatory, and they can also offer superior therapeutic services to the targets of the victimization that still occurs.

Increased Staffing (A1, A2)

Hiring additional staff members naturally increases the level of custodial supervision, which depresses victimization in much the same way as having a police officer on every corner in the neighborhood. We should not forget that increasing the number of prosocial staff members also subtly changes the social environment so as to make it less supportive of predatory behavior. Where budget limitations make it impossible to add staff members, the same effect can be achieved by (1) decreasing prisoner populations through early release, work and study release, and so on, and (2) altering the ecology of prisoner-staff interaction by reassigning staff, increasing the proportion of staff in continuous contact with prisoners, and changing the prisoners' daily schedules. The latter solution requires modifying the staff subculture, which normally encourages correctional officers to minimize and routinize interaction with prisoners—exactly the opposite of the values that are necessary to achieve a prosocial and antivictimization effect.

Cocorrections (A4, A6)

There is evidence (Smykla, 1977) that cocorrectional institutions have lower victimization rates than unisex institutions. It is not clear to what extent this may be due to differences in prisoner characteristics between institutions rather than a reflection of a true structural effect of cocorrections. However, it is reasonable to assume that the normalizing effect of integrating the sexes will reduce victimization in prison, just as it has in some college residence halls. There is no doubt that gender integration is beneficial for male prisoners. Less evidence is available for the effect on female prisoners. In any case, the unbalanced sex ratio (20 or 25 to 1) in correctional systems limits the applicability of this strategy for the reduction of victimization.

Unit Management (A2, A3)

Unit management refers to breaking up large prisoner populations into smaller units, each with its own cadre of staff members. If these small units can be almost completely isolated from other units, victimization can be reduced as caring, prosocial relationships are established among prisoners and between staff and prisoners within each unit. Unitizing large correctional institutions is a low-budget alternative to the widely touted strategy of building chains of mini-prisons. (See Chapter 14 for a discussion of unit management and correctional treatment.)

Lower Incarceration Rates (A5)

Imprisonment rates have been rising in America for a number of years, after a long period of gradual decline. This trend reflects an increased commitment to the incarceration of property offenders as well as the use of longer sentences for violent offenders. To the extent that property offenders are less likely to be able to defend themselves against predatory prisoners, rising incarceration rates translate into rising prison victimization rates. Lowering incarceration rates is a good way to begin a campaign against prison victimization. Most offenders who are not tough enough to defend themselves in correctional settings are probably not enough of a public danger to justify the expense of incarceration.

SUMMARY

This chapter began with the description of four major categories of prison victimization: physical, psychological, economic, and social. Special attention was paid to economic victimization, which occurs as robbery, theft, loan sharking, gambling frauds, pricing violations, protection rackets, deliberate misrepresentation of products, and nondelivery of products. The chapter concluded with the presentation of thirteen interventive strategies designed to reduce the incidence of prison victimization. The most promising among these are minor structural modifications, classification by victimization potential, increased security and staffing, unit management, and decreased incarceration rates.

REFERENCES

Astrachan, A. Profile/Louisiana. *Corrections Magazine*, 1975, 2(September/October), 9-14.

Bowker, L. H. Victimization in correctional institutions: An interdisciplinary analysis. In J. A. Conley (Ed.), *Theory and research in criminal justice: Current perspectives*. Cincinnati: Anderson, 1979.

Bowker, L. H. *Prison victimization.* New York: Elsevier, 1980.

Davis, A. Sexual assaults in the Philadelphia prison system and sheriffs' vans. *Transaction*, 1968, 6(December), 8-16.

Fuller, D., Orsagh, T., & Raber, D. *Violence and victimization within the North Carolina prison system.* Paper presented at the meeting of the Academy of Criminal Justice Sciences, 1977.

Grasewicz, L. *A study of inmate assaults in major institutions.* Richmond: Bureau of Research, Reporting and Evaluation, Virginia Department of Corrections, 1977.

Jacobs, J. B. *Stateville: The penitentiary in mass society.* Chicago: University of Chicago Press, 1977.

Johnson, R. *Culture and crisis in confinement.* Lexington, MA: D. C. Heath, 1976.

Jones, D. *The health risks of imprisonment.* Lexington, MA: D. C. Heath, 1976.

Lockwood, D. *Prison sexual violence.* New York: Elsevier, 1980.

Park, J. The organization of prison violence. In A. Cohen, G. Cole, & R. Bailey (Eds.), *Prison violence.* Lexington, MA: D. C. Heath, 1976.

Smykla, J. O. *A phenomenological analysis of the social environment in a coed prison.* Unpublished doctoral dissertation, Michigan State University, 1977.

Sykes, G. M. *The society of captives: A study of a maximum security prison.* New York: Atheneum, 1966.

Sylvester, S., Reed, J., & Nelson, D. *Prison homicide.* New York: Spectrum, 1977.

Toch, H. *Men in crisis: Human breakdowns in prison.* Chicago: Aldine, 1975.

Toch, H. *Living in prison: The ecology of survival.* New York: Free Press, 1977. (a)

Toch, H. *Police, prisons, and the problem of violence.* Washington, DC: Government Printing Office, 1977. (b)

CHAPTER 5

Stress, Change, and Collective Violence in Prison

LUCIEN X. LOMBARDO

Prison riots have traditionally been explored as if they were singular events—aberrations in the life of prison communities. In studying riots researchers have generally pulled back from the dynamics of day-to-day prison life, focusing instead on the relationship between prison conditions and collective violence. Here, instead, I attempt to relate collective violence to the stresses experienced and coped with by those living and working in prison. I explore the normal conditions of prison life for clues to the development of collective violence. In short, this chapter is an attempt to think about prison collective violence from an integrative perspective that recently published studies concerning the dynamics of prison life make possible for the first time.

Sociological studies of prison riots implicitly assume both the *collective* and *violent* nature of prison disturbances without seeking to explain how either of the crucial defining characteristics develops (Garson, 1972a; Desroches, 1974; Wilsnack, 1976). Inmates and prison staff are assumed to be mutually hostile *groups*, and the violence of a riot is simply a more overt expression of underlying inmate-staff hostility. In this context, riots erupt when the staff loses its ability to exercise power and control over inmates living under conditions of deprivation. When controls break down, inmate frustration finds its outlet in violence.

Wilsnack (1976, p. 73) illustrates this position in developing a theoretical interpretation of riots that integrates survey findings with previous studies:

> For a riot to erupt there must be not only deprived and powerless *inmates* and attention from influential outsiders, but also an uncertain and

unstable administration. If the stability reduces the effectiveness of *staff* control, it may provide a rare opportunity for *inmates* to seize enough power and time to get their message out and to make the right people take it seriously [emphasis added].

Implicit in this formulation of riots is a "frustration aggression" explanation for the inmates' violent behavior. The motivation for rioting is found in the deprivations and powerlessness of inmates (interference with goal-response). The instability and uncertainty of staff allow these long-standing frustrations to surface (reduction of inhibition to aggression). These frustrations are then expressed as aggressive violence directed at the prison administration (an act with the goal-response of injury to an organism; Dollard et al., 1970, pp. 24-26).

This approach leaves essential questions unanswered. For example, why do staff who have run prisons without riots (for years, in most cases) become ineffective? Why do inmates who are constantly deprived and powerless (Sykes, 1958) now react to these conditions with violence? Why are inmates who are normally able to "corrupt guard authority" (Sykes, 1958) not able to continue doing so? Through what processes do outsiders (politicians, the media) contribute to the eruption of violence? We must explore the process by which individual inmates are moved to join in collective action and the reasons that collective action takes the particular violent forms that it does. These are the issues that are discussed below.

The starting point for this discussion is *stress*, as it is experienced and coped with by individual inmates and individual staff. Next, we explore how the mutual interactions of these two groups of stressed individuals shift to collective reactions, setting the stage for violence from and among the inmates and violent retaliation from the prison authorities (Toch, 1977a, pp. 70-71).

PRECONDITIONS AND PROCESS IN PRISON COLLECTIVE VIOLENCE

Analyzing data from prisons that have had riots, those that exhibited nonriot resistance, and those that had no riots, Wilsnack (1976, p. 72) identifies three types of "preconditions" associated with riots: (1) inmate deprivation and social disorganization, (2) administrative conflicts and instability, and (3) pressure and publicity from outside the walls. If we examine each of these preconditions as "stressors" found in the prison environment from the perspectives of inmates and guards who inhabit and work in prisons, some light may be shed on the process by which preconditions become transformed into collective violence.

Before we do this, however, it is important to distinguish among the factors. Some of what Wilsnack calls "preconditions" may well be thought of as parts of a *process* that eventually leads to a riot. Others may relate to the "context"—that is, the particular conditions of deprivation—in which this process takes place.

Such objective conditions as overcrowding, idleness, tight security, and heterogeneous populations that mix inmates varying in age, criminal experience, and race (Wilsnack, 1976) provide individual inmates and guards with motivations and opportunities to develop strategies for coping. The success or failure of these strategies is judged by the individual who employs them. In addition, the relative salience of each condition varies for the individual inmate or guard, and not according to evaluations by observers (Toch, 1977a).

Other factors associated with prison disturbances, however, seem to be involved more clearly in the "process of prison riots"—that is, the process of coping with "objective conditions" in such a way as to promote collective violent action. These *process factors* include increased inmate assaults, assaults on staff, poor communication, publicity about prison conditions, and absences and / or changes in key prison staff (Wilsnack, 1976).

These process factors are not only problems in themselves, but also contribute to the intensity with which inmates and staff experience the "objective conditions" of confinement. These factors tend to be adjustments of some inmates and staff that upset whatever adjustments other inmates and staff have made. Though "objective conditions" can be measured in some ways, they are *subjectively* interpreted partly in terms of the behavior of fellow inmates (Toch, 1977a) and guards (Lombardo, 1981). It is in the alteration of these subjective worlds that process factors may make their contributions to the development of collective violence.

Objective Preconditions: Inmate Perspectives

Such objective prison conditions as overcrowding, heterogeneous inmate populations, idleness, and tight security restrictions contribute to the creation of stressful prison environments (Toch, 1977a) and to prison disturbances (Wilsnack, 1976, p. 69). If such conditions always produce stress, however, why do they not always produce collective violence as a response? Part of the answer may be found in the differential salience of these conditions and in mechanisms individual inmates find to cope successfully or unsuccessfully with the stress these conditions produce.

Toch demonstrates that the *crowding* of prison life exacerbates an inmate concern for privacy and the invasion of personal space by the noise, smells, and behavior of others. Inmates concerned with privacy wish to remove themselves from overstimulating environments. Some attempt to isolate themselves from sources of irritation (Toch, 1977a, 34-35). Others attempt to enclose themselves in social groups composed of similar privacy-oriented inmates (Toch, 1977a, pp. 34-35). Even under normal conditions, however, such isolation and privacy affiliation are difficult to achieve. There are always inmates whose concern for "activity" and being free from the boredom and understimulation of prison life leads them to create the very conditions those concerned with privacy seek to avoid.

It is in this social matrix that the objective conditions frequently associated with prison collective violence have their impact. *Overcrowding* increases the stress produced by an overstimulating environment and makes the possibility of obtaining privacy much less likely. Heterogeneous inmate populations (especially those mixing younger and older inmates) increase the probabilities that all groups will find it more difficult to cope successfully with their environment (Toch, 1977a, pp. 246, 249).

Given the scarce resources of most prisons, *overcrowding* is also related to a decline in opportunities for inmates concerned with activity to keep themselves involved in tasks that provide ego involvement, self-actualization, or simply the release of pent-up energy (Toch, 1977a, pp. 25-26). When available slots in prison programs disappear and waiting lists become longer, *idleness* increases. Idle inmates are more likely to be faced with the disturbing and painful effects of their environment; this results in a heightening of the inmates' experience of stress (see Chapter 3).

Tight security is also capable of having positive and negative effects on different segments of heterogeneous inmate populations. For inmates who are concerned with safety and structure, tight security offers protection from physical assault by other inmates. It also provides certainty and predictability, reducing stress for inmates concerned with these issues. For others, however, tight security means a loss of freedom and a lessened ability to control one's own life. Under such conditions, inmates are more likely to express concerns about the abuse of authority and officer harassment and to make more frequent demands for respect. When tight security measures are not satisfactorily explained to inmates, these concerns may surface as "censorious" behavior (Mathiesen, 1965, pp. 150-151), with inmates criticizing staff unfairness, partiality, and unreasonableness (Lombardo, 1981, pp. 117-119).

From the inmates' perspective, each of the objective factors associated with collective violence (overcrowding, idleness, and tight security) is made more salient by the impact of a heterogeneous inmate population. In diverse groups there is an increased likelihood that individual inmates' attempts to find places within the prison where their environment and individual needs are at least compatible (Toch, 1977a, pp. 179-205) will be doomed to failure and frustration. Though coping strategies have a modest chance of success under normal conditions, a "critical mixture" of abnormal conditions brings new sources of stress to the surface as formerly satisfying living strategies begin to fail.

Objective Preconditions: Guard Perspectives

As they pursue their daily tasks, individual guards also spend time and energy creating work environments that are compatible with their individual needs. Some seek situations in which they can overcome boredom by keeping active (cell blocks, work details). Others seek positions where they can maintain a relative degree of privacy and isolation from what they perceive as the overstimulation of interactions with prisoners and / or administrators (wall posts, administration building assignments). Still others seek assignments where they can exert control, experience autonomy, and make decisions (Lombardo, 1981, pp. 38-47).

In addition to meeting their individual concerns, guards must also cope with the stresses produced by their prison environment: They must seek to reduce pressures and to enhance satisfactions. In this connection, relations with individual inmates take on special significance. Helping inmates cope with their institutional and personal needs is also a way for some guards to cope with their perceived powerlessness. Helping inmates gives guards a sense of control and purpose in a social environment that defines helping behaviors as not acceptable. Exercising discretion in enforcing rules and seeking to establish a "legitimate" basis for inmate cooperation and personal authority provides the guard with an opportunity to achieve recognition from inmates for being fair and enhances guard feelings of self-esteem and self-respect (Lombardo, 1981, pp. 150-155). Good relations with inmates also provide guards with communication networks that otherwise may be lacking (Lombardo, 1981, pp. 125-129).

The "objective conditions" of overcrowding, idleness, tight security, and heterogeneous inmate populations adversely affect the prison guards' ability to maintain their work environment as directly as these conditions affect the inmates' ability to structure their living environment. The time, energy, and attention of the guard are scarce resources—resources upon which overcrowding makes great demands. Under normal conditions guards are often able to help inmates cope with their privacy and safety concerns (see Chapter 17). However, an increase in inmates per officer not only increases the *number of demands* for assistance, it also *diminishes the opportunities* to help by reducing the number and variety of work or housing locations capable of satisfying inmate concerns. With fewer options, officers face more frustrated inmates. In addition, they lose opportunities to make positive contributions, thus reducing their own levels of satisfaction.

Tight security and strict rule-enforcement policies have an adverse effect on guards as well as on inmates concerned with autonomy and freedom. Where guards previously exercised discretion and interpreted individual rule enforcement interactions in light of the characteristics of the situation and the inmate involved (Lombardo, 1981, pp. 78-97), they now must respond "by the book." Any personal legitimacy a guard may have established now erodes. The guard is forced to rely on legalistic responses, which are more likely to evoke hostile reactions from inmates. In addition, tight security means that guards lose the degree of autonomy and control that previously satisfied their own personal needs.

As a general work strategy prison guards frequently adapt directives from prison administrators to the realities of their work situations. In doing so guards maintain an operational smoothness that provides predictability and structure. As overcrowding, tight security, idleness, and heterogeneous inmate populations develop, the guards' ability to make situational adjustments becomes severely circumscribed. As directives limit the guards' ability to control their environment, they must abandon their previous adjustment strategies, and this allows new problems to surface.

Officers reacting in nonpreferred ways to changing conditions and perceived administrative interference do so even though they may know that this increases inmate stress. As officers change "styles," inmates predictably lose some of the indirect autonomy they experienced from officer assistance. Inmates also lose structure as officers vary their previously predictable responses. Where officers were previously able to alleviate stress, they must now contribute to it, causing inmates to seek new avenues of adjustment. This appears to have been a critical factor in promoting the infamous Attica uprising, which followed a decrease in predictability and structure of supervision:

> Inmates not only faced inexperienced officers but might face new ones every day. The inmates could never learn what was expected of them from one day to the next, and the officers could never learn whether an inmate's uncooperative behavior resulted from belligerence, indifference, illness, or some other medical or personal problem. Inmates no longer could adjust to the officer who commanded them, but had to readjust to a

> succession of officers who changed from day to day. Officers, too, were adversely affected by this change. Likely to work with different groups of inmates each day, the officers had no incentive to establish rapport or respect with a group of inmates whom they might not see again for days or weeks. There was neither opportunity nor desire to develop any mutual understanding [New York State Special Commission on Attica, 1972, p. 127].

STRESS AND THE PROCESS OF COLLECTIVE VIOLENCE: FROM INDIVIDUAL TO COLLECTIVE BEHAVIOR

In the early 1970s Jayewardene et al. (1976, p. 33) surveyed Canadian correctional staff members concerning their perceptions of the "process leading inevitably and inexorably to a major prison disturbance." The staff members noted changes in the normal behaviors of inmates seeking to make adjustments to new conditions: There were increases in rumors, in transfer requests, and in inmates reporting to sick call. In addition, inmates sought new job assignments or began to engage in recreational activities where they previously had not (Jayewardene et al. 1976, p. 36). Talkative inmates became reticent and inmate responses to supervision (censorious behavior included) became signs of defiance. Inmates who were generally unpopular and isolated began to become talkative and sought out staff when "trouble" was brewing (Jayewardene et al., 1976, p. 37).

What these staff members were observing is the process by which inmates seek new niches when their old ones begin to be destroyed by change (see Chapter 16 for a discussion of niches). Inmates were still reacting as individuals, but the groundwork for the development of a collective response to stress was being constructed.

In discussing the processes of communication in social groups, Festinger (1968, p. 183) describes situations in which individuals depend on "social reality" to determine the validity of their attitudes, opinions, and beliefs when they are unable to depend on experiences of "physical reality" to test these beliefs. In prison environments that are undergoing change, the certainty, predictability, and structure provided by environmental niches and other coping options represent the "physical reality." Niches provide opportunities for individual inmates to meet their needs in terms of perceived attributes of special prison environments, and without direct reference either to other inmates or to their "status as inmates." The meaning they derive from their experiences is tested against the reality that they as individuals experience to be true. Basing their attitudes, opinions, and beliefs on this "physical reality," the "social reality" of what an inmate is supposed to experience is largely irrelevant.

However, as niches begin to erode under the pressure of overcrowding, idleness, tight security, and heterogeneous inmate populations, inmates' ability to determine their own reality begins to slip away. Increased communication among themselves (Jayewardene et al., 1976, p. 37) becomes a method by which inmates get a fix on the "social reality" of the prison environment. This communication marks the beginning of inmates moving forward and recognizing themselves as a "collective" and a group (Janis, 1968, p. 87).

During conditions of change, correctional officers are also vulnerable to this process. The existence of an officer reference group capable of influencing the attitudes and behaviors of individual correctional officers is something that cannot safely be assumed. Rather than a cohesive group with widely accepted norms and sanctions, the officers may be better described as a highly fragmented collection of individuals. To be sure, their work requires a degree of interdependence, but officers express a high degree of independence in attitude, opinion, and beliefs. Rather than maintaining close personal relationships with their comrades, officers tend to go their own way, seeking to avoid personal contact and communication with each other outside of the institution. Inside the institution, officers create their own "niches" (Lombardo, 1981, pp. 145-149).

In Festinger's (1968, p. 183) terms, these officers interpret prison conditions on the basis of a "physical reality." However, as objective prison conditions begin to change, and as absences and/or changes in key staff, poor communication, and publicity about prison conditions (Wilsnack, 1976, p. 72) begin to impinge on the guard's world, the reliability of this "physical reality" diminishes. Relationships with inmates begin to take on an increasingly "formal" character. And as inmates increase "censorious" responses to guard formality, hostility and mutual suspicion increase. Inmates now behave in ways more likely to be interpreted by guards as challenges to their authority and to their position as guards (Jayewardene et al., 1976, p. 37; Lombardo, 1981, pp. 92-97). By sharing these experiences, guards begin to develop a "social reality" of themselves and inmates at variance with their normal subjective experiences, but confirmed by the experiences of others.

The stage is set for confrontation. Individuals who *live* in the prison are becoming "inmates," and those who *work* in the prisons are becoming "guards," in their own eyes and in the eyes of others. Role-playing behavior based on a new socially determined reality begins to replace coping behavior based on individually determined physical reality. Guards and inmates now begin to behave in collective and symbolic ways, each interpreting and reacting to the behavior of the other in terms of the stereotypical images their new "social reality" has created.[1]

Wilsnack (1976, p. 72) finds increased numbers of interinmate assaults and assaults on prison staff associated with prisons that experienced riots. Such confrontations can plausibly contribute to the development of a collective response by providing the conditions necessary for what Janis (1968) refers to as the "contagion effect." This phenomenon describes the spread of excitement or violence and the development of group identification when the group is faced with an external threat. The conditions for contagion, as identified by Redl and Wineman,[2] are:

(a) an initiator who must openly "act out" in such a way that he obviously gratifies an impulse that the rest of the members have been inhibiting;
(b) the initiator must display a lack of anxiety or guilt; and
(c) the other members who perceive the initiator's actions must have been undergoing for some time an intense conflict with respect to performing the forbidden act (Janis, 1968, p. 87).

Though increasing numbers of violent confrontations between inmates and/or between inmates and guards may in themselves represent last-ditch responses to stress, they are also sources of stress, stimuli for contagion, and occasions for group identification.

Lockwood sees violence as a transition stage in the movement from individual to collective responses to stress. He notes that

> there is a point in the process leading up to outbreaks of [collective] violence where emotion and mass enthusiasm overbalance individual inmate thinking. Small cliques go over as a group to the side of the protestors. The importance of group action is reinforced by the staff techniques of transferring or segregating those who protest. At this particular stage, a man chooses between group loyalty and personal security. If he chooses group loyalty—then the process begins to take place as a group phenomenon [Lockwood, personal communication].

In reviewing antecedents of prison riots, I have thus far traced the erosion of preliminary responses to stressful conditions and the consequent inability of both inmates and guards to develop new solutions to compounded stress. The interpersonal character of these failures leads to the development of social definitions of the problem, mutual hostility of inmates and staff, stereotypical behaviors, and, ultimately, to violence.

STRESS AND COLLECTIVE VIOLENCE IN PRISON

While the collective nature of prison riot behavior might be understood in terms of a shift from individual to group solutions to stress and from "physical" to "social" definitions of stress and coping, the violent content may be, at least in part, an extension of a "subculture" of violence that permeates prisons. Violence and a concern for safety remain parts of a prison's subjective reality no matter how infrequently incidents of violence actually occur. With regard to the objective and subjective reality of prison sexual violence and its impact on victims, Lockwood (1980, pp. 142-143) observes:

> The impact of victimization is not necessarily related to the level of force deployed in an incident or to the "objective" danger of the environment. To an extent the impact of target experience is based on the perception of danger and the expectation of physical harm rather than actual danger and physical harm. Environments themselves viewed as threatening, can be responsible for victim trauma.

Where violence is perceived as a way of life, it is expected that violence will be used to settle disputes. Guards refer to the assumed fact of violence, not its probability, as one of their primary concerns (Lombardo, 1981, pp. 115-117). Jack Abbott, a long-term resident of prisons with expertise in the practice of violence, claims that in prisons

> *everyone* is afraid. It is not an emotional or psychological fear. It is a practical matter. If you don't threaten someone at the very least, someone will threaten you. When you walk across the yard or down the tier to your cell, you stand out like a sore thumb if you do not appear either callously unconcerned or cold and ready to kill. Many times you have to "prey" on someone, or you will be "preyed" on yourself. After so many years, *you are not bluffing.* No one is [Abbott, 1981, pp. 121-122; emphasis in original].

This violent content of prison life is not always available for collective deployment. For this to occur, restraints inhibiting overt expressions of violence must be reduced and justifications for the use of collective violence must be put into place.

One of the most powerful restraints inhibiting outbursts of collective violence in prison is the "status quo," comprising stable conditions (no matter how depriving) within which individuals develop lifestyles that satisfy their felt needs, even where survival is the only need that can be satisfied (Bettelheim, 1943). Stability increases vested interest in the status quo, and prevents depriving conditions from being viewed as arbitrary. Changes in the status quo can draw attention to the perceived *illegitimacy* of the conditions, even where conditions have improved in an objective sense (Fogelson, 1971, pp. 93, 95). Pastore (1952) and Berkowitz (1981) have demonstrated that frustrations perceived as arbitrary or illegitimate promote more aggressive reactions than frustrations perceived as lawful or legitimate.

Staff behavior or institutional policy that alters accepted patterns of adaptation can be perceived as arbitrary and illegitimate by both inmates and staff. When reasonable explanations for staff behavior are not offered to inmates and when previously offered explanations for inmate rule violations are not accepted, the perceived arbitrariness and illegitimacy of staff control is increased. To the extent that staff are not involved in making decisions about their work routines, the legitimacy of administrative changes is not obvious to them. Unfavorable publicity focusing on conditions inside the prison (Wilsnack, 1976, p. 71) strengthens the belief of guards and inmates that existing conditions need not be maintained.

Other restraints inhibiting a violent response to stressful conditions include a concern for personal safety given the perceived overwhelming opposition of the authorities, the fear of arrest (and an extended term of imprisonment), and a commitment to orderly social change and achieving improved conditions through established procedures (Fogelson, 1971, pp. 98-99). Under normal conditions these restraints operate in the prison setting, but as conditions change, they are subject to erosion. With increasing threats to personal safety evidenced by the prevalence of interinmate assaults and the failure of prison administrators to reduce the threat, the potency of administrative control is thrown into serious question. Though inmates know that violent revolt will undoubtedly be crushed, by force if necessary, one of the restraints deterring the outbreak of such violence is severely weakened.

Similar changes weaken the fear of keep-lock and disciplinary procedures. Under normal conditions, a disciplinary penalty of one day or one week may be experienced as a punishment, by some inmates at least. The loss of interpersonal contacts and of social and economic benefits from the maintenance of social relations can cause at least annoyance—especially when one's territory may be taken over by another and when loss of a privileged work assignment may deprive the inmate of a niche. Under conditions of change, instability, turmoil, and danger, a keep-lock may come to mean nothing. Finally, where formal grievance mechanisms do not exist, the chances for achieving orderly change through informal bargaining and administrative responses to crisis situations may have run out. Even where there are formal grievance channels, failure to resolve salient issues satisfactorily often leads to feelings of impotence. Established procedures are redefined as a sham designed and used by administrators to prevent real change.

JUSTIFICATIONS FOR THE USE OF VIOLENCE IN PRISON RIOTS

With the state of flux created by the erosion of established patterns of behavior, the development of mutually stereotypical definitions by staff and inmates, and the loosening of restraints that curb riot tendencies, what is needed to unleash collective violence is a set of justifications for its use. Such justifications may be found in the social processes involved in individuals' reactions to stress and in the process of conversion from individual to collective response.

In analyzing situations in which individuals take action they personally believe is wrong (the infliction of violence on others) but which they pursue in spite of the disapproved effects, Duster (1971) identifies six conditions that contribute to defining the situation as one permitting such contradictory behaviors. Focusing on incidents from the Vietnam war and police involvement with the Black Panthers in the 1960s, Duster refers to these as "conditions for guilt-free massacre," a set of rationalizations with which individuals can shield themselves from responsibility for their actions. These conditions include (1) the denial of the humanity of the victims; (2) organizational grounds for action that supersede individual grounds for action; (3) loyalty to the organization that supersedes every other consideration; (4) the fact that an organization uses secrecy and isolation as a cover for its actions; (5) the existence of a target population; and (6) the motivation to engage in violence (Duster, 1971, pp. 25-26).

Denial of Humanity. Though guards may normally see inmates as people and clients for services (Lombardo, 1981, pp. 26-27) and inmates may perceive guards as solutions to rather than creators of problems (Toch, 1977a, pp. 67-68, 207-211; Lockwood, 1980, p. 130), when stressful conditions remain unresolved such perceptions are likely to change and the underlying "social definitions" of criminal and guard as less than human are likely to emerge. At Auburn such less- or more-than human stereotypes (as sub- or superhuman) dominated correctional officers' preemployment images (Lombardo, 1981, pp. 25-26). Guards have a second group that may be seen as "less than human," the correctional administrators. It is easy for guards to look upon administrators as an outgroup. Lack of meaningful contact turns administrators into "callous calculating manipulators" constantly attempting to interfere in the officers' work environment, usually to the officers' detriment. Officers feel that they are "treated like children" or "like numbers." Feeling dehumanized facilitates their adoption of a rejecting stance toward the administration.

Organizational Goals Supersede Individual Goals. For inmates under preriot stress, conditions within the prison and within the criminal justice system turn from individually experienced stress to shared grievances that call for consensus-based "demands." Though aggrieving conditions may have existed for years preceding violence, the breakdown of normal patterns of prison behavior encourages inmates to view these conditions from a shared, jaundiced, impatient perspective.

For the guard, organizational goals such as rehabilitation, incapacitation, and punishment often have little meaning in the normal work situation. Guards perform their duties in ways that fulfill more immediate personal goals: They try to keep active, find some meaning in their work, or just stay out of trouble (Lombardo, 1981, pp. 38-56). When the status quo becomes upset and organizational goals (expressed through administrative directives) begin to impinge on guards' routine, they may choose one of several available goals and substitute it for their own. The behavior of one officer pursuing an organizational goal may contribute little to disruption of routine. However, many officers working at cross-purposes with each other and with institutional goals may magnify the extent of "institutional breakdown."

Loyalty to the Organization Supersedes Every Other Consideration. Under normal conditions inmate loyalty to peers is minimized by the competition for goods, status, and power. Such divisions serve as social control mechanisms supplementing and sometimes substituting for weak formal mechanisms of control (Cloward, 1977). In developing a collective response, however, loyalties to self or clique become secondary to loyalties to "inmates" as a group, which implies a closing of ranks against the institutional administration and correctional staff.

While officers have little reason to display or express loyalties toward other officers (Lombardo, 1981, pp. 162-164), a combination of perceived threats from inmates (increases in censoriousness and violence), the administration (changes in work routines), and the media (criticisms in the press) leads officers to close ranks. Where officers feel challenged, seemingly on all fronts, loyalty to the guard fraternity can become an overriding concern.

Organizational Secrecy and Isolation to Cover Its Actions. The perception that correctional agencies employ secrecy and seek to maintain isolation is prevalent not only among critics of correctional institutions but also among inmates and correctional officers. When unusual incidents (killings, drug investigations, fires) occur, all groups express dissatisfaction with the explanations offered by administrators. The administration is perceived as acting "as if it had something to hide."

This factor is particularly relevant in understanding guard violence in the aftermath and retaking of prisons. Duster (1971, p. 31) comments that in military and police organizations "public control and scrutiny are to be avoided at all costs on the grounds of inexpertise ('the general knows best') and of subversion ('enemies of the people are among the people')." According to the Attica Commission, officers at Attica held similar opinions concerning court interventions into the correctional process:

> Guards almost universally felt that courts were interfering in matters in which they had no competence. Judges, they felt, knew nothing about prisons or prisoners and could not come to an intelligent decision concerning either [New York State Special Commission on Attica, 1972, p. 125].

The role of the media and reformers (Wilsnack, 1976) in threatening to "expose" abuses magnifies the salience of secrecy and isolation.

A Target Population with Inferior Fire Power. Though inmates know that the ultimate result of any violent collective disturbance will be repression, they also know that their own overwhelming numbers and physical power (guards are usually not armed, while inmates, especially during times of unrest, are frequently armed with homemade weapons) makes the target population (guards and prison administrators) particularly vulnerable. For guards, their target population preceding the riot may be the prison administration. The administrators have no power except that exercised through guards. If guards desert administrators and allow violence to erupt, administrators are left to fight the battle alone. The turnover in prison administrators following outbreaks of violence demonstrates that guards have the ability to massacre by inaction.

Following riots, in retaking the prison and the aftermath, officer violence focuses on inmates as a powerless target population. With inmates locked in their cells, cell-to-cell searches following riots are often occasions for wanton property destruction and even for widespread physical abuse of inmates.

A Motivation to Engage in Violence. For inmates using violence to take over a prison, or for guards using violence to retake the prison, the motivation is frequently expressed in catch phrases. "It's in the national interest" justifies military actions, and "It's in the line of duty" serves as a motivation for normally inappropriate police behavior. Prisoners have to "show we're men" and guards and prison administrators have to "get this place back" and "restore order and regain authority." Such phrases serve to focus and justify violent behavior.

SUMMARY

The subculture of prison violence, coupled with the loosening of restraints against violence and the development of a collective response to stress, provide both to inmates and guards motivations and justifications for their own brand of collective violence in prison settings. When viewed in the context of the ongoing life of prison communities, prison collective violence can serve a large variety of needs for different individuals. But once individuals develop a "collective sense" and violence is set into motion, such individual motivations appear to be superseded by the drama of the event, though individual concerns must still be considered if we are to understand the motives of participants adequately.

Toch's (1969, p. 211) comments on the beginning of the Watts riot of 1965 provide a concise summary of these observations:

> Once collective violence has been initiated, it acquires a momentum of its own; even if people did not suffer from grievances riots would attract and recruit participants. They would do so because they appeal to boredom, anger, frustration, desire for adventure; because they provide a ready-made opportunity to discharge feeling; because they furnish festive activity with the sanction of peers and under the aegis of principle.
>
> As violent crowds form, by-standers are invited to join; if not, they find it natural to fill the gaps within the ranks. Streets become an arena for heroism, a proving ground for bravery. A stage for protest. Boys can achieve manhood heaving rocks or defying police officers; men can

acquire purpose through riot-connected projects. At some points nonviolence requires special explanation and requires special motives. Violence becomes, temporarily, a way of life.

NOTES

1. One of the most graphic (though least consequential) examples of the confrontational potential that lies below the surface of this combination of prison/staff "role behavior" (as opposed to the individual behavior of the persons occupying the roles) occurred during the "simulated prison" experiment conducted at Stanford University in 1971 (Haney et al., 1977). One interpretation for the "prison rebellion" at Stanford is that it was a reaction to the harsh conditions imposed on the students who participated. However, the short time involved and the minimally harsh conditions make this rebellion seem more like the "thing to do." That is, it became assumed that "prisoners" are expected to rebel, and that prisoners are expected to use violence to respond to prison staff. It is possible that the "scripts" the Stanford subjects were following were derived from their expectations and assumptions concerning the behaviors of guards and inmates, rather than from their personal reactions to their immediate situation. They developed a group identity as they reinforced each other in their beliefs about the reality of their confinement. Instead of individuals testing and evaluating their own experiences, these student-inmates and student-guards accepted the "social definition" of their situation and acted out the expected rebellion.

2. See Redl (1966, pp. 155-213) for a thorough discussion of this process.

REFERENCES

Abbott, J. *In the belly of the beast*. New York: Random House, 1981.

Berkowitz, L. On the difference between internal and external reactions to legitimate and illegitimate frustrations: A demonstration. *Aggressive Behavior*, 1981, 7, 83-96.

Bettelheim, B. Individual and mass behavior in extreme situations. *Journal of Abnormal and Social Psychology*, 1943, 38, 417-452.

Cloward, R. A. Social control in the prison. In R. G. Leger & J. R. Stratton (Eds.), *The sociology of corrections*. New York: John Wiley, 1977.

Desroches, F. Patterns in prison riots. *Canadian Journal of Criminology and Penology*, 1974, 16, 332-351.

Dollard, J., Doob, L., Miller, N., Maurer, O. H., & Sears, R. Frustration and aggression. In E. Magargee & J. E. Hokanson (Eds.), *The dynamics of aggression*. New York: Harper & Row, 1970.

Duster, T. Conditions for guilt-free massacre. In N. Sanford & C. Comstock (Eds.), *Sanctions for evil*. Boston: Beacon, 1971.

Festinger, L. Informal social communication. In D. Cartwright & A. Zander (Eds.), *Group dynamics*. New York: Harper & Row, 1968.

Fogelson, R. M. *Violence as protest: A study of riots and ghettos*. Garden City, NY: Doubleday, 1971.

Garson, G. D. The disruption of prison administration: An investigation of alternative theories of the relationship among administrators, reformers and involuntary social services clients. *Law and Society Review*, May 1972, pp. 531-561. (a)

Garson, G. D. Force versus restraint in prison riots. *Crime and Delinquency*, 1972, 18(4), 411-421. (b)

Haney, C., Banks, C., & Zimbardo, P. Interpersonal dynamics in a simulated prison. In R. G. Leger & J. R. Stratton (Eds.), *The sociology of corrections*. New York: John Wiley, 1977.

Janis, I. Group identification under conditions of external danger. In D. Cartwright & A. Zander (Eds.), *Group dynamics*. New York: Harper & Row, 1968.

Jayewardene, C.H.S., McKay, H. B., & McKay, B.E.A. In search of a sixth sense: Predictors of disruptive behavior in correctional institutions. *Crime and/et Justice*, 1976, 4(1), 32-39.

Lockwood, D. *Prison sexual violence*. New York: Elsevier, 1980.

Lombardo, L. X. *Guards imprisoned: Correctional officers at work*. New York: Elsevier, 1981.

Mathiesen, T. *Defences of the weak*. London: Tavistock, 1965.

Newman, G. *Understanding violence*. New York: J. B. Lippincott, 1979.

New York State Special Commission on Attica. *Attica*. New York: Bantam, 1972.

Pastore, N. The role of arbitrariness in the frustration-aggression hypothesis. *Journal of Abnormal and Social Psychology*, 1952, 47, 728-731.

Redl, F. *When we deal with children*. New York: Free Press, 1966.

Sykes, G. *The society of captives: A study of a maximum security prison*. Princeton, NJ: Princeton University Press, 1958.

Toch, H. *Violent men: An inquiry into the psychology of violence*. Chicago: Aldine, 1969.

Toch, H. *Living in prison: The ecology of survival*. New York: Free Press, 1977. (a)

Toch, H. *Police, prisons, and the problem of violence*. Washington, DC: Government Printing Office, 1977. (b)

Wade, A. L. Social processes in the act of juvenile vandalism. In M. B. Clinard & R. Quinney (Eds.), *Criminal behavior systems: A typology*. New York: Holt, Rinehart & Winston, 1967.

Wilsnack, R. W. Explaining collective violence in prisons: Problems and possibilities. In A. Cohen, G. Cole, & R. Bailey (Eds.), *Prison violence*. Lexington, MA: D. C. Heath, 1976.

PART II

Stress Over Time

CHAPTER 6

The First Cut Is the Deepest

PSYCHOLOGICAL BREAKDOWN AND SURVIVAL IN THE DETENTION SETTING

JOHN J. GIBBS

INTRODUCTION[1]

A van backs into what appears to be an ordinary municipal garage. You are ordered off the van, and a door leading into a narrow corridor swings open. The force of the noise from within seems enough to open the door. It's not like the roar of the fans at a football game or the din of machines, people, and tools in a factory. Individual sounds—bells, voices, doors—are more recognizable and seem more personal. Yet it doesn't seem real. It's like a radio station tuning in and out.

You step into the corridor. On one side, there are a half dozen holding cells. Some hold men who are on their way out; others hold men who are on their way in. Each cell holds between five and ten men. Some of these men just sit and stare into space. Others are more active, almost hyperactive. They climb up on the cell bars and shout bitter denunciations. They make exaggerated lewd gestures to intimidate newcomers, and they make comments to humiliate those they consider vulnerable and contemptible.

On the other side, there is a long office that runs the length of the corridor. The office stands about five feet above the corridor floor, and it is separated from the corridor by thick glass. Behind the quiet of the glass, one hears the bustle and hum of the control room. It is similar to a taxi dispatch station or an air traffic control tower. The major concern is the smooth and safe flow of human traffic. In this office, guards process the papers that represent the prisoners with whom their fellow officers are dealing directly in the flesh and in full view.

Someone barks your name. With all the pandemonium, however, you're not sure it was your name you heard. Your name is barked again.

This time there is no question; a guard stationed at a small stand grabs your right wrist and hand, and presses your thumb on an ink pad. You're in jail!

You're in jail. Here the pains of imprisonment begin. This is the first step after you have been arrested and charged. Here you can look out on streets where you walked only a few hours ago, and wonder, as every jail inmate wonders, "What's happening with my case?" Here you will stay while your future is being decided by judges, prosecutors, defense attorneys, jury members, and others.

Now that you're in jail, you're probably concerned about what to expect. This chapter deals with the answers to this question. Its purpose is to explore the stresses present in the jail, and to describe how men cope and fail to cope with them.

Who Goes to Jail

In order to understand the stresses faced by jail prisoners and their reactions to them, we have to know something about the prisoners themselves. Environments are in some ways shaped by their inhabitants, and an investigation of the characteristics of the populations of a setting is one barometer of its human climate.

Jails contain an enormous range of the kinds of people who deal poorly with stress. In part, this is because jails must deal with many of the kinds of people that other institutions and social service agencies will not or cannot assist. Jails have become human dumping grounds. They are places of last resort.

Many people enter jails with symptoms of severe psychological disturbance. The available research indicates that between 48 percent (Swank & Winer, 1976) and 64 percent (Schuckit et al., 1977) of the inmates fit one of several diagnostic categories representing psychiatric disorders. These same studies suggest that a substantial proportion of those who enter jails have a history of some form of psychiatric care. Swank and Winer (1976) conducted clinical interviews with 100 newly admitted jail inmates, and found that 24 percent had a history of psychiatric evaluation, treatment, or hospitalization. Schuckit et al. (1977) report that 44 percent of the 199 new admissions with whom they conducted structured personal interviews had been previously confined in a mental institution.

The results of these studies suggest that the jail is serving a population a good portion of which was once the responsibility of the mental institution. The transfer by default of the social control task from mental institution to jail is a result of legislation and court decisions to reduce the populations of mental hospitals and develop more restrictive criteria for entry. Well-intentioned changes in our view of the treatment and rights of mental patients, coupled with fiscal policies that result in limited services, have created what Adler (in press) calls "a marginal population group, suspended, as it were, in the mid-air between mental hospitals and prison."

If the trend toward decarceration of mental hospital populations and reduced services and concern for the marginal members of our society continues, we can count on an even greater number of disturbed persons being deposited in jails. The available evidence suggests that the proportion of the jail population that represents social and medical problems as well as criminal justice problems has been increasing in recent years,[2] and the problem of inmates who experience psychological disturbances is surpassed in perceived seriousness only by overcrowding (Gibbs, 1981).[3]

Jails are not surrogate mental hospitals, however, and most jail inmates have never been confined in mental hospitals; nor are typical jail inmates in need of psychiatric care. Most are problem prone, however, due to poverty, lack of education, unemployment, and minority group status (see Goldkamp, 1978), and they find jail confinement to be yet one more painful life contingency.

THE PAINS OF JAIL CONFINEMENT

The pains of jail confinement are substantial because the jail prisoner is faced with four interrelated major problem areas: withstanding entry shock, maintaining outside links, securing stability (and sometimes safety) in a situation of seeming chaos, and finding activities to fill otherwise empty time. Some of these problems, to be sure, affect other prisoners. Parolees suffer prerelease and reentry problems (see Chapter 9), though not on a scale that compares with the transition problems of pretrial detainees. Some long-term prisoners and condemned prisoners are crucially concerned with securing emotional support from loved ones and with developing regimens of activity to occupy their time (see Chapters 7 and 8). Entry problems for these men, however, are negligible; their lives are often quite stable, almost suffocatingly so in some instances. These prisoners experience other pressing problems and crises of adjustment, but no group other than pretrial detainees is exposed to high levels of stress from each of the four problem areas noted above. This fact may partially explain why pretrial confinement is regularly described as an unusually disruptive, debilitating, and even traumatic juncture in a person's confinement.

The introduction to this chapter was intended to provide a sense of what it is like to enter a jail as a prisoner. Even veterans of confinement and those who engage in persistent criminal activities that often result in arrest and detention have described entry as a disruptive and disorganizing experience. The rapid transition from street to jail and the attendant change in status from free man to prisoner is unsettling for both the seasoned jail veteran and the novice. From the perspective of some prisoners, it is almost as if they are happily gamboling down the street one minute and pondering their fate in a jail cell the next.

There is ample evidence that the transition from street to jail is a cataclysmic experience for some prisoners. It can result in the manifestation of symptoms of serious psychological disturbance, including self-injury. There is a higher rate of self-injury among prisoners in detention awaiting trail than among prisoners serving sentences (Esparza, 1973; Heilig, 1973; Martin, 1971), and self-injuries usually occur in the initial stage of incarceration (Danto, 1973; Esparza, 1973; Heilig, 1973; Biegel & Russell, 1973; Martin, 1971). Suicide is also more prevalent in jails than in prisons (Danto, 1973).

After the initial shock of detention, the jail prisoner finds himself in a limbo. He is not serving time. He is not on the streets. He is between worlds, occupying a vague position in which he feels impotent. Life goes on in the streets, but he is not there, and his inability to influence what goes on there can have serious implications for his sense of self (see Irwin, 1970).

The jolt of the street-jail transition and the need to maintain a sense of control over the still-warm body of relationships and expectations left on the streets press a man to establish links with those in the community, usually family members. As is the case in many situations of radical disruption, men try to maintain their bearings during the street-jail transition by eliciting support from family and friends on the outside.[4] These significant others are important for both the provision of tangible assistance, in the form of money and information about one's business in the streets, and emotional support that gives a man a sense of hope and adequacy in an uncontrollable and uncertain situation.

The world of the detained prisoner is filled with uncertainty. Going to jail shatters one's sense of predictability, a commodity necessary for psychological health and effective coping (Toch, 1977, p. 81). The jail prisoner is uncertain about how long he will be in jail, about the disposition of his case, the chances of obtaining money for bail, the competence of his attorney, intentions of prosecutors, judges, juries, and the meaning of a hundred other factors related to his legal predicament.

Population shifts occur more quickly in jail than in most other human environments. High population turnover limits the establishment of relationships that can promote a sense of stability and predictability, and impedes the implementation of a set of rules and policies that result in clarity and structure in the jail. The environmental qualities (structure, stability, and clarity) that the jail setting lacks have been shown to be important for reducing anxiety and enhancing self-esteem (Stotland, 1969, pp. 84-85).

Inactivity is another problem faced by the jail prisoner. Jails are notoriously boring places (Sobell, 1974, p. 100; Flynn, 1973, p. 63). In a recent survey of jail administrators and social service providers, the problem of insufficient activities for prisoners ranked third in average seriousness rating. Overcrowding and inmates who experience psychological problems were the only other problems of the 24 considered that received a higher average rating (Gibbs, 1981, pp. 6-7). The results of the same survey show that almost half of the respondents selected boredom as the most common problem faced by jail prisoners (p. 29).

Boredom is painful in itself. However, a more serious problem is that inactivity cuts off one avenue for reducing tension. Tension and anxiety are common problems in jail and the reduction of these consequences of frustration may become a major need, independent of the original source of frustration. If chances for activity are unavailable or limited, this inability to diminish tension can become an added frustration that produces a new cycle of anxiety and tension.

Activity is important for more than the discharge of tension. Men who are accustomed to high levels of activity on the streets may feel that their limbs and minds will atrophy if they do not maintain an equivalent activity level in jail. Other men may wish to stay active to keep their minds occupied. Their goal is to avoid painful and redundant thoughts associated with their new-found status as inmates.

Support and Inventory[5]

For some men, family support is necessary to counterbalance the disequilibrating forces inherent in the jailing process. When a man does not receive the support he feels he needs from his family, a crisis of abandonment may occur. This kind of problem, called "self-linking" by Toch (1975), is the most common crisis described by self-destructive jail inmates.[6] Toch (1975, p. 51) describes self-linking as

> a person's protest against intolerable separation from significant others, against perceived abandonment by them, or against his inability to

> function as a constructive member of a group. The person rejects the possibility of an independent life, feels that this well-being is inconceivable without the continuation of certain vital relationships, and that no satisfactory existence is possible without them.

Imprisoned men need the support of significant others in the community for a number of reasons. During the initial stages of incarceration, support from significant others may help absorb the shock of confinement and provide necessary tangible benefits—bail, counsel, clothing, money, and other necessities.

> My case went to Supreme Court, and my wife didn't appear. My mother didn't appear. They didn't care for me, so what's the sense of me living? . . . So I came back to my cell, and I sat down and started thinking. Tears started running down my eyes. So I said, "Nobody cares for me on the outside. What's the sense of me living?"

> All I wanted was someone to help me out, and that was my mother. And she turned me down. . . . What was the use of me keep on living without nothing to fight for, without any family? Like there was nothing left for me, nothing else to do.

An inherent part of the process of marshaling family and other human resources during stressful times is the evaluation or assessment of the strength of one's resources. For some men, this is a simple task of counting favors owed or markers to be called in. For others, the process takes a more elaborate form; an emotional inventory is taken in which a man assesses his assets and liabilities and makes an estimate of his worth to himself and others. In the process of reviewing his past to determine its value, a man may uncover more debits than credits on his personal balance sheet, and this may further diminish his already failing sense of adequacy.

Men who have been oblivious to the needs of their families and men whose lives on the street centered on drugs and alcohol are especially prone to arriving at negative self-assessments when taking inventory. However, personal reviews of the past are negatively skewed for most jailed men. This may be the case because asset-related incidents are more difficult to recall, or because personal assets are not as concrete as personal liabilities nor as recognizable or verifiable. A man can recall specific guilt-inducing incidents with family and the manifest emotional reactions of significant others at the time of the event; however, it is more difficult for him to determine corresponding assets such as fidelity, honesty, and loyalty. A man's psychological field at the time of inventory thus seems composed primarily of liabilities; from the perspective of a jail cell, transgressions may appear unusually grave, or may dovetail to form a pattern:

> Your mind is like on a highway, and it's going at a very fast pace, just like a car. You know how a car picks up speed? Your mind is going along them terms, and as it's running along this highway, you go back and you pick up incidents. And one incident leads to another incident of your failure in your life. You say, "Well, I've been drinking," and then I remember I did this, and they just keep adding on.

In a setting devoid of activity, a man may go down the same road again and again, and reach a dead end each time. When a man has nothing to take his mind off the process, it can escalate to crisis proportions and can result in a psychological breakdown:

> It bothers me every day. I feel very guilty, and it's something that I can't get out of my mind, that I can't run away from. . . . And I try to tell myself, "The money's gone, you've done it, it's over. So just forget it." But I can't forget it. Every time I think of it, my woman comes back in my mind, the kids come back in my mind. The fact that there were so many things that I needed with the money, that I needed to do with the money, so many constructive things that I needed to do, material things that I needed to do. I just threw it away.

This exposition illustrates the dynamics of one type of crisis commonly experienced by self-destructive jail prisoners. To combat the disequilibrating effect of the street-jail transition and its damaging impact on self-image, one must enlist the support of significant others in maintaining equilibrium or in establishing a new one. In this situation breakdown can occur if (1) the emergency resource (support) is not available and its unavailability sparks negative emotions and thoughts that combine with the initial forces that threatened one's psychological survival, or (2) assessing the strength of one's support evokes a review of personal liabilities that adds to the negative forces that initiated the review. In either case, an attempt to deal with initial stresses results in additional stresses.

Opportunity Costing

The abruptness of the street-jail transition can result in a man feeling that he is physically confined in jail but not that far from the streets. He has not experienced "psychological arrival" (Thyurst, 1957). The temporal, physical, and psychological proximity to the streets, coupled with empty cell time, can make each minute in jail a painful reminder of what a man is missing by being locked up:

> You're in the cell most of the day. You're locked in. And you have nothing to do but think. You get tired of playing cards. That's all they got here is cards. You get tired of that after awhile. You get sick of that. And you got to think. And what do you think about? You think about home, girlfriends, things that you'd be doing, like if it was Friday night or Thursday night, what you'd be doing. And, like, when I lay down, I think of things like that. I try not to, but I can't help it. And I see things that I would be doing. I know what I'd be doing, and I can see this. . . . I just couldn't take it.

Opportunity cost is a consequence of the human limitation of being able to be in only one place at one time. It is the things we could be doing with our time while we are doing what we are doing, and the loss in benefits associated with those other things. As with other forms of psychological inventory, once the process of computing the opportunity cost of confinement begins, it can amplify into a crisis. Under conditions of detention, a man's assessment of his losses may be understandably high, and the future may appear bleak. In such cases, opportunity costing leads to despair.

> Emptiness. It was like being put into a hole, and slowly the dirt is coming in on you, and there's no way you can push the dirt out. That's the way I saw it. When they brought me upstairs and closed that door behind me, I could just see my dream like it was being pushed out of my head. And slowly as it got past my nose and past my eyes, the dream was gone. . . . And now it's all gone. I'm sitting in here and rotting. I'm rotting. I'm actually rotting. For these past days that went by, I could have been out making $84 a week, and for those days that went by I could have come home and said, "Hey, babe, I made $84 this week, and here's money." Where's my paycheck? Where's the money? So I'm rotting in here. . . . So what do you do? You sit here, and you wait and you rot.

Dealing with Uncertainty

While a man is locked up, decisions are being made about when he will return to life outside. Although the jail inmate is often aware of the serious implications of his situation, he is seldom in a position to make informed choices. The jail prisoner suffers from a serious information deficit that, when combined with the instability, noise, and confusion of the jail environment, impairs his ability to make sound decisions.

Decisions about the prisoner's fate are sometimes made in arraignment court, before he even sets foot on a jail tier. It is here that he gets his first taste of the overwhelming confusion and uncertainty that accompanies the street-jail transition. Consider, for example, Hunt's (1972, p. 139) description of arraignment in New York City:

> The judge, brusque and quick, impassive and hardened to the endless stream of unrepentant thieves, whores, addicts, pushers, muggers, armed robbers, knife-wielders, and rapists, would listen, occasionally interrupt with a question or two, then snap out his orders, and ask the clerk for the next one . . . so the accused came up one after another to stand before him, hearing a smattering of phrases fly back and forth, and being led away almost before they knew what he had said.

After arraignment, the jail prisoner is taken from the confusion of the courtroom to the jangle of the jail reception pens. Here his bewilderment sharply increases along with his need for information. He needs some predictability to reestablish psychological balance.

To be sure, the nights in jail are a striking contrast to the disorder and noise of the days. Night, however, does not necessarily bring peace and relief. Instead, the night, with its long, heavy hours of isolation and inactivity, traps a man in his confusion. During the night, a man may attempt to fill his information void and reduce his uncertainty with self-generated data. He creates a number of scenarios and decides which is most probable. His attempt to reduce uncertainty can become a monster of his creation. In building his alternative futures, he may uncover some frightening possibilities. Although these events may be objectively improbable, they may seem very real to sleepless eyes peering through cell bars, and they certainly add to the confusion.

Information about his case is one of the inmate's most compelling needs. While he is waiting in a cell for his day in court, a man's information demands may amplify. He may expect that all of his questions will be answered when he appears before the judge. The anticipation of a clear day in court, however, can create a situation of almost certain disappointment when a court appearance results in even more uncertainty and confusion. For example:

> And like I really don't know the meanings of like different charges. Like this time, I know now, like misdemeanor, felon, this here. And when I go up, and they don't give a chance to ask the lawyer. All he do is call you, read it off to you, and now you come back. Like I figure like, the other guy that hear the charges, he don't have time to discuss with you, and I'll just have to sit and wait. And by waiting, trying to find out information and figure it out, builds up pressure.

For the detainee certain information may become a requisite for psychological survival. Yet, in many instances, the jail setting provides limited information. Efforts to gather information may end in dashed hopes and additional tension. Attempts to make decisions with data of questionable validity in a setting filled with noise and confusion may engender breakdowns that feature declarations of confusion and helplessness.

External Audit and Control

Self-alienation crises, which have been described by Toch (1975, p. 91) as "a reluctant or passive compliance with alien impulses and commands that direct the person to destroy himself," are not uncommon in jail.[7] These crises feature classic schizophrenic symptoms, including breaks with reality, hallucinations, and abysmally low self-esteem. Self-directed messages (such as voices) confirm a man's doubt about himself, highlight his inadequacy and unworthiness, and command him to destroy himself:

> Well, it's kind of funny for me to say, but I'll say it anyway. The voices would say things to me like, "You're no good. You're a faggot. You're a punk. You're this. You're that. Look what you did to the family. You got your mother doing this. You got your whole family in an uproar, worried about you here and there. You're no good."
>
> Well, they always say to me, "There's only one thing that you could do. Get rid of yourself, and then you don't have to suffer no more, you don't have to make nobody else suffer."

Those who are psychologically unstable when they enter jail may be especially prone to succumb to pressure, and schizophrenics are prime candidates. Schizophrenics have been characterized as extremely low in self-esteem, prone to feelings of hopelessness, and likely to find social situations painful and to withdraw from interaction (Stotland, 1969, pp. 152-184). They have also been described as hypersensitive to environmental fluctuations that affect core concerns, and they require a dependable and predictable environment to maintain ego strength and a sense of competence (Bettelheim, 1974, pp. 37, 85). The rapid transition from the community to detention, the confusion and discord of the jail environment, and the uncertain status of detention destroy any sense of mastery the borderline schizophrenic may have had over his world. The threat of forced interaction with others and denigrating messages from authority figures (arrest, indictment, and so on) create a psychologically painful situation from which the schizophrenic may wish to escape. The invocation of failure (the inability to come to terms with arrest and its attendant consequences) sets the stage for self-doubts in the form of self-deprecating voices demanding self-destruction in expiation of failure. The "voices" compute the cost of confinement and review the past for their hosts. The power of these messengers of despair is larger than life, and so too are the dimensions of their condemnation.

> They knew all my secret thoughts. Whenever something would pop into my mind, the voices would go along with it and say, "Yeah, that's right." When I wanted to kill myself, the voices said, "Right, that's what you got to do because it's the only way out, the only way you're going to find any peace."

The self-alienation syndrome involves a man under stress attempting to undercut the strength of doubts that acquire a life of their own. Breakdowns are statements of helplessness, compliance with the commands of voices that condemn and seek to destroy, or attempts to escape the hopeless situation created by engulfing feelings.

COPING WITH DETENTION

Many men cope with the stresses of jail, or at least endure them, without falling apart. The descriptions of adjustment provided by these men show that what one man considers overwhelming odds against psychological survival another may consider a challenge to be met.[8] Of course, many of the difficulties of detention experienced by prisoners who cannot cope are also voiced by men who do. The most prevalent concerns are with inactivity and uncertainty about what is happening with their cases. For men who break down, these concerns emerge as crises of major proportions; for those who do not break down, they take the shape of irritants or stipulated consequences of confinement, and the prisoners often deal with their frustrations by ventilating with peers. In addition, the stresses experienced by copers are often not complicated by serious jail stresses (such as lack of support) to the degree experienced by noncopers.

Group formation is a common reaction to the deprivations of confinement, and it has been noted that peers can play an important role in reducing stress in jail. Rottman and Kimberly (1977) describe a jail inmate culture that helps men deal with some of the problems and pressures faced by jail prisoners, particularly those related to uncertainty and inactivity. The jail studied contained a core of members of subcultures who had a great deal of confinement experience in jails, prisons, juvenile institutions, and other confinement settings. These veterans of confinement are familiar with each other from both the streets and institutional settings, and are similar to the "state-raised youths" described by Irwin (1970).

According to Rottman and Kimberly (1977), there are many benefits associated with subcultural affiliation in the jail setting. Inmate group leaders are purveyors of information that can (a) reduce uncertainty about courts and the activities of other criminal justice agencies and (b) help one adjust to the jail environment.

Peers and Fears

One kind of stress that peers in jail can both generate and ameliorate is fear. In some cases, victims or potential targets are advised, consoled, or protected by fellow inmates. Many protective benefactors advise men under pressure to assume a manly stance, to demonstrate a willingness to fight. In addition, they sometimes provide image-supporting props by convincing their frightened peers that courage is the important commodity, and that it can be gained independent of physical stature and combative skills. For some men, this strategy is successful. Although the mouse is not transformed into a lion, at least he becomes a formidable mouse. For others, the same strategy backfires, convincing them of their resourcelessness and the hopelessness of their situation.

Most of the adolescent inmates who express fear in jail are white inmates who find themselves surrounded by an overwhelmingly black prisoner population. Some of the more resourceful inmates cope with the situation by engineering a transfer to a setting that features a less threatening ethnic mix (the mental observation block). In other cases, astute custodians transfer vulnerable inmates to the less stressful setting. Less resourceful and less fortunate inmates sometimes suffer and break down.

In the Red with Prospects for the Black

Introspection spawned by detention can be a problem, but it can also result in a commitment to change and a promising prognosis. The experiences of some men suggest that a crisis is a turning point that can have a favorable or unfavorable outcome.

Satchel Paige once said, "Don't look back. Something may be gaining on you." Bygones may be bygones. A fatalistic posture is assumed, and the immediate environment is the center of attention. This coping stance is what Irwin (1970, p. 68) identifies as "jailing": "To 'jail' is to cut yourself off from the outside world and to attempt to construct a life within prison." To the "jailer," the past is not prologue; the jail is a life arena that requires no introduction. His world is the day room and the tiers. His status universe is inside. Freedom is desirable, but the street life becomes a bridge to be crossed when he comes to it.

INTERVENTIONS

We can attempt to make some systemic changes to reduce the stresses of jail—uncertainty, lack of activity, the abruptness of the street-jail transition, and separation from significant others in the "outside" community. Some of these stresses could be reduced through changes in legislation, policy, or practice. Effective changes in these areas, however, would involve the participation of more than jail administrators and staff. Courts, prosecutors, defense attorneys, and others would have to commit themselves to change. However, most of these criminal justice actors see themselves as playing very distinctive roles—none of which include responsibility for the combined stresses of detention.

In some states, such as New York, there exist corrections commissions involved in the promulgation and implementation of jail standards (see ABA Statewide Jail Standards and Inspection Project, 1974). These statements are minimum standards that address jail-related issues, notably visitation, recreation, hygiene, inmate programs, and medical care. As adoption of and compliance with such standards becomes more widespread, the lot of detainees may be improved, and some of the stresses of detention—separation from family and lack of activity, for example—might be mitigated. However, even in the area of providing for basic human needs, there are cost, security, and political concerns that impede progress.

One approach to reducing the uncertainty experienced by jail inmates is to increase the information available to inmates about the status of their cases and to expand their knowledge about the operation of the courts. However, increasing client-attorney interactions is no mean task. Many detainees are represented by court-appointed counsel, and the volume of cases handled by each attorney, combined with the distance that must be traveled to the institution, tends to limit contact between the client and his counsel. Requests for more legal resources are common and warranted; however, due to limited municipal and county resources, such requests are seldom met.

There are also other factors that act to restrict the quantity and quality of information available for reducing the detainees' uncertainty. The process of plea bargaining is one such factor. A large majority of criminal cases are settled by pleas of guilty. Rates vary by jurisdiction (Miller, 1977, p. 16-18), but a commonly cited figure for guilty pleas is 90 percent (Newman, 1966, p. 3; Heumann, 1975, p. 515, n. 1). Usually, pleas of guilty are gained through negotiation (Miller, 1977, p. 17), which means that the process of plea bargaining involves an informal exchange between the defense attorney and the prosecutor. The defendant "is present only for the formalities, the signing of the treaty, not its negotiation" (Morris, 1974, p. 53). If the defendant were a participant in the bargaining process, the uncertainty about the status of the case might be reduced; at least, the inmate might feel that he had some control over his fate.

However, plea bargaining has been described as a process of "gamesmanship" (see Miller, 1977; Alschuler, 1968) in which the prosecutor and defense attorney jockey for position. The tactics of the game—"bluffing" about evidence, defenses, witnesses, pretrial motions, overcharging, and so on (see Miller, 1977; Alschuler, 1968)—do not benefit from the presence of the defendant and may even be contaminated by it. It has been suggested that the informal network of relationships surrounding the bargaining process and the nature of the process itself exert some pressure on the defense counsel to be less than candid when he or she does meet with a client. Although numerous proposals have been advanced for the abolition or reform of plea bargaining (see ABA Project on Minimum Standards for Criminal Justice, 1968; National Advisory Commission, 1973; Morris, 1974, pp. 53-54), the economics of the situation are such that one would be ill advised to wait with bated breath for successful implementation (see Miller, 1977, pp. 122-129).

The issues of bail and speed of trial also have obvious implications concerning who is detained and for what duration. The present money bail system has been criticized heavily, and in recent years reforms ranging from use of citation in lieu of arrest to release on recognizance programs have emerged. Even when such reforms are enacted, however, some people are still detained in jails and some suffer breakdowns.

RESEARCH AND REFORM

The first step in increasing the number of people who will receive help with coping when under stress is to study those who have received assistance with their problems. Salient in this context is the work of

Toch (1977), who mapped the environments or human climates of a number of New York State prisons. He discovered that not only do different prisons possess different environmental characteristics, but also within each institution there exist a number of environmentally distinct subenvironments or niches (see Chapter 16), which feature more or less of particular ameliorative qualities for those who are crisis prone or who have suffered breakdown.

Jails may offer comparatively more limited environmental options than prisons, but there is some evidence that different jails will have different environmental qualities. For instance, in the summer of 1974, only 14 of 261 eligible inmates chose to transfer from the Manhattan House of Detention for Men (which had been declared as falling short of conditions of humane detention by a federal circuit judge) to a more modern structure on Rikers Island in which conditions were reported to be comparatively much better. It was reported in the *New York Times* that "a number of prisoners told authorities yesterday that their attorneys and families could more easily visit them if they stayed in the Tombs" (Chambers, 1974). This example not only illustrates the importance of family support and legal assistance to jail prisoners, but also demonstrates that, from the inmate's perspective, some institutions provide more opportunities to satisfy these needs than others. These inmates felt that proximity to family, courts, and lawyers was more important than more pleasant physical surroundings and chances for recreation.

The adolescent mental observation section of Rikers Island Hospital displayed ameliorative characteristics when a particular officer was on duty. The officer was a gentle and empathic man who easily established rapport with inmates who had been diagnosed as having psychiatric problems. Many of the inmates were reluctant to transfer from this setting to a less regimented one because of the importance of having this officer on hand when they were experiencing difficulties. Surely other helpful officers can be identified and developed to alleviate inmate stress (see Chapter 17).

A systematic survey of the environments of jails may result in the discovery of a number of institutions, subenvironments, and personnel with ameliorative qualities for inmates who are experiencing certain difficulties or who are susceptible to certain stresses. Congruent matches between men and environments could reduce the stresses of detention.

NOTES

1. This chapter is based on the findings of a number of research projects. The descriptions of jail breakdowns and coping strategies are based on 105 interviews with self-

destructive jail prisoners and 77 interviews with a random sample of prisoners from the general jail population. All subjects interviewed were male. Information was also collected from institutional files on 415 male inmates who had injured themselves while confined and 1188 who did not suffer self-destructive breakdowns in jail. This research was one component of a study directed by Professor Hans Toch of the School of Criminal Justice, State University of New York at Albany. The research was supported by an NIMH research grant (5 ROI MH 20696-02, "Self-Destruction Among Prison Inmates") from the Center for Studies of Crime and Delinquency and the Center for Studies of Suicide Prevention.

The perceptions of jail personnel presented are based on the results of a survey of jail personnel conducted in 1981 at the Meeting Jail Standards Through Team Effort Workshop. The workshop was sponsored by the New Jersey Warden's Association and the Correctional Social Service Association, and was conducted by Professor Todd R. Clear and Associate Dean Albert Leroy Record of the Rutgers University School of Criminal Justice, Program Resources Center. A questionnaire was administered to 35 participants who represented 11 of the 21 counties in New Jersey.

2. More than four-fifths of the participants surveyed at the jail workshop mentioned above responded affirmatively to the question: "Do you think there has been an increase in the percentage of jail prisoners who have social and medical problems rather than criminal justice problems in the last few years?" (Gibbs, 1981, Table 6).

3. On a scale of 1 to 5 ("not a problem" to "serious problem"), overcrowding received an average serious rating of 4.1. The mean serious rating for the item inmates who experience psychological problems was 3.8 (Gibbs, 1981, Table 3).

4. Initial reactions to the stress and disorganization created by natural disaster are usually family oriented. If a family is together when such catastrophies strike, the chances of physical and psychological damage to its members are generally reduced (see Marks & Fritz, 1954; Hocking, 1970).

5. The breakdown syndromes described, support and inventory, opportunity costing, dealing with uncertainty, and external audit and control, are based on a thematic analysis of tape-recorded and transcribed interviews with 105 men who suffered self-destructive breakdowns while confined in New York City jails. The syndromes have been described also in Gibbs (1975).

6. Of the men interviewed who injured themselves while confined in jail, 16.5 percent expressed self-linking as the problem that was primarily responsible for their act (Gibbs, 1978b, Table 4.3).

7. Approximately 11 percent of the self-destructive inmates interviewed in jail expressed self-alienation as the kind of crisis they faced when they broke down (Gibbs, 1978b, Table 4.3).

8. Interviews were conducted with a stratified random sample of 77 prisoners who did not injure themselves while confined. The interviews were tape-recorded but not transcribed. The coping strategies described in this chapter are based on the interview summaries (see Gibbs, 1978b, ch. 2).

REFERENCES

Adler, F. From hospital to jail: New challenges for the law enforcement process. *Criminal Law Bulletin,* in press.

Alschuler, A. The prosecutor's role in plea bargaining. *University of Chicago Law Review,* 1968, 36, 50-112.

American Bar Association (ABA) Project on Minimum Standards for Criminal Justice. *Standards relating to pleas of guilty*. Washington, DC: American Bar Association, 1968.

American Bar Association (ABA) Statewide Jail Standards and Inspection Systems Project. *Survey and handbook on state standards and inspection legislation for jails and juvenile detention facilities*. Washington, DC: American Bar Association, Commission on Correctional Facilities and Services, 1974.

Bettelheim, B. *A home for the heart*. New York: Alfred A. Knopf, 1974.

Biegel, A., & Russell, M. Suicidal behavior in jail: Prognostic considerations. In L. Danto (Ed.), *Jail house blues*. Orchard Lake, MI: Epic, 1973.

Chambers, M. Only 14 at Tombs choose transfer to Rikers Island. *New York Times*, August 17, 1974.

Danto, B. Suicide at the Wayne County Jail: 1967-70. In L. Danto, (Ed.), *Jail house blues*. Orchard Lake, MI: Epic, 1973.

Esparza, R. Attempted and committed suicide in county jails. In L. Danto (Ed.), *Jail house blues*. Orchard Lake, MI: Epic, 1973.

Flynn, E. Jails and criminal justice. In L. E. Ohlin (Ed.), *Prisoners in America*. Englewood Cliffs, NJ: Prentice-Hall, 1973.

Gibbs, J. J. Jailing and stress. In H. Toch, *Men in crisis: Human breakdowns in prison*. Chicago: Aldine, 1975.

Gibbs, J. J. *Psychological and behavioral pathology in jails: A review of the literature*. Paper presented at the Special National Workshop on Mental Health Services in Local Jails, Baltimore, 1978. (a)

Gibbs, J. J. *Stress and self-injury in jail*. Unpublished doctoral dissertation, State University of New York—Albany, 1978. (b)

Gibbs, J. J. *Jail problems: A report to the participants of the Meeting Jail Standards Through Team Effort Workshop*. New Brunswick, NJ: Rutgers University, School of Criminal Justice, Program Resources Center, 1981. (limited circulation)

Goldkamp, J. S. *Inmates of American jails: A descriptive study*. Working paper 1. Albany, NY: Criminal Justice Research Center, 1978.

Heilig, S. Suicide in jails. In L. Danto (Ed.), *Jail house blues*. Orchard Lake, MI: Epic, 1973.

Heumann, M. A note on plea bargaining and case pressure. *Law and Society Review*, 1975, 9, 515-528.

Hocking, F. Extreme environmental stress and its significance for psychopathology. *American Journal of Psychotherapy*, 1970, 4, 4-26.

Hunt, M. *The mugging*. New York: Signet, 1972.

Irwin, J. *The felon*. Englewood Cliffs, NJ: Prentice-Hall, 1970.

Marks, E. S., & Fritz, C. E. *Human reactions in disaster situations*. Unpublished manuscript, National Opinion Research Center, University of Chicago, 1954.

Martin, S. *Prison suicide study*. Interdepartmental memorandum, City of New York Health Services Administration, 1971.

Miller, H. *Plea bargaining in the United States: Phase I report*. Washington, DC: Georgetown University Law Center, 1977.

Morris, N. *The future of imprisonment*. Chicago, University of Chicago Press, 1974.

Newman, D. *Conviction: The determination of guilt or innocence without trial*. Boston: Little, Brown, 1966.

National Advisory Commission on Criminal Justice Standards and Goals. *Corrections*. Washington, DC: Government Printing Office, 1973.

Rottman, D., & Kimberly, J. The social context of jails. In R. Carter, D. Glaser, & L. Wilkins (Eds.), *Correctional institutions*. New York: J. B. Lippincott, 1977.

Schuckit, M., Herrman, G., & Schuckit, J. The importance of psychiatric illness in newly arrested prisoners. *Journal of Nervous and Mental Disease,* 1977, 165, 118-125.

Sobell, M. *On doing time.* New York: Scribner, 1974.

Stotland, E. *The psychology of hope.* San Francisco: Jossey-Bass, 1969.

Swank, G., & Winer, D. Occurrence of psychiatric disorder in a county jail population. *American Journal of Psychiatry,* 1976, 133, 1331-1333.

Thyurst, J. The role of transition states--including disaster in mental illness. In *Symposium on preventive and social psychiatry.* Washington, DC: Walter Reed Army Institue of Research, 1957.

Toch, H. *Men in crisis: Human breakdowns in prison.* Chicago: Aldine, 1975.

Toch, H. *Living in prison: The ecology of survival.* New York: Free Press, 1977.

CHAPTER 7

Lifers and Long-Termers

DOING BIG TIME

TIMOTHY J. FLANAGAN

This chapter focuses on the special problems and stresses faced by offenders serving long prison sentences, particularly those serving life terms. This focus assumes that a distinctive set of problems associated with long-term imprisonment can be identified and distinguished from the pains of imprisonment that are inherent in incarceration generally, regardless of the length of sentence.

It is always dangerous to divide a population that is as heterogeneous as prison inmates into smaller groups that presumably differ from the balance of the population. The danger is that in identifying a distinctive subgroup for attention, the dimensions on which the subgroup *differs* from the parent group become paramount, and the many areas in which the groups are similar are deemphasized. As a result, the generalizability of the findings and implications may be needlessly reduced. Moreover, we often think we see things that are unique to the subgroup of interest when in fact we are observing a characteristic that is shared with the larger group.[1] In short, while we may be able to identify specific problems and stresses that putatively are unique to long-termers, it is useful to remember that these problems may differ from those faced by all prisoners more in degree than in kind.

Unwarranted atomization of the prison population is cause for concern, but most of the current literature on the psychology of confinement errs in the opposite direction. By assuming that the pains of imprisonment are ubiquitous, much of our current knowledge in this area is not sensitive to the notion that facing and serving a term of life or twenty years may be a fundamentally different experience from facing and serving a term of two, three, or four years.

CONVENTIONAL WISDOM AND THE EFFECTS OF IMPRISONMENT

Before discussing the principal problems and stresses faced by lifers and long-term inmates, the profound change in thinking that has occurred during the past few decades on the issue of the effects of long-term confinement must be recognized. In fact, the conventional wisdom in this area has undergone a reversal of such magnitude that it rivals the debate over the efficacy of rehabilitation efforts in the larger correctional sphere.

Early thinking about lifers and long-term inmates assumed that the effects of extended confinement were relatively predictable and profoundly negative (Flanagan, 1981, pp. 201-203). Extended incarceration was felt to be inexorably linked to deterioration of the personality, growing dependence upon the highly controlled regime of institutional life, and increasing levels of "prisonization" or commitment to the value system of the institution. Some writers recognized variation in the extent to which these effects were manifested, but many took the position that these effects were "inseparable from the long prison sentence" (Fox, 1934) and that few long-term inmates would survive the experience without substantial and irreparable damage.

In the last decade, several investigations attempted to document and quantify the nature and extent of deterioration suffered by long-term inmates. In addition, these studies sought to isolate variables such as facility type, security level, preprison characteristics of the offenders, and other variables that might be related to differential levels of "incarceration effect." This research, which has relied in large measure on the use of objective tests to measure diminution of personal attributes, has yielded virtually no convincing evidence that systematic deterioration occurs as a consequence of long-term confinement (for reviews, see McKay et al. 1979; Wardlaw & Biles, 1980; Flanagan, 1981). Regardless of the life area studied—whether physical degeneration, development of psychopathology, negative attitudinal change, or cognitive impairment—the portrait offered by these recent investigations is that long-term imprisonment per se does not necessarily lead to damage to the person.[2]

Thus the early views on this issue posited a number of serious negative effects of long-term confinement, but later research does not appear to document them. Perhaps the safest course to follow, given these diametrically opposed perspectives, is to suggest that while it is unlikely that both positions could be correct, it is possible that they could both be wrong.

The deterministic view of systematic personal destruction as a consequence of long-term confinement ignores the variation in response to incarceration that clearly exists. According to Toch (1975, p. 5),

> paradoxically, some men flourish in this context. Weaklings become substantial and influential; shiftless men strive and produce; pathetic souls sprout unsuspected resources.

The deterministic view also fails to consider the development of effective adaptive strategies among long-term inmates. To the extent that any organism can fashion modes of adaptation to stressful situations by drawing upon interpersonal or external resources, experiences with stressors can be negotiated successfully. Ample evidence regarding human capacity to devise coping strategies is available from diverse sources (for examples, see Bettelheim, 1943; Cohen & Taylor, 1972).

If the deterministic view fails to consider human variability and adaptability, the recent evidence suggesting a complete lack of incarceration effects suffers from the assumption that "if it can't be measured, it doesn't exist." The former view leads us to commit one type of error, while the latter fosters errors of a different type. It must be recognized that the dimensions that are trapped by standardized inventories may not be the salient dimensions through which the effects of long-term confinement are manifested (Wardlaw & Biles, 1980). Also, the rating scales used in many studies may not be sensitive enough to detect gradual changes in personality dimensions over a lengthy term of imprisonment. In addition, the design of typical studies necessitates reduction of data into comparative measures that may mask variation within the respondent group. Finally, the studies themselves may be deficient. McKay et al. (1979, p. 4) characterized this area as a "methodological nightmare" and concluded that

> this can be better understood by recognizing that it is an area of experience that does not lend itself easily to systematic empirical investigation. The unique and extreme conditions that are associated with incarcerating individuals for significant periods of their lives is not an easy subject for quantitative analysis. The difficulty in identifying and separating meaningful variables which can be manipulated in the natural environment or simulated in the lab is nearly insurmountable. . . . Thus, it should not be surprising to find that much of the significant writing which attempts to communicate the effects of the experience of long-term imprisonment is of a qualitative nature. The phenomenological approach serves well in enabling investigators to reach some minimal understanding of the power and complexity of the experience of long-term incarceration.

The term "phenomenological approach" has been used to describe a number of methods of studying stress and adaptation among long-term prisoners. The common element of these approaches is some measure of subject involvement in the definition of the phenomenon under study. Hence, the research protocol may involve systematic assessment of prisoners' writings about their experiences, participant observation, or open-ended interview methods. Cohen and Taylor (1972, pp. 35-40) observed that the term "phenomenological" has been used in some instances to disparage the products of research on the grounds that studies so labeled lack scientific "objectivity," rigorous control of test stimuli by the researcher, and readily quantifiable measures of reliability and validity (see also Taylor, 1977). Be that as it may, the approach considers the prisoner's report of discomfort and pain as an important problem in its own right that cannot be ignored while we await the development of diagnostic tools to define the nature of the subject's malady with more precision.

THE SPECIAL STRESSES OF LONG-TERM PRISONERS

External Relationships: Ambivalence and Attenuation

Loss of contact with family and friends outside the prison is a major source of stress for all inmates, but for long-term prisoners the fear that these relationships will be *irrevocably lost* creates a unique set of concerns. The problem is that whereas relationships with spouses, other family members, girlfriends, and others may withstand enforced estrangement for a few years, the prospects for maintenance of these relationships over a longer term are dim. Despite the prisoner's realization that life must go on for persons left behind—in the sense that decisions must be made, life changes negotiated, and new lives constructed—this perceived reality does not make the stress caused by the gradual attentuation of relationships easier to bear. Bettelheim (1943) reported that the prisoner seeks to "freeze" a picture of life on the outside—and his or her role in it—in the mind as an aid to protecting the ego. Therefore, any contacts between the prisoner and a bearer of tidings of external change are approached with ambivalence by the inmate. The prisoner desperately seeks to keep contacts with the outside world salient, but adds to the stress of confinement by doing so.

Farber (1944) found that the relationship between degree of suffering of the prisoner and personal contact with the outside was curvilinear—

those who cut off all contact and those who were able to maintain high levels of contact suffered the least, while those in the more common intermediate levels suffered the most. Cohen and Taylor (1972) suggest that very few long-term prisoners are able to maintain high levels of outside contact over a lengthy sentence and that most slip gradually to a level of very low contact.

Several observers have suggested that some long-term prisoners preemptively sever external relationships to avoid the stress or "hard time" produced by the attenuation process. Toch (1975, 1977a) has referred to this as the "decathexis of relationships" but suggests that this response is comparatively rare. The long-term inmates I interviewed reported that whereas they could appreciate the motivation of an inmate who chose this strategy, this position was also seen as selfish and pathological. One man stated that

> cutting ties is a sign of burning out. Guys who take this position (and there are some) can't deal with people beyond the walls. If you concentrate only on the illogical system in here, you will go crazy [Flanagan, 1980a, p. 254].

In sum, maintaining extraprison relationships is a problem for long-term prisoners that differs considerably from the plight of short-termers. The major sources of stress in this area for long-termers are the gradual slipping away of human resources, the ambivalence that they foster, and the fear that these losses will be irrevocable. In two recent studies that sought to identify the principal problems of long-termers, these externally oriented deprivations were rated as significantly more frequent sources of problems and as more intense sources of stress than deprivations relating to the internal conditions of the prison (Richards, 1978; Flanagan, 1980b).

Relationships Inside: Acquaintances and Associates

If maintaining support outside the prison is problematic for long-term prisoners, developing personal relationships within the walls may be no less troublesome. Cohen and Taylor (1972) observed that in the small security wing in which their long-termers were housed, the many demands imposed by friendship with another inmate served as a formidable barrier to the formation of interpersonal relationships. Long-termers are also restricted in their choice of friends because of the dual problems of commonality and continuity. If the inmate is older than many of his colleagues and faces many more years of confinement, there may be few prisoners who share his concerns and perspectives who will be around for long. Toch (1977a, p. 286) has lucidly described the plight of the older inmate who is surrounded by noisy, aggressive youngsters who boast incessantly of the adventures that await them in their impending return to the streets. Given these irritations the prisoner must escape, Cohen and Taylor note that it is not surprising to find the friendship networks of many long-term prisoners limited to a few dyadic relationships or to a solitary existence.

The strained and tenuous nature of social relationships among long-termers may result in a perceived lack of resources for dealing with problems and may enhance the need to maintain "face" at all times. For long-termers who form a wider network of friends within the prison, stresses related to the periodic severance of these relationships are paramount. Unlike the situation faced by the short-term prisoner, there is no wholly satisfactory way of resolving the dilemma of friendship for long-term prisoners. Coupled with the problems related to maintaining extraprison relationships, the friendship dilemma produces a situation in which few resources are perceived, and feelings and anxieties must be bottled up and kept to oneself. The ability of most individuals to handle problems in this manner over a long period of time without high levels of stress as a consequence is questionable.

Fear of Deterioration: The Assault on Self

Concern with deterioration is a source of stress that is most often identified with lifers and long-term prisoners. Cohen and Taylor (1972) wrote that the long-term inmates with whom they worked were obsessively concerned and highly self-conscious about outward signs of personal deterioration. They noted that

> many of these men already suffer from what R. D. Laing has called "ontological insecurity." The term describes the state in which one doubts the integrity of the self, the reliability of natural processes and the substantiality of others. In some forms this insecurity can take the form of dread of the "possibility of turning, or being turned, from a live person into a dead thing, into a stone, into a robot, an automaton, without personal autonomy of action, an *it* without subjectivity" [Cohen & Taylor, 1972, p. 109].

Several distinct factors may give rise to the long-termer's concern with deterioration. First, prisoners are continuously offered unfavorable definitions of themselves by others, and over an extended period of time it may become increasingly difficult to counter these unfavorable definitions, particularly in the absence of the external resources discussed above. Second, several investigators have reported that persons institutionalized for long periods develop difficulty in framing and marking time when faced with an abundance of time to fill and few traditional benchmarks with which to segment time (Calkins, 1970; Cohen & Taylor, 1972; Sapsford, 1978). To the extent that the inmate recognizes the presence of these "barrier effects" and the decreased ability to mark time in him- or herself, this perception may lead to fears that other cognitive processes are also deteriorating.

Finally, the potential cumulative effects of the regimentation, passivity, and lack of personal choice within the prison environment are not lost on long-term prisoners. In essence, long-termers fear that after many years of being told what to do they may well lose the ability to think for themselves and assume the passive role of inmate that is offered. Moreover, the presence of other prisoners in the environment who have "lost it" serves to exacerbate these fears and give testimony to the fact that one is not safe from deterioration. Cohen and Taylor (1972, p. 105) provide a telling example of this problem:

> These men felt that all around them were examples of people who had turned into cabbages because they had not been sufficiently vigilant. Every day they encountered an old sex offender who spent hours merely cleaning and filling the teapot, a mindless activity that the old man appeared to be contented with. And this was their problem: at what price would they achieve peace of mind and contentment? Would they start behaving like the old man, as a way of banishing the ghosts of time, the fear of deterioration, and not knowing what was happening to them? In other words, would the cumulative result of years of working at something which looked like adaptation, in fact really be a process of learning how to deteriorate?

Cohen and Taylor observe that the frank self-consciousness with which these fears are expressed reveals both the stress that this problem induces and one method of "checking onself out" periodically to assess damage. (For a discussion of deterioration as it affects condemned prisoners, see Chapter 8.)

Indeterminacy and the Environment of the Prison

Two additional sources of stress among long-term prisoners are the indeterminacy of prison sentences and exposure to noxious features of the prison environment. While these are problems that are faced by all prisoners, they take on special connotations for the long-term prisoner.

Farber (1944) reported nearly 40 years ago that indeterminacy regarding the length of confinement was positively related to the degree of suffering of the inmate. Indeterminacy varies in degree, however, and we have little empirical knowledge concerning the relative effects of varying levels of indeterminacy. We may stipulate that varying levels of indeterminacy are present in a 2-to-6-year sentence and a 25-to-life sentence, but the effect, if any, of the shift in the magnitude of indeterminacy is not known. In the latter case, the length of time involved raises the specter of dying in prison, which presumably adds a different dimension to the problem. Several investigators have noted that acceptance by a long-termer of the likelihood of dying in prison implies a resignation to fate that is indicative of personal deterioration (Farber, 1944; Cohen & Taylor, 1972; Flanagan, 1980a). In order to fend off this resignation, many long-termers engage in self-deception that is itself stressful.

Finally, there are a number of features of the prison that may induce stress because of a lack of congruence between the inmate's environmental needs and the characteristics of the environment. Toch (1977b, p. 16) reports that many long-term prisoners prize "structure" in their environment. By "structure," Toch means "a concern about environmental stability and predictability; a preference for consistency, clear-cut rules, orderly and scheduled events and impingements." Unfortunately, relatively few prisons characterized by heterogeneous inmate populations are fully responsive to these environmental concerns. Thus, although need-environment disjunctures occur for all prisoners, the implications of research findings are that some person-environment mismatches offer an additional source of stress for long-term prisoners that must be considered in conjunction with the other stresses discussed above.

COPING AND ADAPTIVE STRATEGIES

How do lifers and long-term prisoners respond to the constellation of stresses they face? Are they able to adapt or do they simply endure? Do some fall apart? We know that many long-term prisoners successfully negotiate prison pressures, but the strategies employed are neither easily deduced nor readily classifiable.

Unkovic and Albini (1969) suggest that one adaptive strategy adopted by lifers is adherence to a "philosophy of minimum expectation." This fatalistic perspective assumes that life can be expected to deal no favorable developments during the prison term, hence the prisoner sets the likely release date as a time boundary and fights off depression by expecting nothing positive in the interim. Sapsford (1978) provides a variation on this theme, linking the idea of restriction of future time perspective with methods of coping among lifers. Sapsford found evidence of barrier effects that preclude the long-termer from considering events that might occur beyond the release date. According to this analysis, the long-termer's concept of "life" ends with the date of sentencing and time in prison is a limbo period from which projections far into the future are not made. Cohen and Taylor (1972, p. 91) explain that under the circumstances "it is not surprising that the prisoners live for the present—not from some ideological disdain for future planning, but out of necessity." While short-term prisoners are able to mark time in orthodox ways, such as crossing days off calendars, these techniques have a surrealistic character for lifers and long-termers. As one inmate remarked, "You can't measure 20 years—you don't have a ruler" (Flanagan, 1981, p. 209).

Flanagan suggests that focusing on the "here and now" is a central element of a perspective toward doing time that is adopted by many long-termers. The perspective originates in two distinguishing characteristics of the long-termer group (an older age distribution and the longer sentences they are serving) and is facilitated by association with other long-term inmates. Key elements of the perspective are maturity, predictability of action, and the "prison sense" that comes from years of experience doing time. Adoption of the "long-termer perspective" has several behavioral and attitudinal implications that may be highly functional in enabling the individual to cope with the stresses of confinement.

Cohen and Taylor (1972) propose a typology of adaptive strategies among long-term prisoners that links the selection of coping strategies with the offender's preprison ideological stance. In essence, their model assumes that modes of adaptation to imprisonment are related primarily to the offender's preprison relationship with authority. If the offender's criminal career was characterized by confrontational relationships with authority, continuation of this ideology would suggest that adaptation to prison may take the form of rebellion and escape attempts. Similarly, offenders whose previous relationships with authority were symbiotic in nature ("involving the bending and fixing and rigging of rules rather than the flouting of them"; Cohen & Taylor, 1972, p. 169) may be most likely to cope in prison by "campaigning" and subversion of rules. It is important to note that Cohen and Taylor do not view the relationship of ideology and prison adaptation as fixed. Rather, inmates may shift ideologies in pursuit of a functional adaptive strategy, or be influenced by others either within or outside the prison to adopt a different ideological stance.

The model suggested by Cohen and Taylor reveals the complexity of the question of responses to long-term confinement. Their approach requires us to broaden the inquiry into functional coping strategies among long-termers by enlarging our definition of "successful coping" and by including a great deal of information about individual prisoners in the analysis. By keeping in mind the complexity of the problem, we are cautioned against the development of unitary reform strategies. But while there is no single or simple answer to the problem of reducing the human costs of long-term incarceration, this does not imply that nothing can be attempted.

DESIGNING REFORM

Given the continuing and, in all likelihood, expanding use of long-term imprisonment as a response to crime, the development of environments that minimize the potential human costs of these sanctions is a critical concern. With few and isolated exceptions, however, little attention has been paid to the problem of creating environments and designing correctional regimes for long-term prisoners (Home Office Advisory Commission on the Penal System, 1968; Council of Europe, European Committee on Crime Problems, 1977). A recent paper by the American Correctional Association (1981) reported an investigation of the regime at a Mexican penal colony with an eye to its possible applicability to the problems of long-term imprisonment in the United States. Toch (1977a) suggests that only in a few of the old fortresslike "end of the road" prisons do the environmental features that facilitate doing a lot of time exist, but that other features of these facilities may foster stress among long-termers.

One method of approaching intervention strategies in this area is to consider basic elements or principles that should guide efforts to provide appropriate environments for long-term confinement. These principles could serve as guidelines for the assessment of specific intervention strategies.

The first principle that might guide strategy is recognition of the importance of *choice* in people's lives. An environment in which choices are available fosters the notion that one is in some semblance of control over one's environment. McKay et al. (1979) contend that lack of choice destroys the "illusion of control" that is a fundamental human need. In addition, provision of choice recognizes the diversity within a group, fosters autonomous thinking, and helps to counter the development of institutional dependency.

The implications of the principle of choice are twofold. First, this principle would argue against efforts to prescribe interventions for long-term prisoners *as a class*. An example of this type of thinking is the continuing debate over management of long-termer populations through concentration in a single facility or dispersal throughout the prison system (see Home Office Advisory Commission on the Penal System, 1968). Policy debates of this type assume that a single solution will yield favorable results with a class of persons, and ignore the mismatches that may result. Second, the principle of choice places a premium on diversity in the prison environment and calls into question proposals that would limit this diversity. Toch (1977a), for example, sees orchestrating environmental diversity as central to the development of humane prisons. Moreover, McKay and his colleagues (1979, p. 55) provide examples that demonstrate that choice can be enhanced in an institutional environment "without jeopardizing custodial or security considerations," so efforts in this direction need not be proscribed on security grounds without careful examination.

The second principle to guide intervention strategies for long-term prisoners is the concept of *meaning*. The concept of meaning is central to the maintenance of self-esteem and personal growth. Although the idea of a meaningful life in prison appears on its face to be a contradiction, Toch (1977a) has argued that frank recognition of the fact that many inmates will spend most of their productive years in confinement can foster attempts to build meaningful lives in prison. This principle requires correctional officials to adopt a new perspective toward long-term prisoners. Traditional strategies based on short-run "programs" may be functional for offenders serving shorter terms, but the development of useful prison careers requires planning, linear progression toward long-term goals, and the reinvestment of resources into the correctional system.

Finally, the principle of *permeability* should guide intervention strategies with long-term prisoners. Because the primary sanction inherent in imprisonment—removal from society—is applied to long-term inmates in extreme form, efforts must be made to ameliorate the potential secondary consequences of this sanction. In particular, innovative methods of fostering the retention of extraprison relationships must be developed. These efforts are important for the reduction of stress during the period of confinement as well as for enhancing the prospects of successful reintegration upon release. Albrecht (1979, p. 153) reported a study of the postrelease reintegration of lifers in which he found that the attitude of the prisoner's family toward him and his postrelease position in the social structure were the factors that "vitally determine the extent of effects from imprisonment."

Impediments to Change

Lifers and long-term prisoners are among the most difficult subgroups of the population to think about in the context of change and reform. Historically, other than through the provision of continuous custody, correctional systems have not seen themselves as well equipped to deal with offenders who will spend a large portion of their adult lives in confinement. Moreover, the problems presented by these prisoners, ranging from possible deterioration to maintenance of outside ties, appear to be intractable within the context of the correctional system. Also, the very serious crimes that have brought most long-term offenders to prison do not encourage concern for reforms benefiting this group (Flanagan, 1982). Countering these obstacles presents no easy task for correctional officials. One response to this dilemma can be to do nothing, but the costs of this alternative may be high. Long-term prisoners clearly represent "long-term problems," and the alternative to addressing these problems is to "run prisons in which inmates unobtrusively and very gradually waste away" (Toch, 1977a, p. 288).

The principles discussed above amount to pursuit of a goal of "humane containment" within conditions of maximum security (Cohen & Taylor, 1972). No position has been taken about the propriety or efficacy of long-term incarceration per se, and it is doubtful whether the findings of the research to date would add anything meaningful to such a discussion. Certainly our knowledge of the unique problems and stresses associated with long-term confinement should be considered when questions about the *use* of this sanction are raised. Given the alternatives currently available, however, and the nature of the offenses committed by offenders who receive long prison terms, it is doubtful that awareness of prison impact will carry much weight when the societal decision is perceived as a choice between the use of long-term incarceration and the death penalty. Given this fact, the principles of humane containment must be regarded as a way to guide attempts to ameliorate individual problems, rather than as a means of shedding light on more general social choices. As for solutions directed to the heart of the matter—the use of long-term confinement—the pessimistic conclusion that Cohen and Taylor (1972, p. 188) reached a decade ago remains applicable today: "In the absence of the death penalty, transportation or deliberate physical torture, the only way our society can think of dealing with certain offenders is to send them to prison for very long periods." Moreover, the prospects for developing positive alternatives to this practice may be even less encouraging today than they were a decade ago, since today we have substantial populations of long-term prisoners *and* condemned prisoners (whose confinement is discussed in Chapter 8). In this context, the search for ways of reducing the human costs of imprisonment must be regarded not only as an acceptable goal, but also as the goal most likely to yield rewards in the near future.

NOTES

1. In addition, Toch (1977a, p. 1) warns against imputing causal relationships between observed phenomena and the effects of imprisonment: "It is also impossible to separate the impact of prison on an inmate from the personality the inmate brings to prison. We sometimes think we notice the effects of a man being in prison when we see behavior that the same inmate manifested in nursery school."

2. For exceptions, see Sluga, (1977), Taylor, (1961), and others discussed in Wardlaw and Biles (1980). Wardlaw and Biles (1979, pp. 64-65) observe that all of the studies that report significant negative effects of long-term confinement are "methodologically suspect and of doubtful practical utility," and that "it is interesting to note that those studies which are methodologically superior find it very difficult to measure any quantifiable deterioration." These writers conclude that since there is little basis for selecting between the two sets of findings, decisions about the use of long-term confinement must be made on ethical and moral grounds.

REFERENCES

Albrecht, P. A. [The effects of imprisonment on the self-image of "lifers"] (K. Dell'orto, trans.). In National Criminal Justice Reference Service, *International summaries* (Vol. 2). Washington, DC: Government Printing Office, 1979.

American Correctional Association. *The Mexican penal colony at Islas Marias: Implications for alternative environments for long-term incarceration.* College Park, MD: Author, 1981.

Bettelheim, B. Individual and mass behavior in extreme situations. *Journal of Abnormal and Social Psychology*, 1943, 38(4), 417-452.

Calkins, K. Time: Perspectives, marking, and styles of usage. *Social Problems*, 1970, 17(4), 487-501.

Cohen, S., & Taylor, L. *Psychological survival: The experience of long term imprisonment.* New York: Pantheon, 1972.

Council of Europe, European Committee on Crime Problems. *Treatment of long-term prisoners.* Strasbourg: Author, 1977.

Farber, M. L. Suffering and time perspective of the prisoner. *University of Iowa Studies in Child Welfare*, 1944, 20, 153-227.

Flanagan, T. J. *Long-term prisoners: A study of the characteristics, institutional experience and perspectives of long-term inmates in state correctional facilities.* Unpublished doctoral dissertation, State University of New York—Albany, 1980. (a)

Flanagan, T. J. The pains of long-term imprisonment: A comparison of British and American perspectives. *British Journal of Criminology*, 1980, 20(2), 148-156. (b)

Flanagan, T. J. Dealing with long-term confinement: Adaptive strategies and perspectives among long-term prisoners. *Criminal Justice and Behavior*, 1981, 8(3), 201-222.

Flanagan, T. J. Correctional policy and the long-term prisoner. *Crime and Delinquency*, 1982, 28(1), 82-95.

Fox, L. *The modern English prison*. London: Routledge & Kegan Paul, 1934.

Home Office Advisory Commission on the Penal System. *The regime for long-term prisoners in conditions of maximum security*. London: Her Majesty's Stationery Office, 1968.

McKay, H. B., Jayewardene, C.H.S., & Reedie, P. B. *The effects of long-term incarceration and a proposed strategy for future research*. Ottawa: Ministry of the Solicitor General of Canada, 1979.

Richards, B. The experience of long-term imprisonment. *British Journal of Criminology*, 1978, 18(2), 162-169.

Sapsford, R. J. Life sentence prisoners: Psychological changes during sentence. *British Journal of Criminology*, 1978, 18(2), 128-145.

Sluga, W. Treatment of long-term prisoners considered from the medical and psychiatric points of view. In Council of Europe, European Committee on Crime Problems, *Treatment of long-term prisoners*. Strasbourg: Council of Europe, 1977.

Taylor, A.J.W. Social isolation and imprisonment. *Psychiatry*, 1961, 24, 373-376.

Taylor, L. Long-term imprisonment: Commentaries. In S. Rizkalla, R. Levy, & R. Zauberman (Eds.), *Long-term imprisonment: An international seminar*. Montreal: University of Montreal, 1977.

Toch, H. *Men in crisis: Human breakdowns in prison*. Chicago: Aldine, 1975.

Toch, H. The long-term inmate as a long-term problem. In S. Rizkalla, R. Levy, & R. Zauberman (Eds.), *Long-term imprisonment: An international seminar*. Montreal: University of Montreal, 1977. (a)

Toch, H. *Living in prison: The ecology of survival*. New York: Free Press, 1977. (b)

Unkovic, C., & Albini, J. The lifer speaks for himself: An analysis of the assumed homogeneity of life-termers. *Crime and Delinquency*, 1969, 15(1), 156-161.

Wardlaw, G., & Biles, D. *The management of long-term prisoners in Australia*. Canberra: Australian Institute of Criminology, 1980.

CHAPTER 8

Life Under Sentence of Death

ROBERT JOHNSON

I have written elsewhere that

> death row epitomizes a correctional system based on coercion and resulting in dehumanization. Death row is the most total of total institutions, the penitentiary most demanding of penitence, the prison most debilitating and disabling in its confinement. On death row the allegorical pound of flesh is just the beginning. Here the whole person is consumed. The spirit is captured and gradually worn down, then the body is disposed of. A century ago prisoners were subjected to the discipline of silence. Today on death row, this silence may prove endless [Johnson, 1981, p. 121].

Death row is thus the ultimate prison, and this is the case whether we are speaking of Alabama's death row (which we shall examine in detail) or that of any other state. Death row produces its own trauma, victimization, and violence. It impinges harshly on all its inhabitants, though it seems especially inhospitable to some. All death row prisoners face either execution or, should their sentences be commuted, lengthy confinement; only a handful of those reprieved can hope for parole as a means of egress from prison (see Chapters 7 and 9). All condemned prisoners suffer powerlessness, fear, and loneliness to a degree largely unparalleled elsewhere in the prison. Some grow old prematurely; many describe themselves as "the living dead," an image that conveys the extremity of their confinement.

This chapter draws upon tape-recorded interviews conducted during September 1978 with 35 of the 37 men then confined on Alabama's death row.[1] The interviews were open-ended explorations of the dominant problems and pressures of confinement as experienced by the prisoners themselves. Each interview was unique, of course, but together they allowed the identification of broadly shared features of the death row experience in terms of three existential dimensions: powerlessness, fear, and emotional emptiness or death. Each of these central problems, in turn, was associated with several specific themes that tapped concerns as disparate as perceived staff harassment and characterization of death row confinement as a living death.

A sense of powerlessness was defined as a

> response to a controlling environment marked by seemingly omnipresent rules, regulations, and staff. The person feeling powerless believes he is unable to influence significant aspects of the living environment or to fight back and gain autonomy. A sense of helplessness and defeat is experienced as a continuing or dominant feature of adjustment [Johnson, 1981, p. 16].

Corollary themes included concerns with harassment, defined as persistent interference and annoyance interpreted as a policy or aim of the custodial regime; isolation, the severing of contact among prisoners and between prisoners and the larger world attributed as a policy or aim of the custodial regime; and pressure, with the environment defined as a pressure cooker in which problems envelop and threaten to suffocate the prisoners.

Fear appeared among inmates as a response to an environment that is

> organized and run to facilitate the execution of its inhabitants. The person experiencing fear believes he is unable to defend himself against danger, or to ignore perceived threats or occasions of danger. Danger is often seen as widespread and diffuse, beyond the ability of any person to constructively cope or respond. A sense of vulnerability is experienced as a continuing or dominant feature of adjustment [Johnson, 1981, p. 16].

Corollary themes included a perceived climate of violence pervading the environment; the assumption that physical harm at the hands of guards was a real possibility; and a concern with lawlessness, with death row seen as a law unto itself. There was also death anxiety manifested in a preoccupation with the possibility or details of one's execution, and a more specific staff-precipitated death anxiety, or death anxiety suffered as a consequence of staff behavior drawing attention to the death sentence.

Emotional emptiness or emotional death was defined as a response that occurs

> when one believes he is beyond the reach and support of intimates and has been abandoned or forgotten by them and the free community in general;

> it is a reaction to confinement in a setting in which human needs are discounted. The person feeling emotionally empty experiences loneliness, a deadening of feelings for self and others, and a decline in mental and physical acuity. A sense of apathy, passivity, and decay is experienced as a continuing or dominant feature of adjustment [Johnson, 1981, pp. 16-17].

Corollary themes included a feeling of abandonment, with the person seeing himself as forgotten or neglected by loved ones, prison officials, or the larger world; deterioration, a sensed reduction in acuity—mental, physical, emotional, or a combination of these—seen as an effect of confinement; and the perception that death row confinement offers a living death in which only minimal physical needs are met, such as for food and shelter, while emotional or spiritual needs are ignored.

Each interview was coded by myself and one of two research assistants.[2] Themes were initially coded as absent, present-low intensity and present-high intensity. Intercoder agreement was quite high (66 percent), especially when themes were recorded as either present (including both high and low intensity themes) or absent (88 percent agreement). Interview themes were related statistically to a battery of demographic and criminal history data collected at the termination of each interview.[3]

THEME PREVALENCE AND DISTRIBUTION

Table 8.1 shows the prevalence of themes. The table suggests that concerns relating to powerlessness are strikingly widespread; most prisoners felt helpless to stem abuse by their keepers, to secure contact with one another or with loved ones, or to ignore pervasive tension and stress. A total of 97 percent of the interviewees saw harassment as a feature of their daily lives on death row, and 3 of every 4 men indicated high levels of such harassment as part of their daily round. Half of the prisoners depicted death row as intentionally and arbitrarily isolated from the outside world, and particularly from the prisoners' families and other sources of external support. And 63 percent of the prisoners characterized the custodial regime of death row as producing high levels of pressure, though only 1 in 6 emphasized this perception.

Concerns relating to fear were also widely shared by death row prisoners. Of every four men, three described death row as having a climate of violence, and fully half of the prisoners emphasized violence as a salient dimension of the environment. In fact, every other prisoner viewed real physical harm at the hands of staff as a possibility to be reckoned with, indicating that the violence-toned climate of death row was seen by many prisoners as tangible in its implications for their personal safety. Relatively common statements to the effect that death

TABLE 8.1 Theme Prevalence

	Low	*High*	*Absent*
	%	%	%
Powerlessness			
Harassment	22.9 (8)	74.3 (26)	2.9 (1)
Isolation	34.3 (12)	20.0 (7)	45.7 (16)
Pressure	45.7 (16)	17.1 (6)	37.1 (13)
Fear:			
of Guards			
Violent climate	22.9 (8)	54.3 (19)	22.9 (8)
Physical harm	25.7 (9)	28.6 (10)	45.7 (16)
Lawlessness	34.3 (12)	11.4 (4)	54.3 (19)
of Sentence			
Death anxiety	42.9 (15)	17.1 (6)	40.0 (14)
Staff-precipitated death anxiety	60.0 (21)	8.6 (3)	31.4 (11)
Emotional Emptiness			
Abandonment	28.6 (10)	57.1 (20)	14.3 (5)
Deterioration	40.0 (14)	28.6 (10)	31.4 (11)
Living death	0.0 (0)	31.4 (11)	68.6 (24)

row was a lawless regime—a law unto itself—reinforced these perceptions of danger.

Fear was not limited to the conduct of guards in their role as death row custodians. The death sentence, which casts death row guards as would-be executioners, was a significant source of fear. Of every ten prisoners, six reported death anxiety associated with shouldering a death sentence; seven of ten suffered death anxiety that was attributed to the activities of staff members (staff-precipitated death anxiety) who drew attention to the condemned prisoners' plight. The small minority of condemned prisoners who reported no death anxiety at all were case studies in denial (Johnson, 1981, pp. 91-94).

Concerns relating to emotional emptiness, like concerns relating to powerlessness and fear, were virtually universal. Fully 86 percent of the condemned prisoners felt abandoned by loved ones, staff members, or both. The poignancy of this concern was revealed by the fact that almost 6 of every 10 prisoners emphasized feelings of abandonment as a significant feature of their confinement. Furthermore, 7 of every 10 prisoners diagnosed themselves as suffering physical, mental, or emotional deterioration in what was typically portrayed as the interpersonal vacuum constituting the human environment of death row. One-third of the condemned adopted the metaphor of "living death" to convey the cumulative impact of death row confinement—a round of confinement comprising abuse and neglect, uncertainty and anxiety, loneliness and decay.

The interview themes tended to be equally distributed across background variables, particularly when the standard .05 level of significance was used to demarcate statistically reliable χ^2 values. This suggests that the death row environment was sufficiently stressful and overwhelming to render irrelevant such individual differences as age or formal education. However, when less stringent alpha levels were set (such as .20 or .15), some possible differential trends emerged. These patterns related to race, age, educational achievement, marital status, prior criminal and prison experience, length of time confined on death row, and whether or not the prisoner had contemplated suicide as a response to confinement.

More sheltered inmates—those younger, more formally educated, less acquainted with violence and prison—had more salient concerns than their more experienced and often prison-wise contemporaries. White prisoners, whose backgrounds may generally be more privileged and sheltered than those of their black counterparts, seemed more susceptible to death anxiety (79 percent versus 50 percent, $\chi^2 = 1.77$, $p = .18$) and were more likely to characterize their confinement as a living death (43 percent versus 20 percent, $\chi^2 = 2.01$, $p = .16$). Younger inmates (in their teens and twenties) were more prone to view death row as a lawless regime than were older prisoners (62 percent versus 29 percent, $\chi^2 = 2.52$, $p = .11$); younger inmates also appeared more likely to suffer death anxiety (76 percent versus 43 percent, $\chi^2 = 2.70$, $p = .10$). High school graduates, in comparison with less educated prisoners, were susceptible to a wide range of difficulties: They were more likely to feel isolated (83 percent versus 39 percent, $\chi^2 = 4.56$, $p = .03$), to see a climate of violence surrounding death row (100 percent versus 61 percent, $\chi^2 = 4.44$, $p = .04$), and to envision physical harm as a potential outcome of a violence-toned social climate (83 percent versus 39 percent, $\chi^2 = 4.56$, $p = .03$). Single inmates, in comparison with their married peers, seemed more likely to suffer death anxiety (74 percent versus 47 percent, $\chi^2 = 1.57$, $p = .21$). Men with no prior convictions for violent crimes were significantly more likely to suffer staff-precipitated death anxiety (94 percent versus 47 percent, $\chi^2 = 6.65$, $p = .01$) and seemed more concerned with signs of deterioration (88 percent versus 53 percent, $\chi^2 = 3.42$, $p = .06$). Finally, men with no prior prison experience were prone to see death row as characterized by a climate of violence (92 percent versus 65 percent, $\chi^2 = 1.67$, $p = .20$) and by the potential for physical harm flowing from this climate (83 percent versus 39 percent, $\chi^2 = 4.56$, $p = .03$); these prisoners were also slightly more likely to be preoccupied with signs of deterioration (83 percent versus 61 percent, $\chi^2 = .95$, $p = .33$).

Experience, of course, does not provide anything approaching an immunity from the pressures of death row confinement. Black prisoners, for instance, though arguably exposed to especially harsh and toughening socialization experiences in white America's urban ghettos and backwoods communities, nevertheless felt painfully abandoned both by their loved ones and by the justice system that confined them (95 percent versus 71 percent, $\chi^2 = 2.01$, $p = .16$). Older prisoners may have benefited from their years of experience and cumulated maturity, but were more likely to feel intentionally isolated both from other condemned prisoners and from the larger world (71 percent versus 43 percent, $\chi^2 = 1.73$, $p = .19$). Men who had done prison time before may have accepted many features of death row confinement as painful but routine, yet were prone to class themselves among the abandoned, the unloved and unlovable who must be locked away in the deepest recesses of the prison (96 percent versus 67 percent, $\chi^2 = 3.30$, $p = .07$). Moreover, cumulative experiences of death row confinement produced not adjustment based on familiarity, but added susceptibility. Those held on death row six months or more (at the time of the interview) were more prone to manifest the ingredients of the hurt and despair that make up the typology of death row stress: feelings of isolation (68 percent versus 38 percent, $\chi^2 = 2.22$, $p = .14$) developed in an environment suffused with pressure (74 percent versus 50 percent, $\chi^2 = 1.20$, $p = .27$) and marked by a climate of violence (84 percent versus 63 percent, $\chi^2 = 1.16$, $p = .28$) and producing, finally, a sense of living death (53 percent versus 0 percent, $\chi^2 = 9.35$, $p = .002$).

These differential patterns must be viewed as merely suggestive. The sample is small and the statistics indicate emerging trends, not definitive patterns. The differential patterns of response are plausible, however, and this adds to the credibility of the typology. Of even greater significance may be the fact that prisoners who independently diagnose themselves as victims of extreme stress—those who consider suicide as an escape from death row—display the most pronounced concerns of any group of prisoners. Their concerns include the following: feelings exposed to pressure (75 percent versus 47.1 percent, $\chi^2 = 8.37$, $p = .02$); death anxiety, both due to the death sentence alone (81 percent versus 47 percent, $\chi^2 = 5.74$, $p = .06$) and due to the behavior of staff (81 percent versus 59 percent, $\chi^2 = 4.05$, $p = .13$); and self-diagnosed deterioration (81 percent versus 59 percent, $\chi^2 = 4.05$, $p = .13$). These susceptibilities, when read in conjunction with the findings regarding long-term exposure to the death row milieu, show that the concerns of high-risk persons and experiences are both dramatic and readily captured in the typology.

Dimensions of inmate experience may be directly related to attributes of the death row environment. Powerlessness may be rooted in the physical immobility and social isolation produced by the custodial regime of death row; fear may have its origins in the death work that is the routine business of death row, which pits captor against captive in a life-and-death struggle; emotional emptiness is the probable product of exposure to the lifeless human environment that emerges on death row. Our discussion will explore these relationships, dealing in turn with custody, death work, and the human environment of death row. Implications for ameliorating the psychological survival problems of death row prisoners will conclude the chapter.

CUSTODY

Death row is a prison within a prison in which inmates live in virtual solitary confinement for periods of imprisonment that typically are counted in years rather than weeks or months. Prisoners spend up to 23.5 hours a day alone in their cells. Even men locked in neighboring cells are barely able to make physical contact. As one inmate told me, "You can pass objects to each other and you can virtually touch hands then if you wanted to, but that's as close as we come to each other. At any time—24 hours a day, 365 days a year—that's the situation. You can't even play cards with a guy, like to kill time." The routine of the death row prisoner is thus one of painful solitude.

Custody on death row frequently reaches levels that are unmatched elsewhere in the prison system. In Alabama only one condemned prisoner is moved at a time, and he is always handcuffed (behind his back) and accompanied by two and sometimes three or more guards. Until recently Alabama's condemned even took their exercise alone, in an outdoor cage reserved exclusively for them. Not surprisingly, recreation in this cage often proved unrewarding because it was an obvious extension of the prisoners' confinement. Said one man:

> We get 30 minutes a day to go outside. But that's in isolation, too. You walk around. You got a little place they set aside for us, but it's a cage. And you walk around like an animal does. And you know you're no different. You just go out there in another cage and you walk around.[4]

Tight restrictions are applied to condemned prisoners' contacts with the outside world. Correspondence and visiting lists are small, and packages are limited. Purchases from the prison canteen are also sharply restricted. The isolation of the prisoners alerts them to the joys of communication and consumption. Something as ordinary as a chance to send a written order to the prison store thus becomes a major event. One prisoner described the scene this way:

> They have one day which is a store day. The one day actually is to these people on death row like Christmas and all they actually get is cigarettes and candy or cookies, and that's actually become to be a thing like Christmas. I've surveyed it from watching the guys and everybody gets excited and they are actually more happy on Tuesday when they get that little store package. But, you see this is actually what we have been reduced to as far as being men, trying to be a man, finally enjoying a little thing like a cookie. To me it's actually absurd, this actually affects me to that point and there is no way out of it, there is no way to rebel against it.

Restrictions on visits, however, may hurt the most. Condemned prisoners are eligible for only a few hours of visits a month, and these take the form of arrangements euphemistically classified as "noncontact visits" or "contact visits." During noncontact visits the handcuffed prisoner sits alone in an enclosed metal and glass structure and must shout through paint-clogged apertures if he is to be heard by his visitors. Contact visits are somewhat more congenially arranged; the prisoner can touch his loved ones but must remain handcuffed. It is important to note that ties to loved ones are often crucial to men facing a death sentence; restrictions on the frequency or intimacy of visits amount to tampering with a drowning man's lifeline.

> I get a lot of encouragement from my wife. This is why I basically need to be near her or talk to her more often, because she gives me strength to hold on to this thing. She tells me that she's not going to give up and she believes God can make miracles. This kind of stuff helps me, man. And believe it or not, from talking to her—if I could talk to her once a week, I could get through years of this. But if I am cut off from her . . . Even my mother, if I am cut off from these people, you know, it's going to be my downfall because I, in a sense, depend on them for strength to hold on. And when these people [prison staff] mess with that, you know, when they tell me I can't see this person or I've got to talk to them through a metal partition, it's just ridiculous. I can't accept that. I want to be close to them. I want to know that, hey, these people are concerned about me. . . . This is all that I have and if they are going to take all of this away from me, I'm dead anyway.

Condemned prisoners view the custodial regime of death row as a planned assault on their humanity. The physical setting is seen as punitively isolated and barren; surveillance and security are seen as ways to harass and inflict pain.

> We're treated just like animals put in a cage. You know, like sometimes they come by with their sticks and they poke at you like you're an animal or something. That's the way they feel around here. And once you pick at an animal long enough, he starts fighting back. And we're not in a good place to fight back.
>
> The people here make you feel isolated from the world. After a time, you don't want to trust nobody for nothing. Now you know that if a man gets to feeling like that, he just going to back off into a corner and he is going to protect that corner. That's the way I feel. Since I've been on death row, I feel like I have to protect myself because ain't nobody else going to help me. . . . I feel like I have lost faith in everybody.

DEATH WORK

An obsession with custody unites prison policy in the disparate provinces of cell time, exercise, mail, and visits, and is a central feature of existence on death row. But death row is more than a custodial milieu. It is more like a tomb than a segregation wing, since death row prisoners are held in confinement for execution, not for release. Death row guards, then, are agents of both custody and execution. The violence implicit in this role is well understood by the prisoners. In one man's words:

> We know within ourselves that no matter how courteous a guard tries to be to us, we know what he will do in the end. And so that right there makes us guard against them. This is their domain, where they can come and have some say so, they can tell other people what to do and force people to do what they want. I feel that's why they are here. They just have that ability; they want to kill. They want to see people go through hardships. That's why I say they are mental.

Most prisoners acknowledge that there are a few humane guards among their keepers. But the positive influence of these guards is seen to be undone by their more numerous peers, men who "take it upon themselves to be your judge and your jury and your executioner."

Many condemned prisoners describe death row as a totalitarian regime, with the prisoners totally under the thumb of the guards. Violence is felt to be an ever-present threat, and most prisoners speak of unprovoked harassment and occasional beatings. "They can do anything they want to you," said one man. "Who's going to stop them?" "These people are something else," stated another prisoner. "It's just whatever you get, you just be satisfied with that, because if you voice your opinion about it, you're going to get a whipping." Many prisoners feel safe only in their cells, and a few become paralyzed with fear. Their view of guards as tyrants who administer brutal justice leaves some fearful that their executions could occur at literally any time, at the whim of their captors. Among the very fearful, in other words, more immediate fears merge into the ultimate fear of the execution of their sentence. For example:

> When you're on death row and you're laying down in your cell and you hear a door cracking you'll think of where it comes from. When you hear it crack. And when you hear they keys and everything, when something like this happens, the keys come through there: I'm up. I'm up, because you don't know when it's going to take place. The courts give you an execution date, that's true. But you don't know what's going to take place between then and when your execution date arrives. You don't know when you're going to be moved around to the silent cell over here. That's right down the hall, what they call a waiting cell. Up there, you don't know when you're going to be moved down there. And this keeps you jumpy, and it keeps you nervous, and it keeps you scared.

The climate of violence and fear on death row stems from the influence of the death sentence. Guards fear and hate many of the desperate men they cage; inmates fear and hate many of the men who warehouse them for death. The death sentence is also an independent source of stress for the condemned. Condemned prisoners feel uncertain, vulnerable, and afraid. Death anxieties are widespread, and are nourished by various mundane experiences that remind the prisoners of their predicament. In the words of one prisoner:

> When guards show so much neglect and cold attitudes towards me, that brings the sentence to my mind. When I look at the picture of a beautiful niece of mine that I have there on my table, that brings it on, knowing that I probably will be executed. You know, here it is, I have got beautiful relatives who love me and I love them and that brings it on, you know, me not being about to be with them anymore in life. And when I hear people, you know, over the news, talking about the death penalty like talking about criminals—mainly that they are unfit, that the doors ought to be shut and never opened again—that brings on worries about my sentence. Seems like I live with the death penalty every day.

Tragically, the most powerful source of death anxiety is conduct by guards that draws attention to the prisoners' impending executions. For example:

> I was down here in twenty minutes [after sentencing]. I was looking at that chair and they said, "Bring him on in here." They showed me the chair and they said, "Yeah, we are going to sit your ass in there." You know, they were calling me nigger and shit. They were asking me why I did what I done, and did I want to die. . . . What they want to do, they want to scare you. It fucked me around. The chair, that's just like seeing a childhood ghost. That's what that is, a ghost. I went upstairs, you know, they put me in a room and I didn't say nothing to nobody for a whole day trying to get that, trying to get the chair off my mind. But I couldn't, you know. I was thinking too hard trying to get it off and I wouldn't say nothing to nobody. Didn't nobody ask me too much because I guess the same thing probably happened to them.

Of course, a sentence of death by execution, with or without harassment, is intrinsically stressful and demeaning. Some men, for example, dwell on the painful details of their "last walk." Others are haunted by nightmares in which their executions are ritualistically carried out. The legacy of execution—the ugly image left behind for loved ones to contemplate and remember the prisoner by—also torments many prisoners. Alabama's condemned face death by electrocution, a fate one prisoner described as "the way you do a beast when you are killing him, like a hog at slaughter." Condemned men ponder the raw physical violence of the death sentence, and try to comprehend the experience they may one day face. In this regard one prisoner asked, and answered, a series of disturbing questions.

> How am I going to approach and sit in that chair? How am I going to take it? What's it going to be like? How is it going to feel? I already have an understanding about electricity, you know, it's not hard for me to imagine what an experience it would be. . . . Just think about the insides of your body, you know, how such organs could be burned, you know, thousands of high voltage. Think about the precious brain that is in your head, you know? Think about your eyes? What will become of them through such hundreds of volts being ran through your body? It's just really unpredictable what all can happen through such an experience, and what it will be like to go through it, to die right there, strapped in the chair.

The death sentence is a source of worry, anxiety, fear, even dread of the unknown and of a despoiled death. A few men claim to be unconcerned about their sentence and the media sometimes makes much of them. But most prisoners concur in the sentiments of a fellow prisoner who described the condemned as "pinned to the wall, waiting to be shot." Impending executions in Alabama and elsewhere send waves of fear through death row, touching the hearts and minds of every condemned prisoner.

HUMAN ENVIRONMENT

What kind of human environment emerges when men are confined awaiting execution? We can say that death row is a pressure cooker in which feelings of helplessness, vulnerability, and loneliness are widespread; death row makes men feel trapped, suffocated, even entombed; death row produces physical and mental deterioration that must be strenuously resisted if prisoners are to preserve their sanity and human integrity. Condemned prisoners have few avenues of adjustment open to them and must strive, in the final analysis, to endure pressures that threaten to make deterioration their common fate.

Many death row prisoners engage in a fight against decay and are partially successful in these efforts, in the sense that they lose energy, vitality, and hope only slowly and in small steps. They suffer stress in silence. A few prisoners even become tougher, stronger, and more resilient. Others are less fortunate, however, and break down completely. One such prisoner described lengthy psychotic episodes on death row in the following words:

> I done flipped out three or four times in different tiers, you know? My mind just right up and leave me. I didn't expect the thing to happen. And everything just, you know, how you just go. I can't explain it and everything that's taken place but I just flipped out. . . . I'd be depressed and lost. Like the officers would come by and they'd talk to me, some of them, and say I was lost, man, say, "It was like you was in another world, man," Ya know? I say, "Yeah, that's the way I felt, like I was in another world." I felt sometimes for weeks at a time that I wasn't even here.

The lessons of this person's troubles are disquieting to the men of death row. Observed one prisoner, "We all know we can do just like him: Go crazy." These fears are disturbingly plausible on death row, where deterioration manifests itself in the imagery of an extended sleep that permits gradual disengagement from sanity and life.

Given the threat of deterioration and what it portends, it is fitting that some condemned prisoners see their existence on death row as a living death and see themselves as the living dead. Living death is a dramatic metaphor for life under sentence of death, but it is not overstated. Virtually every prisoner I spoke with felt emotionally dead or dying. Said one man, "You need love and it just ain't there, it leaves you empty inside, dead inside. Really, you just stop caring." What prisoners experience is a physic numbness that resembles "ontological insecurity," a term created by R. D. Laing (1965) to describe the inner world of individuals who fear they are petrifying and becoming frozen in place as lifeless objects or things, alive as organisms but dead as persons. But Laing, it is wise to remember, studies regressed psychotics; we speak here, in the main, of nonpsychotics succumbing to abnormal conditions—conditions that suggest to condemned prisoners that they are more dead than alive. (For a discussion of deterioration as it affects long-term prisoners, see Chapter 7.)

The impact of death row confinement is reinforced by policies and priorities that discount the human needs of prisoners. Medical care is inordinately difficult to come by; psychologists and psychiatrists are rarely in evidence; even the prison chaplain has generally abandoned the condemned. The need for a secure prison effectively rules out the provision of basic human services. In one man's words, "There is no way to get the kind of care you need. You ain't going to get no help from none of them [staff] other than what they have to do. That's it. As far as doing anything individually for you, forget it. That's out of the question." Another prisoner concurred: "They're not gonna do anythin' for you. They gonna let you sit here and one day they gonna kill you, rather than let you sit here, or let you turn into an old man right here in one of these cells."

Where visits are concerned, the priorities of death row are unforgivable. A noncontact visit seems almost like a viewing at a wake. The inmate sits handcuffed and alone in an enclosed chamber, neatly dressed and carefully groomed, almost as if on display for his loved ones—all of this even though his teeth may be rotting for want of dental care. The need to shout across the barrier separating the inmate and his visitors precludes intimate conversation. And since no one can touch or embrace, the experience often proves cold and unfulfilling, even mournful.

A living death, then, is what death row provides its prisoners. Condemned men are offered an existence, not a life—allowed to sustain the body while the person withers and dies. In one man's words, "The living dead is actually what it adds up to. What does a maggot do? A maggot eats and defecates. That's all we do: eat and defecate. Nothing else. They don't allow us to do nothing else."

INTERVENTION

Reducing the pains of death row confinement is no mean task. The physical setting is sterile, the social world tense and explosive, and the morale of both the keepers and the kept extraordinarily low. The public, moreover, is largely oblivious to these facts, and, if informed about them, might well support this regime as an appropriate prelude to execution. One can envision John Q. Public holding forth that no discomfort should be spared the condemned prisoner, who after all has committed the ultimate crime and must therefore wait, in pain if not agony, for imposition of the ultimate penalty. Justice can be an ugly business, he might concede, but justice must be done.

There is truth in this popular syllogism. Significant suffering is an inevitable consequence of the death penalty, and this suffering is clearly intended by the judicial and correctional systems and countenanced, principally through apathy, by the general public. But no punishment that treats the offender like an object is just, and hence the dehumanizing conditions of death row confinement we have reviewed are unjust and must be reformed. Condemned prisoners, to put it plainly, cannot be warehoused for death as if they were so many animals whose bodies have to be preserved solely for their official dispatch in the execution chamber. If the state deems death to be the appropriate penalty for certain crimes, this death must be a dignified one and the offenders awaiting sentence must be confined in a fashion that comports with their human dignity. The mission of death row must be to prepare full-blooded human beings for a dignified death. Broadly conceived, this includes the physical death of execution, which a certain proportion of the condemned are likely to suffer, as well as the civil death of extended death row confinement followed by life imprisonment, which a perhaps larger contingent of prisoners is likely to suffer. Confinement that breeds a living death among the condemned serves neither of these objectives; confinement that preserves their human dignity serves both.

It is an open question whether, in practice, the mission of death row can be changed from warehousing to the preservation of human dignity. In principle there is no reason that it cannot be so altered, however, and it is instructive to examine what a humane death row might look like. In general terms, the suggested reforms parallel those recommended for humane confinement of long-term prisoners (Chapter 7): expanding living options beyond those of maximum custody and lock-down, permitting the development of meaningful activities and programs, and reducing isolation.

First and foremost, a humane death row would be characterized by custody that is not an end in itself, to be maximized at all costs, but by custody that is instead a means to maintain an ordered and secure milieu within which emotional support and personal relationships can develop. Condemned prisoners are hungry for human relationships. They are also confined within a massive arsenal of steel and concrete, and are convinced, almost to a man, that escape is futile. These facts combine to give correctional officers a broader range of control options than those they have heretofore considered. Within the girdle of safety provided by the physical environment and the emotional deprivations produced by confinement, order and security on death row could proceed principally from human relationships rather than from force, and the guiding themes of social control could be support and hope rather than fear and despair. Officer training in human relations, in conjunction with differential classification and placement of inmates within death row, could be used to facilitate these ends. The human service officer (described in Chapter 17) would find among the condemned a source of challenging and rewarding candidates for the deployment of his interpersonal skills. This would be particularly the case among the sizable minority of prisoners his custodial counterparts currently classify as amenable to reduced surveillance. Maturity and hopefulness characterize the person who proves most helpful with the terminally ill patient (Kubler-Ross, 1969); variations on these themes might identify the effective death row officer as well.

Of course, a humane death row is composed of more than helpful and concerned officers. Other opportunities for supporting the needs and aspirations of condemned prisoners must be grasped. These include allowing regular visits, particularly contact visits, which are central to the psychological integrity of many death row prisoners. Programs of work or study that can take place in cells or in small groups can also be developed. Small group recreational activities, if properly supervised, would be rewarding departures from the numbing effects of solitary confinement. Self-help programs, preferably developed by and for the prisoners, would permit collective adaptations to the stresses of death row confinement. Self-help programs are of little or no cost to the prison administration, are pursued with enthusiasm even under the present conditions of almost total lock-down, and promote personal growth through helping others (Johnson, 1981, pp. 123-128). There might be a poetic justice in requiring the pariahs of death row to rehabilitate themselves. There is a practical wisdom in such a policy when condemned prisoners win release from death row, as they often do, and are free to mingle with regular prisoners and staff. Some, no doubt, will eventually reenter the civilian world, and it behooves us to consider this contingency in the management of condemned prisoners.[5]

Solitary confinement must not constitute the extent of the correctional effort on death row. Means to preserve and even enhance the humanity of condemned prisoners are available. Their use would make it possible for at least some condemned prisoners to find meaning and dignity in what is otherwise gratuitous suffering. Surely such a regime of confinement serves both justice and humaneness, the paramount values that define social control in a civilized society.

NOTES

1. One prisoner refused to come out of his cell and speak with me; the other man was temporarily housed elsewhere in the Alabama penal system, participating in an appeal of his sentence. Only male capital offenders are held on death row in Alabama.

2. The interview classification system used in this analysis was developed under NIMH grant 1-R03-MH 34516-01. I am indebted to Christine Cormier and Pamela Marks for their selfless devotion to the arduous job of coding the interviews.

3. The following items were collected at the close of each interview: age, race, formal education, religion, marital status, employment, residence, offense, prior violent crimes, prior arrests, prior prison terms, length of stay on death row at time of interview, suicidal thoughts or attempts during death row confinement, and perception of the likelihood of execution. Also solicited was each interviewee's opinion regarding the fairness of his trial and sentence, as well as of his handling by the police, prosecuting attorney, judge, and defense attorney.

4. All quotations by death row prisoners are drawn from Johnson (1981).

5. Officials at San Quentin Prison have recently signed a consent decree mandating some of the reforms advocated in this chapter. The consent decree calls for a two-part classification system: Grade A (low-risk) prisoners are allowed out of their cells on the tiers of the cell block during the hours of 9 a.m. to 3 p.m., have access to a range of hobby/craft items, and have access to group religious services; Grade B (high-risk) prisoners are confined to their cells except during regular exercise periods. All prisoners, independent of grade rating, have access to outdoor recreation (for nine hours per week) in reasonably equipped quarters, and are eligible to take educational programs, including in-cell tutoring. Visiting conditions assure a degree of privacy, and visits are allowed on a regular basis for sessions lasting for two and one half or more hours. Unfortunately, nothing has been published to date about the extent to which the consent decree has been implemented

or its impact on the experience of death row prisoners. For further details about this important death row reform effort, see Consent Decree No. 79-1630-SAW, Thompson et al. v. Enomoto, U.S. District Court for the Northern District of California, October 23, 1980.

REFERENCES

Johnson, R. *Condemned to die: Life under sentence of death.* New York: Elsevier, 1981.
Kubler-Ross, E. *On death and dying.* New York: Macmillan, 1969.
Laing, R. D. *The divided self.* London: Penguin, 1965.

CHAPTER 9

The Stress Comes Later

MARC RENZEMA

In *The Felon,* Irwin (1970, p. 112) said of 41 felons whom he interviewed shortly before release from prison:

> Most of them express the belief that making it is up to the individual, and now that they had decided to try to make it their chances were very good. Most of those who come back, they believed, don't want to make it. Only four of the sample expressed doubts about their chances of making it.

In the report of probably the most massive study ever undertaken of the impact of imprisonment and postrelease supervision, Glaser (1969, p. 332) states:

> It seems that over 90 percent of the men released from prison initially seek legitimate employment and try to achieve self-sufficiency without engaging in crime.

If so many prisoners and parolees intend to avoid trouble, why were 25.1 percent of the paroles granted in 1975 revoked or the prisoner recommitted within 3 years (U.S. Department of Justice, 1980, p. 8)? Why were 71 percent of those released in 1972 unable to avoid rearrest within 4 years?[1] Although cynicism about reformation and rehabilitation is currently fashionable, there is a great deal of evidence that, reformed or not, the great majority of people being released from prison do attempt to refrain—at least for a time—from behaviors that could cause their return to prison. Some recidivism, it would appear, is unintended—the result of lapses in coping. An intensive longitudinal study of the problems experienced and the means of coping employed in making the transition from the role of prisoner to the role of parolee might suggest some means of easing the transition and of thereby reducing some unintended recidivism.

CONSIDERATIONS SUGGESTED BY THE LITERATURE

Almost since the invention of the prison, there has been recognition of the problems faced by newly released men and women. As early as 1817 a commission of the Massachusetts legislature recommended the construction of a halfway house to ease difficulties of readjustment (Johnson, 1968, p. 331). From the earliest experiments with parolelike supervision of released prisoners, there has been a dual and contradictory emphasis: Released prisoners are to be carefully observed in order to ensure that they commit no new crimes, but ex-inmates must also helped with the task of building a new life despite obstacles that usually include poverty and stigmatization.

That stress during the reintegration process is not just a figment of liberals' imaginations is suggested by the wariness with which prisoners approach other prisoners whose release dates are nearing: The "short-time" syndrome is quite real. Also described as "getting short," "shortitis," and "gate fever," the syndrome is characterized by Cormier et al. (1967) as including irritability, anxiety, restlessness, and a variety of psychophysiological symptoms. (Note that these symptoms also appear among juveniles approaching release, as indicated in Chapter 10.)

Research on the prison-to-parole transition suggests that the first few days *after* release also can be a time of acute stress. For example, Irwin (1970, p. 114) tells us that "the initial confrontation with the 'streets' is apt to be painful and certainly is accompanied by some disappointment, anxiety, and depression." Studt (1967, pp. 1-6) describes the time after release as a status passage without the environmental supports that facilitate most other status passages. Rovner-Pieczenik's (1973, pp. 57-58) review of the literature on employment problems and projects for parolees suggests that most parolees are burdened by both formal and informal barriers to employment that are directly related to the statuses of ex-convict and parolee. The picture of society's inhospitality to newly released parolees is further reinforced by research reports on the administration of parole (Erickson et al., 1973; Glaser, 1964; Stanley, 1976; Studt, 1972; Waller, 1974) and by the memoirs and fictionalized accounts generated by articulate convicts and ex-convicts.

If stress during and soon after release is as common and severe as has been reported, logic suggests that it should be measurable and perhaps remediable. Looking at prison release and parole from a stress perspective would seem promising since it is well known that stress can result in dysfunctional behavior, and many parolees obviously display dysfunctional behavior. Furthermore, although methods of treatment of psychological stress are neither simple nor sure, stress is considerably more tractable than unemployment, prejudice, psychopathy, and most of the other factors to which recidivism has been linked. We can more easily envision giving parolees a few pills, a bit of counseling, and perhaps a pinch of biofeedback training than we can imagine overhauling the economic system, liberalizing public attitudes, and restructuring whole personalities.

Perhaps because of my firsthand observation of men afflicted with "gate fever" and because of a disappointing experience as the evaluator of a relatively unsuccessful program that attempted to ease the prison-to-parole transition, I became quite attracted to the stress perspective. In the research reported in the remainder of this chapter, I set out to measure the extent of stress that occurs during the prison-to-parole transition and to classify patterns of stress and coping. I hoped amelioration would become possible through an understanding of stress and that, ultimately, more parolees would complete their paroles without incident.

TERMINOLOGY

Research dealing with stress is always faced with semantic problems. To one of my respected mentors, stress is what happens when one attempts to land an airplane at 170 knots; he feels uncomfortable describing any less extreme stimulus as a stressor. His view of stress focuses on stimuli; for him, stress is the product of extreme situations.

One of my past colleagues piloted a supersonic fighter every weekend. A couple of years ago he was approaching a landing when a light indicated that one of his landing gear wheels was not locked down. Certainly that little light should qualify as a stress stimulus; however, when I asked my colleague later how he felt on final approach, whether his knuckles were white and whether his kness shook afterward, his response was a matter-of-fact "No." Although his life was in danger, his failure to *feel* stressed and to respond *as if* he were under stress makes improper the classification of this incident as a stress episode. Clearly, personal perceptions and response patterns affect stress. My pilot friend was protected both by his concentration on following emergency procedures and by a nervous system that, he says, has never produced white knuckles and knocking knees, not even during the course of being shot down twice in Vietnam.

To deal with individual difference in perceiving and responding to stress, most current stress research seems to use, either implicitly or explicitly, some variety of "process" model of stress. Process models usually sets out interacting phases of psychological stress. McGrath (1970, p. 15), an authority on psychological stress, labels these phases "demand, reception, response, and consequence." As noted in Chapter 2, "demand" refers to the load or input from the external environment. Demands may be material or social. "Reception" is the process by which demands become motives: It is the process of appraising or personally defining the demands. The necessity of looking at reception was recognized relatively late in the evolution of stress research, but it has been found to be critical. That which can drive some people to suicide may never even become a recognized concern to others. "Responses" may occur at several levels: McGrath labels these levels "physiological, psychological, behavioral, and social-interactive." "Consequences" are response costs and benefits to the individual and to the larger system.

METHODS

I interviewed 53 male New York State parolees during the month before each one's release to parole supervision by parole board decision or by conditional (good-time) release. All parolees were released to New York City and subsequently interviewed there 2 to 4 weeks after release, 3 months after release, and 6 months after release. Each interview consisted of 3 parts. In an initial segment the respondents were simply asked to describe the problems and supports they were *currently* experiencing or anticipating. The second segment was a fixed alternative psychophysiological symptom checklist based on that of Langner (1962). The third segment consisted of 20 open-ended questions, most of which were suggested by the findings of Glaser (1964), Studt (1972), and Waller (1974). In terms of McGrath's paradigm, the interviews sought information on the reception, response, and consequence phases of the stress process.

Although much more complex and defensible sampling procedures had been planned, the study group I finally obtained may be most accurately described as a quota sample. The ratio of parolees to conditional releasees (about 2:1) approximates the proportion released by the two methods from New York State prisons during the 1975-1976 study period. The proportion of the men in the sample from each of eight rural, high-security institutions and from two work-release facilities also is close to the proportion of the general New York City parolee population originating in each institution.

Attrition totaled 19 percent despite payment of $3 to respondents for each postrelease interview and my own considerable persistence in attempting to track down missing interviewees. Of the 172 interviews I obtained, all but 7 were tape-recorded and transcribed. For those not recorded, I took extensive notes during the interviews and used these notes to reconstruct and dictate the content of the interviews as soon as they were completed.

Thematic content analysis was applied to the interview transcripts. About half of the final coding themes had been identified in past research. The remaining themes were derived through attempts to minimize the uncoded material in a 10 percent random sample of interview transcripts. Interrater reliability for each stress and support theme ranged from 87 percent to 100 percent, with a mean of 91 percent. Also coded was extensive life history information in the state correctional services department central office.[2] The parole status at the end of 182 days after release was also coded so that there would be a measure of official recidivism.

RESULTS

Except for the absence of acute postrelease stress, the degree of congruence among the products of my interviews in New York City in the mid-1970s, Glaser's in the late 1950s, those of Irwin and Studt in California in the 1960s, and those of Waller in the Toronto area in the late 1960s, is remarkable. Despite the diversity of parole policies experienced and cultural differences caused by the passage of time and regional and ethnic diversity, the problems appear to be quite similar. My study differs from its predecessors primarily in the analytic framework that was employed, which subdivides findings as follows.

Finding 1: Little Acute Stress

Despite the obvious anxieties of men approaching release from prison, after release I simply did not find the phenomena I was expecting: personality disorganization, irrational behavior, and increased physiological symptoms. I began the research expecting to find relatively frequent and easily identifiable stress episodes. Because the respondents' postrelease environments *were* quite noxious, the absence of gross stress must be attributable more to successful defenses against stress in the reception process than to the absence of demands.

Finding 2: Peak Stress Before Release

By several indices of stress, the most stressful time for the respondents was the period *before* release from prison. The data do not provide a basis for distinguishing between the effects of the prison environment itself and the effects of stresses produced by anticipation of release. On the basis of both the general stress literature and the literature on prisons, it seems likely that both of these elements contribute to "gate fever." Just as the period *before* the dentist drills and the lull *before* the battle are often times of peak stress, it seems that knowing of upcoming problems without having the means to cope with them actively may be worse than the time when one is totally immersed in coping activities. Figure 9.1 shows one indicator of stress during the prison-to-community transition. Other indices, not shown graphically, all are at their highest before release. Most indices are lowest a few weeks after release, and most increased at the second and third postrelease interviews. The general pattern is that of a reversed J.

Finding 3: Changing Patterns of Concern

The respondents were most concerned about the issue that past research suggested would be most significant: employment. In almost three-fifths of the focused interviews, concerns about finding, holding, advancing in, or earning money in jobs were mentioned.

About one-third of all of the interviews contained expressions of concern about money problems, family problems, and problems flowing from conviction and/or imprisonment. Although all of these concerns have been reported in the literature, their shifts in proportions and in salience over time seem to have been ignored. Figure 9.2 shows trends in indices of employment concerns. Numbers of employment concerns seem to be *independent* of prior work experience, age, and job-skill levels. The only factor that consistently is associated with lowered employment concerns is concurrent employment. Not apparent from Figure 9.2 is the relatively low salience of employment concerns to some respondents: While a majority claimed concern about employment, only one man saw finding work as critical to his survival on parole.

Figure 9.3 shows the instability of the indicators of concern about money. The respondents were chronically short of money, but not to satisfy basic needs. The need for money appeared to be most salient in

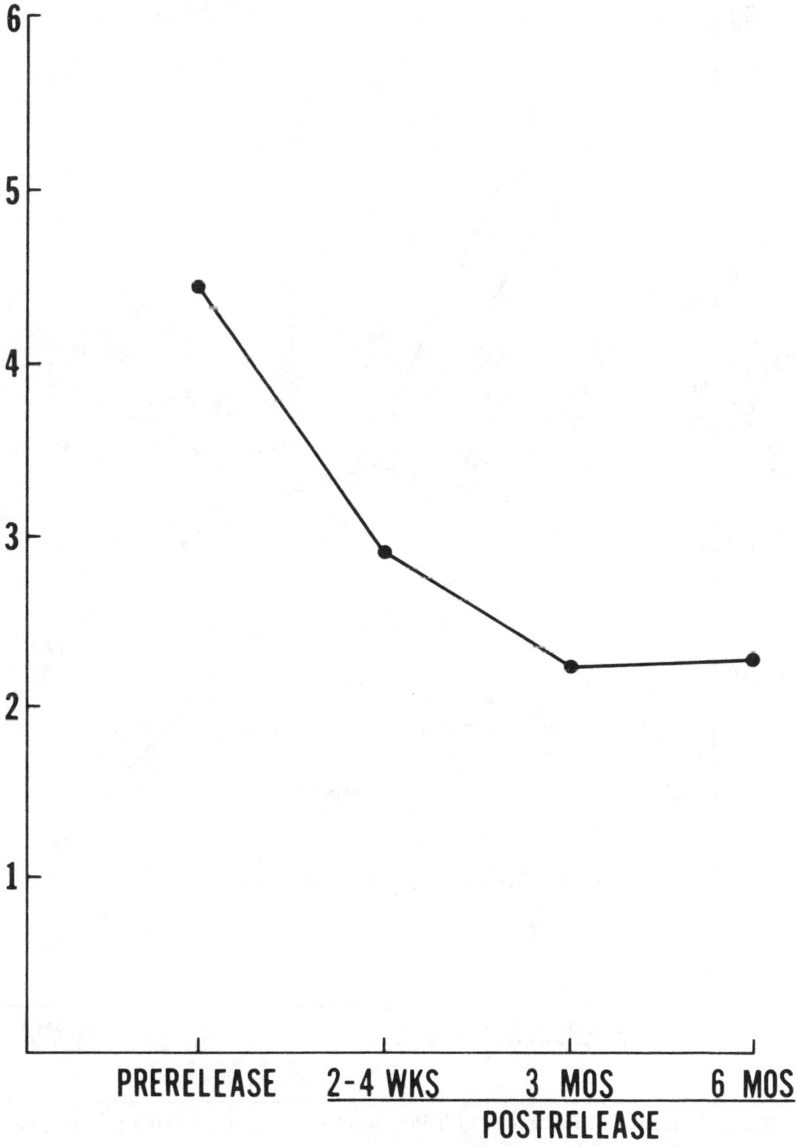

Figure 9.1: Median Number of Psychophysiological Symptoms at Four Interview Times

the first month after release. (Interestingly, employment status and presence of concern about money are statistically unrelated.)

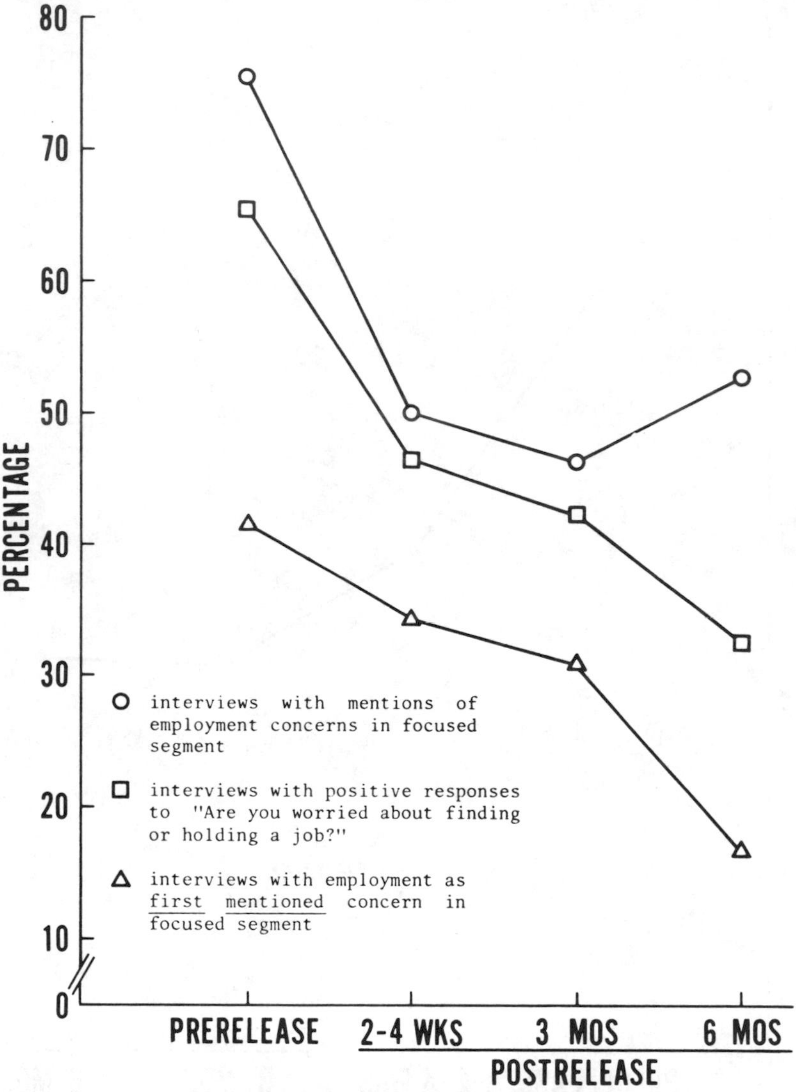

Figure 9.2: Relative Frequencies of Three Measures of Concern About Employment in Four Interview Periods

Figure 9.4 shows concern about stigmatization. It reveals that most men anticipated more discrimination because of their convictions than they later experienced. After release, the respondents tended to blame their job-finding problems much more often on racial discrimination and on their own deficiencies in education, vocational skills, and work experience than they did on their prison records.

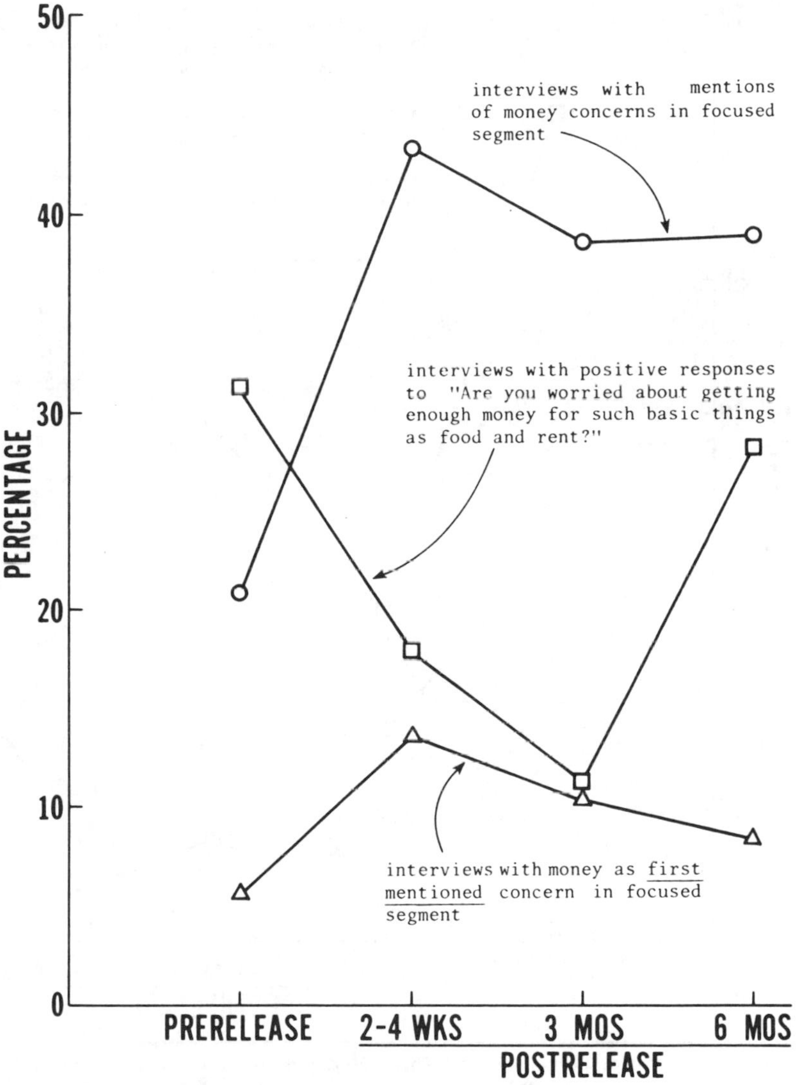

Figure 9.3: Relative Frequencies of Three Measures of Concern About Money in Four Interview Periods

Figure 9.5 shows measures of concern about nonfamily interpersonal relationships. Many respondents worried before release that old friends and associates would lead them astray; they thought that others would make it difficult for them to refrain from crime. After release, most respondents were relieved to find that this was not the case. Unfor-

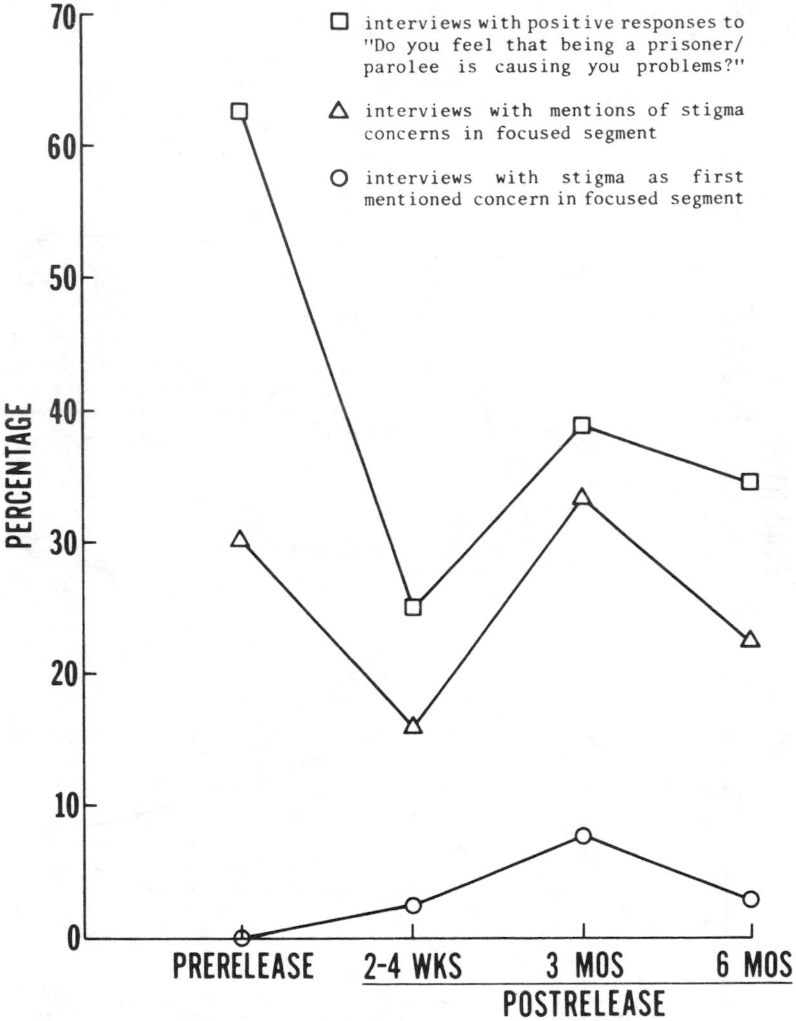

Figure 9.4: Relative Frequencies of Three Measures of Concern About Stigma in Four Interview Periods

tunately, they did find a plentiful supply of conflict at the third-month and sixth-month postrelease interviews. These conflicts, largely unanticipated, tended to be with neighbors, girlfriends, and employers rather than with criminal associates known before incarceration.

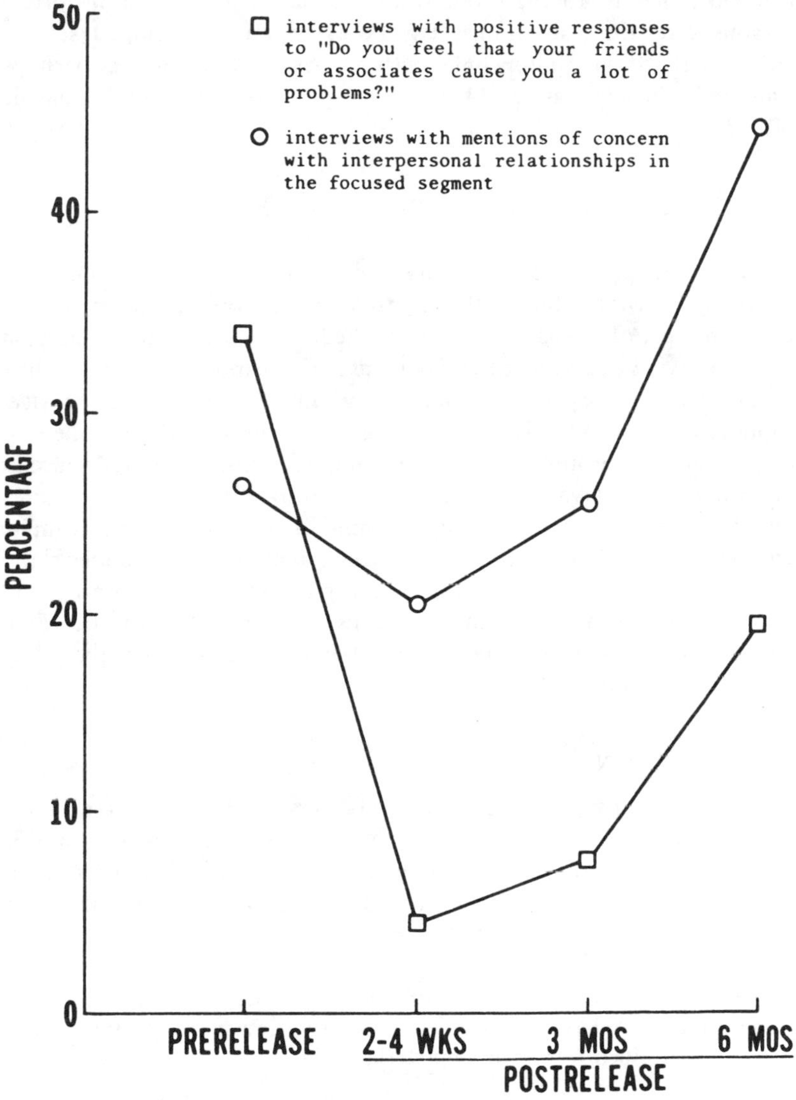

Figure 9.5: Relative Frequencies of Two Measures of Concern About Interpersonal Relationships in Four Interview Periods

Finding 4: Significant Self-Doubt

In terms of the practical applications of my research, probably the most interesting finding is that in 71 percent of the interviews the respondents expressed doubts about their abilities to manage their own behavior, that is, to carry out what *they* defined as the appropriate responses to their situations. Psychologists have developed several techniques for helping people with self-control problems; perhaps training in the application of these techniques would be useful to parole officers.

Finding 5: Complex Support Systems

Levels of perceived emotional and material support remained relatively constant during the postrelease months. Contrary to the classic picture of the parolee as unattached or detached from society, at every interview period at least 85 percent of the respondents felt they had "people [to] . . . talk to about things . . . important." In terms of physical support, only one man reported a crisis in which the lack of money for basic needs made him consider returning to crime. The predominant pattern of support was reliance on multiple resources. Most respondents depended on some combination of employment in both the legitimate and underground economies, petty crime, help from both nuclear and extended families, public assitance, and gifts from friends. Because of the extensiveness and flexibility of means of support, the withdrawal of any one source seemed to be perceived as of no great consequence by most respondents.

DISCUSSION

The disconfirmations of my expectations are as interesting as the positive findings. The traditional picture of the prison-to-parole transition is that the first few days are critical and that the style of subsequent adjustment is determined during the first few days and weeks. For example, Irwin (1970, p. 113) says:

> Many parolees careen and ricochet through the first weeks and finally in desperation jump parole, commit acts which will return them to prison, or retreat into their former deviant world.

Parole officers acting on this belief usually require reports from new releasees at least weekly, then later reduce reporting frequency and the amount of attention parolees receive.

The picture emerging from this study is different. The approach of release was a time of considerable stress; however, this stress diminished quickly when the inmate was released. The period immediately following release was a time of decompression, a time of relaxation. The new releasees were not disoriented, anxious, depressed, or immediately overwhelmed by tasks of coping. However, by three months after release indices of stress were ascending, and by six months after release they were approaching prerelease levels.

I suspect that the discrepancy between the "critical first few days" view and my "stress comes later" view is caused both by the changed nature of the release experience and by my method's sensitivity to concerns that failed to reach full-blown crises. Over half of my respondents had been, at some time during their imprisonments, on furloughs, on work-release, or on both : These people may be presumed to have been less isolated from the community than most parolees who have been studied in the past. Parole policy has also been liberalized. No longer can parole officers routinely bluster, "If you don't get a job by Thursday, I'm sending you back." In the wake of several court decisions in the early 1970s and in the anticipation of possible legal attacks on parole, administration of parole throughout the country has changed considerably. Revocation procedures became more formalized, revocations for violations of parole rules (as opposed to new crimes) declined, and parole became generally less intrusive in the lives of parolees. Although older studies (excepting Irwin, 1970, p. 110) tend to attribute many of the problems of reentry to the parole system itself, parole and its obligations seemed to cause little immediate or long-term concern to my respondents. Perhaps reduced isolation from the community and the changes in parole policies have eased reentry, especially the first few days, for most parolees.[3]

In terms of potential interventions by parole officers, a key finding of this study is that parole was not central in the respondents' lives: Parole would likely have to be greatly improved in both quantity of contact and in the appropriateness of services for it to determine whether parolees succeed or fail in their parole obligations. Neither significant parolee problems nor the resources they used to deal with their problems came from the parole system. However, the generally ascending indices of stress during the postrelease period suggest that the traditional practice of declining intensity of postrelease supervision may be counterproductive. Parole officers should not assume that if the first few weeks of parole are successfully negotiated the parolee is on the way to a successful adjustment, and that any subsequent trouble is either random or freely chosen by the parolee. Rather, continued vigilance is indicated for general signs of stress, for specific frustrations, and especially for the loss of hope.

Loss of Hope

Review of the interviews with the 21 respondents (of 53) who returned to crime or to addiction suggests that more important than either the stressors in the environment or the discomfort they generated was the respondent's ability to maintain hope. When hope of achieving a satisfactory life through legitimate means failed, trouble followed. The most remarkable evidence for this hypothesis came from the five men who voluntarily quit their jobs before violating their paroles. A synopsis of the experience of one of these job quitters illustrates the gradual increase of frustration and hopelessness.

> Parolee #4 went to work as a welder two weeks after release. His pay was above minimum wage, but well short of the wages that a unionized welder would earn. Three weeks after release #4 was saying, "This job ain't suiting me, I'm not satisfied with it, 'specially working at night, but I'm going to hold onto it until I find something better." Other than for his shift assignment and the distance to his job, #4 was initially quite happy and comfortable. He took pleasure in his family. I happened to talk to #4 by chance a few weeks later. He had quit the welding job but had immediately found another job through a private employment agency. He then quit again, explaining at the interview three months after release, "It was pretty good until about a week ago—me and the foreman, ever since I been there, we just didn't meet." Working was apparently beginning to appear pointless: at the same interview, #4 grumbled, "It's hard. I could have had a job, but it wasn't the kind I wanted. I don't want to be behind a restaurant washing dishes." Two weeks later, #4 was arrested and charged with two robberies.

Parolees need help if they are to avoid the existential frustration and the loss of hope that seemed in several cases to be the immediate precursors of failure. Long-term emotional monitoring, emotional support, and occasional material support should prove to be of assistance in combatting incipient disgruntlement. Some avenues for the provision of such support would be sensitization of parole officers to parolee expectations of success and failure, increased use of volunteers to provide success models and specific services, and design of specific "transition experiences." Such experiences might

> ameliorate adjustment shock and bridge the abruption of adaptive demands. This bridging may entail gradual familiarization with a new reality world, intensive reassurance, and opportunities for test and rehearsal [Toch, 1971, p. 397].

Seduction by the Environment

In some cases of failure, loss of hope of legitimate success was accompanied by criminal opportunities so appealing that these criminal opportunities might be considered as stressors. The situation is not unlike that of a person on a fast who is confronted with a richly spread buffet in a room where no one else is present. Although the appetizers, the salads, and even the entrees may be successfully resisted, not to snatch a dessert "just this once" may prove impossible. Given that the odds of escaping apprehension for any given property crime heavily favor the criminal, the parolee's situation is analogous to the faster's. Possible interventions include keeping the person away from the buffet (target hardening), having witnesses in the room (increased surveillance), and making available to parolees the whole armamentarium of techniques found useful in the treatment of self-control problems and substance abuse (including food!) problems.

NOTES

1. This 71 percent statistic is the combined rearrest rate for 5101 men and women parolees, jurisdiction not specified (U.S. Department of Justice, Federal Bureau of Investigation, 1976, p. 46). The difference between the revocation and recommitment figure and the rearrest figure is not surprising. Arrested parolees are not automatically sent back to prison. The arrest figure probably more closely corresponds to parolee criminal activity. While an arrest is not a conviction, it does represent a dangerous skirmish with law enforcement and at least the possibility of a new offense. Claims that using arrests within three years as a measure of recidivism tends to exaggerate new crime can be countered with claims that because a great deal of crime is not solved or reported, arrests underestimate parolee criminal activity.
2. Data coded included criminal history, substance abuse and psychiatric problems, employment skills and history, prior parole violations, educational achievement, IQ, ethnicity, birthplace, and age.
3. Of course, should furlough, work-release, and parole-release policies become more restrictive (in response to public intolerance of crime), problems immediately after release might once again become salient.

REFERENCES

Cormier, B. N., Kennedy, M., & Sendbuehler, M. Cell breakage and gate fever. *British Journal of Criminology*, 1967, 7, 317-324

Erickson, R., Crow, W. J., Zurcher, L. A., & Connett, A. V. *Paroled but not free*. New York: Behavioral Publications, 1973.

Glaser, D. *The effectiveness of a prison and parole system.* Indianapolis: Bobbs-Merrill, 1964.

Glaser, D. *The effectiveness of a prison and parole system* (Abridged ed.). Indianapolis: Bobbs-Merrill, 1969.

Irwin, J. *The felon.* Englewood Cliffs, NJ: Prentice-Hall, 1970.

Johnson, E. H. *Crime, correction, and society* (Rev. ed.). Homewood, IL: Dorsey, 1968.

Langner, T. S. A twenty-two item screening score of psychiatric symptoms indicating impairment. *Journal of Health and Human Behavior,* 1962, 3, 269-276.

McGrath, J. E. A conceptual formulation for research on stress. In J. E. McGrath (Ed.), *Social and psychological factors in stress.* New York: Holt, Rinehart & Winston, 1970.

Rovner-Pieczenik, R. *A review of manpower R&D projects in the correctional field (1963-1973).* Manpower Research Monograph 28, U.S. Department of Labor. Washington, DC: Government Printing Office, 1973.

Stanley, D. T. *Prisoners among us.* Washington, DC: Brookings Institution, 1976.

Studt, E. *The reentry of the offender into the community.* Studies in Delinquency, U.S. Department of Health, Education and Welfare. Washington, DC: Government Printing Office, 1967.

Studt, E. *Surveilliance and service in parole: A report of the parole action study MR-166.* Los Angeles: Institute of Government and Public Affairs, UCLA, 1972.

Toch, H. The delinquent as a poor loser. *Seminars in Psychiatry,* 1971, 3, 386-399.

U.S. Department of Justice. *Parole in the United States 1979.* Uniform Parole Reports, Bureau of Justice Satistics. Washington, DC: Government Printing Office, 1980.

U.S. Department of Justice, Federal Bureau of Investigation. *Crime in the United States, 1975: Uniform Crime Reports.* Washington, DC: Government Printing Office, 1976.

Waller, I. *Men released from prison.* Toronto: University of Toronto Press, 1974.

PART III

Differential Stress

CHAPTER 10

Survival Problems of Adolescent Prisoners

CLEMENS BARTOLLAS

Institutionalization is a painful process for most offenders, though it is clearly more painful for some than for others. Persons from different racial or ethnic groups (Chapter 11), women (Chapter 12), and the mentally ill (Chapter 13) often show distinctive patterns of adjustment and breakdown in confinement. Adolescent offenders, too, have special problems and concerns. For most adolescents, imprisonment is an extremely stressful experience, whether they are confined in adult jails or prisons (Cottle, 1977; Toch, 1975; Johnson, 1978), youthful offender prisons (Johnson, 1978), or training schools (Bartollas et al., 1976). In this chapter I examine the psychological survival problems of boys and girls confined in training schools.

As juvenile inmates see it, institutionalization means that they are told when to arise and when to go to bed, are required to eat institutional food, are frequently escorted to institutional activities, are often supervised by uncaring or even brutal staff, are sometimes required to attend religious services, are subjected to various means to remake or rehabilitate them, are made to jump through a number of staff-imposed hoops to be released from their confinement, and are separated from family and friends. All youths experience the stresses of the loss of liberty, the coerciveness of a punishment-oriented environment, and the deprivations of caring relationships they would have in their home communities. Moreover, they find they must learn to make it in a "strong shall survive" setting. From the day they first enter the training school to the day they leave, they will be tested and confronted by predatory peers. If they have learned how to take care of themselves on the streets, it of course becomes easier to cope with juvenile institutionalization. But if they have not, their period of confinement is likely to be difficult and even traumatic. Some institutional victims make it; some do not and choose to run away, to withdraw into their own world, or even to "hang it up" (commit suicide). In view of what juveniles experience in training schools, it is not surprising that juvenile correctional institutions have more enemies than friends.

To examine more carefully the stresses of institutionalization, this chapter considers the following aspects of confinement: initial traumas, making it with peers, supervision of staff, pains of imprisonment, and coping with confinement. After this review, I will recommend four changes that are needed to make this nation's training schools more humane and less harmful to offenders.

INITIAL TRAUMAS

Youthful offenders hear rumors about state and private juvenile institutions, and sometimes they know youths who have served time in one or more of these facilities. Ranches, farms, and forestry camps usually are considered "easy time," but end-of-the-line facilities frequently provoke considerable anxiety among youths sentenced to them for the first time. The Bartollas et al. (1976, pp. 52-53) study of a maximum security training school for boys in Ohio reported fearful rumors residents had heard about this institution before their arrival:

> I heard that all the staff were black, and that all the guys were big and tough and they messed over you. I also heard there was a lot of homosexuality up here. And that the institution wasn't together. It was more like a racial problem.
>
> I was scared, because when I was at [another institution], everyone was telling me [present institution] was supposed to be a bad place. Everybody was getting pushed around, jumped on all the time, fighting all the time, and all of this. Always being locked up, and they said [present institution] was underground.
>
> I heard that when you first came that they took your handcuffs off, then hit you in the head, shaved your head, and beat you up before they put you in your cell in the ground.
>
> That all the students would jump on you and try to get to you, and that all the staff members ever did was beat you up during the time you were here. And that you had to stay here three years.

Initial Interaction with Peers

New admissions are handled in one of three ways: They are placed in an orientation cottage with other new residents, assigned to a cottage that has residents with similar personality characteristics or world views, or assigned to whatever cottage has space for them. All residents then go through a period of testing from other residents; those who are able to stay in an orientation cottage for a few weeks probably run less of a gauntlet than those residents who are immediately sent to whatever cottage has room for them.

Cottage residents are typically experts in sizing up a newcomer. One strong white youth tells how the diagnosis is arrived at:

> By the way you talk and the way you act, when they talk to you they find out what you've done and they kind of put it all together in their own little way to determine whether you're bad or not. Whether you can fit in with them or not. If you just seem like some silly little kid off the streets, you're the scapegoat—like a few people in this cottage. If you don't know how to handle yourself, then somebody is always picking on you [Bartollas et al., 1976, p. 54].

New residents are forced to walk a fine line. They must appear strong enough that predatory peers will not exploit them; yet if they put up too big a "front," they know that inmate leaders will look upon them as a threat to their social positions and, therefore, will physically and emotionally test them even more.

But regardless of how good newcomers' skills at impression management are, they will be tested. Predatory peers may demand their institutional food, weekend canteen, food brought from home, or cigarettes. In a juvenile state correctional system in the South, a favorite predatory practice is to line up at the "chow line" ahead of new residents and take all the desired foods before the new inmates arrive at the front of the line. The victimization process sometimes takes more verbally or physically aggressive forms: A youth may be verbally accosted, may be "accidentally" bumped by another, may be "palmed" (grabbed on the buttocks), or may be "sucker punched" (struck in the face or stomach without warning).

Unfortunately, some neophytes are sexually assaulted during this initial period. A black youth in a southern training school was greeted with a "blanket party" during his first few days; a blanket was thrown over his head and he was gang raped. In another southern training school, a girl was grabbed in the shower and three other girls sexually penetrated her with a metal object. A lower-class white in a midwestern training school was sodomized by three black residents and was so shattered by this experience that he suffered a psychological breakdown. Another youth in a midwestern state training school was forced to commit oral sodomy on sixteen youths his second night in the institution.

MAKING IT WITH PEERS

The social structure of inmate social systems has a variety of social networks: (1) subgroups of residents based on race, age, criminal conduct, locale, or gang affiliation; (2) informal primary groupings of friends; (3) networks of instrumental relationships revolving around the production or supply of illicit goods and services; (4) social hierarchies in the living unit with expected role behavior of residents who occupy these social positions; and (5) official positions allocated by staff, such as honor unit member (McEwen, 1978, pp. 151-152). The more custodially oriented or coercive the training school, the more likely it is that a power-oriented social hierarchy will dominate the other social relationships. The social roles in most training schools for boys are divided into aggressive, manipulative, and passive groups (Polsky, 1963; Rubenfeld & Stafford, 1963; Breed, 1963; Allen, 1969; Feld, 1977; Bartollas et al., 1976; Sieverdes & Bartollas, 1982b).

Aggressive Roles

The inmate leader is usually given argot names such as "wheel," "bruiser," "heavy," "El Presidente," and "duke," and controls peers through physical attack, exploitation, agitation, and patronage. The inmate leader's lieutenants may be called "vice-president," "tough," "tough boy," "all right guy," "hard rock," "thug," "bad dude," "redneck," and "wise guy." Sexual exploiters are often referred to as "daddy" and "booty bandits."

Manipulative Roles

Residents who "do their own time" in order to reduce the length of confinement are called "slick," "cool," "con man," and "con artist." The "peddler" or "merchant" is the role occupant who trades stolen, illegal, or exploited goods from one resident to another.

Passive Roles

Residents who are prostaff and are uninvolved in the delinquent subculture are called "straight," "straight kid," "quiet type," and "bushboy." Role occupants receiving depreciation from peers are called "messup," "pain freak," "weak-minded," "stone-out," and "lame." Sexual victims, the social pariahs of the inmate social system, are given such names as "scapegoat," "punk," "sweet boy," "girl," and "fag."

Family Social Structure

The social roles in training schools for girls are generally based upon a family or kinship social structure. Giallombardo (1974), in examining three training schools for girls in various parts of the United States, found that aggressive girls tended to adopt the male sexual roles ("butches"), and put pressure on new residents to adopt the female sexual roles ("fems"). Giallombardo identified the following social types: "true fems," "trust-to-be-butches," "trust-to-be-fems," "jive time butches," "jive time fems," "straights," "squealers," "pimps," "foxes," "popcorns," and "cops." Sieverdes and Bartollas's (1982a) study of six coeducational training schools in a southeastern state also revealed the presence of the family social structure in the girls' cottages, but further divided the seven social roles found in these living units into aggressive, manipulative, and passive roles: "bruiser" and "bitch" (aggressive roles), "lady" and "bulldagger" (manipulative roles), and "child," "girlfriend," and "asskisser" (passive roles). Propper (1981) examined three coeducational and four girls' training schools scattered through the East, Midwest, and South, five of which were public and two of which were private Catholic training schools. In contrast to previously held assumptions, she found little overlap between pseudo-family roles and homosexual behavior; participation in homosexuality and make-believe families was just as prevalent in coeducational as in single-sex institutions and homosexuality was as prevalent in treatment-oriented as in custody-oriented facilities.

Variables Affecting the Selection of Social Role

Race, street sophistication, degree of exploitation experienced within training schools, crimes committed in the community, and personality characteristics are the most important variables affecting the social role adopted by the new resident.

In most juvenile correctional institutions, whites adopt the more passive roles while blacks and other minority groups assume the more aggressive roles. (This is often the case in adult institutions as well, as indicated in Chapter 11.) This means that blacks make up the leadership of the cottage and whites serve as the victims or scapegoats. Street sophistication and previous institutional experience are also important in determining where a youth fits in the cottage pecking order. The streetwise youth knows how to carry himself or herself; this youth knows how to respond to a direct confrontation or challenge. But the first-time offender, instead of knowing the techniques of impression management needed to impress peers, frequently emits fear and anxiety about his or her present placement. Furthermore, the more a youth permits himself or herself to be victimized, the lower this youth will be placed in the social hierarchy of the cottage. For example, the sexual scapegoat is sometimes regarded as a social outcast and is avoided by nonpredatory peers in the cottage. Offense is also of consequence in determining a youth's social standing. The youth who has committed a murder in the community is regarded quite differently than the runaway. One youth put this quite well when he said, "He hasn't done shit! What's he doing here?"

Finally, personality characteristics affect where a youth will fit on the social hierarchy: A resident who exhibits aggressiveness and makes "dominance gestures" will take over highly esteemed roles, but those inmates who are passive and make "submissive gestures" will take over the more unacceptable roles (Mazur, 1973).

This inmate social system causes considerable stress, especially for the less advantaged inmates. Those who have the credentials and desire to adopt more highly esteemed roles know that they must claw their way to the top. If they are confronted verbally or physically, they must retaliate immediately and must be certain that they do not exhibit weakness in any way. To impress peers it may be necessary for them to confront staff, with the consequence of prolonging their institutionalization. Once they have earned highly esteemed roles, they cannot relax because there are always others who desire their social position.

Those who lack the credentials to impress peers are faced with being forced into lowly social positions. Although they are aware that they must avoid victimization, they may not be able to protect themselves against predatory peers. Staff generally offer little help, and may even inform potential victims, "If you are a man, you'll protect yourself." In older male institutions there may be a respected inmate who is willing to protect others against predatory peers, but the price of protection is steep—the protégé must become his "boy" or "sweet boy." A sexual victim finds himself on the last rung of the social hierarchy, nearly engulfed in a social role from which escape is very difficult.

The degradation of victim status presents nearly overwhelming stress to a youth. In a revealing incident, a resident was making fun of a scapegoat one day when the scapegoat, to the surprise of everyone, attacked the supposedly more aggressive youth. In the fight that ensued, the scapegoat clearly got the better of the other youth. Staff locked both youths in their rooms until a disciplinary meeting could be held. The youth who had a higher position in the cottage until the fight tried to commit suicide by setting his room on fire; he clearly preferred to die rather than take the place of the scapegoat. This youth did become the cottage scapegoat and later confessed to a staff member that he was committing oral sodomy on half the youths in the cottage.

The Inmate Code

As is the case with adult prisoners, the inmate social system sometimes develops conduct norms, or an inmate code, that all residents are expected to follow. Bartollas et al. (1976, pp. 63-64) discovered that the general inmate code of the maximum security youth institution consisted of the following tenets: "Exploit whomever you can," "Don't kiss ass," "Don't rat on your peers," "Don't give up your ass," "Be cool," "Don't get involved in another inmate's affairs," "Don't steal 'squares,'" and "Don't buy the mind-fucking." In their study of a coeducational correctional system, Sieverdes and Bartollas (1982a) found the existence of the following reference norms: (1) an unwillingness to inform on peers; (2) an expectation that nobody else within the institution is likely to snitch on the respondent or on a third party; (3) a lack of feeling of trust and confidence in staff; (4) a willingness to manipulate and play games against staff members; (5) a perception that staff view the respondent as a troublemaker; and (6) a feeling of antagonism toward staff.

Both McEwen's (1978) study of training schools in Massachusetts before they were closed and Sieverdes and Bartollas's (1982a) study of coeducational training schools in a southeastern state revealed that the most widely accepted informal norm was the one against informing, variously called "snitching," "ratting," "finking," or "dime dropping." Sieverdes and Bartollas also found that a number of sexual, racial, and institutional variables affected the response of residents to the code. Black youths usually upheld the informal norms more than did the white and American Indian youths. Black females were somewhat more supportive of the code than black males, while American Indian males generally adopted the code more than white males, white females, and American Indian females. Residents in the maximum security training school also supported the code slightly more than those in the minimum and medium security facilities. Finally, long-termers and the elites supported the code more than short-termers and lower-status types.

Residents are most troubled by the norms of the code that forbid informing on peers and that advocate resisting the supervision of staff. Should a peer "snitch" on another who stole his radio or cigarettes, or should he settle the matter himself? Should a sexually victimized youth "rat" on his exploiter or should he follow the tenet of the code and remain quiet? In terms of "taking on" staff, residents would literally be cutting their own throats because the "keepers" control institutional privileges and usually determine the length of confinement. The ideal solution is to make it appear to peers that the resident is resistant to the control and norms of staff but at the same time convince staff that he or she has changed and is ready to return to the community.

Supervision by Staff

McEwen (1978, pp. 64-66) found in his study of 23 institutional and community-based programs in Massachusetts that organizational arrangements and expectations of staff either increased or reduced the resistance of residents to staff. The most important variables negatively correlated with the resistance of residents to staff were informal exchanges with staff, no isolation cells, no locks on the doors of living units, no limitation on smoking, permission to wear one's own clothing, youthful staff, and ex-offender staff.

In observing juvenile institutions in five states, the same staff patterns consistently appear in living units: one staff member is exemplary with youth, one receives a very negative response and is sometimes involved in brutality if the correctional system permits physical force, and the rest are on the short end of the ineffectiveness continuum. Exemplary staff members are typically nonprofessionals who are genuinely interested in their charges, have remarkable insight into their needs, are able to reinforce them when it is needed, and are able to discipline them effectively when appropriate.

However, this positive and caring person is usually matched by another staff member who has considerable problems working with adolescents. This person is often overloaded with personal problems and has a tendency to vent repressed anger on residents. The present author has seen these ineffective staff become involved in such incidents as splitting a resident's head open with a pool stick, bashing youths in the head with a flashlight, and giving the room key of a passive inmate to sexual exploiters. These staff members commonly create considerable turmoil among residents; one inmate expressed the sort of angry feelings that are generated when he said, "Man, when I get out of here, I'm going to get that MF."

The remainder of the staff usually came into the institution intending to guide wayward youth back to more constructive lives. However, when they are met with manipulation and hostility rather than appreciation from their charges, they eventually lose interest in their jobs and develop the attitudes of "Don't do more than you get paid for" and "Beat the punishment-oriented system as much as you can."

The supervision patterns of staff pose several problems for the "kept." First, residents quickly discover that staff make all the important decisions relevant to them during their institutional stay. They usually decide when residents will be promoted to the next status or level, when and what privileges will be given, whether or not residents will be permitted home visits, off-campus visits, or work release in the community, and perhaps even when they will be released. Thus it becomes imperative that residents make a "good presentation of self" (Goffman, 1959) to the cottage staff. Most youths handle this challenge by manipulating or "conning" staff (Bartollas et al., 1976; Bartollas & Sieverdes, 1982)

Second, residents are commonly resistant to authority and are therefore apt to resent staff control. Status offenders, especially, are known for their refusal to comply with authority and rules; their typical response to orders is "I ain't going to do it." Sieverdes and Bartollas's (1982b) study of a training school for boys in a southeastern state suggested that the longer a resident remained at the facility, the less likely it was that he would have effective and open communication with staff: 16.7 percent of the early-phase, 37.7 percent of the middle-phase, and 46.3 percent of the late-phase inmates reported that communication with staff was difficult. Sieverdes and Bartollas's (1982a) study of the coeducational training schools in another southeastern state revealed that inmates in the maximum security institution were more hostile to staff than those in minimum and medium security institutions.

Third, inconsistencies among staff members create suspicion and disrespect among residents. Although the institutional rules specify procedures of cottage life, staff members commonly vary in what rules they enforce. For example, one youth supervisor will permit residents to roam the cottage, whereas the other on duty keeps them in one place. The enforcement of rules sometimes varies from one cottage shift to the next, and there is usually also some variation among cottages (McEwen, 1978, p. 71). For example:

> Mr. Simmons does not see the prohibition against smoking, which is an institutional rule, as making much sense. The school rule is that the boys are not allowed to carry their own cigarettes and are only supposed to smoke at specified times during the day, when the masters hand out cigarettes to the boys. The rule at Elms [Mr. Simmons's cottage] is that kids can keep their own cigarettes but that they cannot smoke in specified areas and that they cannot carry cigarettes around the grounds; Mr. Simmons told me that the school superintendent knows of his transgression of the school rule but that he apparently condones it.

On one hand, staff inconsistencies promote gaming and manipulative behavior as residents end up playing one staff member against another.

But on the other hand, the lack of consistency in their environment engenders anxiety and insecurity among inmates.

Fourth, because the institutional release process usually depends on the whims and sometimes capricious judgments of cottage staff, this process creates considerable anxiety among residents. Inmates know that they can be turned down for release because of lack of rapport with staff members, for failure to do their work detail or to keep a neat room, for poor personal hygiene, for an altercation with peers, or for inadequate performance in school. Residents are aware that various staff members may feel differently about their being released and that the vote, therefore, depends on who is present at the meeting. One indignant inmate who spoke about the lack of fairness in the release process summarized consensus when he noted, "You've got to kiss a staff member's ass to get out of here." (Correctional officer behavior in adult prisons is described in Chapter 17.)

PAINS OF IMPRISONMENT

Recent reforms have removed some of the psychic discomforts of juvenile institutionalization. Required short haircuts have disappeared in most settings. No longer are most residents required to wear drab institutional clothing. Residents also have more privacy in personal correspondence than they had in the past; most staff no longer open outgoing mail and only check incoming mail for contraband. With the establishment of coeducational institutions in some states, residents also enjoy the benefits of a more normal social environment than they had in the past. The typical institutional stay is much shorter than it used to be; indeed, a commitment to a training school may now mean a shorter period of confinement than a disposition to a group home. Training schools also are smaller than they were in the past; the large fortresslike training school holding 600 or more residents has largely passed from the scene.

But some psychic humiliations still remain. Residents are still typically run through showers like cattle and given a limited time to dry. When they first come to the institution and when they return from each trip off campus, residents still receive a strip search. The food varies in quantity and quality from institution to institution, but it is generally starchy and bland. Although being locked in one's room at night with an emergency pail is humiliating enough, it can be a terrifying ordeal if residents become ill and are unable to convince staff that they need medical attention. Youths have nearly died at night because of their inability to convince staff that they had a genuine medical problem. Inmates who become sexual victims must deal with this devastating blow to their self-esteem, and must worry that the news of their "degradation status" may be spread around their home communities. One youth, in this regard, said:

> I'm afraid of going home. I'm afraid that it's all around the neighborhood what I've done here. If my mother and brothers and sisters find out about it, I couldn't handle it.

The emotional deprivations of institutional life are among the sharpest pains of imprisonment. In the junglelike setting of many training schools, inmates know that they must constantly guard against "bogarting" peers who bully and push them around. They are aware that the best way to handle institutional life is to keep their distance from others. Some youths are fortunate to have an occasional visit from their parents; other youths have no contact with those at home. It becomes painful to display photographs of a girlfriend or sister when other residents can make derogatory sexual comments about them. Boyfriends or girlfriends are sometimes not even permitted to visit because they are underage. The sexual deprivations of confinement are a painful factor of institutional life because most incarcerated youths have had more or less regular sexual relations since their early teens or so.

The memory of good times in the community is also considered a pain of confinement. Many youthful offenders, especially those who have dropped out of school, stay up a good part of the night and sleep until the late afternoon. They enjoy loafing with friends, listening to music, playing pool, and committing their capers. They often are free to come and go as they please because of the laxity of home supervision. Juvenile offenders, most of whom abused drugs in the community, particularly miss "getting high" because few residents are as resourceful as adult prisoners in getting drugs smuggled into the facility or in making alcohol.

"Prison time" becomes extremely hard to handle the final few weeks before release. It is painful for a youth to be locked up for any length of time, much less for many months or several years. Time goes by very slowly, aggravated by the typically monotonous daily existence of training school life. But when a youth receives his or her release date, time becomes even harder to handle. Allen (1969, p. 300) describes the experience:

> When a boy is within a few weeks or a few months of release, either on parole or on mandatory release, he becomes a "short timer." . . . He counts

the days remaining and tells the others, which is called "signifying" and for which he is chided in a good-natured way by the other boys. This often initiates a period of considerable turmoil, during which many seek out a staff member—sometimes the psychiatrist. There is depression at leaving one's friends, the institution, the staff, the ordered and well-looked-after existence, and the place one has made for oneself. There is anxiety at returning to the community, family, wife, or nothing at all, depending on the case. Initially, there is jubilation and a false sense of euphoria; however, insomnia, hyperactivity, and nightmares indicate that this is a dysphoria rather than a euphoria. A general withdrawal and depression may develop, and irritability, fighting, and generally impulsive behavior may occur.

COPING WITH CONFINEMENT

The Bartollas et al. (1976) study of a maximum-security training school for boys in the Midwest found that most residents exhibited the following emotions about their confinement: righteous indignation, rage, fear and anxiety, shame and humiliation, and despair and hopelessness. The ways in which inmates attempted to cope with their confinement depended largely upon which of these emotions was the strongest.

The most popular mode of adaptation was making the most of institutional life. Residents attempted to satisfy their creature comforts with this adaptation: They tried to get more food, to find ways to avoid unpleasant talks, and to be given all possible institutional privileges. Inmate leaders were the most effective in getting their needs met.

The least popular way to cope with institutional life was to adopt prosocial attitudes and to use the training school experience to prepare for the future; only a few youths over a period of four years were receptive to this mode. A third mode of adaptation was to "play it cool." The inmate was simply "doing time" and gave allegiance to neither staff nor peers. He learned to keep his emotions under control and to do whatever was necessary to shorten the institutional stay.

Rebellion was a fourth way of coping with the training school; in this mode, inmates confronted staff in every possible way. They were filled with rage toward their confinement and instigated others to rebel against staff, to stage a protest, and even to set institutional fires. Withdrawal, another extreme type of adaptation, was usually accompanied by feelings of anxiety, humiliation, and hopelessness. Whites were more prone to this mode of coping than blacks, and victims were the most likely of all to withdraw. Runaway behavior was the favorite means of withdrawal, but other means included drugs, mental breakdown, and suicide (Bartollas et al., 1976, pp. 172-178).

POSSIBLE INTERVENTIONS

It is not difficult to understand why training schools have few friends. There is too much truth in the accusations that they are inhumane and unsafe for residents, that they are schools for crime, and that they are prohibitively expensive. Improvements in juvenile correctional institutions must include steps to assure that they are safe for all offenders, provide positive experiences for residents, enlarge the personal and group decision-making responsibilities of residents, and normalize the atmosphere as much as possible.

The safety of training schools is a first priority. Society is responsible for providing safe settings in which inmates will not be victimized or intimidated by either peers or staff. Some institutions are safer than others, some racial groups are safer than others, and some staff are better than others in protecting residents. But in conducting empirical studies in three states and in interviewing institutional residents in two other states, this author has not found a single training school that adequately protects residents.

How can training schools be made safe? Staff appear to be the most important variable. Some staff are very skillful in protecting residents but, unfortunately, many do not care. The amount of indefensible space also becomes an important variable because predatory peers can use indefensible space to victimize peers. Finally, the more staff can help to turn around the "strong shall survive" nature of the peer culture, the safer the institution will be.

Second, training schools must provide positive experiences for residents. A good relationship with a concerned staff member can help generate a lot of positive feelings in a youth. To learn social survival skills, to develop vocational and educational skills, and to gain positive feelings from doing something well are other constructive experiences that confined offenders usually need. Some residents have felt good about their involvement in a sailing program or a wilderness experience, in a treatment modality such as transactional analysis (TA), or in a vocational shop experience such as automotive design, printing, or welding.

Providing more opportunities for decision making and making offenders responsible for their behavior is a third reform that is needed in most training schools. The danger, of course, is that increasing the amount of responsibility given to residents might result in their creating more of a lawless society within the walls. However, the effective staff person can usually determine when a youth is ready to accept greater responsibility. The development of a logical consequences model, in which residents are taught the consequences of behavior, may be a step in the establishment of a more responsible peer culture.

Finally, correctional administrators should make every effort to simulate a normal atmosphere within the institution. Coeducational institutions are a good beginning because they constitute a more normal setting than a single-sex institution. Frequent contacts with the community, with residents going to the community and with the community (family, friends, and volunteers) coming to the residents, are also necessary in order to make training schools more humane.

Summary

The average training school is clearly better today than it was a decade ago. However, there is still evidence that these long-term juvenile institutions do damage to many residents. The stresses of confinement begin when a youth hears that he or she has been committed to a training school; they do not end until the youth establishes some semblance of a satisfying community adjustment upon release. (This holds for adults as well, as seen in Chapter 9.) Some youths have the credentials to handle the stresses of confinement; other residents find confinement an extremely painful experience. The goals of policymakers must be to make juvenile institutions as humane as possible and to create as little pain as possible for those confined within them. A society that supposedly cares about youth must do a better job of confining those who need secure detention.

REFERENCES

Allen, T. E. Psychiatric observations on an adolescent inmate social system and culture. *Psychiatry*, 1969, 32, 292-302.

Bartollas, C., Miller, S. J., & Dinitz, S. *Juvenile victimization: The institutional paradox.* New York: Halsted, 1976.

Bartollas, C., & Sieverdes, C. M. ***Institutional games played by confined juveniles.*** **Un-published manuscript, 1982.**

Breed, A. Inmate subcultures. *California Youth Authority*, 1963, 16, 6-7.

Cottle, T. J. *Children in jail.* Boston: Beacon, 1977.

Feld, B. C. *Neutralizing inmate violence: Juvenile offenders in institutions.* Cambridge, MA: Ballinger, 1977.

Giallombardo, R. *The social world of imprisoned girls.* New York: John Wiley, 1974.

Goffman, E. *The presentation of self in everyday life.* Garden City, NY: Doubleday, 1959.

Johnson, R. Youth in crisis: Dimensions of self-destructive conduct among adolescent prisoners. *Adolescence*, 1978, 13, 461-482.

McEwen, C. A. *Designing correctional organizations for youths: Dilemmas of subcultural development.* Cambridge, MA: Ballinger, 1978.

Mazur, A. A cross-species comparison of status in small established groups. *American Sociological Review*, 1973, 38, 513-530.

Polsky, H. W. *Cottage Six: The social system of delinquent boys in residential treatment.* New York: Russell Sage, 1963.

Propper, A. *Prison homosexuality: Myth and reality.* Lexington, MA: D. C. Heath, 1981.

Rubenfeld, S., & Stafford, J. W. An adolescent inmate social system: A psychological account. *Psychiatry*, 1963, 26, 241-256.

Sieverdes, C. M., & Bartollas, C. *Adherence to an inmate code in minimum, medium, and maximum security juvenile institutions.* Unpublished manuscript, 1982. (a)

Sieverdes, C. M., & Bartollas, C. *Coping and adjustment patterns among institutionalized juvenile offenders.* Unpublished manuscript, 1982. (b)

Sieverdes, C. M., & Bartollas, C. Race, sex, and juvenile inmate roles. *Deviant Behavior*, in press.

Toch, H. *Men in crisis: Human breakdowns in prison.* Chicago: Aldine, 1975.

CHAPTER 11

Race, Ethnicity, and the Social Order of the Prison

LEO CARROLL

Racial and ethnic minorities have always been overrepresented in American prisons. As far back as 1833, de Beaumont and de Tocqueville (1833, p. 61) observed that "in those states in which there exists one negro to thirty whites, the prisons contain one negro to four white persons." After the Civil War, prisons in the South became overwhelmingly black, while those in the North were populated mainly by first- and second-generation immigrants from Europe (Sellin, 1976, pp. 140-144). Thus, the great "manual labor school," the Massachusetts State Prison in Charlestown, with its largely immigrant population, stood in sharp contrast to the "South Carolina Penitentiary, almost entirely black, with its chain gangs, field hands, work songs and white overseers" (Hindus, 1980, pp. 175-178, 243).

Despite the high visibility and probable significance of these statistical facts, scholars have until recently ignored the impact of race and ethnicity on the culture and social structure of the prison. Clemmer (1940/1958), in his pioneering study of the prison community, notes that about one-fourth of the prisoner population at Menard at the time of his observations were black. However, despite numerous references to race in the remarks and observations of his informants, Clemmer makes no attempt to analyze race relations either among the prisoners or between staff and inmates. Sykes (1958, p. 81), in his classic study of the New Jersey State Prison in Trenton, observes at one point that "the inmate population is shot through with a variety of ethnic and social cleavages which sharply reduce the possibility of continued mass action," but he makes no mention of these cleavages in the rest of his analysis. The same inattention to ethnicity characterizes every major prison study prior to 1970.

Whatever reasons there may be for this inattention to the role of race and ethnicity in the prison,[1] the fact remains that we know little about its influence. Today, however, in many prisons "racial politics set the background against which all prisoner activities are played out" (Jacobs, 1979, p. 14). Indeed, the contemporary crisis in corrections is largely "attributable to the changing pattern of race relations" (Jacobs, 1979, p. 7). The black challenge to the traditional pattern of white dominance, which extended into the prison in the early 1960s, plunged prisons into a turmoil from which they have yet to emerge.

TOTAL INSTITUTION OR SLUM?

Following Goffman (1961, pp. 14-48), it has been common to view the prison as a total institution. From this perspective the prison is seen as set off from the larger society and impervious to its influence. Upon entry, prisoners are stripped of their preprison identities and, through a ritual series of defilements, confirmed in a new identity, that of the convict. Through their interaction within the walls, prisoners are said to develop a subculture designed to alleviate the pains of imprisonment and interaction is seen to be structured in terms of the normative prescriptions of an inmate code of solidary opposition to staff (Sykes & Messinger, 1960).

As plausible as this view is, conceptualizing the contemporary prison as a slum community would seem to be as valid, and perhaps more so, than characterizing it as a total institution. Over half the residents of the contemporary prison are drawn from racial and ethnic minority groups, and most were residents of ghettos prior to their incarceration. Many slum dwellers have been characterized as untrustworthy and perhaps dangerous in the eyes of others; this is true of all prison inmates. Slums provide a cheap source of labor to marginal enterprises in the service economy and are characterized by high levels of unemployment and underemployment. Prison industries are prohibited from competing with private industry and produce goods at low cost for use by the state; there is a high level of unemployment in the prison and wages for the employed are abysmally low. Of course, slums are not typically surrounded by walls, though ghettos in the Middle Ages were. Thus this obvious physical difference might be interpreted as a reversion to an earlier form of ghettoization because of the proven disreputability of the residents of the particular slums we call prisons.

Suttles (1968), in his analysis of the Addams area of Chicago, portrays the social order of a slum community as one of "ordered segmentation." Cultural differences and the fact that many peers are known to share disreputable characteristics produce a high degree of mistrust and suspicion. In the absence of trust, people withdraw into small territorial groupings segregated first by ethnicity and then by sex and age.

Despite their seemingly common status, prisoners are sharply divided along racial and ethnic lines. In a recent study of federal youth institutions, Slosar (1978, pp. 86, 111) found race to be the most important determinant of friendship and leadership choices. White inmates chose white friends and leaders 2 to 6 times more often than would be expected by chance. Blacks exhibited even greater ethnocentricity, choosing black friends and leaders between 19 and 35 times more frequently than chance. Self-segregation by race appears even in small residential units with as few as 3 minority group inmates; an equal ratio of minorities in a cottage with 30 residents results in virtually separate and parallel racial subcultures (Feld, 1977, pp. 181-188). Administrative policy may make for a high degree of demographic integration in cell and work assignments, but biracial interaction cannot so easily be compelled. In those areas subject to formal controls, it is rare: it is nonexistent in areas of life beyond the boundary of administrative policy. Certain areas in the cell blocks, break areas in the industrial buildings, and select spots in the yard become identified with particular cliques and are used only by them. As the cliques are almost always racially and ethnically homogeneous, the prison is thereby balkanized (Carroll, 1974, pp. 147-172; Moore, 1978, pp. 109-110).

It is hard to imagine a convict code of solidarity spanning the social distance that prisoners of different races place between themselves. One recent study reports the existence of racially specific norms encouraging the exploitation and victimization of outgroup members (Bartollas et al., 1976, pp. 62-67); Irwin (1980, p. 184) observes that "loyalty to other prisoners has shrunk to loyalty to one's clique or gang." Loyalty, however, was probably always coterminous with primary group cohesion, and the inmate code has probably always been more fiction than fact. Like public morality in the slum, the code may be "not so much the heartfelt sentiments of people as much as a set of defensive guarantees demanded by various minority members . . . a means of protecting themselves from one another" (Suttles, 1968, p. 4). The increased heterogeneity of the contemporary prison has made it more difficult to create and maintain personalized relations between and among groups that undergird the public fiction. To comprehend the social order of today's large prison we must therefore understand the diverse cultural orientations of prisoners, how these define the experience of imprisonment, and how they shape adaptations to its pains.

BLACK PRISONERS AND DISCRIMINATION

In *The Society of Captives*, Sykes (1958, p. 64) delineates five "pains of imprisonment"—"deprivations or frustrations of prison life today . . . which the free community deliberately inflicts on the offender for violating the law [and] . . . the unplanned . . . concomitants of confining large groups of criminals for prolonged periods." In delineating these pains, Sykes was emphasizing what he perceived as the "hard core consensus" among those confined, though he recognized the fact that there was diversity among prisoners in the saliency of those concerns. In today's prisons, the diversity stands in sharper relief than the consensus.

Through three centuries of oppression in the United States, black Americans have developed a sensitivity to discrimination and victimization. Expecting whites to victimize them, lower-class blacks are inclined to view every use of power with skepticism. This tendency is reinforced by their experience with the criminal justice system. Researchers may debate the existence of discrimination in arrest and sentencing (see, for example, Hagan, 1974; Kleck, 1981; Zatz, 1981), but from the perspective of many black prisoners the evidence is clear and compelling. The rate of incarceration for blacks is nearly 10 times that for whites, 544 versus 65 per 10,000. Black males, who constitute but 5.4 percent of the population, make up 45.7 percent of the prisoner population (Christianson, 1981, pp. 364-368).[2] It is scarcely surprising that in the minds of many black males prison "simply looms as the next phase in a sequence of humiliations" (Jackson, 1970, p. 9).

The very structure of the prison—its walls and bars, its rigid hierarchy, its whiteness—seems designed to foster an image of a racist conspiracy. At Attica at the time of the riot in 1971, there were only 2 minority employees on a staff of over 500, with a prison population that was 63.5 percent black and 9.5 percent Puerto Rican (New York State Special Commission on Attica, 1972, pp. 24, 490).[3] The commission made the following observation regarding race relations:

> There was no escape within the walls from the growing mistrust between white middle America and the residents of urban ghettos. Indeed, at Attica, racial polarity and mistrust were magnified by the constant reminder that the keepers were white and the kept were largely black and Spanish-speaking. The young black inmate tended to see the white officer as the symbol of a racist, oppressive system which put him behind bars [New York State Special Commission on Attica, 1972, p. 4].

While affirmative action policies have increased the number of minorities employed in corrections since 1971, the observations of the

Attica Commission remain accurate with respect to most prisons today. A report on a recent disturbance at the Brushy Mountain State Penitentiary, for instance, notes that 55 percent of the prisoners are black but 100 percent of the officers are white; among the staff there is only 1 black, a teacher (Rawls, 1982a).

The sense of discrimination is confirmed through the daily round of discretionary decisions to which prisoners are subject. Research suggests that black prisoners are more likely to be seen as dangerous and threatening by white custodians. As a result, they are kept under closer surveillance than white prisoners. Their visitors and cells are more likely to be searched, they themselves are more likely to be denied passes to go from one part of the prison to another, and small groups of them are likely to be told to "break it up." Black prisoners are written up for disciplinary offenses in significantly larger numbers than white prisoners, particularly in those categories in which the guards have the greatest discretion (Carroll, 1974, pp. 115-143; Held et al., 1979). There is also some evidence that black prisoners, at least in some jurisdictions, are subject to discrimination in consideration for release on parole (Carroll & Mondrick, 1976; Clark & Rudestine, 1974, p. xx; Peterson & Friday, 1975).

All minority prisoners are concerned with discrimination, but for blacks it is the most salient concern. Johnson (1976) reported the results of clinical interviews with 325 men who had either mutilated themselves or attempted suicide in confinement and with a random sample of 146 prisoners used as a comparison group. Black prisoners in the comparison group were strikingly different from Hispanic and white prisoners in their concern with being victims of inequity and abuse by the criminal justice system and in tending to express fear of being unable to control their anger and resentment at this perceived victimization (Johnson, 1976, pp. 74-77). Much the same inference can be drawn from the work of Toch (1977). He identified eight environmental concerns of prisoners; the most prominent for blacks was freedom: "A concern about the circumscription of one's autonomy; a need for minimal restriction and for maximum opportunity to govern one's conduct" (Toch, 1977, p. 17). Prisoners exhibiting a high degree of concern with freedom are those who see themselves as placed in childlike roles, deprived of their due respect, continually harassed in both serious and petty ways, and tending to experience anger at their lack of autonomy and perhaps rage at their inability or fear of expressing resentment (Toch, 1977, pp. 97-104).

The debasement and degradation of being an inmate pose serious threats to self-esteem. Black prisoners in the late 1960s and early 1970s were able to protect themselves from these threats by using the perspectives of black nationalism to integrate their role as blacks with their role as prisoners in such a way as to place themselves in the vanguard of a worldwide revolutionary movement against oppression (Carroll, 1974, pp. 95-98). Undoubtedly this prison-reinforced ideology affected the concerns of black prisoners and is reflected in the findings of Johnson and Toch. Nationalism, however, was superimposed and to some degree in conflict with more enduring strains of black culture, strains that extol perseverance rather than revolution (Carroll, 1974, pp. 95-98; Johnson & Dorin, 1978; Dorin & Johnson, 1979). Pervasive victimization gives rise to a view of life as a jungle, an almost paranoid suspiciousness of one's environment and the motives of others (Grier & Cobbs, 1969, p. 172). Both cunning ad toughness are highly valued and assiduously cultivated. The concern for safety and the instability of the family gives rise to a strong peer group orientation that is also indispensable to the maintenance of self-esteem, providing an audience to validate the young ghetto male's claims of masculinity and personal worth (Anderson, 1978; Liebow, 1967). This orientation is also the source of special relations of mutual aid and affection, which are frequently given the status of kinship, as in "going for cousins" (Anderson, 1978, p. 21). The appraisal of one's future as being filled with trouble, failure, and despair results in a "present-time orientation," the absence of a delayed gratification pattern (Liebow, 1967, pp. 64-71).

The adaptiveness of the black ghetto subculture to the prison was evident in the social organization of black prisoners in Rhode Island in the early 1970s (Carroll, 1974, pp. 98-113). Virtually every black inmate in Rhode Island's small prison was a member of an Afro-American Society. The organization was begun by some "revolutionaries" who saw it as a means to convert their "brothers." Most black prisoners remained semiconverts, however. They were "half-steppers," "talking the talk" of nationalism but not "walking the walk." This produced continual strain and conflict between the public leaders of the group and their presumed followers. The operative basis of black unity, however, was not the leaders' political ideology, but cohesive, personalized relations among cliques. Most black prisoners had several "partners," inmates whom they knew well, with whom they could rap easily, and who would go "all the way" for them. Some of these peers were "street partners" and others were "jail house partners" but, regardless of the origin of the relationship, the obligations of partnership remained. In consequence, the entire black population was bound together by an interlocking structure of diffuse relationships of mutual aid and obligation.[4]

Relationships similar to those between "partners" have been described as the building blocks of a black street gang (Keiser, 1969, pp. 13-14, 18), and in large prisons they may also provide the foundation for a larger structure. Jacobs (1977, ch. 6) has documented the development of street gangs in Stateville Penitentiary following a crackdown on gang activity in the streets of Chicago. In his view, the intrusion of the gangs changed the very principles by which inmates sought to "do time"—from "doing your own time" to "doing gang time"—and transformed the nature of the inmate social system as gangs gained a monopoly over the sub rosa economy.[5]

> When the gangs emerged at Stateville in 1969, they placed the old con power structure in physical and financial jeopardy. For the first time those convicts with the good jobs were not necessarily protected in their dealings, legitimate or illegitimate. Seeing strength in numbers, the gang members attempted to take what they wanted by force. . . . For the first time in history the old cons who "knew how to do time" found their lives disrupted and in danger. Gang members moved in to take over the "rackets." One informant described an instance where a half dozen "gang bangers" simultaneously put knives to his throat. Rather than cut the gangs in, many of the dealers went out of business [Jacobs, 1977, pp. 157-158].

Gang members also used their numbers to gain considerable freedom from custodial control. Jacobs (1977, pp. 161-162) describes how gang members at Stateville confronted officers attempting to discipline one of their members, with the result that the officers frequently backed down. In one case a gang leader negotiated his appearance at a disciplinary court with two captains. The same pattern of group-based confrontation existed in Rhode Island, even in the absence of street gangs (Carroll, 1974, p. 130). The result was a contradictory pattern of enforcement in which the guards were more inclined to keep the black inmates under surveillance but less inclined to punish them severely.

There exists a fair amount of research to support the hypothesis that black prisoners are more resilient to the stresses of confinement than are prisoners from other ethnic backgrounds. Harris (1975, 1976) for instance, found black prisoners to have higher levels of self-esteem than white prisoners. He also found that while the number of months imprisoned was related to a significant decrease in the self-esteem of white inmates, it was unrelated to any change in self-esteem among the blacks. Consistent with this finding are those of several studies of psychological distress. Jones (1976, pp. 70-71, 80-83) reports that among inmates at the Tennessee State Penitentiary a much lower percentage of black prisoners than white prisoners reported symptoms of general psychological distress, and that while one-third of the white prisoners have considered suicide, only 3 percent of the black prisoners have. In his more focused study of self-injury in New York's correctional system, Johnson (1976, pp. 41-55) found black prisoners to be grossly underrepresented among those who had experienced psychological crises and breakdowns. This relationship between race and breakdown remained unaltered when a wide variety of variables were held constant, which adds support to a cultural interpretation. Blacks apparently also feel safer in prison than do whites. Nearly 40 percent of the white prisoners in Jones's (1976, p. 164) study believed they could be the next victim of a random knife attack, as compared to only 12.5 percent of the blacks.

It is plausible to infer that the subculture of the black urban ghetto is functional for survival in the walled ghetto of the prison. The ghetto inhabitants' sense of themselves as victims, reinforced daily by the facts of their existence, provides a rationale that shifts responsibility for their acts from themselves to the system. Having been raised to be cunning and tough, they feel less vulnerable, and through their extensive involvement in peer groups they are able to monopolize the available goods and services and, to some degree, can counter the power of the guards. Moreover, their "present-time orientation" inclines them to do "easy time" by absorbing themselves in the prison rather than trying to "live with their heads on the streets while their bodies are in jail."

LATIN PRISONERS AND FAMILY

In a recently published study that examines the continuities and parallels between life in the barrio of East Los Angeles and life in prison, Moore (1978, p. 103) echoes the words of George Jackson: "In actual experience, pintos [Chicano prisoners] can see their lives as a set of recurrent, accelerating interactions with Anglo institutions that inevitably climaxed in the disaster of prison." True as this may be, it nonetheless appears that the subculture of the barrio does not insulate Latin prisoners from the stresses of confinement to the same degree that the ghetto subculture insulates black inmates. Indeed, in certain respects the core values of Latin culture may increase prison stress.

Latin prisoners are distinctive in the saliency of their concern with family. In Johnson's (1976, pp. 71-75, 170) clinical interviews, the most common theme expressed by his random sample of Latins (70.8 percent of them) was self-linking, defined as "a protest against intolerable separation from significant others [usually family], against perceived abandonment by them, or against inability to function as a constructive group member." Moore (1978, p. 111) in a survey of Chicanos who were members of prisoner self-help groups, confirms this finding; she finds that family is mentioned as the greatest worry by some 60 percent of the Chicano prisoners.

These concerns are a direct reflection of the familistic basis of Latin culture. Latins view the world in terms of extended kinship networks and "even with respect to identification the Chicano self is likely to take second place after the family" (Murillo, 1971, p. 99). Even *machismo,* the Latin ideal of masculinity, is a derivative of familism. *Macho* connotes virility, aggressiveness, fearlessness, and risk-taking, but not independent self-sufficiency. The *macho* male is bound to his family by complex ties of duty and dependency. A man provides for his wife and children; he is deferential and respectful to his elders. In return he is heavily dependent upon his family, especially his wife and/or his mother, for nurturance and emotional support. This dependency perpetuates a sense of adult masculinity which, by Anglo standards, has a "curious childlike quality" (Mintz, 1973, p. 75).

Separation from family thus poses a serious threat to the identity and self-esteem of many Hispanic prisoners. Moore (1978, pp. 100-106) describes how a Chicano prisoner may become morbidly preoccupied with the well-being of his family as a result of a missed visit or a delay in the mail. Johnson (1976, pp. 81-93) traces the complex and circuitous route by which such concerns lead to self-injury. (Self-injury and attempted suicide are comparatively common among Latin prisoners [Beto & Claghorn, 1968] and disproportionately high in comparison to their numbers in prison [Johnson, 1976].) Crisis-prone Latin inmates, overwhelmed with anxiety about family, seek to place staff in the role of parental surrogates. Non-Latin staff are inclined to view such concerns and tactics as unmanly and perhaps as manipulations to gain special treatment. Self-mutilation may be an attempt by the prisoner to convince the staff that he is, in fact, a man and that his requests are serious and urgent (Johnson, 1976, pp. 89-93).

In other ways, however, the culture of the barrio can be functional, and Latin adaptations to imprisonment may be seen as "variants of adaptations to the streets" (Moore, 1978, p. 98). Of particular importance, again, is the street gang. Moore's description of Chicano gangs in East Los Angeles in many ways parallels Suttles's (1968) description of Italian and Mexican gangs in Chicago. Barrio gangs are territorially based to the extent that *"mi barrio"* refers equally to neighborhood and gang. Gangs are also age graded. New cohorts are formed every few years as the result of conflicts between teenage boys from different barrios. While territoriality decreases with time, the gang remains a primary reference group into adulthood, being reinforced by marriage to female relatives of fellow gang members and by ritual kinship ties such as godparenthood (Moore, 1978, pp. 35-36). The strength of barrio ties extends deeply into the prison. Even after years in prison, Chicano prisoners spend much of their time with friends from their neighborhoods, and turn to them for aid in dealing with personal problems and stresses of prison life (Moore, 1978, pp. 119-121). In a sense, the gang becomes a family surrogate that extends its support into the prison (Davidson, 1974, p. 84).

Although Chicano gangs arise from conflict and remain fighting gangs, they are also heavily involved in the marketing of heroin. As described by Moore (1978, pp. 88-92), the heroin market in Los Angeles is more decentralized than it is in other areas, and suppliers and dealers go into and out of business with relative frequency. A number of factors account for this. Of primary importance is the closeness of sources of supply, the poppy fields in northwestern Mexico. Extended kinship ties often mean that a distributor can gain a supply on credit, and the relative impurity of Mexican heroin means that the organizational chain cannot be very long, as there cannot be too many cuts made. Organizational relationships are not those of a bureaucratic hierarchy, but those of kinship and friendship among a group of men who are from the same gang or perhaps have done time together.

Encounters with the Anglo system of criminal justice have provided a basis for coalescence among Chicano gangs in prison. Since 1967, the dominant Chicano groups in California prisons have been two supergangs that, while resembling street gangs, had their origins inside the prison in conflicts over the control of the narcotics trade. The "Mexican Mafia" originated as a gang of "state-raised youths" with ties to Southern California who attempted to organize the drug traffic in San Quentin by strong-arming Chicano loners who were mostly from small towns in central and northern California. *La Nuestra Familia* emerged in response to these attacks. For years conflict between the two gangs was responsible for a spiraling wave of violence in the California prisons.[6] Prison officials have been able to stem this tide only by segregating the gangs into different institutions, sending Mafia members to San Quentin and Folsom, and Familia members to Soledad or Tracy (Irwin, 1980, pp. 189-191; Moore, 1978, pp. 114-116).

The high degree of conflict and violence associated with Chicano prisoners in California and other areas of the Southwest is perhaps due to their involvement in the narcotics trade and to conflicts between territorial groups outside the prison. It is not typical of other areas, nor even of youth institutions in California, where Chicanos appear to form the most cohesive and solidary group. Jacobs (1977, pp. 148, 156) found the Latin Kings to be the best organized and most disciplined of the gangs at Stateville and to pose few control problems for the staff, and Dishotsky and Pfefferbaum (1981, p. 1060) observe that at the Karl Holton School "only the Chicanos were sufficiently cohesive to develop an institutionwise, clandestine organization with a single leader co-ordinating policy aims." Moreover, Chicanos seem to be little involved in interethnic conflict in prisons.

WHITE PRISONERS AND SAFETY

Judging by reports of psychological distress, suicidal ideation, rates of self-injury, and completed suicides, incarceration today seems more painful for white prisoners than for their black and Latin counterparts (Johnson, 1976, pp. 42-49; Jones, 1976, pp. 69-85). The stress for whites does not seem to be related to any single focal concern. Like Hispanics, white inmates show great concern for their separation from significant others, and like blacks, a goodly number see themselves as victims of unjust treatment. But in addition to these stresses, there are several distinctive concerns expressed by white prisoners. In comparison to blacks and Hispanics, white prisoners are more prone to express a disinterest in day-to-day prison life and to direct their anger and resentment at themselves rather than at the system (Johnson, 1976, pp. 75-79). As Jacobs (1977, pp. 17-18) has observed, "'Whitness' simply possesses no ideological or cultural significance in American society." Lacking in class or ethnic consciousness, white prisoners lack a group-supported rationale to deflect blame from themselves. Forced by their incarceration to take a personal inventory, many white inmates develop a view of their lives as devoid of value and of themselves as despicable and inadequate. They are also particularly vulnerable to threats to their external relations, which are probably less secure than those of Latin prisoners. Unlike blacks, many whites seem to make a "quasi-psychotic attempt to reside physically in the prison while living psychologically in the free (real) community" (Johnson, 1976, p. 122).

Another theme found by Johnson (1976, pp. 68-71) to be more common among white prisoners than others is "fate avoidance," fear that one is unable to stand up to prison pressure, especially the pressure generated by threats from other inmates. Confirming this, Toch (1977, p. 127) found safety to be the second most common concern of white inmates; it was mentioned in 44 percent of prisoner interviews and was the primary theme in 20 percent.[7] Quite possibly, the backgrounds of white prisoners have not provided them an equal opportunity with ghetto and barrio dwellers to develop the skills functional for survival in the prison. To some extent, these concerns with safety may also reflect common white stereotypes of ethnic minorities and a consequent exaggerated fear of life in an institution where minorities are the numerical majority. The concern is, however, also based on a realistic, albeit somewhat self-fulfilling, perception of their fate.

Whatever solidarity may have developed among white convicts in the past was presumably a product of their common deprivation in prison. As this deprivation has decreased with humanitarian reforms of the prison, so apparently has the sense of solidary opposition to staff. White prisoners today are not an organized collectivity so much as a congeries of small cliques with diverse orientations to the prison and the outside (Carroll, 1974, p. 85). Similar observations have been made in both juvenile and adult facilities in all regions of the country (see, for example, Bartollas et al., 1976; Davidson, 1974; Dishotsky & Pfefferbaum, 1979, 1981; Feld, 1977; Jacobs, 1977; see also Chapter 10, this volume). Irwin (1980, p. 147) compares the withdrawal of the white prisoners to the tactics of slum residents who, as depicted by Suttles (1968), restrict the range of their interaction to their households and close relatives. Toch (1977, pp. 179-205) describes the retreat of many white prisoners into subsettings within the larger prison in which the inmate can relax with a small number of others of similar interests and orientations. For a disproportionately large number of white inmates, however, the only avenue of retreat is protective custody, where they may be kept in a cell for 23 hours a day. In the mid-1970s at Coxsackie, a youth prison in New York, 90 percent of those in protective custody were white; these prisoners accounted for one-fourth of the white prisoner population (Lockwood, 1980, p. 73). These figures reflect a national trend.

In some institutions, most notably in California but also in Illinois and elsewhere (Jacobs, 1979, p. 18), the threat posed to white inmates by minority numbers and solidarity has produced counterorganizations along the lines of the Ku Klux Klan and the American Nazi Party. Generally small, these groups tend to make up for lack of numbers with their high cohesion and virulent racism. In the youth institution studied by Dishotsky and Pfefferbaum (1979, 1981), for example, 17 percent of the white residents belonged to a neo-Nazi group. However, members of this group, which was the most internally cohesive and displayed the highest level of cross-ethnic hostility, accounted for over half the white inmates designated as leaders. In this institution and others there seems to be the potential of replacing convict solidarity, rooted in opposition to staff, with a similarly defensive solidarity rooted in racial and ethnic hatred.

INTERGROUP RELATIONS

The level of violence in the contemporary prison is exceedingly high, whether judged by the standards of the outside or by those of prisons in the past (see Chapter 4). Using anonymous prisoner reports, Fuller et al. (1977) estimate that approximately 77 of every 100 prisoners in North Carolina are assaulted every year,[8] and in state prisons the annual homicide rate is at least double that in the nation as a whole (Bowker, 1980, p. 27). Much of this violence crosses racial and ethnic lines. Of the incidents documented by Fuller et al. (1977), 40 percent were interracial; of these, 82 percent involved a black aggressor and a white victim. The black victimization rate was 45 percent lower than the rate for whites.

This pattern of victimization is quite common. Indeed, in some institutions, blacks seem to dominate whites totally. In a juvenile institution in Columbus, Ohio, with equal numbers of black and white residents, Bartollas et al. (1976, pp. 53-81) found that a boy's status was determined by and inversely proportional to the level of exploitation to which he permitted himself to be subjected. The status hierarchy is described as an "exploitation matrix" and its racial composition is portrayed as follows:

> At the top is normally a black leader called a "heavy." He is followed closely by three or four black lieutenants. The third group, a mixture of eight to sixteen black and white youths, do the bidding of those at the top. This group is divided into a top half of mostly blacks, known as "alright guys," with the bottom half comprised mostly of whites, designated as "chumps." One or two white scapegoats make up the fourth group in each cottage. These scapegoats become the sexual victims of the first three groups [Bartollas et al., 1976, p. 72].

This degree of dominance seems unusual by comparison to other studies (for example, Carroll, 1974; Feld, 1977) and may have been related to a rather active cooperation of the staff in maintaining black hegemony (see Bartollas et al., 1976, pp. 106-125).[9] The sexual domination of whites by blacks in prison is, however, a matter of general agreement, with a number of studies reporting that somewhere in the vicinity of two-thirds of all sexual assaults involve black aggressors and white victims (Carroll, 1974, 1977; Davis, 1968; Jones, 1976; Lockwood, 1980; Scacco, 1975). Most researchers have seen this pattern as indicative of racial antagonism. Lockwood (1980, pp. 106-107), however, in what is the most detailed study of the problem, reports that

> neither aggressors nor their peers emphasized racial antagonism in interviews. The idea also fails to explain the significant number of blacks becoming targets and victims of aggressors. We should also consider that most rape victims of black aggressors in the street are black. If sexual aggression were primarily motivated by racial animosity, we would expect to find the same victim-aggressor pattern on the street as we find in prison.

Lockwood (1980, ch. 6) argues that the root cause of the problem is the threat that incarceration poses to the sexual identity of young males and results from the response to that problem on the part of some males who have been socialized into a subculture of violence. True as this may be, racism still must remain an important element. How else can we explain why "most informants reported young slender white men were the highest object of desire" and that "the white target brings the highest status to the aggressor" (Lockwood, 1980, p. 32). Moreover, Lockwood's comment on the difference in the racial composition of sexual assaults overlooks the symbolism of the penitentiary for blacks.[10] As we have seen, to many blacks the prison represents white dominance and oppression. In raping a white inmate, the black aggressor may in some measure be assaulting the white guard on the catwalk.[11]

Sexual aggression is only one dimension, however, of the conflict and violence in the prison. There has always existed an illegal economy through which inmates have sought to meet their needs for desirable food, good coffee, and cigarettes, not to mention alcohol and drugs. In the past twenty years, the affluence of the surrounding society has spilled over the walls and created a more visible and pronounced stratification within. In some institutions, prisoners who can afford them are permitted luxuries such as televisions, stereos, musical instruments, virtually unlimited supplies of food and books, even street clothing. And, as the result of more liberal visiting policies and the power and connections of gangs, drugs, alcohol, and cash have become more readily available. All of this has stimulated increased economic competition and conflict (see Chapter 4). In the larger prisons, well-organized gangs struggle to control a share of the sub rosa economy, and in all prisons small cliques, usually differentiated by race, prey upon one another (Irwin, 1980, pp. 206-212).

Unlike sexual aggression, the violence surrounding economic conflict tends to be instrumental, and leaders attempt to control and moderate it. Jacobs (1977, pp. 155-156), describes how the leaders of rival gangs at Stateville reached an accommodation by pledging to abide by a set of "international rules." A similar agreement was arrived at between a white "Mafia" clique and black leaders in Rhode Island (Carroll, 1974, pp. 188-190). Due to the mistrust that surrounds such arrangements, they tend to be tenuous, and are heavily dependent upon the personal relations between the leaders who enter into them and their ability to control the behavior of their followers. The release or transfer of a leader, any challengers to his position within the gang, or independent actions by small cliques can prove sufficient to destroy the precarious equilibrium and can plunge the prison into violence.

For a brief period of time in the early 1970s, it appeared that prisoners might bridge racial and ethnic cleavages. Black and white inmates, politicized by the civil rights and antiwar movements, came to see racism as a facet of the prison administration's efforts to divide and conquer prisoners. A series of unity strikes at San Quentin, followed by a number of other dramatic prison-related events across the country, focused attention on the prison and drew groups as diverse as the American Friends Service Committee and the Black Panthers into coalitions with prisoner organizations. Reform was pursued both through the courts and by direct action of strikes and nonviolent demonstrations in prisons from California to Massachusetts. While some significant victories were won, notably in the area of disciplinary procedures and minimum health and safety standards, the diversity of goals and tactics made common action tenuous, and the movement ultimately collapsed in the face of a strong custodial reaction. Leaders were segregated or transferred, followers were harassed, and political organizations, in the most generic sense of the term, were banned. Irwin (1980) argues that this movement, though indirectly causing an increase in violence against staff, afforded the only possibility to develop a new and peaceful order in the prison. He argues that in repressing this movement "the administrators stopped the development of alternative group structures that could have prevented the rise of hoodlum gangs involved in rackets, formed on racial lines, and engaged in extreme forms of prisoner-to-prisoner violence" (Irwin, 1980, p. 151).

Whether or not Irwin is right in his speculation, it is clear that the resurgence of custody has not been accompanied by a decrease in violence and rapacity. In the late 1970s, in the words of a long-term observer of prisons, "*anarchy within the walls replaced unity; atavism replaced ideology; prisoners destroyed their own*" (Dinitz, 1981, p. 9; emphasis in original).

A NOTE ON INSTITUTIONS FOR FEMALES

Females constitute only about 3 percent of the adult prisoner population in the United States (Hindelang et al., 1981, Table 6-21) and institutions for females have been studied infrequently. What is known of race relations in these institutions, however, suggests a much different order than is found among males.

In an early article on the sub rosa life of residents at a girls' training school, Otis (1913) noted that lesbian[12] relationships are common and usually interracial. Most recently, Carter (1973, p. 40) has reported that

> the single most important factor determining this distribution (between sex roles) is race. Within the institution, race becomes a highly visible constant for imagined sex differentiation. Blacks, grossly disproportionate to their numbers . . . become butches, and whites, equally disproportionately, become femmes. The most common and desirable arrangement is a relationship consisting of a black butch and a white femme.

Giallombardo (1966, pp. 174-184), while not discussing the role of race in the family structures she details, does present two prison "family" kinship diagrams in which the race of the participants is indicated. Nearly three-fourths of the make-believe kinship relations are interracial, including five of seven marriages.

On the basis of such descriptions, it would seem that race relations among female prisoners may be characterized by intimacy and warmth rather than tension and hostility.[13] Carter (1973, p. 40) makes the interesting observation that when racial segregation does occur it seems to be an indirect result of segregation by sex roles—when butches want to discuss things femmes should not hear—but that the high correlation of race and sex role makes it difficult to determine which axis is primary. This is certainly an area in which more research is needed.

CONCLUDING REMARKS

Racial tension and hostility, although exacerbated by the pain of prison life, is endemic to American society. It is unrealistic to expect to cure in the prison what is one of society's most serious and persistent problems. Nevertheless, some measures can be taken to moderate the current high level of racially tinged antagonism in our prisons. Some of these steps may be relatively minor, such as classifying prisoners according to their environmental concerns as assessed by Toch's (1977) Prison Preference Inventory and placing them in congruent environments. Especially vulnerable prisoners could be placed in sheltered environments or niches (see Chapter 16). Such classification could have a major impact in some institutions, particularly where minorities are not a numerical majority. In most cases, however, improving race relations will require major changes in the organization of the prison.

There is an extensive body of research in the field of race relations that rather uniformly concludes that, under certain conditions, interracial contact reduces racial prejudice even among highly prejudiced persons (see Carroll, 1974, p. 217, n. 12). The situation in most contemporary prisons is the antithesis of these conditions, but where it is not there is evidence to suggest that contact reduces prejudice among black and white prisoners (Foley, 1976).[14] Attempts at intervention need to focus on those features of the prison's physical and social structure that impinge on these conditions.

The first condition to be met is that the contact situation must be one in which the participants are defined as equals and in which the social climate favors interracial association and egalitarian attitudes. Obviously, prison inmates cannot be defined as the equal of officers, but more could be done to minimize status distinctions, as is being attempted at the new Minnesota Correctional Facility (Rawls, 1982b). More important is the elimination of racial discrimination. Among other things, this will require that prisons be lawful. There must be reasonable rules, clearly stated and firmly enforced in a manner consistent with minimum guarantees of due process. Disciplinary decisions must be subject to review and there must be a grievance system for both staff and inmates so that meaningful action on complaints may be taken in advance of serious problems. Parole eligibility guidelines should be developed and implemented, and inmates denied parole should be informed of the reasons for denials in specific terms. These procedures, and others, must be seen as legitimate. Ultimately, legitimacy can be gained only by efficacious implementation, which depends on continual, credible communication among staff and between staff and inmates.

Minority prisoners may never entirely suspend their belief in racial discrimination, but they certainly will not become less bitter as long as those who keep them in prison are almost entirely white and Anglo. Active efforts must be made and, where they are being made, must be increased to recruit minorities into staff positions at all levels. Recruitment is not enough, however. The little research that exists suggests that black officers may be subject to rather severe discriminatory practices by their largely rural white superiors (Jacobs & Grear, 1977; Jacobs & Kraft, 1978). Affirmative action must be accompanied by continuing staff training that focuses on interracial understanding and cooperation among the staff members themselves. Moreover, it is to be emphasized that minority staff are not needed primarily to understand minority prisoners any more than white staff are needed primarily to understand white prisoners. The primary needs are for a racially and ethnically integrated staff to serve as a model of effective cooperation, to promote a climate that encourages interracial understanding, and to ensure that all prisoners are defined and treated as equals.

The recruitment and retention of black and Hispanic staff will be greatly facilitated by relocating prisons nearer cities in which large numbers of black and Hispanic people live. With so many prisons overcrowded, decrepit, and obsolete, and with the necessary public support emerging,[15] we appear to be entering a new era of prison construction. These new facilities should be near larger population centers, not on abandoned military posts in remote rural areas. Moreover, they should be smaller, housing perhaps no more than 300-400 prisoners in relatively autonomous living units of 15 to 20 prisoners. This will facilitate security and order maintenance, of course; it will also facilitate credible communication between staff and inmates.

A second characteristic of contact situations that reduces prejudice is that they require, or at least encourage, mutually interdependent relationships to promote interaction that is personal, intimate, and of sufficient duration to overcome stereotypes. The most obvious issue that could draw prisoners into such association is that of meaningful sharing of power. In suggesting this, I am under no illusions about the amount of support that exists for inmate self-government. But it seems that the failure of such experiments has usually been a self-fulfilling prophecy. Initiated under pressure from prisoners or by a lone administrator with a vision, fragile arrangements have been doomed to failure. Where prisoners have been unopposed thay have achieved some notable successes, as when a biracial organization of convicts ran the Walpole prison in Massachusetts for three months during a guard strike in 1973 (Irwin, 1980, p. 246). Even programs now branded as failures seem to have had some beneficial effects. A study at Walla Walla, for example, found that participants in the inmate self-government system established in the early 1970s showed significant increases (over a nine-month period) in self-esteem, self-confidence, acceptance of others, and acceptance of law and order—the last two showing the biggest gains (Regens & Hobson, 1978). With respect to racial antagonism, Feld (1977, pp. 186, 204-205) found that collaborative decison making concerning the establishment of rules and the imposition of sanctions was particularly useful in defusing racial violence, which became translated instead into verbal aggression. Collaborative efforts may also be used to reduce the antagonism that sometimes spills over into sexual violence (see Chapter 15).

Ideally, the construction of smaller facilities, and the renovation of existing prisons to create smaller and more autonomous units, will make prisoner participation in decision making less threatening to custodians and administrators. We can then experiment with different types and degrees of collaboration to determine which are most feasible. (Collaboration in service of voluntary treatment programs is one possible agenda, as indicated in Chapter 14.) Only through collaborative efforts do we have a chance to reduce racial hostility and violence; the result may be prisons that are reasonably stable, safe, and possibly even constructive living environments. Our only other choice is to repress conflict, maintaining order by a reign of terror. This is an unacceptable and unworkable option and, in the long run, we will all suffer its consequences.

NOTES

1. Jacobs (1979, pp. 19-20) speculates that the oversight may have been due to the general acceptance of segregation and discrimination against which prison relations may have appeared normal or even progressive, and/or to theoretical "blindness" due to the concepts dominating the discipline at the time and thus filtering perceptions. Fascinating as the second explanation may be, I find it hard to accept in light of the intense interest in race and ethnic relations in American sociology back to the 1920s and before. Another factor of possible importance is the overpowering fascination with the prison as an institution that tempts all observers to see other influences on prison behavior as subsidiary.

2. Blacks constitute about 47 percent of the prisoner population and are a majority in 17 states and the District of Columbia. This percentage has been rising steadily (see Christianson, 1981). The percentage of prisoners who are Hispanic is difficult to estimate because they are counted as white. Those states with majority black prisoner populations are: District of Columbia (95.8), Maryland (75.7), Mississippi (66.7), New Jersey (61.5), Alabama (59.8), Georgia (59.8), Virginia (59.5), Illinois (57.9), South Carolina (56.8), Delaware (56.3), Michigan (56.1), Pennsylvania (54.5), North Carolina (54.2), New York (53.6), Ohio (52.3), Arkansas (51.9), Florida (51.4), Missouri (50.0) (Hindelang et al., 1981, Table 6-19).

3. *De jure* racial segregation in prisons continued in the 1970s. Jacobs (1979, p. 5) presents a list of cases in which racial segregation in prisons was held to be unconstitutional. The most recent was Battle v. Anderson, 376 F Supp. 402 at 410 (E.D. Oklahoma, 1974).

4. Davidson (1974, p. 55) presents a rather negative view of black prisoners at San Quentin. Nothing that their private behavior is frequently at odds with their public displays of unity, he concludes that "they are concerned for themselves, not for any group." While agreeing that the public demonstrations of unity are often only a veneer, I find his conclusion slights the real sense of mutual obligation found among "partners."

5. Of the four gangs at Stateville, three are black—the Black P. Stone Nation, the Devil's Disciples, and the Vice Lords—and one is Hispanic, the Latin Kings. During the 1960s the black gangs had been politicized, at least to the degree that they realized that

black nationalist symbolism and ideology could be used to gain money and power. They continued to use this tactic within the prison but never allied with other groups such as the Black Panthers, who regarded the gangs as counterrevolutionary (Jacobs, 1977, p. 155). This is the same tension I found in Rhode Island, but on a larger scale.

6. In 1969 the rate of violent incidents in the California prison system was 1.08 per 100 prisoners per year. By 1974 the rate had risen to 4.3. Much of this increase was due to the feud between the Chicano gangs (Park, 1976).

7. By way of comparison, safety was mentioned as a concern by 30.7 percent of the black prisoners, but was the primary theme in only 4.1 percent of the interviews (Toch, 1977, p. 127).

8. The rate based on official records was much lower, 6.8 per 100.

9. Bartollas and Sieverdes (1981), in a recent study in another state, report a similar pattern but note that it does not exist to the same degree.

10. Hispanic prisoners, as I have discussed, probably suffer sexual identity problems more than others; yet only 14 percent of the aggressors identified by Lockwood (1980, p. 27) were Hispanic. This is perhaps due to their comparative lack of anger and resentment at being victimized. It is not apparently due to a lack of participation in homosexual activity (see Davidson, 1974, pp. 74-77).

11. Not all white inmates succumb to threats of sexual aggression or retreat to protective custody. Some retaliate. In nearly one-fifth of the homicides in prison, homosexuality is the primary motive (Sylvester et al., 1977, p. 48). These homicides often involve a young white aggressor and an older black victim (Jones, 1976, p. 151-152).

12. There is some question about how frequently these relations involve genital sex. Many, perhaps most, seem to be symbolically sexual, involving emotional intimacy and displays of affection, but not physical sex.

13. Bartollas and Sieverdes (1981) have recently presented evidence to the contrary. They found a stronger association between race and victimization among females than among males in six coeducational facilities for juveniles.

14. It should be noted, however, that this study has a number of methodological flaws. Many of the requisite conditions (such as equal status, cooperation, intimacy) are not observed but are assumed to exist. The living units compared (dormitories, two-man cells, and eight-man cells) are radically different, and it is quite possible, indeed likely, that the prisoners in the different units were quite different from each other despite random assignment with respect to race. The retest occurred after only three weeks, nearly one-third refused the retest, and many who took it had to be coaxed by the researcher.

15. A recent Gallup (1982) poll shows that 57 percent of the American people believe their states need more prisons and 49 percent are willing to pay more taxes to build them.

REFERENCES

Anderson, E. *A place on the corner.* Chicago: University of Chicago Press, 1978.

Bartollas, C., Miller, S. J., & Dinitz, S. *Juvenile victimization: The institutional paradox.* New York: Halsted, 1976.

Bartollas, C., & Sieverdes, C. M. The victimized white in a juvenile correctional system. *Crime and Delinquency,* 1981, 27, 534-543.

Beto, D., & Claghorn, J. Factors associated with self-mutilation within the Texas Department of Correction. *American Journal of Corrections,* January/February 1968, pp. 25-27.

Bowker, L. *Prison victimization.* New York: Elsevier, 1980.

Carroll, L. *Hacks, blacks and cons: Race relations in a maximum security prison.* Lexington, MA: D. C. Heath, 1974.
Carroll, L. Humanitarian reform and biracial sexual assault in a maximum security prison. *Urban Life,* 1977, 5, 417-437.
Carroll, L., & Mondrick, M. E. Racial bias in the decision to grant parole. *Law and Society Review,* 1976, 11, 93-107.
Carter, B. Race, sex and gangs: Reform school families. *Society,* 1973, 11, 36-43.
Christianson, S. Our black prisons. *Crime and Delinquency,* 1981, 27, 364-375.
Clark, R., & Rudestine, D. *Prison without walls: Report on New York parole.* New York: Praeger, 1974.
Clemmer, D. *The prison community.* New York: Holt, Rinehart & Winston, 1958. (Originally published, 1940.)
Davidson, R.T. *Chicano prisoners: The key to San Quentin.* Prospect Heights, IL: Waveland Press, Inc., 1974 (reissued 1983).
Davis, A. J. Sexual assaults in the Philadelphia prison system and sheriff's vans. *Trans-action,* 1968, 6, 8-16.
de Beaumont, G., & de Tocqueville, A [*On the penitentiary system in the United States and its application in France*] (F. Lieber, trans.). Philadelphia: Carey, Lea & Blanchard, 1833.
Dinitz, S. Are safe and humane prisons possible? *Australian and New Zealand Journal of Criminology,* 1981, 14, 3-19.
Dishotsky, N. I., & Pfefferbaum, A. Intolerance and extremism in a correctional institution: A perceived ethnic relations approach. *American Journal of Psychiatry,* 1979, 136, 1438-1443.
Dishotsky, N. I., & Pfefferbaum, A. Racial intolerance in a correctional institution: An ecological view. *American Journal of Psychiatry,* 1981, 138, 1057-1062.
Dorin, D., & Johnson, R. The premature dragon: George Jackson as a model for the new militant inmate. *Contemporary Crises,* 1979, 3, 295-315.
Feld, B. C. *Neutralizing inmate violence.* Cambridge, MA: Ballinger, 1977.
Foley, L. A. Personality and situational influences on changes in prejudice: A replication of Cook's Railroad Game in a prison setting. *Journal of Personality and Social Psychology,* 1976, 34, 846-856.
Fuller, D., Orsagh, T., & Raber, D. *Violence and victimization within the North Carolina prison system.* Paper presented at the meeting of the Academy of Criminal Justice Sciences, 1977.
Gallup, G. Most Americans receptive to wholesale prison reform. *Providence Sunday Journal,* April 4, 1982, p. A-11.
Giallombardo, R. *Society of women: A study of a women's prison.* New York: John Wiley, 1966.
Goffman, E. *Asylums: Essays on the social situation of mental patients and other inmates.* Garden City, NY: Doubleday, 1961.
Grier, W. H., & Cobbs, P. M. *Black rage.* New York: Bantam, 1969.
Hagan, J. Extra-legal attributes and criminal sentencing: An assessment of a sociological viewpoint. *Law and Society Review,* 1974, 8, 357-383.
Harris, A. R. Imprisonment and the expected value of criminal choice: A specification and test of aspects of the labelling perspective. *American Sociological Review,* 1975, 40, 71-87.
Harris, A. R. Race, commitment to deviance and spoiled identity. *American Sociological Review,* 1976, 41, 432-441.
Held, B. S., Levine, D., & Swartz, V. D. Interpersonal aspects of dangerousness. *Criminal Justice and Behavior,* 1979, 6, 49-58.

Hindelang, M. J., Gottfredson, M. R., & Flanagan, T. J. (Eds.). *Sourcebook of criminal justice statistics—1980.* U.S. Department of Justice, Bureau of Justice Statistics. Washington, DC: Government Printing Office, 1981.

Hindus, M. S. *Prison and plantation: Crime, justice and authority in Massachusetts and South Carolina, 1767-1878.* Chapel Hill: University of North Carolina Press, 1980.

Irwin, J. *Prisons in turmoil.* Boston: Little, Brown, 1980.

Jackson, G. *Soledad brother: The prison letters of George Jackson.* New York: Bantam, 1970.

Jacobs, J. B. *Stateville: The penitentiary in mass society.* Chicago: University of Chicago Press, 1977.

Jacobs, J. B. Race relations and the prisoner subculture. In N. Morris & M. Tonry (Eds.), *Crime and justice: An annual review of research* (Vol. 1). Chicago: University of Chicago Press, 1979.

Jacobs, J. B., & Grear, M. Drop-outs and rejects: An analysis of the prison guard's revolving door. *Criminal Justice Review,* 1977, 2, 57-70.

Jacobs, J. B., & Kraft, L. J. Integrating the keepers: A comparison of black and white prison guards in Illinois. *Social Problems,* 1978, 25, 304-318.

Johnson, R. *Culture and crisis in confinement.* Lexington, MA: D. C. Heath, 1976.

Johnson, R., & Dorin, D. Dysfunctional ideology: The black revolutionary in prison. In D. Szabo & S. Katzenelson (Eds.), *Offenders and corrections.* New York: Praeger, 1978.

Jones, D. A. *The health risks of imprisonment.* Lexington, MA: D. C. Heath, 1976.

Keiser, R. L. *The Vice Lords: Warriors of the streets.* New York: Holt, Rinehart & Winston, 1969.

Kleck, G. Racial discrimination in criminal sentencing: A critical examination of the evidence with additional evidence on the death penalty. *American Sociological Review,* 1981, 46, 783-804.

Liebow, E. *Tally's corner: A study of Negro streetcorner men.* Boston: Little, Brown, 1967.

Lockwood, D. *Prison sexual violence.* New York: Elsevier, 1980.

Mintz, S. An essay on the definition of national culture. In F. Cordasco & E. Bricchione (Eds.), *The Puerto Rican experience.* Totawa, NJ: Rowan & Littlefield, 1973.

Moore, J. W. *Homeboys: Gangs, drugs and prison in the barrios of Los Angeles.* Philadelphia: Temple University Press, 1978.

Murillo, N. The Mexican-American family. In N. Wagner & M. Haur (Eds.), *Chicanos: Social and psychological perspectives.* St. Louis: Mosby, 1971.

New York State Special Commission on Attica. *Attica: The official report.* New York: Bantam, 1972.

Otis, M. A perversion not commonly noted. *Journal of Abnormal Psychology,* 1913, 8, 112-114.

Park, J. The organization of prison violence. In A. K. Cohen, G. F. Cole, & R. G. Bayley (Eds.), *Prison violence.* Lexington, MA: D. C. Heath, 1976.

Peterson, D. M., & Friday, P. C. Early release from incarceration: Race as a factor in the use of "shock probation." *Journal of Criminal Law and Criminology,* 1975, 66, 79-87.

Rawls, W., Jr. Fortress prison harbors violence that erupted in death of 2 blacks. *New York Times,* February 9, 1982, p. 15 (a)

Rawls, W., Jr. Prison in Minnesota, considered best ever built, opens to first convicts. *New York Times,* March 25, 1982, p. A-16. (b)

Regens, J. L., & Hobson, W. G. Inmate self-government and attitude change: An assessment of participation effects. *Evaluation Quarterly,* 1978, 2, 455-479.

Scacco, A. *Rape in prison.* Springfield, IL: Charles C. Thomas, 1975.

Sellin, J. T. *Slavery and the penal system.* New York: Elsevier, 1976.

Slosar, J. A., Jr. *Prisonization, friendship and leadership.* Lexington, MA: D. C. Heath, 1978.

Suttles, G. D. *The social order of the slum: Ethnicity and territory in the inner city.* Chicago: University of Chicago Press, 1968.

Sykes, G. M. *The society of captives: A study of a maximum security prison.* Princeton, NJ: Princeton University Press, 1958.

Sykes, G. M., & Messinger, S. M. The inmate social system. In R. A. Cloward et al., *Theoretical studies in social organization of the prison.* New York: Social Science Research Council, 1960.

Sylvester, S. F., Reed, J. H., & Nelson, D. O. *Prison homicide.* New York: Spectrum, 1977.

Toch, H. *Living in prison: The ecology of survival.* New York: Free Press, 1977.

Zatz, M. S. *Differential treatment within the criminal justice system by race/ethnicity: A dynamic model.* Paper presented at the annual meeting of the American Sociological Association, Toronto, August 1981.

CHAPTER 12

Women in Prison

A CASE STUDY IN THE SOCIAL REALITY OF STRESS

JAMES G. FOX

The adaptations of women in confinement have not been described adequately in the voluminous corrections literature. Until recently, most scholarly work on female prisoners had focused on the nature and structure of the female prisoner social system (Giallombardo, 1966; Heffernan, 1972), without examining individual adaptations, prison-related stress, or personal crisis. In addition, little is known about the underlying sources of stress and how these problems affect the prison adjustment of women.

The extensive body of literature on male prisoners offers only limited help in understanding the special adjustments made by female prisoners. Factors such as racial conflict and violence (Carroll, 1974; Fox, 1982; Irwin, 1980; Jacobs, 1977), normative violence (Gibbs, 1981; Irwin, 1980; Toch, 1969), and predatory sexual aggression (Lockwood, 1980), typically associated with male institutions and examined in Chapters 4 and 11 of this book, are rarely manifested within the female prisoner community. While the nature and extent of violence in male and female prisons may differ, violence between line custodial staff and female prisoners, as well as violence among prisoners, appears to be increasing steadily. What was once appropriately characterized as a cooperative and caring prisoner community (Giallombardo, 1966) has slowly evolved into a more dangerous and competitive prison social climate.

The differences between male and female prison experiences are best understood within the context of structural and cultural influences, such as historical imbalances in priorities given to women's prisons, differen-

---

Author's Note: *This research was supported, in part, by Grant 78-NI-AX-0033 from the National Institute of Justice, U.S. Department of Justice. Points of view or opinions stated in this document are those of the author and do not necessarily represent the official position or policies of the U.S. Department of Justice.*

tial cultural and social expectations (prior to and during imprisonment), and theoretical perspectives that influence the treatment of male and female offenders (Klein, 1973; Klein & Kress, 1976; Weis, 1976). Other influences shaping the prison experience of women have been the proportionately smaller number of women in confinement[1] and sex-based correctional programs emphasizing traditional "women's work" and ascribed sex roles.

This chapter will attempt to characterize the nature of the prison experience of women and illustrate the reactions and crises that emerge in a changing women's prison social climate. Data supporting the observations provided in this chapter were drawn from two different studies, spanning a five-year period, conducted at Bedford Hills Prison in New York (Fox, 1976, 1982).[2] These data sources offer a unique opportunity to consider the relative impacts of change in prison policies on the adaptive strategies evolved by members of the prisoner community.

As I have mentioned, it is difficult to assess the nature of women's prison experiences without first examining the myriad structural and cultural influences governing their collective and individual adjustments. An awareness of these influences not only allows us to better distinguish between male and female responses to confinement, but it also provides a conceptual framework for understanding the special difficulties faced by women in prison.

SEX, CULTURE, AND WOMEN'S PRISONS

The correctional treatment of women and girls has always closely paralleled the prevailing views of criminologists and cultural perspectives toward women in general. Most traditional approaches to the study of female social deviance have been based on male, middle-class standards of conduct that were primarily concerned with women's "spoiled identity," sexual behavior and sexuality, and morality (Bullough, 1973; Pomeroy, 1975; Smart & Smart, 1978). Early writers saw female deviants as having an abundance of "masculine" biological features (Lombroso & Ferraro, 1895), as having failed to acquire feminine traits (Belby, 1942; Thomas, 1923), and as being "inherently deceitful in nature" (Pollack, 1950). Only recently have attempts been made to explain female crime and social deviance as related to economic opportunity and exposure to sexism (Klein, 1973; Klein & Kress, 1976; Weis, 1976; Feinman, 1979).

Concern with the virtue and sexual conduct of women has led to discriminatory application of the law (Nagel & Weitzman, 1972; Temin,

1973) and to correctional treatment programs aimed at reforming the "fallen women." Even today, vocational education programs in sewing, typing, food service, hair styling, and child care remain major programs in many women's prisons (Potter, 1979; Glick & Neto, 1977). While there are several women's prisons that offer "nontraditional" programs, such as welding, electronics, and auto mechanics (Potter, 1979), there has been only limited support for this trend from the correctional management hierarchy, which appears to be concerned more with program shortages in dangerously overcrowded male institutions.

Women's corrections has taken a distinctively different path of development from that of male prisons.[3] Before the emergence of the American penitentiary system in the late eighteenth century, prison conditions and the treatment of female prisoners were considerably harsher than those of male prisoners (Freedman, 1974; Young, 1932). The period from 1790 to 1870 was characterized by severe overcrowding of women's quarters, inadequate medical care, and extremely hostile attitudes toward female deviants. Women of all ages were typically crowded together in a single wing of a male prison under the supervision of male guards, who occasionally used their authority to coerce sexual favors (Young, 1932, Smith, 1962). Harsh punishment, generally considered to be restricted to recalcitrant male prisoners, occurred frequently within early female prisons (Young, 1932). As overcrowding mounted, the frequency and intensity of disciplinary measures escalated to meet the internal control interests of the prison administration. Feinman (1976, p. 47) reports that "strapping, cold douches, handcuffing to stationary objects, and overnight solitary confinement" were common methods of social control during the early years of women's corrections.

The period from 1870 to 1930 is best known for the construction of separate institutions for women and girls, and a gradual shift in public attitudes toward the treatment of female prisoners. Feinman (1976, p. 41) argues that these changes were brought about by the efforts of reform and feminist movements of that era, which saw women as having been the victims of limited economic opportunities and the objects of male sexual interests. Since these early feminists viewed female offenders as having been corrupted by male influences, they believed that women should direct and supervise their reform (Feinman, 1976).

The development of women's prisons in New York followed trends established in other states. The House of Refuge at Hudson (later renamed the New York State Training School for Girls) opened in 1887, the Western House of Refuge at Albion was opened in late 1893, and the New York State Reformatory for Women was opened in 1901 at Bedford Hills. As a part of the reform movement, the New York Prison for

Women, located in a separate unit at Auburn, was moved to Bedford Hills in 1933.

The custodial methods used in all of New York's female institutions were focused on efforts to establish "homelike" environments where prisoners were expected to adopt conventional female roles and responsibilities (McKelvey, 1936; Feinman, 1976). As a part of their treatment, prisoners were housed in cottages under the supervision of female parent figures. The cottage system not only fostered dependency through artificial mother-child relationships, it also served to emphasize caring and nurturing roles (Barrows, 1919).

The scope of correctional objectives during the early period of women's corrections is illustrated in a historical document describing the mission of the House of Refuge at Hudson:

> The Refuge was also designed to be a haven for females . . . either too young to have acquired habits of fixed depravity, or those whose lives have in general been virtuous, but who having yielded to the seductive influence of corrupt associates, have suddenly to endure the bitterness of lost reputation, and are cast forlorn and destitute upon a cold and unfeeling public, full of compunction for their errors, and anxious to be restored to the paths of innocence and usefulness [Pickett, 1969, p. 56].

The progression of women's corrections into the 1980s has produced few fundamental changes in correctional treatment or custodial methods. The vast majority of women's prisons remain modeled after institutions reflecting stereotyped sex roles and cultural expectations of caring and nurturing.

ORGANIZATIONAL CHANGE: HELP IS ON THE WAY

Major changes have occurred at Bedford Hills Prison and were evident within the five-year period (1973 to 1978) marking my research. For example, during the 1973 study (Fox, 1976) there were few vocational training opportunities except laundry, sewing, cosmetology, key punch operation, and office skills.[4] At that time, the Bedford Hills population was at an all-time high of 365, of which only a very small percentage were engaged in full-time educational or vocational training programs. Most were resigned to finding a way to pass idle time to offset the monotony of the prison routine. Consequently, the informal social system within the prisoner community became the dominant influence shaping women's prison experiences. Prison management was excessively paternalistic, and only a small number of correctional officers (who had transferred from Albion) enjoyed access to the "inner circle" of top management. As a result, most correctional decisions were made informally and were typically *reactive* in nature.

By 1978, the population had climbed to over 400, but a much greater percentage of this population was engaged in full-time or part-time programs. Management had become more closely modeled after that found in male prisons, and an effort was being made to approach organizational problems in a *proactive* manner. Furthermore, many prison operations were becoming formalized, and a greater emphasis was being placed on standardized policies and procedures.

Vocational training opportunities included auto mechanics (sponsored by Sears, Robuck and Company), electronics and video, and a wide selection of programs previously offered only in male institutions.[5] Visiting policies had also changed drastically. In 1973 severe restrictions were placed on the number of authorized visitors at one time, which often resulted in prisoners being forced to choose among family, friends, and their children. An innovative approach to this problem was the creation of the Sesame Street program, in which small children (who typically found it very difficult to conform to restrictions placed on their noise and activity) were supervised by other prisoners in a special play area within the visiting room where they were allowed to play while their mothers were visiting with other members of the visiting party. The mothers could observe the children at play and the children were subjected to relatively little restraint, so that they were subsequently able to view visits with their mothers in a more positive light.

While prisoners' rights litigation (particularly in the area of sex discrimination) was a major factor in bringing about a greater number of program opportunities, it also served as a catalyst to the emergence of new social roles within the prisoner community. Outside volunteers provided a variety of services, created a new channel of communication to the "outside world," and served as alternative role models for women previously "locked" into conventional prison roles. As a result of such influences, the prisoner community underwent substantial evolutionary changes in just five years, establishing different social dynamics and expectations. In 1973 the idleness within the prison tended to foster a heavy reliance on "kinship" relationships (Giallombardo, 1966; Heffernan, 1972; Fox, 1976) as solutions to prison adjustment problems. The kinship network, consisting of numerous loosely structured "family" units, routinely gave interpersonal comfort, shared limited resources, and provided crisis intervention for acute adjustment problems lying outside the scope of prison services.

During 1973, 52 percent of the Bedford Hills prisoners held membership in a kinship unit, and 45 percent had formed a close personal relationship with another prisoner in an attempt to deal with the impersonal nature of confinement. By 1978, the proportion of prisoners holding membership in the kinship system had fallen to 27 percent, and only 25 percent of the Bedford Hills prisoners were involved in a personal relationship with another woman. In addition, the basic structure of the kinship units had also changed. The larger "extended" family (5 to 8 members) found in 1973 no longer was the modal type of social organization. In 1978 most prisoner "families" were smaller (2 to 5 members) matriarchal social units providing a structure for the socialization, supervision, and guidance of less "streetwise" prisoners. Previously, the family system existed as an oppositional (and alternative) social system, dividing the prison organization into a formal and informal world. By 1978, the major function of kinship units was to address special needs that could not be met legitimately with conventional prison resources.

Another important and obvious change was the substantially higher levels of "political" awareness among members of the prisoner community. Radical perspectives toward prisoner care and custody were virtually nonexistent in 1973, but in 1978 the Bedford Hills prisoners' radicalism surpassed that of comparable male prisoners (Fox, 1982, p. 107). Female prisoners had begun to question the legitimacy and propriety of correctional decisions; in the past this was primarily a male prisoner response.

While many changes in the prisoner community appeared to coincide with changes in prison management policies, policy changes were often abrupt and lacked support from the front-line staff as well as from within the prisoner community. Many earlier responses to day-to-day problems were not always applicable to problems newly posed by prisoners and prisons, and past expectations of staff responsiveness were being increasingly frustrated. New rules, court decisions, and administrative policy changes stimulated hostile and aggressive responses from prisoners who had acquired new roles and status within the prisoner community. Physical confrontations between custodial staff and prisoners increased to record levels; prisoners demanded respect from front-line staff where they previously had collaborated in an informal "mother-child" arrangement. During the transition, some strong-willed prisoners thrived on a newly emerging form of prisoner empowerment and prestige, but most were unable to make the rapid transition and were left with few group-supported coping devices in a quickly changing prison social climate.

STRESS, CRISIS, AND COPING: LET IT ALL OUT

While the structural and cultural influences discussed earlier in this chapter contribute to the frustration of many women in confinement, they do not *directly* induce stress. Stress appears to be highly dependent on the interaction of accumulated tension and situational influences. Clearly, individual differences in stress tolerance and the presence of predispositional factors are also at play. However, for most prisoners, culturally conditioned expectations (and the various patterns of social interaction they stimulate) serve, primarily, to lower individual tolerance levels to the point where many women in prison are emotional time bombs, ticking off days and hours of stress, waiting for release.

As reported in an earlier survey of women in crisis (Fox, 1975), pent-up feelings, most commonly discharged in highly unpredictable and explosive ways, are frequently self-destructive. When situational influences (such as a child's poor health) emerge, individual and collective coping strategies may no longer be effective. Emotional outbursts often are the last signal of approaching breakdowns, rage, or loss of control. The specific ingredients of stress-related crisis are difficult to isolate. However, several common stress-producing events and circumstances were described by a majority of the women interviewed during each of our Bedford Hills studies. These descriptions illustrate individual responses and adaptations to prison-related stress and provide a glimpse into the day-to-day world of women in prison.

"I Can't Take Much More"

Chaos and confusion stemming from perceived inconsistency in rule interpretation and enforcement were among the most frequently identified sources of stress among Bedford Hills prisoners. The women told us that arguments between prisoners and officers related to rule enforcement and the slowness (and manner) in which officers responded to routine requests. They argued that these pressures reduce the prisoners' tolerance of frustration to the point that they felt compelled to react overtly or seek refuge in tranquilizing drugs.

The specific trigger mechanism of stress varied from prisoner to prisoner, but the reactions tended to be very similar. Again and again we were told that stress, tension, and pressure demand immediate release. Most women directed their release outwardly, aware that it merely postponed their crisis or served, perversely, to escalate it. Others turned inward, seeking solitude and escape from a world perceived as being unjust, uncaring, and unresponsive to their demands.

This aspect of Bedford Hills living appears to have changed little during the five-year period. In fact, the introduction of new security procedures may have increased custody-related stress within the prisoner community.[6] For example, one woman told us how a relatively simple request escalated into a confrontation with an officer in her housing unit and how accumulated tension overcame her ability to maintain self-control:

> There was this officer on my floor. Like, I went to my room and she closed my door, and I asked her to open it back up because I still needed some hot water. So she said, "Well, you wanted to stay in all night, didn't you tell me that?" I said, "Yes, I told you that, but I also said that I wanted some hot water, and I guess you didn't hear what I was saying." And my voice was getting kind of loud and hoarse. And all this built up because she kept on bothering me, and all this tension was building up inside of me. I kept saying to myself, "Please don't let me break on this lady." So, I had to get medication that night. When medication time came, she opened my door. I didn't come on nasty, but she came on again to me. So, I tried to explain what had happened. I said, "I told you in a nice way, I'm not getting nasty on you." She said, "No, you didn't say anything like that! And don't do me any favors!" When she said that, I said, "Let me tell you something! You're not doing my fucking time for me! Who in the hell do you think you are? This is your fucking job! You're supposed to open and close my door, that's what you get paid for!" I got all over her case. I called her a slimy bitch, that's how mad she got me. When I get nervous I start shaking, and I just wanted to take her and choke her. So naturally she wrote me up.

Another commonly described source of stress was some officers' tendency to assert their authority in arbitrary ways during routine supervision of prisoner activity. Several women told us that some officers provoked hostile prisoners into becoming verbally abusive by addressing them in an antagonistic manner. These encounters were seen as being a part of the day-to-day attack on prisoners' self-esteem and womanhood.

One woman, who had served on the Inmate Liaison Committee, felt that aggression was a predictable and appropriate response to pervasive prison pressures:

> You have some women who are really abusive, and not in a sense where that's how they've always been. That's their only means of protection. In here, everything has to be either aggressive or you have to be vulgar, or

> you have to be abusive. You have to be something that's hard, nothing feminine or soft. It's got to be hard, because that's how people treat you in here.

Prisoners typically saw their options as being limited to returning perceived abusive behavior (and being written up) or accepting the burden of accumulated tension and stress. They felt pushed to their limits, but saw no reasonable way out. While some reacted aggressively, accepting the known consequences, others saw the burden of stress as being part of their Bedford experience. In most instances, this acceptance was short-lived and often became self-destructive.[7]

"Just Give Us a Little Respect"

In addition to interpersonal conflict between prisoners and line custodial staff, prisoners told us that loss of their adult status and attacks on their self-image were among the more stressful aspects of their imprisonment. In our later interviews, infantilization, a process by which adult prisoners are reduced to dependent, powerless, and passive "children," continued to be a major concern of Bedford Hills prisoners. However, the widespread (normative) use of the term "girl" to refer to prisoners, regardless of age or maturity, had been substantially reduced. Because many prisoners saw officers' demeanor and tonal inflections as subtle attempts to communicate on a parent-to-child level, they openly demanded to be recognized as adult women.

One woman, for example, told us that officers view prisoners as being something less that adult women, and explained how this practice triggers her anger:

> Some of these officers don't know how to talk to you as a woman. Sure, some women don't demand respect, but I do. Like the way some of them talk to you, like, "Do this, do that." All nasty like. Who in the hell do they think they are? They're no better than me. Just because they are a C.O. and I have a number, they are no better than me. I'm no less a woman than they are. I get so aggravated, so angry. I just go right into anger, and they feed right into it.

Another prisoner felt that officers had to earn respect from prisoners, as opposed to expecting it as a function of officer authority:

> I give you respect because you're doing your job. But don't disrespect me, because I'm still a woman no matter what I'm in here for. Some officers say, "It's not my fault that you're in here." That really does it, I don't take

> that from anybody. I'm a woman, and I give you respect, but don't disrespect me just because I'm an inmate. Don't make it sound like I've got to do this or that because I'm just a "little girl."

A third woman explained how systematic status reduction had affected her view of herself, and she resented this encroachment into her self-image:

> I find myself sometimes, if I'm writing a letter, I'll say, "the girls here. . . ." The officers make you feel as if you're definitely not equal. They look down to you, so you begin to look at yourself as a child. You're told when and what to do, when to go to bed, when to eat, when to shower, when to do everything. You begin to feel as though you're not a woman. And then people start acting like children. At those times, I have to realize that I'm doing this merely for the fact that I'm in here. At other times I can't deal with it, and I'm really messed up for the whole day.

Some prisoners remained indifferent to these pressures. Most frequently they preferred to have authority lines clearly drawn from them or they saw little payoff in confronting a standard that had been in effect since they arrived. However, a growing number of younger women refused to accept the "little girl" label and regarded the way they were being treated as a serious and unwarranted intrusion into their selfhood.

"My Children Won't Even Know Me"

Women in prison suffer one stress-producing experience that is generally not shared by their male counterparts. Women who have given birth shortly after their imprisonment or who were separated from their children as a result of their prison sentence[8] experience anxiety and guilt that often lower their stress threshold. Over 60 percent of the Bedford Hills prisoners had children under 12 years of age. Most had arranged for their children to be cared for by relatives or friends, but a small proportion were forced to place their children in foster care, with little chance of regaining custody.

Unlike the direct prison pressures I described earlier, concerns about children typically gave rise to painful feelings during moments of solitude and introspection. Conversations with other prisoner-mothers, recent correspondence with temporary guardians, and wandering thoughts about their children's welfare predictably triggered a flood of painful emotions.

One prisoner, for example, whose parents care for her two-year-old daughter, told us that being unable to visit her child is one of the most difficult and demoralizing experiences of her confinement, even though she is able to cope with it:

> It's very hard. My daughter is two now, and it's hard. It's something that I hope won't affect her future. It's really hard, because I think of my daughter often, and sometimes I wish things could . . . I hope that things will turn out for the better, because I want her back, and I want to have a really good future together. It's been hard not being able to see her, but I've learned to accept it.

Another woman, with three young children at the time of her imprisonment, recalled that the separation experience was more difficult when she first entered prison six years before, because visiting restrictions at the time made it nearly impossible to have meaningful visits with children:

> When I first came here in 72, you couldn't hold a child in the visiting room. My baby was two months old, my daughter was a year old, and my oldest was three. It was hard. As the years progressed, we can take our children in our laps and sometimes we can visit with three of them. The pressure was alleviated.

The same woman explained that prisoners' feelings over losing legal custody of their children could cause depression in other women with an understanding of their situation:

> There are a lot of women who can't cope with the problem of being a mother in here. And a lot of women lose their children, and if you're in a group where there's a lot of emotion, you react to that emotion too. When a woman loses a child, like if she's doing a life sentence, the state takes over the child, we feel her reaction. We relate to that situation because we are mothers ourselves.

Among the major concerns expressed by women with children was a fear that their children would no longer think of them as their mother, or that the children were not receiving adequate care. The concern over the erosion of the mother-child bond was seen by some women as compounded by their child's (potential) rejection of "a mother in prison." To prevent this rejection from emerging, several women stated that they told the temporary guardian to tell the children that their mother was in a "hospital." Concerns about care and maternal affection frequently fostered "worst-case scenarios," in which prisoners imagined that their children were needlessly suffering. This image tended to provoke enormous anxiety and stress, as prisoners could neither gain tangible evidence of neglect or mistreatment nor muster the power to protect their children.

A prisoner with three children, one living with friends and the other two with relatives, told us that she has to accept the pain of seeing her daughter relate to the guardians as mother and father. Still, at least she has the consolation of knowing that her daughter is being treated well:

> I have three children, and I talk to my children. They come and visit me. My youngest daughter is with Mary and Joe, who I knew before I came here. It's gonna be a little hard when I get out of here. That's because my daughter calls Mary and Joe "mommy" and "daddy," OK? You have to realize that the child's only five months. So to Mary and Joe, that's their daughter. It's gonna be hard. I assured her that when I come home, I wouldn't just take the baby. I would let her get to know me first. I don't want to affect her mentally, you know, to take her away from someone she loves, and she loves them, I mean really loves them. I'll be holding her when they visit me, and when Tina gets tired of me, she hollers, "Mommy." So you see, for mothers in here, it's hard. . . . I'm more fortunate than most, because I know my child is all right. I don't have to worry about her being abused, neglected, or starving.[9]

INTERVENTION STRATEGIES: STILL WATERS RUN DEEP

Women's corrections has changed more during the past ten years than during any other period in its recent history. Some institutions, such as Bedford Hills, have begun to move away from correctional approaches based on stereotyped sex roles and cultural expectations. But tradition is difficult to overcome. Prisoners and custodial staff often cling to old standards and norms. Demands for change compete with demands for stability and maintenance of the status quo. Quite often when change *is* accomplished, there is a lack of support for it, and therefore the change produces even greater stress and disruption.

Stress of this sort characterizes the transitional period between 1973 and 1978 at Bedford Hills. Change intended to reduce many of the hardships of prison life often provoked greater levels of stress and interpersonal conflict. As stress increased, confrontations between prisoners and custodial staff escalated, and greater force was used to stifle growing dissatisfaction and unrest. All of the standard control-oriented custody measures, including the use of physical force, were used to enforce new rules, procedures, and policies. As stress increased, prisoners became even more critical of their treatment by staff. With few constructive outlets, the stress-conflict-stress cycle pushed some women into aggressive and crisis-provoked reactions.

Whereas custody typically had relied heavily on persuasion (at the cost of being overly paternalistic), these methods were being replaced by strict control policies guided by central office security management personnel. For prisoners with low frustration tolerance, the added burden of transition pressures sometimes led to acute personal crises. For these women, past coping strategies were often ineffective in dealing with high levels of stress.

Most Bedford Hills prisoners were not prepared for the changes they experienced in security practices and policies. To many, recent "gains" made in expanded correctional program opportunities carried too high a price. They argued that Bedford Hills was being converted into a prison setting in which male-oriented policies, intimidation, and force were becoming daily events. Equality was seen as carrying unnecessary and counterproductive consequences. Many prisoners felt they should receive equal program opportunities without losing those correctional services and approaches that responded to their special needs as women.

Interventions that could have reduced stress and personal crisis were generally available at Bedford Hills, but the magnitude of situational pressures tended to overload these resources. For example, a clinical program aimed at dealing with personal crises was available under the auspices of the prison mental hygiene service. Women in early stages of crisis could be temporarily assigned to a special "satellite" unit located in the prison hospital, removed from the stressful conditions of regular housing units. After a period of relaxation and counseling, the prisoners were returned to their regular (sometimes modified) assignments.

There were also a substantial number of activity groups, such as Lifers, Hispanic Council, New Directions, and the Committee Against Life for Drugs, that allowed prisoners to focus their energies on specific special interests. In addition, expanded correctional programs were a significant factor in reducing interpersonal conflict and deflecting self-defeating responses generated within the informal kinship structures.[10] The liberalization of visiting rules also alleviated stress for prisoners who now received regular visits from their children, family, or friends. Changes in rules allowing prisoners to wear personal clothing in their housing units appeared to have addressed problems associated with depersonalization and loss of individuality. However, while these interventions appear to have had a significant impact in reducing stress that originated from traditional correctional philosophies and treatment modalities, the movement to "bring Bedford Hills into line" with New York State's male institutions is ultimately a step backward in the history of women's prisons.[11]

The social reality of stress at Bedford Hills emerges out of a tradition of differential treatment of women and a mixture of attitudes, ranging from hostility to indifference, determining organizational policies and objectives. Until top correctional management is willing to objectively appraise its policies and priorities for women in prison, there will remain a high likelihood that current levels of turmoil, stress, and counterproductive reactions will continue to emerge from within the prisoner community. A reduction of stress, and of the destructive impacts it produces, may only be accomplished through a fundamental change in the nature of women's prison experience. This change must assure equal opportunities in correctional services and programs without sacrificing the care and custody requirements of female prisoners. "Equal treatment" must not become a basis for establishing unwarranted and unreasonable custody and security measures resulting in substantially greater stress and hardship within the female prisoner community.

NOTES

1. Female prisoners constitute about 4 percent of the nation's state prison population (U.S. Department of Justice, 1982). While the rate of population increase for women in prison has been growing in recent years, corrections officials continue to use the "small numbers" argument to justify differential treatment (see Singer, 1973).

2. Bedford Hills is the only major institution for women in New York State. Both studies relied heavily on focused interview methods, survey data, and observations. Interviews used to illustrate female prisoner concerns were taken from the most recent study.

3. The historical development presented here is, by necessity, extremely condensed. For a more complete treatment of these developments, see Lekkerkerker (1931), Henderson (1910), Freedman (1974), Pickett (1969), and McKelvey (1936).

4. See New York State Department of Correctional Services, (1971, 1972, 1973).

5. See New York State Department of Correctional Services (1976, 1980).

6. A male captain, with substantial experience in male prison security, was temporarily assigned to Bedford Hills to bring its security procedures in line with departmental standards. During the first few weeks of a new "lock-in," "stand-up" count, the clearance of the count was delayed for periods up to two hours. Consequently, food service, medical appointments, and educational and vocational training programs were routinely delayed, causing substantially greater hardship on prisoners and staff.

7. See, for example, Fox (1975).

8. For a more complete discussion of the special problems of mothers in prison, see McGowan and Blumenthal (1978), Gibbs (1971), Palmer (1972), and Stanton (1980).

9. Names used by respondents have been changed by the author to eliminate any possibility of identifying participants of the study.

10. During the 1973 study, we found that a substantial proportion of women had acquired "jail house" tattoos of other prisoners' names and initials, linking them to informal kinship ties and close personal relationships within the prisoner community. These women had entered the prison unmarked, but left with the highly visible stigmata of their prison experiences (see Fox, 1976).

11. During the early stages of the 1978 study, one top-level central office security manager commented, "If the Bedford Hills inmates want equality, then they should be

treated like everybody else." In this scheme, "everybody else" was men, and the "treatment" was greater custodial regimentation and control.

REFERENCES

Barrows, I. Reformatory treatment of women in the United States. In C. Henderson, *Penal and reformatory institutions: Correction and prevention.* New York: Russell Sage, 1910.

Belby, J. Female delinquency. *Arch. Med. é Iden.*, 1942, 12.

Bullough, V. *The subordinate sex: a history of attitudes toward women.* Urbana: University of Illinois Press, 1973.

Carroll, L. *Hacks, blacks and cons: Race relations in a maximum security prison.* Prospect Heights, IL: Waveland Press, Inc., 1974 (reissued 1988).

Feinman, C. *Imprisoned women: A history of the treatment of women incarcerated in New York City: 1932-1975.* Unpublished doctoral dissertation, New York University, 1976.

Feinman, C. Sex role stereotypes and justice for women. *Crime and Delinquency*, 1979, 25(1), 87-94.

Fox, J. Women in crisis. In H. Toch, *Men in crisis: Human breakdowns in prison.* Chicago: Aldine, 1975.

Fox, J. *Self-imposed stigmata: A study of tattooing among female inmates.* Unpublished doctoral dissertation, State University of New York—Albany, 1976.

Fox, J. *Organizational and racial conflict in maximum security prisons.* Lexington, MA: D. C. Heath, 1982.

Freedman, E. Their sisters' keepers: An historical perspective on female correctional institutions in the United States: 1870-1900. *Feminist Studies*, 1974, 2.

Giallombardo, R. *Society of women: A study of a women's prison.* New York: John Wiley, 1966.

Gibbs, C. The effect of the imprisonment of women upon their children. *British Journal of Criminology*, 1971, 11(2), 113-130.

Gibbs, J. Violence in prison: Its extent, nature and consequences. In R. Roberg and V. Webb (Eds.), *Critical issues in corrections: Problems, trends and prospects.* St. Paul, MN: West, 1981.

Glick, R., & Neto, V. *National study of women's correctional programs.* Washington, DC: National Institute of Justice, 1977.

Heffernan, E. *Making it in prison: The square, the cool, and the life.* New York: John Wiley, 1972.

Henderson, C. *Penal and reformatory institutions: Correction and prevention.* New York: Russell Sage, 1910.

Irwin, J. *Prisons in turmoil.* Boston: Little, Brown, 1980.

Jacobs, J. *Stateville: The penitentiary in mass society.* Chicago: University of Chicago Press, 1977.

Klein, D. The etiology of female crime: A review of the literature. *Issues in Criminology*, 1973, 8(2), 3-30.

Klein, D., & Kress, J. Any woman's blues: A critical overview of women, crime, and the criminal justice system. *Crime and Social Justice*, 1976, 5, 34-49.

Klein, P. *Prison methods in New York State.* New York: Columbia University Press, 1920.

Lekkerkerker, E. *Reformatories for women in the United States.* Batavia: J. B. Walters, 1931.

Lockwood, D. *Prison sexual violence.* New York: Elsevier, 1980.

Lombroso, C., & Ferrero, W. *The female offender.* London: Fisher & Urwin, 1895.

McGowan, B., & Blumenthal, K. *Why punish the children? A study of children of women prisoners.* Hackensack, NJ: National Council on Crime and Delinquency, 1978.

McKelvey, B. *American prisons: A study in American social history prior to 1915.* Chicago: University of Chicago Press, 1936.

Nagel, S., & Weitzman, L. Women as litigants. *Hastings Law Journal,* 1972, 23(November), 171-198.

New York State Department of Correctional Services. *Annual report* (published annually). New York: State Division of Education, 1971-1973.

New York State Department of Correctional Services. Equity justice. In N.Y. State Department of Correctional Services, *Report of Operations and Development for 1976.* New York: Author, 1976.

New York State Department of Correctional Services. *Drop in and check out our vocational education offerings.* New York: Author, 1980.

Palmer, R. The prisoner-mother and her child. *Capital University Law Review,* 1972, 1, 126-144.

Pickett, R. *House of refuge: Origins of juvenile reform in New York State: 1815-1857.* Syracuse, NY: Syracuse University Press, 1969.

Pollack, O. *The criminality of women.* New York: A. S. Barnes, 1950.

Pomeroy, S. *Goddesses, whores, wives, and slaves: Women in Classical antiquity.* New York: Schocken, 1975.

Potter, J. Women's work? The assault on sex barriers in prison job training. *Corrections Magazine,* September 1979, pp. 43-49.

Singer, L. Women and the correctional process. *American Criminal Law Review* 1973, 11(2).

Smart, C., & Smart, B. *Women, sexuality, and social control.* London: Routledge & Kegan Paul, 1978.

Smith, A. *Women in prison: A study in penal methods.* London: Stevens & Sons, 1962.

Stanton, A. *When mothers go to jail.* Lexington, MA: D. C. Heath, 1980.

Temin, C. Discriminatory sentencing of women offenders: The argument for ERA in a nutshell. *American Criminal Law Review,* 1973, 11(Winter), 355-372.

Thomas, W. *The unadjusted girl.* New York: Harper & Row, 1923.

Toch, H. *Violent men: An inquiry into the psychology of violence.* Chicago: Aldine, 1969.

U.S. Department of Justice. Prisons and prisoners. In Bureau of Justice Standards, *Bulletin.* Washington, DC: Government Printing Office, 1982.

Weis, J. Liberation and crime: The invention of the new female criminal. *Crime and Social Justice,* 1976, 6, 17-27.

Young, C. *Women's prisons: Past and present.* Elmira, NY: Summary, 1932.

CHAPTER 13

Mentally Ill Offenders

PRISON'S FIRST CASUALTIES

PAUL J. WIEHN

Can the mentally ill offender survive in prison? How many mentally ill men and women inhabit our jails and prisons today? What can be done to better address the needs of such inmates during these times of rising prison populations and tight budgets?

Unfortunately, mental health within correctional systems is an area that seems to generate more questions than answers. While the debate over the validity of rehabilitation as a correctional theme subsides, by default, with the advent of determinate sentencing, the core problems of mentally ill prisoners remain unchanged. As prison populations continue to rise, the task of surviving in prison becomes increasingly more difficult (see Chapter 3). The mentally ill, who may adapt marginally during better times, are among the early casualties of increasingly bleak prison environments. These casualties, in turn, quickly fill prison hospital beds and protective custody cells and make greater demands on a system already stretching to accommodate greater numbers of prisoners. In the past few years there has been a growing awareness that caring for and coping with the mentally ill offender is a major problem in most correctional facilities. Indeed, there is reason to believe that mental illness is the number-one health problem behind bars as it is in the larger society.

This essay describes some of the difficulties of mentally ill inmates and discusses some ways to intervene to relieve human suffering in prison. The discussion is primarily a reflection on the author's clinical work during the past decade in an adult maximum security prison for men in Connecticut. As such, it may not precisely cover the problems of mentally ill men, women, and youthful offenders in state and federal prisons with markedly different size, population characteristics, penal philosophies, and environmental conditions. Still, Goffman (1961) reminds us that total institutions share many common properties, manage people in similar ways, and elicit predictable response patterns from their residents. Consequently, I expect that my observations will be of at least some relevance to a wider range of mentally ill prisoners.

MENTAL ILLNESS IN PRISON

Psychiatrists in courtroom and prison settings have for many years been assigned the job of determining who is and is not mentally ill. More recently, allied mental health professionals have participated to a greater degree in this process.[1] Perhaps no other forensic mental health issue has generated as much debate and confusion. It has become commonplace in the courtroom, particularly in cases in which the life of the accused may be at stake, for psychiatrists hired by the state and the defense to present sharply contrasting pictures of the defendant.

In prison, the decision to punish an inmate for particular behavior or to grant a reprieve and refer for treatment may depend upon the recommendation of the mental health professional. Halleck (1971), a leader in the field of forensic psychiatry, argues that psychiatric involvement in the area of criminal responsibility has been fraught with problems, misconceptions, and dubious assumptions. The same arguments that apply to psychiatrists testifying in criminal insanity proceedings also hold for psychiatrists intervening in prison disciplinary hearings. Clinicians may operate as if mental illness is an affliction and presume that their expertise in human behavior allows them to know precisely when one is ill enough to be relieved of responsibility for one's acts. Social, economic, and environmental factors that may offer more valid explanations of behavior are ignored. The net result is mitigation of harsh punishment for a few selected offenders while the plight of all other disturbed offenders receives little attention. Halleck (1971, p. 151) contends that "by investing an incredible amount of energy in trying to help a small group of offenders, psychiatrists have done little more than lend our correctional system a deceptive facade of decency."

The mentally ill in prison can be identified by applying much the same criteria used to diagnose mental illness in the free world. The inmate may be depressed, suicidal, anxious, agitated, or characterized by disordered thinking and behavior. Some request help on their own initiative; others are referred by a guard, counselor, work supervisor, or just about anyone in a position to be aware of the inmate's situation (see Chapter 17). In prison, where even the relatively strong and healthy have difficulties, inmates with acute symptoms and debilitating mental illnesses have much poorer chances of successfully coping and surviving. This group of offenders' claim to treatment has little to do with reasons for coming to prison or prospects of postrelease success, but rather is rooted squarely in the criminal justice system's responsibility to minimally ensure the health and welfare of those entrusted to its care (Toch, 1979).

A case study may highlight the dilemma of the mentally ill inmate:

> Lenny sat in my office telling me that he is depressed and once again hearing voices. He is a 24 year old, single, black male serving a 1½ to 3 year sentence for larceny. In the past 10 years Lenny has had 20 psychiatric hospital admissions. When he came to prison the previous year he was confused, agitated, and incoherent much of the time and spent his first three weeks in the prison hospital before transferring to a maximum security state hospital for a seven month stay. With medication, participation in a supportive therapy group, and placement in a special housing unit, Lenny has been able to hold his own since returning to prison two months ago. On this day we talk for awhile, and Lenny's primary concern seemed to be a parole board appearance coming up in a few weeks. With his record of arrests and hospitalizations, his chances are probably not very good. As we close our session we agree to discuss parole board strategy more the next day at his group meeting. If denied parole, I suspect that Lenny will stop trying to cope with prison and will find a way to transfer back to the state hospital. In general, the mentally ill do not fare well in the competition for prison rewards and frequently they experience greater difficulty obtaining early release. The hospital offers more safety, lower demands for performances and a less competitive environment.

During the "golden age of treatment" in American prisons we witnessed the deployment of a variety of programs directed at drug addicts, alcoholics, youthful offenders, sexual offenders, and resocialization of criminal personality types. In these efforts to offer assistance to large categories of offenders, many of us were guilty of false optimism. We expected to experience some measure of success but never came to grips with the fact that most treatment programs were merely grafted onto a core of prison life that was and is inherently antitherapeutic.[2] We often avoided the critical issue of obtaining truly voluntary participation and failed to establish reasonable treatment outcomes, depending instead on termination of criminal careers as the primary objective of correctional treatment. (A notable exception to this pattern is discussed in Chapter 14.) In working with Lenny and other chronically mentally ill inmates, there is a need to pursue more focused and pragmatic treatment goals. Primary interventions need to be directed at symptom relief and sustaining levels of functioning that allow inmate-clients to cope better within a stressful environment.

TRADITIONAL SOLUTIONS: MENTAL HEALTH OR CORRECTIONS

The traditional response to mental illness in prison has in many ways paralleled our response in society as a whole. A strong bias exists in favor of sending mentally ill inmates away from the prison for treatment, just as people in need of mental health care were often sent to remotely located mental institutions. As the flow of patients began to reverse itself during the past couple of decades, most communities found themselves ill equipped to provide the necessary services. Correctional facilities that failed to develop on-site mental health services are now simultaneously faced with tight admission policies in public mental hospitals and record numbers of inmates in need of psychiatric care.

I recently visited a women's correctional facility that was seeking assistance in coping with mentally ill inmates. Unlike many fortresslike male institutions, this facility consists of a dozen older, cottage-style buildings spread across more than 900 acres that occasionally reveal some remnants of the original farming operation. With a population climbing above the 200 mark, this institution has pretrial detainees, jail inmates, and women serving prison sentences.

Mentally disturbed inmates are housed in the prison segregation unit, along with inmates being punished and those viewed as escape risks. If an inmate becomes disturbed and disturbing, she may be moved to the basement, where two seclusion rooms (nicknamed "the dungeon") are located. There are no other inmates or staff routinely in the area, but correctional officers can partially monitor the activity below through a one-way intercom system. A small medical unit is located in the same building, but I was told that is not equipped to handle psychiatric cases. The institution does not employ any mental health staff on a full-time basis (a psychiatrist under contract makes a weekly four-hour visit). Inmates are occasionally transferred to a state hospital for treatment, but once they return to the prison they often revert back to their previous symptomatic state in a relatively brief period of time.

Staff at the facility estimated that at any given time, five to ten inmates appear sufficiently disturbed to require active psychiatric treatment. In this respect the situation seems potentially manageable given the addition of appropriate staff. However, on the day of our visit we were cautioned that any suggestions that might involve expenditures of funds would most likely not be favorably reviewed at the central office. Given this set of circumstances, which is not unusual, there is every indication that survival will remain very difficult for the mentally ill female prisoners housed in this and similar institutions (see Chapter 12).

The power to transfer inmates to another institution is viewed as a key management tool by correctional administrators. In a maximum security institution, transfer to a less secure and more comfortable facility is one of the primary rewards for good behavior. Inmates are also transferred for a variety of other reasons, including mental illness, protective custody, service as an informant, or because they are viewed as chronically maladapted or as prison ringleaders.

> Jerry's case history reveals extensive use of administrative transfer powers. Jerry is a 37-year-old, single, white male who was serving a 3-to-5-year sentence for robbery when he was arrested for assaulting and seriously injuring a correctional officer. Although he was beginning to show definite signs of mental illness, he was transferred to a prison in an adjacent state shortly after receiving a consecutive 10-to-20-year sentence. Jerry remained in this facility barely a year before being moved to a third prison in another nearby state. During the next three years he would be transferred 6 times from this prison to the secure psychiatric unit at the state hospital. Staff at the prison described rambling, incoherent speech, incidents involving self-multilation and destruction of personal property, throwing human feces, and an inability to coexist with other inmates. Jerry was judged to be psychotic and commitable under the applicable state statutes. Hospital staff viewed his behavior as manipulative and sociopathic in nature, and would recommend upon each discharge that he be allowed to serve his time in the prison with medication provided during difficult periods.
>
> Jerry made persistent requests to return to his home state, and these were finally honored. However, he remained there only 3 weeks before being moved to the federal prison system. During the next couple of years he resided in federal facilities in North Carolina, Pennsylvania, and Illinois before being returned once again to his "home institution." Jerry's 6-year odyssey included 20 transfers involving 8 institutions located in 6 different states.

To be sure, Jerry is not an easy inmate to manage or treat. He can be hostile, demanding, aggressive, assaultive, uncooperative with treatment, and sometimes quite disturbed. Where transfer options exist, it is difficult for either prison administrators or treatment personnel to pass these by in favor of trying to cope with the problems inmates such as Jerry present on a daily basis. This process of transferring back and forth between prison and hospital has sometimes been referred to as "ping-ponging" or "bus therapy" (Wilson, 1980). It highlights one of the central problems in the delivery of services to mentally ill inmates. Neither the correctional system nor the mental health system wants the burden of caring for mentally disturbed offenders, particularly those with tendencies to act out and be aggressive. Although transfers are routinely presented and justified in terms of inmate needs and benefits, institutional needs are often the catalytic agent in the transfer process.

A few larger states and the federal system have correctional psychiatric facilities that care for mentally disturbed inmates. These hybrid institutions may be able to employ greater numbers of specialized staff and sustain a more therapeutic environment. In large correctional systems with many facilities, age, offense, length of sentence, and special needs and problems may dictate differential institutional assignment. Yet in most states the choice of institutional assignment is much narrower or nonexistent, and a fairly heterogeneous group of inmates, including the mentally ill, are faced with the task of surviving together.

SURVIVAL PROBLEMS: MORTIFICATION, VICTIMIZATION, ISOLATION

The adjustment process for those men and women who come to prison with histories of mental illness can be a very difficult one. The mortification of new arrivals (as described by Goffman, 1961) affects even those inmates with prior experience with incarceration. The abrupt and almost total loss of self-determination, autonomy, and freedom of action, coupled with separation from family and other support systems, frequently produces considerable stress and psychological disequilibrium. Mentally ill and emotionally disabled inmates appear less capable of managing the giving up and taking on the characterize the transition to prison life. Well-managed admission programs that provide needed information and allow for gradual entry into the prison environment can mitigate the culture shock associated with entry to prison. Even with this kind of programming, in my institution better than half the requests for mental health services come during the inmate's first few days or months of imprisonment.

Harold is a 32-year-old black man serving a 1-to-3-year sentence for burglary. He is short in stature, slender, and wears very thick glasses due to a lifelong vision problem. This is his first trip to prison, although he has had several minor skirmishes with the criminal justice system. The probation officer's report lists 6 psychiatric hospital admissions over a 10-

year period during which Harold was described as agitated, paranoid, and experiencing auditory and visual hallucinations. Harold would recover quickly in the hospital but he would not always follow up with recommended outpatient treatment.

When Harold arrived at the prison, he was placed in a dormitory-style housing unit. If the prison had been less crowded, he would have found a place in the regular admission unit, which contains only single cells. Nevertheless, Harold seemed to do well for the next couple of months. He referred himself to the Mental Health Unit and, after describing his past difficulties, received daily medication and regular visits with a psychiatrist and social worker. Eventually he began to complain of side effects from the medication and elected to stop taking it. During the next couple of months Harold had five changes of housing, spent several weeks in the prison hospital, received two misconduct reports (including one for cutting his wrists), and briefly visited the segregation unit. The incident prompting his first "ticket" for "causing a disturbance" is described by the housing officer filing the report:

> Inmate Harold _______ was pacing very fast throughout the dorm, backroom and dayroom areas from midnight to 1:00 a.m. When I told him that he cannot be in the backroom area or pace because other inmates were trying to sleep, he spoke incoherently. He continued to pace very fast throughout the dorm causing a disruption among other inmates.

Harold was placed in a small, treatment-oriented unit and, once again with the help of regular medication, he is doing quite well. In my office recently I asked Harold to recall what had been most difficult about adjusting in prison. He mentioned the noise, the crowds, and not knowing many inmates. He also spoke of being harassed by other inmates about his glasses and about once being "punched in the face by a white guy" for singing in the bathroom. Harold walked away from these incidents and never made any complaints to authorities, assuming, probably correctly, that doing so would only bring greater problems.

Inmates who become disturbed and disturb others are more likely to become victims in prison. They may be driven from a housing unit by fellow inmates intent upon doing their time without experiencing unnecessary hassles and annoyances. Maneuvers employed to accomplish this objective include threats, theft of personal property, fire setting, and assault. Often removal of an inmate can be achieved by having a well-connected inmate pass along the information to a housing officer or captain that an assault is likely to occur if the offending inmate is not placed elsewhere in the institution. Staff, being anxious to avoid problems and maintain control, respond to this type of information.

In studying patterns of victimization in two New York institutions, Toch (1977) found that inmates with histories of emotional disturbance were much more frequently in the target group than their more emotionally stable peers. He suggests that aggressive, predatory inmates may seek out the easiest prey—the weak, those with low self-esteem, or those with obvious anxiety. The "payoff" of victimization can be to "demonstrate" the "weakness" of the victim, thereby "proving the strength" of the aggressor (Toch, 1977, p. 146). (For a general discussion of prisoner victimization, see Chapter 4.)

The adjustment crisis of the offender experiencing mental health problems can result in both physical and psychological isolation. When Harold began to have difficulties, he made trips to both the hospital and the segregation units, the two living areas within the prison offering the most physical isolation from the general prison population and the least opportunity to socialize with peers. Although placement in an isolated unit may initially bring a reduction in stress or an opportunity for the offender to regain stability, isolation—whether selected or imposed—can exact a steep toll from those who remain in that status. The offender may acquire any one of a number of negative labels such as "snitch," "punk," "psycho," "homo," or the like in conjunction with a move to segregation or protection. Access to potentially useful vocational, educational, religious, and counseling programs may be eliminated or greatly reduced. With mentally ill offenders in isolation, we are often confronted with the incongruous situation of a group very much in need of services housed in areas with the least access to the resources of the institution.

BREEDING GROUNDS FOR PSYCHOSIS

While the mentally ill appear to be entering our prisons and jails in record numbers, clinicians have long suspected that correctional institutions also contribute directly to the emergence of major psychiatric disturbances (Halleck, 1967). Harsh living conditions, overcrowding, fear for personal safety, idle time, separation from usual support systems, and uncertainty of release are stress factors common to the prison environment. Over the years, "prison psychosis" has crept into the psychiatric nomenclature to identify severe decompensation specifically related to the stresses of incarceration. More recently, the problems of returning Vietnam veterans and POWs have been studied, with one result being a better understanding of the relationships among environment, trauma, and current and future mental health. Compared to other groups so affected, prisoners have won little sympathy for their plight since many citizens view them as undeserving of special care.

When Francisco came to prison in 1976 to serve a 1-to-5-year sentence for larceny, he was young, healthy, and had no prior criminal record nor any history of psychiatric problems. Unskilled, uneducated, and unable to speak English, he had not managed well in the urban Northeast in the three years since he left his native Puerto Rico. An enlistment in the army and a later enrollment in an auto mechanics course both quickly ended in failure.

Francisco's initial adjustment to the prison was uneventful, and he was described as cooperative but somewhat indifferent to suggestions that he pursue education or job training. An incident in which he leapt from a tier in a cell block onto a group of officers escorting a friend from the unit appears to represent a significant turning point in his period of incarceration. Francisco was removed to the segregation unit, charged with assault, and given an additional 1-to-3-year sentence. Later the same year he assaulted a correctional officer who was escorting him back from a parole hearing, and subsequently received yet another additional sentence. Last year in a scuffle he broke the jaw of an officer and once again added more time to his sentence.

Over a four-year period Francisco became an almost permanent fixture in the segregation unit. Here he began to display some signs of serious mental illness, such as paranoid thinking and rambling and illogical speech. He vigorously resisted all efforts to provide treatment. He was eventually transferred to a state hospital, but was returned to the prison a month later after being diagnosed as malingering and manipulative by hospital staff. Two years later he was again transferred to the hospital. He remained five months this time, and was returned with a firm diagnosis of paranoid schizophrenia.

A review of Francisco's six years in prison reveals a pattern of progressive deterioration. When he arrived, his primary deficits appeared to be cultural, vocational, and educational. Six years later, despite significant efforts inside and outside the prison to provide treatment and assistance, Francisco displays the type of disturbed behavior and thinking that is characteristic of the mentally ill. Francisco's case is a good example of someone who was not able to manage the adjustment and survival pressures of incarceration. His difficulties brought him to the compressed world of the prison segregation unit, where hostility and aggression are a part of daily life.[3] After six years, Francisco is much further from release than he was the day he walked through the prison gate.

DILEMMAS OF PRISON TREATMENT

Identifying and describing the mentally ill in prison is not difficult compared to the problem of finding ways to effectively intervene to help them. The fact that such variables as size and population of the facility, daily living conditions, and access to jobs and training are normally beyond the control of prison mental health workers limits this treatment response and serves as an ever-present source of frustration for staff. My own institution has experienced an almost 50 percent increase in population during the past 5 years, with a significant negative impact on the quality of prison life, the operation of treatment programs, and the survival prospects of the mentally ill. We are told that not only is there no relief in sight, but that we should expect things to get much worse before they get better. The situation in the prison reminds me of a scene on the beach with little children building and defending sand castles against an incoming tide: No matter what you do or try, the critical forces are working against you.

The problematic aspects of providing treatment to correctional clients have been discussed in some detail in the prison literature. For Szasz (1977, 1979), genuinely voluntary psychiatric interventions for the benefit of the criminal-client are not possible under the current system. Halleck (1967, 1971), a more pragmatic commentator on prison mental health issues, views "double agent" problems as difficult but potentially manageable. Simultaneously working for a client and an institution requires a clarification of confidentiality as it commonly exists in relationships between therapists and clients in free society. The limits of confidentiality need to be defined for the inmate-client at the outset, and measures such as separate records need to be employed to protect sensitive information.

The relationship between prison mental health staff and the prison "gatekeeping" staff can present significant problems. In systems where inmates are indeterminately sentenced, referrals for psychiatric examination prior to prerelease hearings are quite common. This association of clinical staff with releasing authorities induces some inmates to seek treatment in order to obtain a more favorable report, while other inmates may avoid treatment out of fear that a disclosure might jeopardize future release decisions. The therapist as "gatekeeper" introduces a coercive element into the therapeutic relationship that is incompatible with collaborative change strategies (Toch, 1979). In addition, valuable clinical time is siphoned away from treatment into report writing and other bureaucratic activities.

The prison therapist often has to make difficult choices between the short-term and long-term interests of his or her client (Halleck, 1967). I received a call recently from a housing officer, informing me that one of my clients, Charlie, was "going off the deep end again." Charlie is a chronically mentally ill man who has been cooperating with treatment and has been doing fairly well for six months. In this instance, Charlie was described by the officer as agitated, screaming in the cell block for hours and disturbing other inmates, who the officer feared might take some action in the way of reprisal. When interviewed a short time later by myself and a psychiatrist, Charlie was subdued and denied having problems in his housing unit. However, he appeared confused, his speech was slightly pressured, and he had difficulty staying with the subject matter. We offered Charlie a few days in the prison hospital, but he responded that he wanted to return to his cell. In this situation we were faced with a choice between placing him in the hospital against his wishes, and possibly losing the good rapport that had taken months to develop, or returning him to a situation in which he would be vulnerable and would have a good chance of being harmed. In this case we elected to take charge of the situation, and we placed Charlie in the hospital. At other times, where the risk involved is more tolerable, decisions are made to withhold treatment in order to avoid further restriction of the freedom of the inmate-client.

Friction between mental health staff and correctional administrators is a common by-product of efforts to provide services to prisoners (Wilson, 1980). In many ways mental health and corrections are strange bedfellows. Psychotherapy in its many varieties is normally permissive and emphasizes expression of feelings. Corrections has traditionally been repressive and tends toward emphasizing control at all times. The question of whether disturbed inmates who represent significant management difficulties in the institution should be approached as mental health cases or custodial problems is a frequent source of conflict. With many inmates, such as Jerry and Francisco, whose cases were discussed above, this becomes a very difficult question to answer unambiguously.

Even where this friction is resolved in favor of liberal use of psychiatric labels and interventions, prison mental health workers (the author included) often do little more than treat prison casualties and ignore the destructive role played by the conditions of confinement. In this capacity the mental health professional may actually strengthen an oppressive status quo:

> There can be little doubt that many individuals whom the psychiatrist is asked to help live in highly oppressive environments. When the psychiatrist works with such patients, he learns some bitter lessons: he learns

how hard it is for him to do much to change an oppressive environment; he learns how much more help he would provide if he were able to change the environment; and he learns that he helps his patient little, or may even hurt them, if he ignores their environment [Halleck, 1971, p. 29].

TREATING THE MENTALLY ILL OFFENDER

The decision to rely on either transfer or on-site treatment in responding to mentally ill inmates largely determines the direction that mental health services will follow in a correctional institution. The adoption of an active transfer policy requires institutional diagnostic services and readily available access to outside hospital beds. With this approach, the needs of mentally ill offenders are met by what is essentially a prison diversion program. A commitment to provide active treatment to the mentally ill in prison increases the need for staff, space, and program content.

It is very difficult to state with any degree of certainty what constitutes adequate mental health staffing for a correctional institution. Needs will vary with the size of the facility and types of offenders served, living conditions, existence of court diversion programs, and prevailing penal philosophies. However, in almost any institution a commitment to treatment requires, at the very minimum, the designation of at least one full-time mental health professional as responsible for addressing the needs of mentally ill offenders.

A brief history of correctional mental health services in Connecticut may provide an illustration relevant to the staffing issue. In 1960 a psychologist was hired to work at the old maximum security prison in Wethersfield; he became the first full-time mental health worker in the system. His first priority was to arrange mental health transfers for a large number of mentally disturbed inmates who he found locked away in a dungeonlike unit for chronically maladapted inmates. During the next two decades the prison moved to a new facility in Somers and the mental health staff grew to its present complement of six full-time clinicians, five part-time psychiatrists, and a secretary. Services are also provided by supervised graduate-student interns and volunteers from the community. This expansion was undoubtedly aided by pressures to provide treatment created by indeterminate sentencing. However, expansion is also very much dependent upon establishing a professional core group capable of lobbying for the needs of the mentally ill within the institution, attracting other professionals to prison practice, and pursuing relationships with universities and agencies that are in a position to provide assistance.

Staff expansion created a need for office space outside of the prison Medical Department and eventually led to the recognition of the Mental Health Unit as a separate department within the institution. Such recognition tends to be a validation of inmates' needs for mental health services on an ongoing basis. Over a 20-year period at Somers, a mental health policy and practice evolved that relies less on transfers and medication and more upon sustaining staff-client contacts.

Space, often in short supply in prisons these days, is critical in the delivery of mental health services. While almost every prison, regardless of age, contains a unit that provides closer confinement or additional punishment, few have areas designed to meet the needs of the mentally ill. Adequate space for mental health programming includes not only office space and group counseling rooms, but also access to prison hospital beds and, ideally, a supervised outpatient treatment unit.

It is difficult if not impossible to respond appropriately to the type of crises and psychiatric emergencies that routinely occur in maximum security institutions without access to a medical-psychiatric unit with 24-hour supervision. The capacity to remove the inmate-client from the prison proper to at least a neutral environment is often essential in terms of better assessing the situation and beginning appropriate treatment. In many cases this kind of environmental intervention may resolve the immediate crisis, which often involves an inmate harming him- or herself or others, and it provides time for the resolution of the underlying problem. When confronted with the issue of suicide, whether in the form of threats, gestures, or actual attempts, resources normally found in hospital units are needed. In prisons lacking hospital-treatment units, the mentally disturbed are thrown together with other maladapted inmates in essentially punitive areas that offer little beyond isolation from the prison population and closer observation by custodial staff.

Overcrowding at Somers has served to increase my awareness of how important it is to have suitable space in which to operate. For 12 years the Mental Health Unit has occupied the second floor of the prison hospital building. This area has traditionally been quiet, secluded, and conducive to providing treatment to inmates who come in on an outpatient basis. In the past couple of years, space on the floor has been appropriated to accommodate the overflow population. This has brought a dramatic change in the atmosphere on the hospital second floor and, as a result, it is no longer a suitable location for a mental health clinic. A colleague, a psychiatrist with more than 20 years of service to the institution, arrived at work recently to find that what had been his office the day before was now a living unit for 6 inmates. Since the psychiatrist's office is next door to mine, I have more than an average interest in these developments. Mental health staff have had the opportunity to experience and observe the very oppressive impact of overcrowding in an institution. (We have also learned that in prison there is no such thing as a long-term lease on space.)

Crowding and limited treatment facilities may promote a heavy reliance on drugs to treat and control inmates. Where drugs are used inappropriately or exclusively because few additional resources exist, criticisms are justified (Wilson, 1980). However, few practice settings—inpatient or outpatient, private or public—can effectively provide treatment to severely disturbed patients without using antipsychotic and antidepressant medications.

All mental health service providers, including those operating in prison, struggle with problems of how best to respond to the group of patients who seem to need medication to remain sane but for one reason or another refuse to take it. In prison the problem is compounded by the fact that there is no family or alternate support system on hand to share responsibility for the inmates' welfare. Medication itself is often viewed negatively by correctional staff, and taking medication is considered a sign of weakness within the inmate subculture. The decision to hospitalize, medicate, or commit an inmate involuntarily is always a difficult one. It involves not only a diagnosis but also an assessment of the risks involved to the inmate and others if treatment is not provided in a timely fashion.

Of course, conventional forms of psychotherapy, however congenial or uncongenial, may not be sufficient to assure the survival of mentally ill prisoners. At Somers the outpatient treatment unit has become the core of programming for mentally ill offenders. A study of the adjustment process in prison by Seymour has highlighted the importance of prison "niches," or environmental sanctuaries (see Chapter 16). Seymour (1977, p. 181) notes that "occasionally niches are officially or formally supplied," as in mental health units, hospitals, or specialized treatment units. Only rarely do mentally ill inmates find their way unassisted to the more informal prison niches, which include a good job, preferred housing, a lesser security status, or simply spending time in safe, quiet areas. In 1978 the Connecticut Department of Correction received a grant from the Law Enforcement Assistance Administration to restructure special management housing units (segregation and protective custody) at Somers. A tier in E-Block that had served as an isolated, passive sanctuary for mentally ill inmates was officially designated a treatment area. A program director, a counselor, 8 treatment officers,[4] a school teacher, and a recreation director were hired to form the program staff. A psychiatrist and psychiatric social worker served as part-time staff and clinical consultants. This 21-bed, single-celled unit, renamed the Transitional Treatment Unit (TTU), has become a primary formal niche for mentally ill inmates at Somers.

In the development of the TTU over the past four years, there has been liberal adoption of techniques commonly employed by hospital units and halfway houses. The primary treatment planning and decision-making vehicle within the program is the weekly case conference attended by supervisory and line staff, clinical consultants, and the inmate-clients whose situations are being reviewed. This meeting allows for considerable participation by both the inmate and the line officer, who often have little input under more conventional types of prison planning and decision making. Operating much like a halfway house on the outside, the primary goal of the TTU is to assist an inmate to adjust via gradual and systematic exposure to the demands of prison life. A firm commitment has been made to accept only those who voluntarily request admission, and not to retain anyone who asks to leave the program.

In its brief history the TTU has experienced its share of problems. The obligation to provide services to adjoining protective custody units with growing numbers of inmates has reduced the resources available to the treatment unit. Increased population, increased tension, and generally deteriorating living conditions have made it more difficult to return inmates with mental health problems to the general prison population. A few chronically ill inmates are never able to "graduate," while other program participants, after receiving a taste of general population, elect to transfer to a protective custody unit. There is also a stigma within the prison associated with E-Block, which presents an added burden to program participants. As for staff, transfers and promotions have produced a fairly high staff turnover rate.

Despite these difficulties and shortcomings, the TTU represents a major advance in mental health programming at Somers. It represents an effort to move beyond counseling and medication, and to influence significantly the environment where the inmate-client spends much of his time. A viable alternative to frequent hospitalization or mental health commitments was created. By providing safety, structure, and concerned, daily attention from staff, the TTU improves the survival prospects of mentally ill inmates.

CONCLUSION

Can the mentally ill offender survive in prison? The answer to this question depends to a large degree on whether the offender is given tolerable living conditions and access to needed services. There is little doubt that in correctional systems where special facilities and programs exist, the mentally ill manage to survive. The knowledge that today many correctional institutions still do not provide mental health services to prisoners places a damper on hopes for much overall improvement in the near future. The mass media in recent years have described the plight of the mentally ill in this country, particularly that of ex-hospital patients who are becoming increasingly visible on the streets of our cities. Despite this attention and some public concern, there does not appear to be any bolstering of community mental health systems to meet these needs. Mentally ill offenders have little visibility, and their situation does not generate public concern. With the retrenchment of federal programs in the human services area, there is less likelihood that innovative mental health experiments such as the TTU will be initiated in correctional facilities.

On the positive side, both the American Medical Association and the American Correctional Association have adopted guidelines for psychiatric care in prisons and jails and are involved in accreditation programs. With the development of minimum mental health standards for correctional institutions, there is a better chance that the need of certain prisoners for treatment will be recognized as a legal right (Wexler, 1976). Over the long term, greater involvement by the courts may offer hope for improvement in the delivery of services to mentally ill offenders.

NOTES

1. For example, in Connecticut, mobile Court's Diagnostic Clinic teams—consisting of a psychiatrist, a psychologist, and a psychiatric social worker—perform many of the competency evaluations.

2. An important exception to this statement would be the relatively small number of prison treatment programs loosely modeled upon the "therapeutic community" concept advanced by a British psychiatrist, Maxwell Jones (1953). Perhaps the best known of these programs was Asklepieion, which was initiated by Dr. Martin Groder at the federal maximum security institution in Marion, Illinois. These programs incorporated elements of peer counseling and self-government and clearly recognized the critical impact of the environment on prison treatment.

3. Francisco's case is also a good example of how diagnostic differences between correctional and mental health staff contribute to an indecisive and ineffective plan of management and treatment. Once the nature of his difficulties became better understood by all involved with the case, Francisco's adjustment within the prison began to significantly improve to the point where he is now able to live outside of segregation for the first time in a number of years.

4. Treatment officers are uniformed staff who must meet additional requirements in terms of experience and college education and must pass a competitive written and oral examination. The TTU is staffed with at least two treatment officers seven days a week on

the first and second shifts (8 a.m. to midnight). On the third shift the unit is managed by a correctional officer.

REFERENCES

American Medical Association. *Standards for psychiatric services in jails and prisons.* Chicago: AMA Correctional Program, 1979.

Commission of Accreditation for Corrections, Inc. *Manual of standards for adult correctional institutions.* Rockville, MD: Author, 1977.

Goffman, E. *Asylums: Essays on the social situation of mental patients and other inmates.* Garden City, NY: Doubleday, 1961.

Halleck, S. *Psychiatry and the dilemmas of crime: A study of causes, punishment and treatment.* New York: Harper & Row, 1967.

Halleck, S. *The politics of therapy.* New York: Science House, 1971.

Jones, M. *Social psychiatry: The therapeutic community.* New York: Basic Books, 1953.

Seymour, J. Niches in prison. In H. Toch, *Living in prison: The ecology of survival.* New York: Free Press, 1977.

Szasz, T. *The theology of medicine.* New York: Harper & Row, 1977.

Szasz, T. Insanity and irresponsibility: Psychiatric diversion in the criminal justice system. In H. Toch (Ed.), *Psychology of crime and criminal justice.* New York: Holt, Rinehart & Winston, 1979.

Toch, H. *Living in prison: The ecology of survival.* New York: Free Press, 1977.

Toch, H. (Ed.). *Psychology of crime and criminal justice.* Prospect Heights, IL: Waveland Press, Inc., 1979 (reissued 1986).

Wexler, D. *Criminal commitments and dangerous mental patients: Legal issues of confinement, treatment and release.* National Institute of Mental Health, DHEW Publication (ADM) 77-331. Washington, DC: Government Printing Office, 1976.

Wilson, R. Who will care for the "mad and bad"? *Corrections Magazine,* 1980, 6(1), 5-17.

PART IV

Stress Reduction

CHAPTER 14

Try Softer

ROBERT B. LEVINSON

James A. Michener could have had prisons in mind when he wrote, "Character consists of what you do on the third or fourth try." Even more to the point is something that Lily Tomlin once said: "Ever wonder why someone doesn't try *softer*?"

Authors of the preceding chapters have discussed ways in which the pains of imprisonment can be understood and ameliorated. For the most part, the focus has been on the negatives. In this and the remaining chapters of the book an effort will be made to explore ways the positives can be used to enrich correctional environments.

The question that immediately comes to the minds of administrators is: How much will it cost? If we are going to do *more*, then it must be more expensive. Maybe. It is possible to rearrange the distribution of currently available resources with the likely result that if we are not doing more with less, at least we are doing more for the same costs.

The viewpoint from which this chapter is written needs to be made explicit. My background in the field of corrections is primarily (all but two and a half years) in the Federal Prison System. Consequently, examples and data will, in large measure, come from that source. Unfortunately, this makes it all too easy for some state and local corrections workers to dismiss the following prose on the basis that "everyone knows the Feds are different!" Maybe. It is a truism that many of today's federal prisoners were yesterday in state institutions, and vice versa. The inmates are not all that different.[1] Staff are recruited, initially, from the same local areas. We are insulated from local political pressure and this, perhaps, is what allows us to try some things. Possibly among the things we have attempted to do there may be something helpful; after all, everyone doesn't have to discover the wheel for themselves.

Author's Note: *The opinions expressed herein are those of the author, and do not necessarily reflect the policies of the Federal Prison System.*

One of the thousand small cliches we all live by proclaims prisons to be schools for crime. While there are no studies to support this conventional wisdom—at worst those leaving prison are about the same as they were before entering—the despairing slogan "nothing works" continues to dot the correctional landscape despite its repudiation by its own author (Martinson, 1978).

This is not to say that prisons are pleasant places. (The idea of the country club correctional center is about as viable a notion as the existence of the Loch Ness monster—many people believe in it but nobody has ever seen one.) As the preceding chapters testify, there *is* pain in imprisonment. Losses of freedom, of privacy, of decision-making prerogatives are all tormenting; and each is inherent in incarceration. Yet the picture is not totally bleak; the majority of inmates leave prison never to return.

This chapter explores some of the ways institutions can be organized and treatment programs conducted to increase the likelihood of postrelease success.

80 Percent Failure

According to an article in the *New York Times* (McDowell, 1982), the failure rate is 80 percent in this business—of course, this article was in the book review section and the number cited dealt with the financial failure rate of all books that are published. A group of university graduate students (most of whom were members of a psychology honor society) "informed" me that anywhere from 50 percent to 100 percent of those who enter prison will return for an advanced course; the actual facts are presented in Table 14.1.

The figures in the table are for the Federal Prison System (Beck, 1980). The *success* rate for state correctional systems is in the same range—60 percent to 70 percent (Glaser, 1964). Additionally, only 16 percent of the men convicted in state superior courts during 1980 had prior prison commitments. Free society's school of hard knocks instructed 100 percent of all first offenders in the intricacies of crime.

Table 14.1 also reveals an overall 8 percent increase in success rate (chi square = 27.88; $p < .05$), suggesting that something significant occurred during the recent 8-year period.

ORGANIZING FOR TREATMENT

The concept of treatment in a correctional setting has a broader scope than "it's what the mental health worker does" (Levinson, 1978). The

TABLE 14.1 Number (and percentage) with No Arrest or Warrant Issued During the First Year After Release, by Salient Factor Score Category

Release Sample (n)*	Salient Factor Score Category**				
	Poor	Fair	Good	Very Good	Total
1970 (1806)	271	302	367	290	1230
percentage	(51)	(64)	(76)	(91)	(68)
1978 (1894)	148	283	492	515	1438
percentage	(53)	(67)	(80)	(90)	(76)

*Excludes cases with one year or less (if the 456 better risks were included in the 1978 data, the success rate would be 77 percent).
**Categories indicate likelihood of postrelease success (Hoffman & Adelberg, 1980).

following sections discuss treatment programming in prison, examining such issues as staffing patterns, role functions, and so on. But before these can be presented, a context needs to be established that undergirds the structure of an effective correctional enterprise.

Functional Units

The typical correctional institution—say, one of 500 beds—is generally organized along hierarchical lines. That is: one warden/superintendent, two or three deputy or associate wardens, ten to fifteen department heads, an even larger number of professional personnel and first-line supervisors, support services staff, and the largest number of workers in the correctional officer ranks. For every staff member there are anywhere from one to four or more inmates.

Long-established procedures are followed in assigning prisoners to living quarters—usually on a bed-available principle—and to case managers (counselors, social workers)—generally on a random basis. There is also a classification committee—staffed by department heads—which is the decision-making group that periodically reviews each inmate's progress and determines initial and subsequent programs or custody levels, recommends transfers, and, ultimately, advises the paroling authority concerning release to the community (Levinson, in press).

In addition to custody and corrections personnel, other staff have inmate care as a primary concern. Their enterprise encompasses maintaining the institution; providing heat, light, ventilation, water, electricity; supplying physical and mental health services; and providing food and clothing. Running a prison has all the attributes of being the mayor of a small city, with the added burden of furnishing close supervision for all the residents, 100 percent of whom happen to be adjudicated felons.

The typical prison organizational structure requires all staff members to be knowledgeable about every inmate. It also means that each prisoner has to be able to deal effectively with all personnel. The likelihood of both conditions existing in any continually effective fashion is slim. Department heads, sitting as decision makers on the classification committee, will know a few inmates—usually the most notorious ones—while the majority of prisoners will have their fates determined by second- or third-hand information contained in written reports. There is a better way!

Rather than one 500-inmate institution, why not conceptualize the correctional facility as five 100-bed mini-institutions? Perhaps an analogy will help make the point.

Flivvers Limited

Let us suppose there is an automobile manufacturer called Flivvers Limited (FL). Assume that FL wants to produce cars that will function well on the freeways of the world. FL is also aware that buyers like different kinds of cars—powerful, medium size, and compacts. FL's management could construct a single factory and set up the assembly line so that all of its workers are required to perform some operation on every car, as the Flivvers pass before them in random order. The managers find, however, that this method lowers quality control and increases the number of recalls. So FL establishes several subsidiaries, one for each model—Bearers, Seattles, and Tallyhoes. In this way some of the expensive effectuation equipment can be shared while workers specialize and develop expertise in producing exemplary automobiles of each type. Moreover, if there is trouble with the brakes on the Bearers, FL can still go on producing acceptable Seattles and Tallyhoes without having to close down the whole business. (Let us detour at this juncture before we drive this analogy into the ground.)

Unit Management

The concept of a functional unit (Levinson & Gerard, 1973) includes: (a) a relatively small number of offenders—75 to 125; (b) who are housed together—generally throughout the length of their institutional stay; (c) who work in a close, intensive relationship with a multidisciplinary, relatively permanently assigned team of staff members whose offices are located on the unit; (d) with these personnel having decision-making authority for all within-institution aspects of programming and disciplinary actions; and where (e) the placement of an offender in a particular living unit is contingent upon a need for the specific type of treatment program offered. Our theoretical 500-bed prison would consist of five 100-inmate functional units.

There are a number of advantages in the care, control, and correction of prisoners under the unit management organizational structure; these include:

(1) Care: This involves differential allocation of resources (for example, staffing patterns and types of security housing can be aligned with the needs of the different kinds of inmates); personnel development is enhanced by placing significant decision-making authority at a lower level in the staff hierarchy, which fosters the identification of promising future administrators and highlights training needs; and bolstering morale by establishing closer working relationships between line and supervisory personnel across the various disciplines (Toch, 1980).

(2) Control: Since transfers between units are discouraged, this reduces the amount of within-facility movement (that is, "problem cases" are not passed around); the opportunity for regular and continuing contact between staff and inmates encourages the development of better relationships *within* units; a variety of sports and other kinds of interunit tournaments lead to development of pride in one's unit, thereby reducing the likelihood of prisoners finding a common cause for organizing against staff; and, by grouping similar inmates in the same living unit, victims and predators are separated, which decreases the number of assaults and other management problems (Bohn, 1980).

(3) Correction: The semiautonomous nature of the functional units permits maximum flexibility in program design and allows later modifications without disrupting the entire institution: by placing the decision makers closer to the "users" (inmates), planning, implementing, managing, and program evaluation are all in the hands of those who are most knowledgeable about the prisoner population; program fragmentation is diminished since the same unit team works with the offender from time of arrival to release from the institution; and, as a consequence, inmates receive more appropriate program assignments, thereby improving their chances for successful postrelease adjustment (Quay, 1973).

Because of the complex interactions inherent in correctional institutions, it is difficult to establish a one-to-one correlation between a particular program innovation and a positive change in inmates' postrelease success rates. However, the 8 percent increase (noted in Table 14.1) coincided with the introduction of functional unit management in the Federal Prison System—in 1970—and its establishment throughout the system—accomplished by the mid-1970s. Correctional systems not connected with the Federal Bureau of Prisons have also reported success after adopting organizational modifications based on unit management (see Butler, 1979).

Treatment Philosophy

Having an administrative structure that supports the objectives of treatment programming provides a powerful palliative for alleviating the pain of imprisonment. The philosophy of treatment that then guides program activities becomes a major force in creating a facilitative institutional climate.

One way of construing an entering prison population is in terms of three broad categories:

(1) There are some offenders who, from the moment the cell door clangs shut behind them, will never commit another offense.
(2) There are others whom the prison experience will not change regardless of the quantity and/or high quality of programs to which they are exposed.
(3) There is a middle group of inmates who can leave prison improved or unchanged.

It is with this third category of offenders that correctional programs can have their greatest impact.

Medical Model

Conceptualizing correctional treatment in terms of a medical model has become a most popular philosophical stance. This presupposes that criminals are "sick" (infected by a sick society?) and are sent to prison to be "cured" (rehabilitated). Consequently, the inmate's problem must be "diagnosed" and the appropriate "treatment" "prescribed." Responsibility for achieving the prisoner's rehabilitation is assigned to the staff; the inmate is there, passive—to be acted upon. If, following release, the prisoner recidivates, the staff and its rehabilitation methods have failed.

There are a number of problems with this formulation, the most basic issue being that its initial premise is wrong. While some few inmates may be mentally ill—estimates vary from about 3 percent to 5 percent—and some larger proportion may have debilitating emotional problems—another 10 percent to 12 percent—the vast majority of prisoners are no more "sick" than you or I. Further, unlike the use of penicillin to cope with pneumococci, there is no pill for criminality and correctional programs cannot be injected. As someone once said: You don't have to be sick to get better!

The typical inmate is incorrectly characterized if viewed as a passive recipient of correctional programming during the period of incarceration. In order for programs to be effective, prisoners must make an emotional and/or intellectual commitment to them. Staff have the obligation to make available appropriate, attractive, quality programs; inmates have the responsibility to become genuinely involved with both the selection of, and the participation in, these activities.

Training Model

Rather than the medical analogy, a training model seems more accurately descriptive of a correctional programming philosophy. Offenders enter prisons with a variety of deficits. That is, some are socially or morally inept; others are intellectually or vocationally handicapped; some have emotional hang-ups that stem from internal psychological problems and/or have externally generated deficiencies as a consequence of environmental or family circumstances; and still others have a mixture composed of varying proportions of some or even all of these. The role of staff is to help prisoners help themselves—assist them in identifying where their deficits are and encourage them to participate in programs that are designed to help fill in the gaps. The major onus rests with the inmates; the degree to which they actively involve themselves bears directly on whether or not the prison experience will serve as an impetus for positive postrelease change.

From this philosophy of imprisonment flows the idea that the function of staff is to help train inmates in the use of alternative ways of responding to the pressures of living in the free community. The focus is not on seeking methods to eliminate "wrong" behavior; the emphasis becomes one of helping prisoners develop a more appropriate repertoire of responses. Punishing wrong actions without instruction as to what is acceptable does little more than build resentment and a desire to get even.

Thus, unlike working on flivvers, the training model requires an interaction between correctional workers and the subject of their attention. Under the medical model the ball is always in the staff's court; staff serve up what they believe to be the right treatment programs and inmates react. But the training model has both correctional personnel and prisoners in the game together and on the same side; if inmates are not active contributors, everyone loses—especially the offenders.

TRYING SOFTER

What would a prison look like that attempted to incorporate into its daily operations the ideas mentioned in this chapter? In his book *The Future of Imprisonment* (1975), Norval Morris, then Dean of the University of Chicago Law School, outlined a model prison. The Federal Bureau of Prisons, at its facility in Butner, North Carolina, tried to implement the Morris proposals (Ingram, 1978). The remainder of this section deals with the degree of success of that effort.

The Morris Model

The central concept around which Morris focuses his model of imprisonment is that positive change cannot be coerced. Since being released is one of the most powerful motivating forces acting upon prisoners, any attempt to tie together performance in treatment programs with release eligibility results in "game playing." Rather than an authoritarian management structure, a "collaborative" style is advocated by Morris—one in which both staff and inmates work together in a team effort.

Among the key elements in the Morris model are:

(1) offering prisoners a humane and secure environment in which they (a) follow a graduated release plan and (b) are aware that their release date is unaffected by their degree of program participation (but would be subject to possible revision if they were found "guilty" of committing serious violations of prison regulations), thereby (c) permitting inmates to focus attention on acquiring self-knowledge and self-control through voluntary participation in appropriate, attractive program activities;

(2) establishing a fixed release date for every prisoner in order to (a) remove any coercive elements in program enrollment and (b) increase the degree of sincerity of such participation;

(3) selecting "deep end"[2] prisoners on a random basis from a "pool" of eligible inmates already in the system; and

(4) assessing the degree of success of this imprisonment model, based on measures of behavior while confined and during postrelease, by an independent evaluation group (not part of the prison's administration).

The Federal Bureau of Prisons attempted to conform as closely as possible to the Morris model.

Butner

The evaluation of the Federal Prison System's effort to implement the Morris model was conducted by independent researchers from the

University of North Carolina (Bounds, 1979). Inmates confined at Butner and a control group housed in other federal prisons made up the research population.

Populations

Morris's selection criteria for establishing a "pool" of deep-end eligible prisoners for the model prison were that they be prisoners who: have records showing at least two convictions for violent crimes; are betwen the ages of 18 and 35; and are scheduled for release on parole within one to three years of selection. Excluded were women, prisoners requiring mental hospital care, and offenders of great notoriety or leaders of gangs or militant groups or organized crime. Individuals were to be randomly selected from this "pool" and sent to the model institution. (Those not selected remained at their present prison and constituted a control group.) After a period of exposure to the model prison, the prisoner could chose to return to the sending institution with no negative consequences. The bureau tried to come as close as possible to the Morris proposals in establishing the criteria and procedures used to select the prisoners for Butner.

Of the 718 individuals in the research population (Butner and control inmates) for whom there were valid data on prior commitments of at least 6 months duration, about 69 percent had at least 2 such confinements; 56 percent of this research population had commitment offenses in the 2 top severity-of-offense categories. Over 41 percent of the Butner inmates were residents in a maximum security federal penitentiary at the time of the parole hearing that determined their eligibility for the model facility. Of Butner's population, 32 percent had a current offense of a violent nature; 58 percent of the total research population (Butner plus controls) were under age 35; and 71 percent of Butner's inmates were within the 12-to-36-month time-to-release criterion (the remainder were "short"—less than 12 months—thereby reducing their period of exposure to the Butner program relative to the control prisoners).

Programs

No prisoner at Butner was required to participate in any program other than assigned work, small living groups,[3] and a testing session to assess needs. This evoked concern among some staff that there would be almost no program participation by the inmates, a fear that proved groundless.

The program day was divided into periods of three and one-half hours apiece, with each individual assigned work for at least one of these time modules. The remaining two time periods could be programmed for another work shift, education and/or vocational training, or leisure-time activities. Unlike Morris's recommendation, the inmates' rate of pay for their work was not commensurate with free-world salaries; on the other hand, the prisoners received room and board without cost.

Program Phases

As described by Morris, the Butner inmate moved through a three-phase program: initial, continuation, and release.

The *initial phase* of Butner's program lasted 90 days, during which the newly arrived inmate was oriented to the program, background information was gathered, and a graduated release plan was developed by the staff. This phase ended with the inmate's formal decision to remain at the model facility or to return to the institution from which the prisoner had been transferred—only 18 percent elected to be returned.

The *continuation phase* at Butner closely approximated Morris's model. It began at the end of the initial phase and concluded six months prior to the inmate's release date. During this time the prisoner performed in accord with initially spelled-out expectations, complied with prison rules, and followed a program plan jointly developed during discussions between the individual and the unit (classification) team.

The *release phase*—the third and final stage—as implemented at Butner fell short of Morris's concept of placing the prisoner in a community halfway house run by the same prison staff the individual worked with while incarcerated. At Butner a prerelease program of approximately three months duration was to be followed by three months in a community-based program; 85 percent of Butner's inmates were released through a halfway house.

Morris's idea of graduated release was made operational at Butner through the prisoner's graduated release plan. This document scheduled in detail the times when increased levels of liberty and personal responsibility would be granted. The time frames were established by the unit team. These "steps toward release" required only that the inmate maintain a level of behavior that complied with Butner's rules. Receiving reduced custody and an increase in privileges was not contingent upon the individual achieving goals specified in the mutually agreed-upon program plan. (The prisoners were dissatisfied with their level of participation in developing their graduated release plans, primarily because they felt the steps did not come soon enough.)

Prison Environment

The Morris model envisioned an institutional "climate" in which prisoners could make decisions regarding self-development and program participation and not have to worry about personal safety. Within a manifestly secure perimeter, there was to be freedom of movement and a sense of personal protection.

The University of North Carolina evaluation team established that the conditions Morris advocated existed at Butner. There are no prison bars inside the institution, nor a pass system or checkpoints to monitor inmate movement. Prisoners, staff, and visitors walk around freely. There are women staff members, inmates wear civilian clothing, and there is a willingness on the part of institution personnel to have open communication with the prisoners.

Results

The data collection period began July 1, 1976, and ended April 30, 1979. The randomly selected Butner inmates were essentially equivalent to the control group housed in other federal prisons with respect to most characteristics that might affect outcome measures. They were individuals with substantial records of crime, yet young enough to present a continuing threat of danger to society unless deflected from their criminal careers.

No statistically significant differences were found between the two groups studied, either in the number or the severity of disciplinary reports received. In light of the more "relaxed" atmosphere at Butner, this might be viewed as a positive indicator for the model approach. Moreover, Butner experienced no escapes, no killings, relatively few serious assaults on staff or inmates, no mass protests involving work or food strikes, and no known traffic in hard drugs.

The Butner prisoners had a statistically significant higher rate of program enrollments and completions than their counterparts in the control group. Equating for time of exposure to their respective "institutions," Butner inmates, on the average, enrolled in two more programs and completed nearly three times the number finished by the control prisoners.

Data on the relative postrelease success rates of the Butner and control groups are being gathered by another independent research group from the University of North Carolina (Witte, 1981).

An Added Fillip

One managerial option not incorporated in the Morris model or the Butner project deserves mention. This involves the use of an internal management classification system. All prisons have a procedure by which newly arrived inmates are assigned to living quarters. Typically, this process is accomplished either by random assignment or—in these days of overcrowded institutions—on a bed-available basis. Such an approach misses a valuable opportunity.

The research literature has repeatedly demonstrated (see, for example, Bohn, 1980; Smith & Fenton, 1978) that significant reductions in management problems accrue when a systematic, program-relevant method is used for making living quarters assignments. Basically, these approaches subdivide an institution's incoming population into three categories: victims, predators, and a middle group. Housing assignments (and, to the degree possible, program scheduling) are set up so that there is maximal separation between the victimization-prone and the predator groups; the middle category inmates have their own living unit but are also used to balance bed space throughout the institution.

The bottom line—to use the current cliche—is that the kind of systematic rearrangement of procedures described above can be initiated in correctional systems without huge additional expenditures of funds. Frequently, a rational, goal-oriented redistribution of available resources is all that is required, *and* the presence of someone who is willing to try a different way.

IMPLICATIONS

Morris's specification that his model of imprisonment be tried, initially, with "deep end" offenders was based on the premise that if it worked with these individuals, it would be appropriate for the "better bets." A serendipitous spin-off is that this approach suggests a different way to deal with the more difficult to manage prisoner.

The typical response by correctional administrators when dealing with "deep end" felons is to tighten down. What the Morris model seems to be suggesting—for certain of these more troublesome individuals—is that trying softer may offer a constructive alternative. This is not to imply that this approach is a panacea. It may well be that a correctional system needs the more traditionally run institutions to back up a Morris-type facility for those inmates for whom the model approach does not work. What the Morris model does do is increase the options for both inmates and correctional administrators. It offers another way to organize a correctional facility, another way to try.

Thus the Butner project illustrates an alternative to the way we do the many day-to-day things that go on in every prison. The procedures are not new; how they are organized results in the meaningful difference. What is unique is the guiding philosophy within which these activities take place.

CONCLUSION

Philosopher Martin Buber characterized the essence of a human being as the capability of "entering into relations with the world and things" (Friedman, 1965). Partly because the act of incarceration destroys previous relationships and reduces the opportunities for new ones, confinement becomes a painful experience. The degree of discomfort varies; for those with few meaningful relationships in the free world, imprisonment may be somewhat less distressful, while many inmates separated from rich personal involvements find being incarcerated excruciating. This may partially account for "the suicide rate inside the bars [being] 16 times as great as that of a city with a population comparable to that of the jails" (Ostrow, 1981); that is, self-destruction is the number-one killer of jailed inmates (Charle, 1981).

The pain of imprisonment can be reduced. Creating conditions of confinement that not only provide prisoners with a safe, humane environment but also encourage positive relationships among inmates and between offenders and personnel can be accomplished.

For those who operate from a "what's in it for me" frame of reference, increasing the level of human dignity extant in prisons means that fewer brutalized individuals will be walking the community's streets when 95 percent-plus of those presently confined are released. More abstract, but equally significant, if the measure of a civilization is how it treats its prisoners (to paraphrase Goethe), trying softer may move us all closer to being civilized. As someone once said: "Being tough doesn't work because being lenient is not the source of the problem."

NOTES

1. In 1979 the State of Illinois Department of Corrections was in the early stages of developing a systemwide classification system (which they have subsequently accomplished). As part of their developmental procedures, the form developed by the Federal Bureau of Prisons was used by their staff to assess 200 randomly selected inmates from the Stateville institution. A comparison of these Illinois state prisoners with inmates in a comparable federa prison (data collected on 1113 inmates) is shown below:

Percentage of Inmates by Security Needs

Security Level	*SL-1 (min.)*	*SL-2*	*SL-3*	*SL-4*	*SL-5*	*SL-6 (max.)*
Illinois (Stateville)	12	14	34.5	38	1.5	0
Federal (Lompoc)	9	15	21.0	37	17.0	2

2. The selection criteria proposed by Morris called for individuals who (a) had records of at least two convictions for violent crimes; (b) were between the ages of 18 and 35; and (c) were scheduled for release on parole within one to three years of selection for participation in the project.

3. As conceived by Morris, these are groups of 6 to 8 inmates and 2 to 4 staff members who would share meals and have discussions 6 days a week. Butner's approximation was weekly meetings among 3 to 20 prisoners led by a correctional counselor—a specially trained correctional officer who works with a caseload of inmates on a variety of their problems and no longer is responsible for custodial duties. In the view of the university evaluators, the small living groups were never used to the degree advocated by Morris due to organizational limitations and the unavailability of appropriate training for the group leaders.

4. According to FY 80 data, a significantly lower number of assaults was recorded at the one federal penitentiary (Lewisburg) that utilized an internal management classification system than at the other similar prisons; that is, Lewisburg experienced 22 assaults, compared with Leavenworth, 47; Lompoc, 45; and Terre Haute, 40. Statistically significant differences (chi square = 83.4; $p < .001$) were also found in the frequency of disciplinary reports received by Lewisburg inmates in the victimization-prone, middle, and predatory category living quarters:

Severity of Incident Reports	*Frequency of Incident Reports*		
	victim	*middle*	*predator*
Greatest severity	8	0	16
High severity	31	33	49
Moderate severity	109	60	177
Low moderate severity	3	8	5
Total	151	101	247

REFERENCES

Beck, J. L. *Measuring recidivism rates for federal offenders.* Bureau of Prisons, Washington, D.C. (mimeo)

Bohn, M. J. Inmate classification and the reduction of institution violence. *Corrections Today,* July/August 1980, pp. 48-55.

Bohn, M. J., Waszak, R. A., & Story, B. R. Transition to functional units. *FCI Technical and Treatment Notes,* 1974, 4(1).

Bounds, V. L. *Evaluation of a model of imprisonment tests at the Butner, FCI: Final report.* Chapel Hill: Institute for Research in Social Science, University of North Carolina, 1979.

Butler, T. F. *Functional unit management: A concept of correctional institution organization and management as implemented at the Norfolk Naval Station Correctional Center.* Norfolk Naval Station, Norfolk, Virginia. (mimeo)

Charle, S. Suicide in the cellblocks. *Corrections Magazine,* August 1981, pp. 6-16.

Friedman, M. (Ed.). *The knowledge of man.* New York: Harper & Row, 1965.

Glaser, D. *Effectiveness of a prison and parole system.* Indianapolis: Bobbs-Merrill, 1964.

Hoffman, P. B., & Adelberg, S. The Salient Factor Score: A non-technical overview. *Federal Probation,* March 1980, pp. 44-52.

Ingram, G. L. Butner: A reality. *Federal Probation,* March 1978, pp. 34-39.

Levinson, R. B. Non-correctional program aspects for convicted offenders. In American Correctional Association, *Proceedings of the 108th Congress of Corrections.* College Park, MD: Author, 1978.

Levinson, R. B. A clarification of classification. *Criminal Justice and Behavior,* 1982, 9(2), 133-142.

Levinson, R. B., & Gerard, R. E. Functional units: A different correctional approach. *Federal Probation,* December 1973, pp. 8-16.

McDowell, E. The paperback evolution. *New York Times,* January 10, 1982, Book Review Section, p. 7.

Martinson, R. Martinson revisited. *Criminal Justice Newsletter,* December 4, 1978, p. 4.

Megargee, E. I., & Cadow, J. The ex-offender and the "monster myth." *Federal Probation,* March 1980, pp. 24-37.

Morris, N. *The future of imprisonment.* Chicago: University of Chicago Press, 1975.

Ostrow, R. J. Article in *New York Times,* November 27, 1981.

Quay, H. C. *The differential behavioral classification of the adult male offender: Interim results and procedures.* Washington, DC: Bureau of Prisons, 1973.

Smith, W. A., & Fenton, C. E. Unit management in a penitentiary: A practical experience. *Federal Probation,* September 1978, pp. 40-46.

Toch, H. (Ed.). *Therapeutic communities in corrections.* New York: Praeger, 1980.

Witte, A. D., Long, S. K., Eakin, K., Karr, P., Bass, C., & Smith, S. H. *Follow-up evaluation of the Phase I Butner Experiment: Post-release criminality and labor market performance.* Chapel Hill: Department of Economics, University of North Carolina, 1981.

CHAPTER 15

Reducing Prison Sexual Violence

DANIEL LOCKWOOD

Violent sexual incidents among men in prison fall into two groups. In the first category, the aggressor employs violence to coerce his target. Force serves goals decided upon *before* incidents commence. The primary causes of this violence are subcultural values upholding men's rights to use force to gain sexual access.

The second category of incidents is the type in which targets react violently to propositions perceived as threatening. In such cases, the target shares some responsibility for the resulting harm. These incidents often resemble free-world victim-precipitated homicide because words or gestures perceived as offensive provoke retaliatory insults, threats, or violence. Since incidents in prisons seem to be divided almost equally between these two categories, it is clear that programs to reduce prison sexual violence should be aimed at targets as well as at aggressors.

The case study that follows illustrates this point. The man speaking, whom we will call Frank, is a small, almost baby-faced, 19-year-old from Buffalo. Convicted of murdering a homosexual who picked him up when he was 16, attacked by a sexual aggressor while awaiting trial in the Erie County jail, approached by other aggressors whom he fought off when he began his 10-year sentence in Coxsackie, Frank's world is dominated by aggression. His boyish face belies the fact that he has become a "violent man," ready to make preemptive strikes for self-defense, almost eager to engage in public displays of courage to bolster his pride and self-image. The incident in which we now see Frank occurs

---

Author's Note: *The cooperation of the New York State Department of Correctional Services is gratefully acknowledged. Support for this research came from the LEAA-funded project, "Interventions for Inmate Survival," under the direction of Hans Toch (Grant 75-NI-99-0030) and an LEAA Graduate Research Fellowship.*

in a mental health facility for prisoners. Frank's aggressor, who becomes his victim after Frank stabs him, we will call Davis. Davis, an older man, also has an extensive history of violent behavior. As Frank tells us:

> And so he comes in and he sits down. And then he just keeps on staring at me. And I'm not going to run for nothing. And so I just sat there and kept on staring. And so he was sitting right over here and I was looking over there out the window and this guy was staring at me. And so all of a sudden he started laughing and licking his lips and I said, "What the hell does that mean?" I'm still not going to go anywhere. Because, if this dude is going to jump up, then I'm going to hurt him. So then, anyway, he started laughing and licking his lips and everything. And then I told him, I forgot what I told him, but it got him mad. And then he walked out of the room and he said, "I'll get you." And I said, "Get me now." And I stood up. And then I walked back into the room and I crouched into the boxing stance. And then he looked at me and then he walked back out of the room.

Analyzing Frank's thoughts and feelings at the different steps of the incident, we find a typical transactional pattern: A stare, perceived as a threatening overture, is responded to by an insult and a challenge to fight. Frank feels that his pride and his manly image preclude backing away from perceived threats. As he says, "I'm not going to run for nothing." Now Davis, once he is insulted, responds to Frank's insult with his own challenge of "I'll get you." Thus two men escalate their transaction from stares and gestures to threats and counterthreats. It would be helpful if we could train men to respond to threats and insults in ways that do not escalate into violence. Unfortunately, notions about managing such incidents without force are scarce in the prison culture, as we see when Frank turns to a peer for advice. As he tells us, he said to his friend:

> "Look, I'm having some kind of a problem, this dude is supposed to be a boxer." And the guy gave me a blade on the end of a comb . . . and said to use it. And I said, "Are you serious?" And he said, "Yes, you're not afraid of hurting anyone, are you? I don't care how much you don't like hurting anyone on the streets, when you come to jail, you have to hurt somebody."
>
> I never used a weapon like that except a pipe [any improvised weapon used as a club]. So I went to the ward and I had the blade. At night you leave your clothes in the dorm in the sitting room, and you lay there and go to sleep. And I laid there and went to sleep. But I had forgotten that I had laid the blade in my pants so that I couldn't reach it. So in the middle of the night he (Davis) gets up and goes to kiss me on the cheek. And I jumped up and I felt like I was going to puke. I started to choke and everything. And I hit him and he came back and hit me over the head. And just by the style of the way this guy hit me I know that this guy did box. And so I said,

"Shit, if I don't do something to this dude, then he is going to fuck me up." So I just started getting mad and I hit him and hit him again. And then he hit me again and knocked me over the bed. I walked into the day room and he hit me and the officer saw the end of it. . . .

The next morning they put me in the room and it was like nothing ever happened. . . . And I had this blade in my pocket and I went over and talked to him and I said, "Listen, there is nothing going on between me and you. And there is never going to be, I don't care how big an army that you get. Nobody is going to make me a homosexual or I'm going to kill them." And then I took the blade out and he ducked and I went for his throat and I hit him on the arm. I cut him across there. I wanted to kill him.

The incident between Frank and Davis shows an escalating sequence of steps typical of target reactions to unwanted sexual overtures. However, even though the participants themselves are prone to violence, with the proper social learning the transaction might have been resolved peaceably.

Let's consider the opening moves, for example. Davis makes a sexual overture to Frank; Frank responds by insulting or snubbing Davis; Davis then makes a verbal threat and tries to withdraw; Frank then challenges Davis and makes a physical threat by raising his fists; Davis then leaves. What we have is an outcome that is neither planned nor wanted by either of the participants. Had Frank responded in a way that communicated his feelings in a less hurtful manner, Davis might not have been stimulated to threaten him. As we shall suggest later, programs aimed at reducing violence can train participants to respond assertively to unwanted approaches in ways that diminish the chances of subsequent escalation to threats of physical violence. Had Frank or Davis received such training, they might been able to communicate their differences in a manner less likely to provoke threatening responses.

Typical of institutional life, Frank goes to a peer, a fellow prisoner, for help once trouble starts. Unfortunately, peer culture, without positive direction, promotes violence as a means to solve problems. Frank, who has never knifed anyone before, gets a weapon and is told to use it. He learns from a fellow prisoner, one who can strongly influence his behavior, that extreme violence is acceptable and necessary. Had peer culture representatives been trained and organized to handle such incidents nonviolently themselves, the fight may have been avoided.

SOLUTIONS TO THE PROBLEM

Any remedy for prison sexual violence faces stiff obstacles. Aggressors with histories of violence ruthlessly exploit others. Targets use force to protect themsevles and to promote masculine images. Threatened men often are reluctant to go to staff because existing official remedies can cause more problems than they solve. Other prisoners usually help only their friends, and many targets of aggression are social isolates. Given the need for creative and effective measures to deal with the situation, the search for solutions must be far-ranging.

One useful approach is to apply human relations training to the problem. This technique has among its goals increasing interpersonal skill, relieving interpersonal or intergroup tension, and developing individual and group problem-solving skills. It is relatively simple to apply this approach, following such "cookbooks" as Pfeiffer and Jones's *A Handbook of Structured Experiences for Human Relations Training* (1971-1974), Simon et al.'s *Values Clarification* (1972), or Hawley and Hawley's *Human Values in the Classroom* (1975). One example of this approach being applied in prisons in the Quaker AVP, or Alternatives to Violence Project. Project members have trained nonprofessionals, including prisoners, to lead prison inmates and guards through structured human relations exercises especially adapted to the prison scene. The preparation of the trainers takes only a few weekends. A brief apprenticeship with an experience trainer follows, and then volunteers run workshops themselves. While there are no evaluations of the effectiveness of the human relations approach to the field of corrections, a study by Bowers and Soar (1960) showed that the techniques did work to improve behavior in public high schools. After teachers received human relations training, the behavior in their classrooms improved significantly relative to similar classes taught by teachers who had not received such training. There is a need to conduct similar evaluative research in adult institutions; in the interim, the program deserves to be tried.

In regard to prison sexual violence, human relations training could be directed to targets seeking nonviolent responses to aggressive approaches. In group sessions, for example, inmates could use role playing to learn and practice techniques for being assertive in nonviolent ways. The exercises could be designed specifically to defuse the escalating sequence our illustration exemplifies. Ideally, such an action project would be based on analysis of actual incidents. A specific approach that could be adopted to the prison setting is Gordon's (1974) Effectiveness Training Program. Among Gordon's strategies are "owning the problem," "no-lose conflict resolution," and "influencing skills." These techniques are easy to apply and disseminate. Providing they are accompanied by at least some inculcation of nonviolent values, they could prepare men to handle sexual approaches. Imagine, for example, how effectiveness or assertiveness training could have helped the prisoner describing this dilemma:

> The job that I had, we were seeing each other pretty often. And we lived together and we worked together and we ate together. He just felt me out the first week, and the second week he was a little aggressive coming up to me and just staring. Sometimes I would just be laying and reading a book or playing with my guitar and he would just come up to me and just stare at me. I felt tense and nervous and I didn't know what to tell this guy. I couldn't continue playing my guitar or anything. I had to stop and I had to confront this guy. And I felt lost, really lost, because I didn't know how to deal with him and how to tell him to leave me alone.

Human relations training would, of course, leave intact aggressors' exploitative violence. One way to address this difficulty would be social literacy training. Developed by the noted Brazilian educator, Freire, "literacy" in this sense means "naming problems, analyzing the causes, and acting to solve the problem" (Hyman et al., 1979). An approach such as social literacy may be indicated because prison sexual aggression is often hidden, even though our research shows it to be one of the most prevalent and serious problems men face in prison. As with other life problems, few speak openly about the situation and few formal programs counteract it. As one prisoner in Attica stated:

> This thing has not been discussed. We haven't had lectures on that, but we've had them on everything else. We have lectures on getting mail and sending mail out and getting packages, and what the procedures are on getting a haircut, but nothing on the biggest number one problem in the institution itself. Nothing at all.

Social literacy training requires analysis of the total system in which the behavior occurs, so that the persons involved can understand the forces causing the difficulty. The program comprises the following steps: (1) study of the group's thoughts, language, and action by an outsider: (2) definition of "central conflicts" by the outsider and leaders of the group; (3) analysis of the causes of the problem by group members; and (4) solving the problem by group members.

Social literacy offers some specific problem-solving techniques that could be employed in prison to reduce sexual violence. Some of these techniques, which have been successfully used in other settings, are the following: (1) creation by group members of a "survival guide," giving the formal and informal rules of getting by; (2) carrying out a "stress hunt," in which group members question each other about what bothers them the most and then rate the responses; (3) enacting simulations such as *Tame It,* in which group members role play typical incidents, analyze causes, and role play situations.

According to one evaluation (Alschuler, 1978), a program of this kind significantly reduced discipline problems in a large public school. We have no knowledge of the efficacy or even the use of this program in prisons. It would seem, however, that social literacy could provide a readily available, well-structured plan that would stand a good chance of reducing violence. Little expense or organizational change is required. Because the specific recommendations of action come from the persons living in the setting, participants would be motivated to carry them out. Social literacy, then, could be a promising approach to the problem of prison sexual violence.

Social literacy proposes a *process* for alleviating difficulties among groups, leaving the specific *form* of the improvement to the people from the group chosen to work on the difficulty. This is the strength of this approach. If the decision-making process is correct, if it is viewed as legitimate by group members, if it involves them, if it captures their attention, and if it causes them to be subjected to pressure from significant peers, then specific reforms are likely to have an impact. For the same reasons, limited inmate self-government (including therapeutic communities and enterprises such as the "group-treatment model") and the "just community" can also reduce sexual violence. What this approach calls for is a democratic system among prisoners, who are given power and responsibility to govern their own affairs. Decisions are made in open group meetings, which also serve as a forum for public criticism of staff and other prisoners. As in social literacy, community pressures arise in the form of a culture of the group that shapes the social environment.

Why should a democratic group reduce violence and exploitation in prisons? Violence-promoting values can be changed by active participation in a governing body. As an advocate of the just community writes, "intensive community life is essential to the development within the individual of an adult principled moral perspective" (Scharf, 1978, p. 189). This same premise is held by drug rehabilitation communities such as Synanon and Daytop Village. Open discussion and shared decision making also foster collaboration between staff and inmates. Staff know more about life among their clients, are frequently called upon to do more, and can often exert a greater influence. Giving power to the group and using the power from the group generally means that staff need to punish less. As a result, information about victimization is shared more freely, since there is less chance of aggressors being harmed by free talk from informants. Inmates are more willing to talk about violence and exploitation by others when they know that these individuals will not be automatically punished, which brings retaliation and peer disapproval of "ratting." As Feld (1977) points out in his study of a juvenile cottage run according to therapeutic community principles, inmates will tell staff about others' behavior if those offenders are not punished: It is the probability of punishment that sustains norms against "ratting."

Moreover, when regular group meetings are held and when these meetings are taken seriously (because participants have power to make significant decisions), inmates or staff can deliberately focus attention on selected events, such as victimizing incidents. Thus staff or other inmates can respond to every verbal threat or proposition perceived as offensive by making it an item of group discussion. "Crises" in group life can and should be used to achieve social learning. Rules can become established and peer pressure can reinforce constructive norms in democratic problem-solving groups. Such organizations can also focus attention on items perceived by participants to be important. Sexual approaches that are perceived to be a problem by targets can thus be confronted and addressed by the groups. If such organizations are properly run by trained staff (and staff must always be centrally involved in this process), individual incidents featuring threats can be used to create rules leading to safe environments.

Staff-guided self-government is not new to prison. For example, Feld (1977) presents a systematic evaluation of this democratic approach in *Neutralizing Inmate Violence.* He examines three ways of organizing reform school cottages: the custody model, the individual treatment model, and the democratic group treatment model. Violence and exploitation were greatly reduced in the democratically run cottage, even though the social characteristics of the young men in the three cottages were about the same. The boys in the cottage that was set up on democratic community principles complained far less about interpersonal difficulties than did the other boys. The "just community" approach to correctional organization, which allows for inmates' control of internal discipline, proposal of furloughs, and the definition of program objectives, has also been shown to improve institutional climates (Scharf, 1978). If offenses, with the exception of major felonies, are referred to community meetings, the process can reeducate transgressors as well as resolve conflicts they may have precipitated.

When critical incidents are given to groups of prisoners to handle, it is important that a plan be instituted to promulgate nonviolent values. Otherwise, self-government can perpetuate violence and there is danger that individual violence will be replaced by group violence. In the following interview excerpt, the "ward president" of a prison therapeutic community describes the dangers of having groups manage incidents without commitment to nonviolent approaches:

> It was an attempted rip-off. We had ward government and I was ward president at the time. We had two cliques. Now, I don't know who tried to rip the guy off—I had suspicion of who it was, but like somebody attempted to rip him off. Somebody punched him in the mouth and his mouth was bleeding and what not. Anyway, we had a meeting on the ward. . . . He came to me. I was the ward president. . . . And his lip was ripped and he was bleeding and it was still bleeding so it was just a few minutes before. I called a meeting and sort of ran, like, "I am not interested in who, how, when or why, but there is not going to be no fucking rip-offs on the ward." I had five or six guys with me that were willing to be, like, strongarms if there was any kind of trouble. Like, if I was going to be jumped then everybody was gone.

Situations such this can be avoided by active staff involvement in setting the tone of the group. Threats and violence must never be permitted. Staff, who are themselves members of democratic communities, must take the lead in setting limits on permissible solutions to victimization. One such limit, of course, should restrict conflict resolution to nonviolent methods.

Though holding promise of reducing sexual violence, the successful formation of democratic prisoner organizations faces certain obstacles. Staff, as Feld (1977) points out, must be "strong, limit-setting individuals" who are also humanitarian and democratic. In selecting their staff, administrators must find persons whose basic personality orientations support democratic group organization. Where civil service requirements make this impossible, supervisors must struggle to change deeply entrenched attitudes. Prisoners also must alter their views, especially those notions having to do with forcibly interfering with the behavior of other prisoners. It is essential to overcome these obstacles; sexual aggression is fundamentally caused by values supporting the violent exploitation of others. Aggressors holding such values can best be controlled by other prisoners exerting peer pressure in democratic, nonviolent groups. Violent responses to sexual aggression, the second contributor to conflict, are caused by feelings of fear and the need to take self-defensive measures. Properly organized prisoner groups should have the capability to create and maintain tolerably safe environments.

We need to have readily available a variety of techniques to counteract violence in institutions. In this chapter we have reviewed several of these, and have shown how they might be applied to the specific problem of prison sexual violence. Unfortunately, our inquiry has been limited by the lack of controlled research on the topic of managing and preventing violent disputes. Considering the potential for victimization whenever we bring together violence-prone persons in residential institutions, humaneness calls for well-worked-out plans for reducing violence and exploitation. At this time, to be sure, the literature on the topic is sparse. What we know about violence reduction needs to be put in a form that can readily be understood by those in the field, and the basic science on the topic needs to be expanded.

REFERENCES

Alschuler, W. *Discipline, a socially literate solution.* Unpublished manuscript, National Institute of Education, Washington, D.C., 1978.

Bowers, N. D., & Soar, R. S. *Studies of human relations in the teaching-learning process.* Final report: evaluation of laboratory human relations training for classroom teachers, a project supported by the cooperative Research Program of the U.S. Office of Education, Washington, D.C., 1960.

Feld, B. C. *Neutralizing inmate violence: Juvenile offenders in institutions.* Cambridge, MA: Ballinger, 1977.

Gordon, T. *Teacher effectiveness training.* New York: Peter Wyden, 1974.

Hawley, R. C., & Hawley, I. L. *Human values in the classroom.* New York: Hart, 1975.

Holsti, O. R. *Content analysis for the social sciences and humanities.* Reading, MA: Addison-Wesley, 1969.

Hyman, I., et al. *An analysis of studies on effectiveness of training and staffing to help schools manage student conflict and alienation.* Unpublished manuscript, National Institute of Education, Washington, D.C., 1979.

Lockwood, D. *Prison sexual violence.* New York: Elsevier, 1980.

Pfeiffer, J. W., & Jones, J. E. *A handbook of structured experiences for human relations training* (4 vols.). La Jolla, CA: Universities Associates, 1971-1974.

Scharf, P. Democratic education and the prevention of delinquency. In U.S. Department of Health, Education and Welfare, National Institute of Education, *School crime and disruption: Prevention models.* Washington, DC: Government Printing Office, 1978.

Simon, B., Howe, W., & Kirschenbaum, H. *Values clarification.* New York: Hart, 1972.

Toch, H. *Living in prison: The ecology of survival.* New York: Free Press, 1977.

CHAPTER 16

Environmental Sanctuaries for Susceptible Prisoners

JOHN HAGEL-SEYMOUR

One of the more obvious features of behavior in prison is its variation. Some prisoners experience threats to personal safety and well-being and seek isolation. Other prisoners suffer threats to their integrity and independence and erupt in episodic rage.[1] Still others experience little stress in prison and evidence consuming interest in programs, legal work, or maintaining ties with the outside world.

A second, less obvious but clearly visible, feature of prison behavior is that most of it takes place in restricted prison subsettings. In part, subsetting differentiation in prison is attributable to clear and dramatic differences in prisoner responses to stress. Some subsettings are designed or administratively controlled so that prisoners are insulated from some environmental stimuli and exposed to others. Segregation cells provide privacy and safety. Honor companies provide amenities, larger cells, and increased lock-out time. Hospital units provide environmental prostheses and, for old and invalid prisoners, offer a respite from exposure to the young and vigorous. Purposively prosthetic environments are rare in prison, however. Formal administrative intervention on behalf of special-needs prisoners is also uncommon. More frequently, prisoners will survey the settings available to them and select those most congruent with their needs. A job in the law library provides time and resources to pursue legal work. A hall porter job secures maximum out-of-cell time and minimal surveillance. An officers' quarters clerical job provides high levels of supervision and maximum safety.

The phenomenon of subsetting variation has been identified in numerous studies of prison life (Cloward, 1960, pp. 20-48; Glaser, 1969, pp. 170-171; Goffman, 1961, pp. 219-222; Heffernan, 1972, p. 165; Sykes, 1971, pp. 87-95; Williams & Fish, 1974). Several empirical studies have also documented the role of prison subenvironments in mediating prison stress (Glaser, 1969, pp. 88-90; Moos, 1975; Wilson & Snodgrass, 1969, pp. 472-478). However, subsetting differentiation has been mentioned almost parenthetically, or stereotypically. Prison subsettings are viewed as arenas in which prisoners act out their roles as merchant, politician, mafioso, or even rat. Traditional portraits of prisoner adaptation have been concerned with depicting the "workable assignment," with jobs that permit access to contraband and to power, with connivers and swagging in the foreground. When the focus switches to the physical environment, prison subsettings have been viewed in an even less differentiated fashion. In large part, studies of prison environments have focused on the prison itself, and on generic and plausibly painful environmental stressors such as noise, density, levels of staffing, and degress of sanitation (Benton & Obenland, 1973; Nagel, 1973; Flynn, 1976, pp. 115-129).

Neither focus is entirely misplaced. In typing the kinds of transactions prisoners describe within prison settings, we have located a small but distinct group of prisoners who were interested primarily in participating in the illegitimate prison opportunity system, and whose environmental concerns revolved about acquiring what power, wealth, and status was available in prison at reasonable personal risk. And the climates of prisons are indeed sensitive to gross levels of resources and to accompanying problems of crowding, understaffing, and deteriorating services (see Chapters 3-5). Under sufficiently irresponsible management and sufficiently life-threatening prison conditions, the institutional environment may be virtually deterministic in its effect on levels of unhappiness and violence within the prison.

However, most prison systems are not so managed, or at least not most of the time. And most prisoners' day-to-day concerns do not revolve around status, power, or honor in the prison world. Rather, prisons are living environments that confine a variety of people, held in a stressful though largely habitable and differentiated environment that presents varying potentials for the expression and inhibition of personal needs. Although the arenas that prison provides for action are, in free-world terms, small, poorly equipped, and frequently threatening, they are of remarkable variability. This variability, if translated into recognizable sets of environmental attributes, has important implications for human survival in prison. What makes prison *stressful* is a function of the individual's needs for autonomy, safety, self-expression, and personal growth in an environment not primarily designed to provide for them. And what makes prison stress *manageable* is the tendency of people to create or find a suitable match within the larger environment and to assert freedom, garner safety, and find outlets for self-expression.

Our research has indicated that prisons may be best conceived as mosaics of smaller subsettings, which are not primarily differentiated by levels of material comforts or prisoner-attributed prestige, but which reflect varying emphases on sets of ecological dimensions. Toch (1977) has extracted some dimensions salient to prisoners and has defined them as freedom (from restrictions, circumscription of conduct), safety (from physical violence), privacy (from social and physical overstimulation), structure (environmental stability and predictability), support (programs and services that facilitate self-improvement), emotional feedback (love, appreciation, caring), and activity (distraction, filling up time). These dimensions, distilled from prisoner interviews, are transactional in that they represent not only important characteristics of the prison environment but the environmental preferences of their inhabitants. They represent the prisoners' understanding of the kind of life they may be able to live in prison, as well as the objective setting characteristics they see.

The extraction of these dimensions permitted us to begin to explore the concept of congruence, or the fit of prisoners with heightened environmental preferences to settings with corresponding salient ecological dimensions. We developed a typology of human-environmental transactions in small-scale prison settings using male prisoners' assessment of felt stress and their perceptions of those prison living, work, or program assignments that proved most important as influences on stress (Seymour, 1980). One type of transaction, in which the prisoner perceives his setting as ameliorative, was designated as "niche."[1] Niches include a graduated range of subsettings, from carefully selected informal housing, program, and work assignments to supportive and creative oases for inmates who lack the competence to survive in more informal settings. As we use the term niche it is a perceptual construct, involving a prisoner with imported skills, interests, and liabilities, and a prison setting that represents the self-assessed optimal solution to the problems and preferences of that prisoner. It is the ameliorative transaction, with the setting providing relief from fears and concerns rooted in situation-aggravated vulnerabilities, that gives the setting its essential quality and its meaning as niche. Niches can be detected for any ecological dimension, although niches for safety, freedom, and privacy are the most common.

AN EXAMPLE OF AN INFORMAL NICHE: SETTINGS FOR FREEDOM

The most commonly expressed environmental preference of prisoners is, not surprisingly, for freedom. Almost 40 percent of prisoners expressed a dominant concern for freedom. Although not as ubiquitous as freedom expression itself, autonomy niches were common. Almost 30 percent of detected niches were niches for freedom. This finding was surprising to us. We had expected autonomy expression to be largely antithetical to prison adjustment. Stressed freedom concerns might, we hypothesized, result in frustration, episodic rage, and sequestration of prisoners in harsh and deprived prison segregation units. However, the prevalence of freedom concerns also suggests that the prison must accommodate them in some fashion. After all, the prison must be managed, the industry program must produce goods, the flower beds must be cleaned, breakfast prepared, the lid kept on. Some prisoners are provided considerable autonomy within the walls as an adjunct to their prison jobs, and staff similarly temper rules and surveillance to stimulate compliant behavior.

Autonomy niches are settings that reduce the sources of formal control, in which egalitarian staff-prisoner communication is encouraged, or in which the formal disciplinary machinery is deemphasized. Additional characteristics of settings that assuage stressed freedom concerns include enhanced freedom of movement, the ability to choose or reject participation in activities, or the degree to which such settings reflect the free and open life of the streets. Ameliorative characteristics of such settings also include other physical and social resources that permit the displacement, camouflage, or even expression of resentment.

Several common themes arise in prisoner descriptions of autonomy niches. The most frequently mentioned characteristic of a setting that is ameliorative of stressed freedom concerns is physical distance from sources of freedom restriction. Prison assignments are preferred if they facilitate the avoidance of officers, particularly officers who are perceived as asserting control in ways that threaten prisoners' personal dignity. Staff often collaborate with prisoners in creating positions in which the security apparatus is not as apparent or as pervasive as in most areas of the prison. Such settings typically are beyond the prison security perimeter, on outside gangs, farms, gate crews, gardening crews. Outside the prison walls mutual avoidance is easier, with officers overlooking events and behaviors that would mandate intervention within the prison. Horseplay and boisterous behavior are less problematic and out of place in the milieu outside the walls. For example:

> [On the farm] you don't have people telling you all the time to do this and do that and you can have time to just sit down and relax out there. It is a lot better outside on the farm than it is inside. . . . I was kept inside for three months, and I got into all kinds of trouble. See outside the time goes by faster and there ain't nobody out there always nagging you.

For many prisoners, the pervasiveness of supervision may not be as critical a concern as the manner in which supervision is exercised. Freedom-concerned prisoners can make gross distinctions among supervisory styles, and often describe supervision as inflexible, inconsistent, and frequently inhumane. On the other hand, an officer or supervisor may be described as a rare exception, and as "all right."

> I admit that, when I first came in here, I had the idea that the police was like the Gestapo. And I had a lot of trouble. When they finally kicked me out of school I met an officer who was different. Like in the block he would talk to me, and he would be really pulling for me to straighten myself out. Now this don't happen every day here, but this guy was pulling for me. And it made a difference.

Occasionally, the administration does include the inmate's sensitivity to stressed freedom concerns as part of its classification agenda. In several work and program assignments in various prisons, prisoners who are labeled intransigents are trained and supervised by supervisors who both understand the limits of their charges and are relaxed in the face of their occasional hostility. Work supervisors can more commonly provide flexible supervision than can officers, because supervisors can establish a work-place milieu. Work supervisors have a clearly defined training role that permits leniency without a violation of norms requiring impersonal relations with the prisoners. One such supervisor comments:

> I try to keep a low-pressure environment without losing control. They know where the line is drawn, but I also tell them there is a reason why I enforce it. The work [foundry] is decent and it is acceptable, and there is such a thing as pride in doing hard and at times somewhat dangerous work. And for this reason this degree of pride that they exhibit in what they are doing helps to perpetuate this kind of low-pressure setting. . . . I have a lot of success with the particular type of inmate, the one who can't seem to fit in, who gets into trouble all the time. I don't let myself be taken in by the horseplay and the screwing up. These men have a low opinion of themselves and it's necessary to correct that.

An inmate comments:

> Brick mason is a shop where you can learn something. The instructor will teach you. Like I had a lot of problems before, but this guy is good, it's like going to work. . . . My instructor, he will come to each individual and show him how to lay the foundation and how to start a project and he is all right. He doesn't push nobody and as long as everybody gives him respect,

> you know, he will respect us. That is the way I believe more of the officers should treat you.

A third theme that emerged from ameliorative transactions described by freedom-stressed prisoners is that of mobility. Most prisoners cannot walk unimpeded through a maximum security prison for even short distances. Officers continually interrupt such movement to check the legitimacy of a prisoner's presence. Settings that permit relatively free movement through the prison are prized as liberating. Inmates with institutional passes, such as runners, clerks, and maintenance workers, find that mobility allows a more varied prison life. Such prisoners can move about, interact with fellow prisoners, and reduce their restlessness and boredom.

> A lot of the time you might have a whole lot of hostility build up because you got to stay in one place and you don't have anything to do. But this way [as an administrative runner] you can move around. You have access to all the blocks, and you can see people when you want, and nobody bothers you.

Choice itself, the freedom just to choose an activity, however mundane, is also described as an ameliorative influence. Although classification procedures accommodate some inmate requests for housing, work, or program assignments, they do so idiosyncratically. Transfers to new housing areas or jobs may at one time reflect the personal needs of the prisoners and at other times reflect such criteria as security rating, educational attainment, and time to release. Where actions and settings are so controlled, even small self-chosen acts may take on ameliorative properties.

> It's one of the few places where I can do what I want [cell porter]. It's little things that I like. I can do my job, without anyone always harassing me. I can relax. I don't like to be told what to do. I like to choose what I like to do, and all I do is sweep the tier and nobody ever tells me anything. I'm pretty free here.

In its most extreme form, demands for freedom may not be satisfied by such setting characteristics. There are some prisoners who have experienced extreme trauma with parental, school, and criminal justice authorities such that they see themselves constantly challenged, disrespected, and humiliated. They may, in turn, reciprocate by refusing casual officer requests, performing work perfunctorily or not at all, or baiting or goading authority figures. Their world is one in which constant freedom striving is required, and yet is doomed by the backlash it invites. Brehm and Sensenig (1976) and Heilman and Toffler (1976) have postulated a state of "psychological reactance" that defines a motivation state aimed at expressing and maximizing freedoms that are threatened. In settings in which prisoners pay the price of reactance, they experience significant trade-offs, often losing activity, wages, good time, and parole eligibility. However, some freedom-concerned prisoners still perceive ostensibly low-freedom settings as ameliorative. Settings such as disciplinary segregation, idle companies, and mental observation units reinforce a prisoner's self-image as special and hence autonomous.

> I'm in here [idle] for not giving up. . . . They tried to force this job on me. So they come out and told me that I got to take this, but I don't want to take this. So when you don't want it they put you down here. . . . I do not want to work. They say, "Take this," and why should I? I want to do what's beneficial to me. What I want, not what they want. So I'll stay here.
>
> [Segregation] I don't want to submit. I don't want the administrators to think that they are doing something for me. . . . If you have these jobs and things then you put yourself in these positions. Then they can control you.

Although some freedom-oriented prisoners perceive special housing units to be an honorable and adaptive mode of adjustment, for most prisoners segregation is not a niche, but rather intensifies qualities of the prison experience that they find stressful. The milieu is uncompromisingly custodial and communication within it is absent or disturbingly one-sided. However, for the small group of prisoners with special freedom concerns, such settings provide opportunities to advertise defiance to the prison world and to express an honorable volatility that allows the inmates to view themselves as feared and righteous.

A final theme that emerged from interviews with freedom-concerned prisoners is that of "normalcy." Prisoners concerned with freedom frequently seek settings that are most reminiscent of the streets and least evocative of confinement. This characteristic is a gestalt including combinations of the ameliorative themes we have already mentioned. In "normal" settings prisoners can follow their own pace, choose their activities, risk spontaneity, shed careful self-control, and marshal amenities for relaxation. Although prisoners might occupy such settings for only a short time during the day, the settings are often described as providing an important respite from the surrounding abnormality of prison life.

> When your work is done you can sit around the shack [coal gang] and you can talk and play cards and be human. That is the good thing about it. It is a general thing—you can go out there and do your time and be away from everybody. And you don't have to worry about the harassment, the hassle of being in line and so forth. We don't work in formation or anything and, well, we cook out there. I mean we have a hot plate, a coffee pot. It is more like, you know, you are on a job and you can do as you please.

Our review of setting characteristics related to freedom concerns illustrates that prisons are complex environments providing a surprising array of settings, staff, and prisoner resources. Characteristics of settings that resonate to the concerns of the freedom-stressed prisoner include the opportunity to avoid officers or to elect supervision from particular officers. Other characteristics include the ability to advertise autonomy through reactance, or to experience it through choice, mobility, or normalcy. Occasionally the niches are stumbled into by sensitized prisoners who recognize them for what they are. Less frequently, niches represent a collaborative effort by staff and prisoners to create a reasonably tolerable way of life for both. Even officers who otherwise eschew a treatment role assist prisoners in acquiring a better fit with the prison. Such assistance is most dramatically revealed in the creative construction of shelters and isolated settings for the fearful prisoner in search of safety. Yet, even with respect to freedom, the prison provides a measure of tolerance and accommodation. Authorities alter custodial routines, modulate surveillance, and orchestrate assignments for the sole purpose of enhancing adjustment. They do so unsystematically, irregularly, and without a clear sense of the ecological factors being manipulated. The fact that they do so at all, however, suggests that officers frequently recognize a human service component to their job (see Chapter 17), and that environmental variables can be manipulated naturally and effectively by those familiar with a setting.

FORMAL NICHES

Informal niches are naturally occurring subenvironments. Although prisoners in such niches engage in a creative process by perceiving and then organizing elements of their surroundings into a passable way to live, the raw materials for the niche are largely available to all. And although staff occasionally assist in the niche search and creation process, these informal subenvironments are not defined by the administration as ameliorative. If staff view their efforts as interventionist at all, they see themselves as simply assigning the prisoner to a place where he might settle down.

Formal niches, or institution-maintained special settings, however, also exist and are most readily apparent in assignments of some prisoners with skewed safety concerns. Many such prisoners find relief from fear in mainline prison settings, but a sizable group does not. For the latter, the process of orientation and environmental manipulation that characterizes niche search and creation may demand too much. Or they may find coping in even the safest mainline prison setting too dangerous. Ultimately, safety-concerned prisoners are ushered into occupational-vocational rehabilitation units, special tiers for the physically weak or socially immature, therapeutic communities, and traditional protection units in special housing galleries. (A less restrictive approach to reducing fear is described in Chapter 15.) These settings, which can be defined as "formal niches," are far less numerous than informal niches. They are designed for subpopulations with relatively dramatic vulnerabilities and for those for whom the mainline prison environment does not provide a reasonable refuge.

An Example: A Formal Niche for the Elderly and Handicapped

One special subpopulation of prisoners often requiring special supports in prison is that of the aged and invalid offender. Even in the free world, retirement and old age often result in a decrement of environmental control (Eisdorfer & Lawton, 1973; Lawton, 1974). In addition to problems created by physical decline, special problems in adjustment can be caused by the situations in which the old and invalid find themselves. Schulz and Aderman (1973) have demonstrated that erratic or isolative behaviors of elderly patients in institutions often derive from feelings of helplessness resulting from personal failures at mastery caused or aggravated by environmental barriers to control. Lowered personal expectations and inadequate environmental structures combine with individual liabilities to hasten passivity and decline. Seligman (1975) has cited cases in which old age and institutionalized helplessness have resulted in precipitous death among otherwise healthy individuals.

In prisons, environmental barriers and a modal population of young, vigorous offenders often aggravate the disabilities of the elderly or handicapped offender. Bergman and Amir (1973) claim, for example, that the physical and mental condition of aged offenders deteriorates rapidly in prison. They note that younger, aggressive prisoners often frighten, ridicule, or harm older prisoners. Older prisoners are described as disproportionately likely to become depressed and dependent on staff for support. Studies by Adams and Vedder (1961), Baier (1961), and Barrett (1972) have also emphasized that the older prisoner is presented with unique problems of adjustment in prison, which require special attention.

Relatively speaking, older prisoners are much more likely to express a concern for structure and predictability than are younger prisoners (Toch, 1977, pp. 248-249). Some older prisoners find a significant degree of stress amelioration in informal niches, in settings with other prisoners whose behavior is defined as "mature," noninterfering, and predictable. The settings are usually described as providing environmental clarity and insulation from ambiguous, excessively novel, or conflicting demands. Although some elderly and handicapped prisoners are found in such informal niches and others are left in settings that possess no ameliorative properties, a large percentage of elderly offenders in New York several years ago were confined in a formal niche, in a separate institution in the lower Hudson Valley. This facility was designed to provide environmental clarity and consistency for the "elderly and handicapped" prisoner. In large part, the facility succeeded, since prisoners confined in it perceived it to be significantly ameliorative. Nearly all prisoners praised the setting as undemanding yet safe. Its routine provided lengthy periods for rest and relaxation during the day, considerable privacy, and many opportunities for withdrawal, in a homogeneous and therefore controlled setting. Socially, prisoners highlighted the lack of a youthful group in the unit, the nonideological and temperate climate, and the paucity of strong or violent prisoners. The population is generally described as quiet, small, and self-contained, so that elderly prisoners can live without fear.

Three major themes emerged from prisoners' descriptions of ameliorative transactions with this setting. The first theme is that of disengagement. This theme is reminiscent of a prominent theory of gerontology that maintains that under normal life conditions there is a mutual withdrawal between an aging person and other people, leading to a new and positively valued life-cycle equilibrium. Successful disengagement is viewed as a correlate of adaptation rather than as a societally imposed casting off of the useless (Cumming & Henry, 1961). Freedom from obligations, a simplified and structured life, and a conservation of interests and energies combine to make withdrawal harmonious and secure. The prison setting in New York, with its emphasis on minimal programs, self-directed behavior, and a placid, stable, and orderly milieu, supports and encourages this sort of adaptive disengagement. In the words of one inmate:

> I was very old and I was taking it easy, and resting, anytime I want. Which in prison you can't accomplish so easily, you know. And there is no waiting for eating. In prison, if you ate anything, the regulations and rules, standing at the line and waiting to be served, and all the pushing and haggling and arguing, as they are always doing in a crazy house. All that was finished. All you have to do here is go anywheres you want, without surveillance of any kind.

Prisoners' concerns for finding and following the path of least resistance are met by staff willingness to place as few obstacles in that path as possible. The prisoner is permitted the individuation of childhood again, even if the behaviors are dependent, passive, or withdrawing.

> I don't do much, mostly read a little. I don't write to anyone or anything, I don't have any family anyway. I do what elderly people do. Sometimes I play a game of checkers. Now I don't work, that's all behind me. I'm taking it easy here; this is the only place I've run across where they let me. The officers you know. It's the best place for older people, like a nursing home.

Disengagement involves a simplified life and a reduction of tension through the minimizing of interactions. But it requires safety and structure for its success. In an unpredictable environment disengagement can be maladaptive. Under such conditions, a response may be withheld or delayed to the point where an elderly person has no control over potentially dangerous environmental forces. A prosthetic environment for social disengagement provides not only freedom but structure and safety. Virtually all prisoners in the setting we refer to have served time in traditional prison environments and describe safety as a major source of satisfaction with the setting.

> Clinton, now there's a tough place. It's for the young inmates mostly. They are all talking about the same thing and they don't let you alone . . . there's always one or two who give you trouble, and at this stage all I want is to avoid trouble. I'm past that old ball-busting stage. . . . I'm here, I'm treated ok, and I don't want to have nothing to do with anybody. Here you can do that. . . . I can't do anything at my age, anyway. I like Nick Carter and mystery books, and they have movies here I can get to. In prison I used to avoid the movies, they were too dangerous and messed

up. Here it is like being put out to pasture. I can sit in the wards and the hallways and the kids don't harass me.

Not only are elderly prisoners disengaged from activities, staff, and the outside world, but they are disengaged from mainline prisoners as well. They are alienated from the mores and values of youth, and while some youthful prisoners in traditional prisons avoid the elderly, others either antagonize or patronize them. The desires of older prisoners for withdrawal and social simplification are frequently perceived by younger prisoners as passivity and moral compromise. Young prisoners, as young men, have fewer investments and commitments, are often less secure with themselves as men, and hence are more prone to seek rather than to avoid trouble (Jensen, 1977; Johnson, 1966). Age homogeneity in the elderly and handicapped unit is perceived by prisoners as allowing them to do time undisturbed, with fellow prisoners who are similarly inclined.

People here are all old, and very polite to one another, and friendly, and everybody gets along. But like at Green Haven, the young guys they all got their own attitude, and they are jumpy. If you just look at them they get nervous and jump off, like they had to prove themselves every day. It is very dangerous in the penitentiary, not at all like here.

A second theme reflecting satisfaction with the setting is that of convalescence. Poor health and old age not only stimulate disengagement, but are themselves liabilities in prison. In traditional prison settings, the old and the invalid are housed on the "flats," the ground-level tier. Those with serious and chronic health problems may be housed permanently in a prison hospital, or in an invalid company. Prison health care is often of low quality, though, and bureaucratic needs combined with suspicions of malingering present obstacles to the ill in obtaining what care is available. The formal niche represents the most generous and comprehensive response to the physical health problems faced by the elderly in prisons. In the elderly and handicapped unit, all nonambulatory prisoners live on the ground floor. The dining hall and visiting room are located conveniently, proximate to the living units, and rooms and corridors are designed without major security obstructions. A vocational rehabilitation counselor is available to provide assistance and therapy to the prisoners, nurses are on duty at all hours, and a physician visits the facility daily. A number of prisoner aides, trained to perform nursing and therapeutic tasks, assist in bathing the elderly, with meals, with the transportation of the nonambulatory, and other related tasks.

The setting also provides physical prostheses ranging from well-lighted and pleasant rooms and wheel chair ramps to geriatric-use bathrooms, and kitchens designed for easy and nontaxing use. The physical limits of old age are recognized in a way they cannot be in the inflexible and case-hardened environments of traditional prisons. Accessible dispensaries and infirmaries adjacent to individual rooms provide health care and reassurance. Many prisoners wait at the infirmary to talk with nurses or to meet with the physician even though they have no urgent medical problem.

> The nurses are cheerful and helpful. . . . In prison, just to get on sick call is a big deal, dropping slips and all. Most of us go on sick call (they don't call it sick call here, it's always open) every day. . . . It's nice to see a doctor, maybe there's something new for arthritis, and we sit and talk with the nurses. It makes me feel good knowing they are here.

A final theme illustrating ameliorative transactions of the prisoners with the setting revolves about the degree of community found in the unit. Disengagement does not call for solitude. Aging has been described as a process leading to a decrease in the number and variety of attachments, but an increase in intensity of bonds based on similarities and common sentiments (Cumming, 1963). Prisoners who have few family members with whom to correspond and little useful work of interest find that participation in informal friendship groups is important. Such prisoners find either a single confederate or a small group with similar value systems with whom to associate.

> If you want a discussion on an intellectual level you can find some people here. If you want a discussion on a political level you can find people here. If you want to play any games, which are more or less entertaining, like chess or checkers or pinochle or bridge, you find the people here. There are enough chess players here, or bridge players. . . . You can't find this in another institution.

Not all prisoners like the elderly and handicapped unit, and those prisoners who like the unit do not always like all its characteristics. Disengagement can mean a slipping into passivity and inactivity that some prisoners find wasteful. Convalescence may encourage dependency on health care that can create a negative perception of unambiguously good services. Cultural compatibility for most may result in stress for the few different prisoners, for whom the setting was not designed. Prisoners who express greatest dissatisfaction with the setting are youthful, albeit disabled, prisoners who find themselves in a world of relative inactivity, in which cooperation between staff and prisoners is an integral dimension of the social environment. However, with few exceptions even these prisoners perceive the environment as less stressful, more privileged, and less intrusive than any previously experienced in prison. The program is seen as a predictable island of permissiveness in which the elderly are allowed to retire to their rooms to read, or go to the yard to harvest tomatoes, or to walk, and to make their daily morning journey to the pharmacist or doctor without administrative hurdles.

IMPLICATIONS

Prison stress consists of a judgment on the part of the prisoner that his experiences with the environment involve the possibility of harm or loss. Stress is common because the physical environment is designed to frustrate free-world needs and contains unfamiliar possibilities of harm. Stress, in turn, conditions a prisoner's response to the environment and determines what stress-reducing potentials reflected there will be seen as meaningful. But these meanings differ. The referents of stress may include the extent and quality of supervision, the degree to which the setting is open to outsiders, its racial composition and culturally determined climate, the kinds of activities permitted or banned. Prisoners sort themselves out, and if they are sufficiently competent, they locate settings that are most congruent with their needs and ameliorative of stress. Such settings, niches, reflect for a particular prisoner faced with particular problems of living a specifically identifiable subsetting that the prisoner perceives as providing reasonable solutions to his problems and a significant degree of stress amelioration.

Not all stressed prisoners locate niches. A prisoner may carry a carefully husbanded rage from subsetting to subsetting, finding no relief. Some prisoners expect the worst from custody, assist in confirming their expectations, and are placed in punitive, alienating, or claustrophobic settings. A prisoner traumatized by a sexual approach in reception company may view the prison world in an understandably undifferentiated fashion, and such a prisoner may see all refuges as temporary and fragile. Similarly, a prisoner facing a life sentence or an imminent divorce may find subsettings only marginally relevant to his most important concerns.

The prevalence and variety of niches in prisons suggests that ameliorative transactions in subsettings are far from epiphenomenal. The existence of substantial residual stress among inmates does not necessarily suggest that prison is seriously and irremedially stressful, but instead may tell us that some resources go unallocated or are allocated to the wrong prisoners. Settings with dramatically ameliorative properties go unrealized because they are preempted by the strong and resilient who prize the settings because they provide personal growth, cultural revival, easy time, privileges, or other commodities unrelated to stress reduction. Moreover, niche search and niche creation are not nurtured or even recognized in organizational policy and practice. Some prison staff, as shown in Chapter 17, are aware of the existence of differentially ameliorative settings and of variegated prison stress. In many informal niches, there is a considerable degree of staff collaboration in, or tacit acceptance of, ameliorative setting properties. But most prison staff are unaware of the ease with which they could create humane environments in tough places, and of the stress-reducing supervisory styles prevalent among some of their peers (Johnson & Price, 1981).

In training, prison staff can be sensitized to the ecological dimensions of prison life. This does not require a therapeutic or exceedingly esoteric curriculum. Such training can simply use the officer's own perceptions and experiences to highlight the diversity of environmental needs and resources that are characteristic of prisons. What is important is that prison staff acquire a sensitivity to environmental effects and a perspective that permits an identification of hidden or subliminal impacts felt by the users of a setting. With such a perspective officers can begin to view their own supervisory styles, availability, and skills as resources within the prison environment and as important facilitators of prison coping. As both users and primary manipulators of prison settings, prison staff can be more aware of the social climates that persist in places, and of the referents of stress and stress reduction. The increased involvement of staff serves both to realize staff's capabilities and interests and to institutionalize niches for inmates. It could reduce often ritualized and extreme solutions, such as segregation placement. Informal niches are more varied and immediate and are solutions that involve the imagination of line staff. For instance, qualities such as staff concern are particularly important to prisoners seeking emotional feedback, the softness and subtlety of supervision is a major preoccupation of freedom-concerned prisoners, and a protective and paternalistic stance is an issue for prisoners concerned about physical safety. Staff, playing roles as diverse as friend-protector or laissez-faire and respect-emphasizing supervisor, elicit counterpart roles played by prisoners with corresponding concerns.

It is this environmental sensitization that provides the bridge between stress amelioration and community, though niche creation begets its own problems. Niches are often creative and imaginative, but they are not always adaptive. They may include settings that permit the expression of chronic resentment or provide insulation from both threat and challenge. It is evident that some niche inhabitants make intentional and unintentional trade-offs to secure perceived stress reduction. Safety entails sacrificing activity and support, freedom requires self-reliance and a sacrifice of dependency benefits (feedback), and most formal (and some informal) niches in which staff-assistance is most manifest include a measure of stigma. Prisoners frequently view obvious self-classificatory efforts as weakness. Settings formally designated for the uncontrollable, the weak, and other special-need prisoners are often viewed as hiding places. But the dangers of overly insulated and stigmatizing special classification are minimized if the implications of niches are extended to everyone. When staff view the challenge of facilitating adjustment through encouraging environmental fit as a primary job responsibility, they recognize and legitimate human differences and make helping activities more routine (Johnson & Price, 1981). There is a payoff for both staff and prisoners in participating in the management of prisons as humane environments, because both have a stake in ensuring safe, flexible, responsive, and controlled prison settings.

NOTE

1. The categories of subsetting-prisoner transactions are distinguishable along two dimensions: (1) the degree of stress experienced by the prisoner during the imprisonment and (2) the degree of satisfaction felt by the prisoner with the subsetting. "Benign transactions" are those in which relatively unstressed prisoners viewed the setting as providing easy time, benefits, or possibilities for growth and involvement; "mismatched transactions" are those that stressed prisoners find either irrelevant or harmful; "environmental indifference" occurs where nonstressed prisoners find the subsetting unimportant (Seymour, 1980, pp. 146-152).

REFERENCES

Adams, M., & Vedder, C. Age and crime: Medical and sociological characteristics of prisoners over 50. *Geriatrics*, 1961, 16. 177-180.

Baier, G. The aged inmate. *American Journal of Corrections*, 1961, 23, 4-34.

Barrett, J. Aging and delinquency. In J. Barrett, *Gerontological psychology*. Springfield, IL: Charles C Thomas, 1972.

Benton, F. W., & Obenland, R. *Prison and jail security*. Urbana, IL: National Clearinghouse for Criminal Justice Planning and Architecture, 1973.

Bergman, S., & Amir, M. Crime and delinquency among the aged in Israel. *Israel Annals of Psychiatry and Related Disciplines*, 1973, 10, 33-48.

Brehm, J., & Sensenig, J. Social influence as a function of attempted and implied usurpation of choice. *Journal of Personality and Social Psychology*, 1976, 4, 703-707.

Cloward, R. Social control in the prison. In R. Cloward et al., *Theoretical studies in social organization in the prison*. New York: Social Sciences Research Council, 1960.

Cumming, E. Further thoughts on the theory of disengagement. *International Social Science Journal*, 1963, 15, 377-393.

Cumming, E., & Henry, W. *Growing Old*. New York: Basic Books, 1961.

Eisdorfer, C., & Lawton, M. P. (Eds.). *The psychology of adult development and aging*. Washington, DC: American Psychological Association, 1973.

Flynn, E. The ecology of prison violence. In A. Cohen, G. Cole, & R. Bailey (Eds.), *Prison violence*. Lexington, MA: D. C. Heath, 1976.

Glaser, D. *The effectiveness of a prison and parole system*. Indianapolis: Bobbs-Merrill, 1969.

Goffman, E. *Asylums: Essays on the social situation of mental patients and other inmates*. Garden City, NY: Doubleday, 1961.

Heffernan, E. *Making it in prison: The square, the cool and the life*. New York: John Wiley, 1972.

Heilman, M., & Toffler, B. Reacting to reactance: An interpersonal interpretation of the need for freedom. *Journal of Experimental Social Psychology*, 1976, 12, 519-529.

Jensen, G. Age and rule-breaking in prison: A test of sociocultural interpretations. *Criminology*, 1977, 14, 555-568.

Johnson, E. Pilot study: Age, race and recidivism as factors in prison infractions. *Canadian Journal of Corrections*, 1966, 8, 268-283.

Johnson, R., & Price, S. The complete correctional officer: Human service and the human environment of prison. *Criminal Justice and Behavior*, 1981, 8(3), 343-373.

Lawton, M. P. Social ecology and the health of older people. *American Journal of Public Health*, 1974, 64, 257-260.

Moos, R. *Evaluating correctional and community settings*. New York: John Wiley, 1975.

Nagel, W. *The new red barn: A critical look at the modern American prison*. New York: Walker, 1973.

Schulz, R., & Aderman, D. Effects of residential change on the temporal distance of death of terminal cancer patients. *Omega, Journal of Death and Dying*, 1973, 4, 157-162.

Seligman, M. *Helplessness: On depression, development and death*. San Francisco: Freeman, 1975.

Seymour, J. *Niches in prison: Ameliorative environments within maximum-security correctional institutions*. Unpublished doctoral dissertation, State University of New York—Albany, 1980.

Sykes, G. *The society of captives: A study of a maximum security prison.* Princeton, NJ: Princeton University Press, 1971.

Toch, H. *Living in prison: The ecology of survival.* New York: Free Press, 1977.

Williams, V., & Fish, M. *Convicts, codes and contraband: The prison life of men and women.* Cambridge, MA: Ballinger, 1974.

Wilson, J., & Snodgrass, J. The prison code in a therapeutic community. *Journal of Criminal Law, Criminology and Police Science*, 1969, 60, 472-478.

CHAPTER 17

Alleviating Inmate Stress

CONTRIBUTIONS FROM CORRECTIONAL OFFICERS

LUCIEN X. LOMBARDO

In the closed world of the prison, the person who wears the uniform of the correctional officer carries within him or her the potential for helping inmates and alleviating inmate stress as well as the potential for abusing inmates and creating stress. Throughout the 200-year history of prisons in America, however, it has been extremes of the latter potential that have captured public, legal, and academic interest. From Elam Lynds's penchant for the whip exhibited at Auburn Prison of the 1830s (de Beaumont & de Tocqueville, 1964, pp. 162-163), to the tortures of Arkansas (Holt v. Sarver, 1970), to the abuses inflicted upon inmates at Attica (New York State Special Commission on Attica, 1972), guards have been portrayed as the natural antagonists of inmates.

Sociological studies of prison communities have emphasized the guards' role in the maintenance of order, the containment of conflict, and the exercise of power (Sykes, 1958; Mathiesen, 1965). These studies recognize the guards' contribution to inmate stress by focusing on the "pains of imprisonment" inherent in prison organization and the guards' general contribution to the "custodial regime." Indeed, the famous simulated prison experiment conducted at Stanford University reportedly found in the guards' role the inherent "pathology of power" and the ever-present potential for abuse of power (Haney et al., 1977).

Though the abuses of correctional officer authority cannot be denied, they form but part of the more complex relationship between the correctional officer and the genesis of inmate stress, a relationship that is gaining more attention as the prison is explored as a human environment within which, and with which, guards and prisoners interact (Toch, 1977; Johnson & Price, 1981; Lombardo, 1981). In this environment correctional officers carry out their mundane day-to-day duties, encountering opportunities to ameliorate as well as enhance the stress experienced by inmates.

PERSPECTIVES ON CORRECTIONAL OFFICERS AND INMATE STRESS

In the human environment of prison, relationships between guards and inmates may be examined from two general perspectives. First, guards and inmates may be studied as representatives of groups: "the guard" and "the inmate." Here the relationship between the *average guard* and the *average inmate* affects *average amounts* and *types* of stress inmates experience. Alternatively, one may focus on individual guards and their interactions with individual inmates. Here the guard's ability to increase or reduce inmate stress experienced at a personal level becomes salient. Sykes (1958, p. 63) notes this problem and opts for the former perspective. He observes:

> It might be argued that in reality there are as many prisons as there are prisoners—that each man brings to the custodial institution his own needs and his own background and each man takes away from the prison his own interpretation of life within the walls. Yet when we examine the way the inmates . . . perceive the social environments created by the custodians, the dominant fact is the hard core of consensus expressed by the members of the captive population with regard to the nature of their confinement. The inmates are agreed that life in the maximum security prison is depriving or frustrating in the extreme.

However, inmate stress that the individual officer can affect is *not* experienced as a consensus. Though guards as a group may contribute to the overall stressful impact of prison environments on inmates, the fact that guards as guards (not as individuals) cause stress by just being there is not something the individual can change. What individual guards do attempt to control are their immediate environments (a cell block, a work assignment, a section of the yard), their methods of handling inmate problems, and their concern about the needs of inmates with whom they interact. As one guard in a maximum security prison put it:

> The inmates know what I stand for. Not the hard core type program that says things are definitely this way. And I don't say, "Anything is OK with me," either. I feel I allow myself flexibility to handle most situations and still maintain the respect of the inmates around me.

What this officer was defining was his way of reacting to individual inmates and situations he encounters and his own individual style, not his role as guard. The importance of focusing on individual correctional officer styles as variations on a more general theme was noted by Glaser (1969, p. 87):

> The reasons for liking or disliking an official vary with his position. For custodial officers, what seems to have been a trait of fairness and predictability was the major influence upon inmate preference or prejudice, with manner of expression, whether friendly or hostile, next in importance.

FROM CUSTODIAN TO HUMAN SERVICES PROVIDER

The tasks of correctional officers have traditionally been associated with the purposes of the institutions for which they work. This organizationally based perspective tied the guard's duties to such concerns as custody, maintaining internal order, and security. In more progressive institutions, rehabilitation was added to the list (Jacobs, 1975, pp. 6-9). This approach casts the correctional officer in a ministerial role, simply carrying out the tasks assigned by the prison administration.

It is increasingly recognized, however, that the guard's tasks are more complex than previously understood and that they often reach well beyond the limits of formal assignments. It is also more apparent that the motivations and perceptions of the individual officer play an important part in determining "what he (or she) does," extending officer activities into areas formally outside his (or her) domain (Johnson, 1977, 1979). This aspect of the correctional officer's duties has been labeled "providing human services" (Johnson, 1979; Johnson & Price, 1981; Lombardo, 1981).

HUMAN SERVICES VERSUS TREATMENT

As experienced by correctional officers, provision of human services in a prison setting has three major components: (1) providing goods and services for inmates; (2) acting as referral agents or advocates; and (3) contributing to the institutional adjustment of inmates (Lombardo, 1981). Providing inmates with human services should not be confused with providing treatment; these services share characteristics that differentiate them from treatment.

First, *providing services to inmates is generally reactive in nature.* This means that the character of a particular intervention is determined by the needs of the individual inmate involved. It is the inmate who most often initiates the request for help. The officer approaches the situation with no set solution and no predetermined criteria for a successful outcome. A success in human services can be judged only by the consumer of the service. If the inmate is satisfied, it means that he or she feels that the difficulties have been alleviated. Then and only then is service provision a success. Treatment, on the other hand, is generally *proactive.* It is something that every inmate is assumed to need, whether the need is expressed or not. The criteria by which treatment is judged are provided by the service provider, not by the recipient. In treatment, personal inmate problems are not solved until the recipient of the treatment can convince the treater that they are.

In treatment, clients are usually by definition different, deviant or disturbed. They exhibit general characteristics that the treater can diagnose and label. Treatment strategies are often determined by such diagnoses. The correctional officer providing human services, however, does not work with types; *he or she works with individuals,* recognizing and acknowledging the individuality of the inmate experience and reacting to it. In providing human services the correctional officer is flexible and creative, not rigid and ritualistic.

Second, *human services are concerned with the inmate's present state,* his or her here-and-now experience and condition. Whether the inmate becomes a better person in the future, or changes his or her way of life, is largely irrelevant. What matters is that the inmate can live more comfortably in the prison setting, not that he or she learn to adjust to the world in which he or she will live when released.

Finally, when correctional officers provide human services in prison, *they do so outside of, and frequently in opposition to, regulations limiting their formally recognized assignments as guards.* Guards are not treatment personnel; they are not paid to help inmates, nor is the giving of such help expected either by the prison administration or by inmates. As Jacobs (1975, p. 9) observes, "No guard will be reprimanded or dismissed for failure to communicate meaningfully with inmates." The point is that they will not be rewarded for meaningful communication either.

PROVIDING HUMAN SERVICES AND INMATE STRESS

Goods and Services

Some correctional officers see themselves as providers of goods and services who make certain that inmates' basic needs are met. Providing food, clothing, and medication and ensuring cleanliness and quiet dominate such an officer's concerns. Sykes (1958, p. 68) assumed that the prisoners' basic needs for food, clothing, and shelter are usually met, and that the deprivation of goods and services is experienced by inmates in relation to amenities of life and not just its necessities. However, necessities can be differentially provided. Though an inmate does have clothing, clothing wears out. Though inmates are fed regularly, inmates locked in their cells for disciplinary or medical reasons receive their food through arrangements made by officers. Even the extra food and clothing obtained by inmates from the outside must pass through the hands of officers who control the inspection and delivery systems.

In operating distribution services in regular and orderly fashion and not allowing obstacles (even those set up by other officers) to impede inmate access to necessities, officers not only prevent the deprivation of basic goods and services, but they satisfy another inmate concern, a need for structure and organizational stability. As Toch (1977, p. 89) observes:

> Stability is provided by the smooth operation of administrative machinery and formal organizational process. Such organizational stability is important as a protection against arbitrariness.

When an officer promises to intervene on behalf of an inmate who has requested that he or she be allowed to receive his or her prescribed allotment of clothing or shoes, most officers are aware of the importance of keeping their word. As one officer put it, "If you say you'll do something for an inmate and you don't, you're marked. They'll see you every day and know who you are. You're in for trouble." The immediate concern of officers for avoiding trouble from inmates meshes with the concern of inmates for credibility or stability in communication with staff (Toch, 1977, pp. 92-94). Officers who do not "take care of business" or live up to their word create stress in those inmates who need certainty. Officers who do what they promise reduce stress for these inmates by providing guides for action.

One final aspect of the provision of goods and services by correctional officers relates to inmate shelter. Beyond the officer's role in helping to assign inmates to their individual cells, he or she provides an environment in the cell house in which the inmate can live without unwanted and unwarranted intrusions. Here correctional officers have opportunities to deal with stress produced by the lack of privacy, the undesired invasion of personal space by the observations, sounds, and smells of others (Toch, 1977, pp. 27-32). By responding to inmate complaints about "dirty" or "loud" neighbors (8.5 percent of 541 disciplinary reports filed by a sample of 50 officers at Auburn Prison were for "loud talking after the quiet bell"; Lombardo, 1981, p. 94), officers reduce the impact of crowded conditions for those inmates concerned with peace, quite, and sanctity of their living area.

Referral Agent and Advocate

A second aspect of the human service theme involves the correctional officer in the handling of inmate institutional problems. Here the officer aids the inmate in a variety of ways, such as by setting up appointments with counselors or by calling the correspondence office or commissary to check on the status of an inmate account. Though the problems presented to the officer may directly relate to obtaining the goods and services discussed above, or to institutional adjustment problems discussed below, what is important here is that the officer acts as an intermediary, connecting the inmate to the institutional administration. Johnson (1979) discusses the relationship between custodial staff and treatment personnel and the obstacles to their successful collaboration in mobilizing human services resources. In two of New York State's prisons he found that "these resources were, for the most part, sparingly deployed; guards made comparatively few referrals to treatment staff and were in turn rarely called upon to provide assistance to clients" (Johnson, 1979, p. 56). When institutional problems are removed from the treatment context, however, officers appear to be very responsive to inmate requests. At Auburn Prison, 44 percent of a sample of 50 officers interviewed indicated that they become directly involved in solving inmate institutional problems (Lombardo, 1981, p. 64). Block officers and supervisors of work groups generally have more opportunities to respond to such needs. To quote one officer:

> You're dealing with the inmates' everyday problems, money, packages, visits, mail, telephone calls. You've got to call right away and lots of times you can't get the right people. If a guy's borderline, you've got to be careful because he might go into a rage.

In acting as referral agents or advocates, these officers are responding with sensitivity to two sources of stress in inmates: (1) a need for support and (2) a need for autonomy (Toch, 1977, pp. 70-80, 97-122). When one is powerless but still wants the environment to be responsive to one's needs, one often depends on the help of others who have power. By providing a conduit through which inmates can obtain information and services from those charged with delivering them, officers are providing that needed support. Such support not only alleviates the immediate problem, but prevents the accumulation of minor annoyances that may lead to more serious inmate adjustment problems. From this long-term perspective, the officer is providing the inmate with a degree of autonomy, albeit with indirect autonomy. Where inmates know that they are free to approach individual officers with problems, the inmates may feel that their environment is less oppressive.

> I have a lot of inmates come to me with problems. Maybe you call to see how a guy should make arrangements for something. One guy was shaking and upset. He said he was in a big jam and he didn't want to go to the P.K. He gave me a check he'd gotten in the mail. (The people in the correspondence office had overlooked it.) I took the check, gave the guy a receipt and put it in his account. It's not a big thing, just little things to take the edge off. Sometimes if you're helpful you can correct things and save trouble. When they can't handle it, they just swing out.

As Toch (1977, p. 104) has observed, "A key factor in rage is not being able to express rage, plus the knowledge that one is actually *afraid* to act." At least in their relations with officers who are sensitive to such issues, inmates need not be afraid to act when they have problems.

AIDING INSTITUTIONAL ADJUSTMENT

Officers working in cell blocks, industrial shops, or with work gangs of inmates often become aware of inmate family, personal, and mental health problems. In these situations, officers are involved with the same group of inmates on a day-to-day basis, and mutual trust between officers and inmates is more likely to develop. Officers see themselves as psychiatrists, doctors, social workers, or father figures capable of providing inmates with a personally satisfying caring relationship. As Toch (1977, p. 55) observes:

> "Help" here means Feedback. Where staff members respond formally to requests for services, they risk being seen as cold, uncaring or disinterested.

One officer who worked in the Special Housing Unit (segregation) at Auburn Prison demonstrates a keen sensitivity to the stressed inmate's need for a supportive relationship:

> One guy was having problems with his wife and tied a sheet over the bars in the back. He had one foot on the bed and one on the toilet and timed it

> so I was coming around. He didn't want to hang himself. I ran for help and when I came back he was untying the sheet and another officer was folding it up. . . . His wife knew he'd be away for a long time and she was playing around and he couldn't stand that.

In dealing with inmate personal problems and providing feedback, officers are very aware of another inmate concern—the need to have their problems kept confidential. Divulging one's personal weakness to another carries the risk of exposure, and exposure of a personal flaw in prison is likely to subject one to the aggressive overtures of other inmates (Lockwood, 1980). Those officers who do have opportunities to confront inmate stress emanating from personal adjustment difficulties are aware of the consequences of exposure:

> I went by a guy's cell and he was crying. He says for me to go, but if he tips, he might hurt six or seven people. I opened his cell, walked in and started talking to him and got him calmed down. I knew the guy long enough and convinced him good enough to stop crying. He punched the wall four or five times and I talked him into going to sick call and handled it alone. Once you run into a situation like this, don't say anything. Other inmates asked me what was happening when I went by. I told them, "Nothing's going on." You don't spread the word on a thing like that. If the inmate knows this, it takes the edge off and he feels better.

Though human services work performed by correctional officers is generally reactive, there are times, especially in the area of inmate adjustment problems, when officers will take the initiative and attempt to discover if particular inmates in particular circumstances are having difficulties. An officer attuned to unexpressed inmate concerns will go out of his or her way to inquire about an inmate's condition (1) if he or she is somewhat well acquainted with the inmate and (2) if he or she has had an opportunity to observe the inmate in question over a period of time. These conditions allow the officer to inquire into the inmate's condition without invading the inmate's privacy.

TRADITIONAL GUARD FUNCTIONS AND INMATE STRESS

Though the human services aspects of the correctional officer's tasks have an obvious and direct relationship to the expressed needs of inmates, the traditional aspects of the guard's job also have enormous potential for alleviating inmates stress. By providing order and security and by enforcing rules in particular ways, officers may affect inmate experiences with and concerns for physical safety. Officers similarly enhance the predictability of institutional life. They may heighten inmates' perception that they have the ability, in some respects at least, to control their own fate while institutionalized.

The security and rule-enforcement functions of correctional officers are traditionally associated with the creation of stress in inmates by virtue of the limitations they place on autonomy and freedom. However, new perspectives suggest that security and rule-enforcement practices also contribute to providing safe environments, to providing stable and nonarbitrary environments, and to defining the boundaries within which freedom can be exercised (Toch, 1977; Johnson & Price, 1981; Lombardo, 1981). For at least some inmates, these activities are associated with the reduction of stress. As with human services work, it is not the general content of the correctional officer's *role* that matters to the inmate. It is the individual officer's interpretation of that role, and the application of the interpretation to individual situations that affect the inmate's experience of stress.

Security and Inmate Stress

In 1958 Gresham Sykes (p. 78) observed that with

> his expectations concerning the conforming behavior of others destroyed, unable or unwilling to rely on the officials for protection, uncertain of whether or not today's joke will be tomorrow's bitter insult, the prison inmate can never feel safe.

Though little has changed in the last thirty years to alter inmate expectations concerning their safety, recent research has begun to shed some doubt about both the unwillingness of inmates to seek help from staff and the inability of officials to deal with inmate safety needs.

When correctional officers define their tasks with such phrases as "Keep them from killing one another," and "Keep stealing, gambling, and homosexuality to a minimum," they are illustrating their awareness of the positive as well as the negative aspects of controlling inmate behavior. One officer from a maximum security prison displayed such sensitivity to inmate safety concerns when he said:

> Security [in correctional officer work] doesn't mean keep them from going over the wall. It means you try to make the guy feel secure, that he's not going to get killed or hurt. You make it so an inmate can sit next to another inmate in the mess hall or auditorium and feel comfortable. So he doesn't have to worry about something happening.

Lockwood's (1980, p. 130) study of targets and aggressors involved in prison sexual violence reveals that as many as two-thirds of these incidents may be known to the staff, and that as many as one-half of these incidents are reported to staff by inmates. Lockwood (1980, p. 134) points out that staff may intervene by "paying special attention" to men identified as aggressors and to their potential victims. This "special attention" may include the officer's communicating in very subtle ways to potential aggressors that the officer is aware of the aggressor's activities. This communication puts the inmate on notice that more formal action may be taken should the behavior persist (Lombardo, 1981, pp. 84-85).

In addition, correctional officers may informally put other staff on notice about potential problems, especially those staff members who have day-to-day interactions with the inmates involved (Lockwood, 1980, p. 134). Correctional officers may also provide inmates with "niches" (Toch, 1977, pp. 179-205; Lockwood, 1980, p. 136; see also Chapter 16, this volume) where inmates can achieve a greater sense of safety. Here the officer acts as the inmates' advocate, cutting through red tape to make appropriate arrangements. For example, as one officer reports:

> I had a guy two years ago, pacing in the shop all day long. Just before he went to the blocks he said "[officer] put me on the roof" [segregation]. He said he'd kill a guy in the block if he went back. Another guy was trying to pick on him and he's trying to go along with the program and he wouldn't take any more baloney. He was going to prove he's a man, but he wouldn't do it because "it's not worth it for these animals," he said. I called the sergeant and he put him there. He respected me for trusting him and so he told me when he was going to do something. It saved him a new sentence and me a hassle.

Though it is the officer's formal security (order-maintenance) role that is being fulfilled, it is the informal, personal relationship that allows the officer to alleviate the inmate's safety concern.

Rule Enforcement and Inmate Stress

For some correctional officers the difficulties involved in treating inmates fairly are a particularly troublesome part of their work. For others, inconsistencies in departmental and institutional policies, rules, and regulations are seen to cause problems (Lombardo, 1981, p. 114). In citing these difficulties, correctional officers are reacting from their perspective to what inmates perceive as a lack of "structure" in the environment. For inmates, structure means that their environment is dependable from one day to the next, that the people with whom they interact will be predictable, and that communication with important people will be credible (Toch, 1977, pp. 81-96).

There is little that an individual correctional officer can do to improve communication between prison administrators and inmates, especially when he or she feels that the administration's communication with officers is worse than that with inmates (Lombardo, 1981, pp. 125-129). However, by turning to inmates as a source of information and acknowledging the existence of general communication difficulties, the officer may reduce the inmate's feeling that he or she is being singled out for unfair treatment.

That correctional officers do contribute to meeting the inmates' need for structure becomes apparent in the approaches of some officers to their formal rule-enforcement task. In their individual work settings, the blocks, yards, or shop areas, many officers strive for consistency. They make the point that developing mutually understood expectations concerning what is and is not acceptable to them as individuals goes a long way toward alleviating their own (the officers') and the inmates' difficulties. This sometimes involves letting inmates know that decisions that affect them are not being made arbitrarily and offering reasonable explanations to inmate complaints. As an officer in charge of assignments on a work crew reports:

> A new guy comes into the shop, that's where they start. If we get two or three guys at a time, the one with the higher number gets the porter's job. It just so happened that two black guys got the toilet area and a white guy got put up farther. The black guys asked about this. I showed them the number system and they accepted it.

With regard to enforcing specific rules, many officers deal with the inmate perception of unfairness and inconsistency by not relying on formal authority to back up their commands. Many officers feel that minor rules governing inmate behavior are unnecessary and that variations in enforcement strategies from officer to officer must appear unfair to inmates. Others perceive inconsistencies in communication of rules to inmates as well as variations in inmate attention to rules over time. Responding to these concerns, most officers will warn an inmate about a possible violation or just "let him know" there may be a problem (Lombardo, 1981, pp. 87-91), thus giving the inmate the opportunity to respond appropriately. Officers who behave in this way not only remove some of the pressure created by a sometimes chaotic environment, but also informally provide inmates with a degree of freedom to operate within rules that formally limit their autonomy.

FORCES PUSHING GUARDS TO ALLEVIATE INMATE STRESS

Guards who establish helping relationships with inmates do so without formal authority or incentives and are often in opposition to the perceived desires of prison administrators and other officers. The question that needs to be addressed is, why do they establish these relationships? What brings some correctional officers to concern themselves with the problems of inmate stress?

Part of the answer lies in the officer's need to come to terms with the reality of his or her work. Officers often experience a sense of powerlessness within their organization. Since they are not asked to contribute to solving administrative problems, are limited (by directives) to formal handling of inmate behavior, and are excluded from being involved in treatment, many officers find that helping with inmate institutional and adjustment problems becomes the one informal task for which their contributions become meaningful. Inmates also become a "reference group" for some officers, providing officers with validation of their authority and a sense of appreciation for their helping efforts. Helping inmates in trouble often presents a challenge that tests officers' ingenuity in a job that otherwise merely tests their ability to withstand boredom.

Finally, some officers find that helping inmates cope with stress helps them to cope with their own. If the officer appears inconsistent, unfair, uncaring, and hostile, it is very likely that he or she will hear complaints from inmates who react to his or her personal behavior. Those officers who do not exhibit such traits will hear complaints about the behavior of those officers who do, and about the institution in general. From the officer's perspective, to reduce inmate problems is to reduce one's own problems. Informally allowing inmates a degree of personal autonomy also helps officers increase their own control over their work. Protecting inmates from each other protects the officer from the danger involved in breaking up physical conflicts. Officers as well as inmates reap the benefits when correctional officers meet the challenges of helping inmates cope with stress.

REFERENCES

de Beaumont, G., & de Tocqueville, A. *On the penitentiary system in the United States.* Carbondale, IL: University of Southern Illinois Press, 1964.

Glaser, D. *The effectiveness of a prison and parole system.* Indianapolis: Bobbs-Merrill, 1969.

Haney, C., Banks, C., & Zimbardo, P. Interpersonal dynamics in a simulated prison. In R. L. Leger & J. R. Stratten (Eds.), *The sociology of corrections: A book of readings*. New York: John Wiley, 1977.

Holt v. Sarver, 309 F. Supp. 362, E. D. Ark., 1970.

Jacobs, J. B., & Retsky, H. G. Prison guard. *Urban Life*, 1975, 4(1), 5-29.

Johnson, R. Ameliorating prison stress: Some helping roles for custodial personnel. *International Journal of Criminology and Penology*, 1977, 5(3), 263-273.

Johnson, R. Informal helping networks in prison: The shape of grass-roots correctional intervention. *Journal of Criminal Justice*, 1979, 7(1), 53-70.

Johnson, R., & Price, S. The complete correctional officer: Human service and the human environment of prison. *Criminal Justice and Behavior*, 1981, 8(3), 343-373.

Lockwood, D. *Prison sexual violence*. New York: Elsevier, 1980.

Lombardo, L. X. *Guards imprisoned: Correctional officers at work*. New York: Elsevier, 1981.

Mathiesen, T. *The defenses of the weak*. London: Tavistock, 1965.

New York State Special Commission on Attica. *Attica: The official report*. New York: Bantam, 1972.

Sykes, G. *The society of captives: A study of a maximum security prison*. Princeton, NJ: Princeton University Press, 1958.

Toch, H. *Living in Prison: The ecology of survival*. New York: Free Press, 1977.

CHAPTER 18

Management Strategies to Reduce Stress in Prison

HUMANIZING CORRECTIONAL ENVIRONMENTS

RONALD I. WEINER

As our prisons become more clearly complex organizations operating under conditions at best described as uncertain, the need for correctional managers capable of coping with complexity becomes ever more pressing. Managerial reliance on a paramilitary structure manned by tough guards who kept prisoners under constant surveillance and control seems to be giving way to a different correctional reality. Prisoners are more complex and demanding; their willingness to challenge authority, including through the use of violence and force, is a well-known feature of prison life. External assaults on correctional institutions by the judiciary have complemented the "revolt of the client," further challenging institutional policies and practices (Haug & Susman, 1969). Budgetary restraints and cutback management have eroded resources in personnel and program areas. Correctional personnel are becoming better organized and even militant in their demands for better job benefits and working conditions.

In addition to these forces, correctional managers also face an increasing lack of community support for reintegration programs designed to help inmates enter the community (Weiner, 1981). Community options in the form of probation, work-release programs, community treatment programs, educational release, and parole are not as accessible to correctional administrators as they once were. Prison sentences for more offenders for longer periods of time overtax constant or diminishing resources available to correctional managers. As conditions in our communities worsen as a result of economic instability, we can expect to see more violence and crime, as well as hardening of attitudes toward those who choose lawlessness as a way of life (Brenner, 1976). Instead of a trend decreasing our demand for prisons and imprisonment, we are witnessing a revival of interest in the prison as the primary tool used by our society to deal with criminal behavior.

The forces affecting prisons are extremely complex and demand a correspondingly complex set of skills on the part of contemporary correctional administrators if they are to keep prisons running, let alone manage these organizations efficiently and effectively. It might be useful to focus on some of the managerial skills and strategies that could help prison administrators accomplish their tasks in the face of environmental stress and uncertainty.

KNOWLEDGE BASE REQUIREMENTS

Any administrators confronted with uncertainty and a turbulent environment need to develop a knowledge of open-systems concepts and management techniques. The open-systems manager requires training to provide him or her with three layers of knowledge: (1) *methods knowledge* (knowledge of techniques useful in devising answers to multifaceted problems); (2) *realities knowledge* (knowledge of conditions and trends affecting the nature and operation of the organization); and (3) *goals knowledge* (flexibility in redefining goals, policies, and procedures that are desirable for the changing organization).

In order to use knowledge intelligently, the manager of an open-systems organization must keep under constant review the boundary transactions of forces generated from within the organization and those generated by forces impinging on the organization from its external environment. Competence in collecting information and analyzing its potential impact for the organization is a major requirement of organizational survival, particularly for a prison, which has the potential to erupt into spontaneous violence at any time. In other words, survival of a prison may often depend on the correctional manager's "ability to learn about the environment accurately enough and quickly enough to permit organizational adjustments in time to avoid extinction" (Thompson & McEwen, 1958, p. 29).

The manager must be attuned to the fact that stress is an inevitable part of living and working in a prison environment. Inmates are not alone in their plight of experiencing high levels of stress. One management-relevant organizational stressor is the officers' awareness that the prison administration or governor's office might be unwilling to negotiate for their safety in the event a riot actually occurs (Wicker, 1975). Inadequate resources in the form of personnel shortages may add to the anxiety of working in an already tenuous environment, placing officers in doubt, with reason, as to whether sufficient colleagues are available to assist or help out in the event of a crisis.

The manager must be concerned with *all* inmate and staff stress because conflict is an inevitable by-product of stress. The greater the degree of organizational, interpersonal, and individual stress, the more likely it is that conflict will be handled in dysfunctional ways. The management of stress, and ultimately of conflict, is a vital function of the change-capable correctional administrator (Nelson & Lovell, 1969).

The traditional rigid, mechanistic organizational design model of the prison is likely to enhance the stress reactions of both staff and inmates. A highly structured, coercive, and conflict-ridden environment produces "an alienative response characterized by distrust and psychological distance between the managers and those who are managed" (Nelson & Lovell, 1969, p. 10). As a large, complex organization, a prison does not necessarily have to operate in a highly centralized authoritarian manner with a tight span of control. Many large-scale organizations operate efficiently and democratically, with communications that are open, in contrast to limited and controlled, and a management style that is of a consultative rather than of a command or decision-relaying nature (French & Bell, 1973, p.184). Rigid organizational structures endemic to prison systems can create tensions for both staff and inmates. More important, we know that such structures tend to enhance the inmate social system and prevent staff from having any positive effect on the attitudes, values, and behavior of the inmates they must supervise (Thomas & Petersen, 1977, p. 41). Coercive tactics, rigid rules and organizational procedures, and uncaring or indifferent managerial and staff attitudes and behaviors may also contribute to antisocial feelings and behavior on the part of inmates that persist upon release to the larger society (Thomas & Petersen, 1977, p. 65).

Correctional officers are the main human resource of any prison organization. As indicated in Chapter 17, they can be used to exercise power and authority in ways that can enhance stress for themselves, the inmates, and ultimately the prison, or they can be used to help solve problems of the institution. It is only recently that attention has been drawn to the role the correctional officer plays in minimizing or reducing the suffering inmates experience in the coercive environment of the prison setting (Lombardo, 1981; Toch, 1977; Johnson, 1979; Johnson & Price, 1981). Lombardo's (1981) superb study of guards at work reveals what has long been known but has been ignored by many correctional administrators—that most officers see themselves first and foremost as human service providers acting as the institution's front line problem-solvers and referral agency (Lombardo, 1981). Officers take both a passive and a proactive stance in trying to assist inmates with personal problems. Prison bureaucracy and organizational policy, however, have done little to legitimize the human service role carried out by the correctional officer. In many respects activities of this kind performed by officers in the cell blocks are seen as extraorganizational, rather than as a functional and legitimate requirement of the role for which officers should be both accountable and rewarded.

THE MANAGEMENT OF STRESS IN PRISONS

What can be done by managers to alleviate or minimize the dysfunctional dimensions of prison life and the attendant stresses experienced by both inmates and officers?

(1) Humanize the Work Environment. Managers of contemporary prisons have the power to change the culture and character of the prison. The essence of a correctional management system that satisfies the primary tasks of security and custody while pursuing subtasks of humane care for inmates and improved conditions of work for staff is an open-system model. Such a model trains supervisors to cope with complexity, encourages communication and information flow throughout the organization between officers and inmates and between officers and administrators, involves strategies to deal with the management of conflict through the use of problem-solving approaches rather than through compromise or compliance, acknowledges stress as inevitable, and develops plans for minimizing the effects of stress on the organization, the staff, and the inmates by their mutual efforts to aid one another while living and working together in the prison setting.

Correctional administrators will need to redesign the role and function of correctional officers to include human service work as a vital and necessary facet of their job. "People work" with prisoners will need to be rewarded and encouraged by prison administrators. Encouragement and expectations for role enhancement to include human service work will also require adequate training programs designed to aid officers in acquiring the knowledge and skills they can use to perform more effectively (Johnson & Price, 1981; Weiner & Johnson, 1981). Unless officers perceive that the administration cares about their needs and their work-related concerns, it is very unlikely that officers will feel inclined or encouraged to demonstrate a similar regard for those to whom they are responsible for acting as custodians.

Efforts to change the organizational climate of the prison must involve the creation of a leadership climate such that officers feel secure in their relationships with their supervisors. A set of clear performance expectations, knowledge of their roles, consistent support, and mutual confidence between supervisor and officers enhance the sense of well-being of employees doing correctional work. Many officers do not understand what is expected of them and view administrators as obstacles to their work (see Chapter 17). Staff also need feedback of a positive nature—they need to know what a job well done looks like.

Every employee must develop the knowledge and skills necessary for resolving conflicts and differences in constructive ways. Training programs in conflict-resolution techniques would promote the idea that correctional staff work jointly with inmates to resolve differences or grievances, whether they occur between officers and inmates or between the inmates themselves. Creating a structure and climate that permit conflict resolution to occur within the prison setting would enhance the communication systems among the diverse members of the prison community and lessen the chances for unmonitored tensions to turn into full-scale riots (see Chapter 5). Research studies conducted in other organizational settings have found that most effective conflict-resolution processes employ a confrontation-problem-solving approach, using an "open exchange of information about the problem as each participant sees it and a working through of differences to reach a solution that is optimal to both" (Burke, 1970, p. 50). Blake and Mouton (1971, p. 56) refer to such a model as the "fifth achievement," in which creative problem solving permits "threats to be anticipated, and risks that result when people fail to react to be reduced."

Expanding the role repertoire of the correctional officer to include human service work combined with knowledge and skill of conflict-resolution approaches is an essential ingredient for improving the quality of work conditions for the officer. Through the development of the officers' capacities and their opportunity for further growth and security, we create more favorable attitudes among staff leading to the potential for job satisfaction.

(2) Create Alternative Institutional Structures. The traditional organizational structure of most prison settings provides little opportunity for the organization to adapt itself to changing environmental conditions. Given the range of different types of inmates and correctional officers, we can attain a more flexible system by developing a variety of organizational structures and climates within the confines of a single institutional setting. Experience and research (for example, see Levinson & Kitchener, 1966) have shown that officers and inmates can be matched effectively by personality type and that inmates can also be matched to each other in terms of personality attributes in determining housing or cell assignments.

Different units can also be managed differently. Some institutional units may require tight organizational structure, with rigid rules and no input on the part of inmates regarding their living arrangements. Other self-contained living units may be more open and flexible, with fewer rules and more input by inmates regarding decisions affecting them. In some units, victimization may neither be allowed nor tolerated. Other units may be provided with leeway to become more high-risk environments. It is impossible, of course, to dictate how such differential environments would be designed given differences among institutions. Nevertheless, it seems both feasible and desirable to experiment on the degree to which such settings could be created and to examine the effects such environments migh have on reducing stress among inmates and staff and, under certain conditions, providing viable contexts for treatment (see Chapter 14).

(3) Design Strategies for Handling Job Stress. Programs aimed at improving employees' physical and psychological health and emotional ability to resist stress are increasing significantly in both the public and private sectors. Organizational stress-prevention programs have not, however, caught on fully in the field of corrections, although they clearly have the potential to aid both employees and inmates in coping with the harsh demands of prison life. One of the basic management tools used in industrial and organizational settings is the "employee-assistance program" (Kets de Vries, 1979), which, in conjunction with other stress-prevention programs, can significantly improve employee health. As a first step in planning such a program for a correctional institution, the role of a stress-management coordinator needs to be created for purposes of program planning, development, implementation, and evaluation. This person may be a seasoned correctional officer who is trusted by his or her colleagues for competence and interpersonal skills. The role of the coordinator is to oversee the operation of the employee assistance program and other stress-prevention programs developed by the organization.

A similar program could be developed for the inmates as well, with inmates serving in the role of inmate-assistance program counselors. By creating a focal role for inmates to work in close conjunction with highly trained correctional officers, concern for the welfare and vulnerability of inmates could be legitimized throughout the institution. Both an employee-assistance program and an inmate-assistance program would be ideal for identifying "high-risk" employee and inmate subgroups who are especially vulnerable to stress. A referral network within the institution and in the community could be deployed to provide an array of human services to employees and inmates demonstrating stress reactions. Training programs could disseminate information on how to spot stress reactions so that supervisors and coworkers would feel supported in their efforts to recommend help for those in need. The more legitimacy is given to the needs of the officers, the more likely it is that officers will be able to recognize stress reactions among their captive clients; by encouraging inmates to assist one another as a legitimate and desirable function, the institution also does a great deal to decrease the salience of exploitation and victimization in inmate social relationships. (An important variation on the inmate self-help theme, including a supportive role for staff, is examined in Chapter 15.) In this sense, staff and inmates might "function more as partners in the resolution of a problem and share in the responsibility for the decisions made. Clients would find their role less demeaning, and staff would find theirs less of an emotional burden" (Maslach, 1978, p. 121).

Changing the climate of the institution from one that is uncaring and exploitative to one that emphasizes the welfare of the officers and the inmates is an important step in humanizing our prisons. The traditional prison has operated as a large and impersonal bureaucratic organization, with limited concern for the physical or psychological needs of the correctional officers who work in them. Creating work environments in which officers feel valued and respected for the highly complex and demanding nature of their work will necessitate allowing them greater opportunities to participate in decisions directly affecting them. Creating mechanisms that involve officers and inmates working together, where appropriate, to solve institutional problems provides opportunities for collectively defusing potential crisis situations (see, for example, Chapter 5). Providing opportunities for inmates to work as peer counselors under the guidance and supervision of correctional officers decreases the potential for dehumanization of the client as a response to stress. Greater contact in a shared helping role would also enable both staff and inmates to provide one another with positive feedback when justified.

(4) Open-Systems Thinking. Other promising stress-reduction strategies rely upon open-systems thinking. For example, bridging the gap between the work place and the home is a significant factor in helping the employee to deal with the demands of the job. Programs that encourage spouses, children, and other loved ones to better understand the work and demands confronting correctional officers are extremely important, not only to the officers, but to family members, who can describe some of their own stressful reactions to the prison work situa-

tion (Cooper & Marshall, 1976). Employee-assistance programs can facilitate the process of helping officers' families provide them with greater psychological support and vice versa. By facilitating family life so that husbands and wives feel supportive toward one another, we create a greater likelihood to reducing stress in their lives (Burke & Weir, 1977).

Programs that encourage stronger family ties among inmates and their families play a similarly vital role in reducing the potential for stress reactions among inmates. Research has clearly shown that inmates are more likely to engage in acts of self-destruction when they feel abandoned by loved ones (Toch, 1975; Johnson, 1977). The benefits of encouraging programs of visitation and other family events far outweigh the risks associated with managing the problems of illegal contraband.

Opening the institution to the community by encouraging various programs of education, recreation, cultural enrichment, entertainment, vocational development, and perhaps even the importation of some business or industrial enterprises that provide work can also significantly decrease the stressful conditions inherent in our prisons. Expanding the institution into the community can make reintegration an ongoing process rather than an event reserved for those inmates who are about to be released. As a means of facilitating this process, correctional officers can be assigned responsibility for exploring opportunities in the community as a regular part of their duties. In a sense, the officer could become an organizational link (Pruden, 1971) for the institution, opening it to its environment by developing resources that could be imported back into the institution. Such diversification of the officers' work roles and work environments could significantly reduce many of the stresses inherent in remaining constantly behind the walls of a penal institution.

Efforts on the part of correctional administrators to deal with problems of stress must focus on both personal and organizational strategies. The two facets are intimately linked. For example, if officers feel they personally have no power to cope with the pressures they are experiencing, they may feel hopelessly trapped at work. On the other hand, the absence or presence of organizational support available to the officer can make a tremendous difference in the quality of the officer's coping efforts "if he feels that the organization is in there pitching with him closely, and working just as hard as he is in solving the problem" (Burke, 1976, pp. 243). It is quite possible, if not probable, that the same holds true for inmates, in terms of how much support they believe is available from officers and their own ability to cope with stressful conditions.

(5) Miscellaneous Stress-Reduction Options. Career development programs, job rotation and training programs, efforts to spell out clearly the criteria for evaluation and promotion, and responsiveness to complaints are but a few of the organizational strategies found to be effective in reducing stress (Kets de Vries, 1979). Other management actions found to be useful for reducing the experience of distress include job enrichment, work redesign, and performance planning programs. While heavily oriented to the profit-making private sector, the use of these approaches in correctional institutions might significantly enhance the role of and decrease the stress of, the correctional officer (see Quick & Quick, 1979; Newman & Beehr, 1979).

On the individual level there are a variety of stress-preventive techniques that have been found to be effective. Some of these programs are symptom directed (autogenic training and biofeedback techniques), while others are more generalized (relaxation techniques). Psychotherapy programs are effective on an individual level to help more seriously stressed employees cope with the demands of the work environment (see Chapter 2).

For any of these programs to work, we need enlightened correctional administrators. The change-capable correctional administrator so vividly described in 1969 in a study by the Joint Commission on Correctional Manpower and Training has yet to be achieved as the norm in our correctional institutions, but it offers the best hope we have for humanizing our prisons in the face of increasing complexity:

> It is the individual manager himself who must recognize the essentiality of continuing development and of the struggle against the spector of personal obsolescence. Ultimately the goal is to build a self-renewing correctional system in which positive and negative feedback continually adjusts the system's path, keeping it pointed toward existing goals and helping it to establish new ones. A self-renewing system will require self-renewing managers [Nelson & Lovell, 1969, p. 95].

The skills required for the "self-renewing" correctional manager include the ability to understand and manage human systems. Perhaps conceptual skills are the most significant, for they represent the ability to see the organization as a whole and to recognize how the various functions and constituent groups of the organization interrelate and depend upon one another. Such conceptualizations allow the manager to understand that what he or she does with correctional officers and inmates today will determine how safe our penal institutions and communities will be tomorrow. An observation made by Gaylin (1978, p. 35) perhaps best describes the essence of this link and captures the thrust of my remarks in this chapter:

> When we alienate a group of our population, when we deprive them of whatever those resources are that build dignity and compassion, we are, in time, destroying ourselves. The unity of man is no romantic myth. It is a biological factor that we ignore with peril.

REFERENCES

Blake, R., & Mouton, J. The fifth achievement. *Personnel Administrator*, May/June 1971, pp. 49-57.

Brenner, H. Estimating the social costs of national economic policy: Implications of mental and physical health and criminal aggression. Employment paper 5. In *Achieving the goals of the Employment Act of 1946—30th anniversary review volume 1.* 94th Congress, 2nd session, October 26. Washington, DC: Government Printing Office, 1976.

Burke, R. Methods of resolving interpersonal conflict. *Personnel Administrator*, July/August 1970, pp. 48-55.

Burke, R. J., & Weir, T. Marital helping relationships: The moderators between stress and well-being. *Journal of Psychology*, 1977, 95, 121-130.

Cooper, C. L., & Marshall, J. Occupational sources of stress: A review of the literature relating to coronary heart disease and mental ill health. *Journal of Occupational Psychology*, 1976, 49, 11-28.

French, W. L., & Bell, C. H., Jr. *Organization development: Behavioral science interventions for organization improvement.* Englewood Cliffs, NJ: Prentice-Hall, 1973.

Gaylin, W., Glasser, I., Marcus, S., & Rothman, D. *Doing good: The limits of benevolence.* New York: Pantheon, 1978.

Haug, M., & Susman, M. B. Professional autonomy and the revolt of the client. *Social Problems*, 1969, 17(Fall).

Johnson, R. Ameliorating prison stress: Some helping roles for custodial personnel. *International Journal of Criminology and Penology*, 1977, 5(3), 263-273.

Johnson, R. Informal helping networks in prison: The shape of grass-roots correctional intervention. *Journal of Criminal Justice*, 1979, 7, 53-70.

Johnson, R., & Price, S. The complete correctional officer: Human service and the human environment of prison. *Criminal Justice and Behavior*, 1981, 8(3), 343-373.

Kets de Vries, M. Organizational stress: A call for management action. *Sloan Management Review*, Fall 1979, pp. 3-12.

Levinson, R., & Kitchener, H. Treatment of delinquents: Comparisons of four methods of assigning inmates to counselors. *Journal of Consulting Psychology*, 1966, 30(4), 364.

Lombardo, L. X. *Guards imprisoned: Correctional officers at work.* New York: Elsevier, 1981.

Maslach, C. The client role in staff burn-out. *Journal of Social Issues*, 1978, 34(4), 111-123.

Nelson, E. K., Jr., & Lovell, C. *Developing correctional administrators.* Washington, DC: Joint Commission on Correctional Manpower and Training, 1969.

Newman, J. E., & Beehr, T. A. Personal and organizational strategies for handling job stress: A review of research and opinion. *Personnel Psychology*, 1979, 32, 1-43.

Pruden, H. O. The interorganizational link. *California Management Review*, 1971, 14, 39-45.

Quick, J. C., & Quick, J. D. Reducing stress through preventative management. *Human Resource Management*, Fall 1979, pp. 15-22.

Thomas, C. W., & Petersen, D. M. *Prison organization and inmate subcultures.* Indianapolis: Bobbs-Merrill, 1977.

Thompson, J. D., & McEwen, W. I. Organizational goals and environment: Goal setting as an interaction process. *American Sociological Review*, 1958, 23(February), 23-31.

Toch, H. *Men in crisis: Human breakdowns in prison.* Chicago: Aldine, 1975.

Toch, H. *Living in prison: The ecology of survival.* New York Free Press, 1977.

Weiner, R. I. The need for interagency cooperation in corrections: Problems and prospects. *Federal Probation*, 1981, 45(December), 35-38.

Weiner, R. I., & Johnson, R. Organization and environment: The case of correctional personnel training programs. *Journal of Criminal Justice*, 1981, 9(December), 441-450.

Wicker, T. *A time to die.* New York: Ballantine, 1975.

PART V

Epilogue

CHAPTER 19

What Do the Undeserving Deserve?

JOHN P. CONRAD

I

For the last ten years or so, I have been uneasily available as an expert witness on penology. My testimony has been taken in a number of cases concerning prison conditions, mostly originating in claims that the Eighth Amendment of the Constitution has been violated. My uneasiness arises from my skepticism that there is any need for penological expertise in these cases. Most of the issues on which my views have been sought should and can be settled by the application of common sense, the prevailing standards of plain decency in human relationships, or both.

I am available for this kind of testimony because of many years of work in prison systems and more years of observing them as a well-informed outsider. I also know that most working prison staff are reluctant to testify about the shortcomings of their colleagues. Undoubtedly there are many who are better qualified than I to pronounce opinions in court on these matters, but I am one of the few who will. When litigation is the only remedy for horrifying and needless abuse of the powers of prison authorities, I am not willing to withhold my views if they will contribute to the success of the plaintiffs' case.

To come to terms with the ambiguities of this role, I remind myself that the intrusion of the courts into the management of prisons has put prison officials on their mettle. Some gross violations of fundamental humanity no longer occur in American prisons. Some advocates of a return to the old "hands-off" doctrine that used to prevail in the federal courts have argued that the activism of the judiciary in penal affairs amounts to the presumption that judges think they can manage prisons better than wardens. Whether that is true or not may be debatable, but it is certain that some judges have shown that they know more than some wardens about what human beings should be allowed to do to each other.

Preparation for testimony begins with a conference between the attorneys and myself about the general thrust of what I can authoritatively say about the state of affairs in the prison with which the litigation is concerned. Sooner or later in such a discussion, someone will ask me hopefully, "Can you testify about the harm that confinement under these conditions might do to a prisoner?"

I always have to answer that, although I am not a psychologist, I have read the relevant literature and I am unconvinced that it has ever been demonstrated that permanent harm consistently results from exposure to prison conditions that are generally regarded as horrifying. Human beings are resilient creatures, capable of adaptation to appalling adversities. Survivors of Auschwitz and of Russian "corrective labor camps of the strict regime" have been able to function successfully after their liberation. Closer to home, I have known many men who have lived for years in solitary confinement in prisons not known for their indulgence to convicts. Some of these men have sunk into an apathy from which they could not emerge, but some have survived to succeed in productive occupations after their release from prison. A strong personality will cope with deprivation of an extreme nature. A weaker individual will be impaired for the ordinary functions of life. Many of the recidivists who return again and again to captivity have been irreversibly damaged by their experiences in prison. Unfortunately, an empirical account of this damage and of the persons most vulnerable to it that would enable the expert to assess its extent is currently beyond the capability of social science, though volumes such as this one contribute to the achievement of this goal.

The point at which punishment becomes excessive or cruel and unusual, however, need not be located by scaling the damage done to the minds and souls of those who are locked up in dirty cell blocks under the control of untrained and callous guards. Misery is not limited to prison walls. It cannot be settled that a lifetime of unemployment in the South Bronx or in North Philadelphia is more or less miserable than two or three years—or even a lifetime—in some American prison systems. That most prisoners say they prefer misery outside the walls to that which they endure inside is belied by the numbers of them who find their ways back to their cells. The notion that flourishes in some minds that time in prison should somehow be "less eligible" than the worst conditions of freedom is unacceptable. The state can do little to remedy the conditions in a metropolitan slum. It has full responsibility for controlling the conditions in a prison. It can and must set limits to the misery that it inflicts on the citizens it must punish.

This point is anything but obvious to many people in charge of prisons. Physical and verbal abuse, filth, constant personal danger, and general degradation are mindlessly and heartlessly tolerated in too many penitentiaries on the premise that nothing positive can be done with most criminals and certainly all of them deserve the conditions they have brought on themselves.

By their acts, by the harm done to their victims, prisoners must be accounted as the least deserving members of society. No amount of understanding of the causes of their crimes can gloss over the wickedness of a murder or a rape or the callous brutality of a street mugging. The consensus that people who commit crimes like these must be punished is compelling. For most such criminals, nothing less than confinement in prison is sufficient punishment. The question that I will address in this essay is not whether excessive or cruel and unusual punishment harms the person subjected to such outrageous treatment. That issue is irrelevant in a civilized nation. The issue I will address is the kind of prison that we, as American inheritors of a magnanimous tradition, should be willing to maintain. We have had much trouble with this issue. It is difficult indeed to decide how much harm may be inflicted without compromising our own standards of decency. We can answer this question realistically only when we understand what has been happening in our prisons during the last 35 years, a generation during which so many values have been reevaluated.

II

In 1958 Gresham Sykes published *The Society of Captives*, a widely admired account of the prison community as he studied it at the New Jersey State Prison at Trenton. It was a sociological tour de force, adapting Robert Merton's (1957, pp. 140-157) typology of modes of individual adaptation to the interpretation of the responses of prisoners to the measures used to control them. The studies on which the book was based took place during the aftermath of the wave of prison riots that spread through the country during the years 1951-1953. The basic questions that Sykes tried to answer were, *How is control possible in the maximum security prison?* and the related question, *What is the basis for an equilibrium in the prison community?*

I have always thought his answers left something to be desired. At no point did he consider the race problems of the prison, even then a looming element of destabilization (see Chapter 11). Nor did he allow for the power of the paroling authority in controlling behavior by its control of the time of release. In spite of these deficiencies, Sykes succeeded in capturing the qualities of the social organization of the prison of those times with a sure grasp of some of its most salient characteristics.

An essential element of Sykes's analysis was the prisoner's need to alleviate the pains of imprisonment. These pains, he said, although at the "psychological level," were no less fearful than a "sadistic beating, a pair of shackles in the floor, or the caged man on a treadmill" (Sykes, 1958, p. 64). We may indulge that comparison as understandable overstatement by a researcher who has never discussed the experience of months on a treadmill with a man who has been subjected to it. But in his dispassionate review of the pains of imprisonment, Sykes was close to the mark. I think his account of them is still a fruitful basis for study of the prison community (see Chapter 1). As Sykes (1958, pp. 65-78) laid them out, the "pains" were deprivations. Prisoners were seen as involuntary monks, doing their penitence by undergoing the loss of entitlements that free citizens expect as a matter of course.

For Sykes's purposes, the significant deprivations had to do with liberty, goods and services, heterosexual relationships, autonomy, and security. The problem common to all prisoners was to reduce as far as possible the impact of each of these deprivations on their daily lives. Clandestine procurement of various amenities, collusion with subverted guards, and other expedients enabled resourceful prisoners to cope with their deprivations. An impressive literature of prisoner adaptation has accumulated over the years that have intervened since the publication of *The Society of Captives.*[1] None of these deprivations has been changed. during the 24 years since Sykes's report, though their form has changed. Public opinion and the professionalization of penology have alleviated some of the rigors while increasing others. As I shall show presently, as to the deprivation of security, the rigors have immensely increased.

The deprivation of liberty is the essence of imprisonment. The isolation of the prisoner from the world outside—from family and friends, but perhaps even more important, from free contacts with others—constricts existence and stunts natural perspectives. So long as we use imprisonment as a sanction, the deprivation of liberty is inescapable, but the nature of the isolation has changed in most prisons. In large prison systems, classification may loosen the restrictions of confinement; transfers from one prison to another provide changes of scene, usually in the direction of more freedom. Some prison systems include "community residential facilities," as, for example, those maintained by New York State, in which prison time is served under conditions that allow for daytime and weekend freedom in the community. Work-release programs also serve the valuable purpose of reducing isolation while technically retaining custody of the offender. These developments have moved slowly, but we may expect them to increase in number and improve in quality as the cost of keeping prisoners in complete isolation from the outside world continues to soar.

The deprivation of goods and services enforces poverty on the prisoner. With no income, or at most a nominal wage of a few dollars a month, prisoners live in the barest poverty. They will not go hungry or unhoused or unclothed; they will have medical care if needed, and occasional free entertainment. This condition has been slowly improving since Sykes's time. Not enough prisoners earn a wage that is more than derisorily minimal, but their keepers are generally agreed that at least they should work and receive enough for innocent luxuries and to save for their postrelease needs. In recent years we have begun to see prison systems take the initiative in employing prisoners at wages that allow some of them to make choices as to how they will spend their money, or for what they will save it. This policy has been in effect in the United States Bureau of Prisons for many years. It is gratifying to note that steps have been taken in several states to employ prisoners on realistic terms under the Free Venture program.[2] Prisoners will never become rich from their legitimate earnings in prison, but the prospect is conceivable, if still dim, that there will be less inducement to connive or to prey on other prisoners to get the simple amenities that most citizens in free life take for granted (see Chapter 4).

In Sykes's time, the deprivation of heterosexual relationships was absolute. The idea of conjugal visits was regarded with puritanical revulsion.[3] Partly because of the notoriety given to accounts of homosexual rapes in prison, partly because of accounts of more liberal policies with respect to sexual contacts in foreign prisons, and certainly in view of the sweeping changes in standards for sexual activity in American society, our prisons are moving toward solutions to the deprivation that once seemed so proper and so unavoidable. Not only are conjugal visiting arrangements increasingly accepted, but the practice of allowing furloughs to qualified prisoners has become rather widespread. These developments would have seemed inconceivable at the time of Sykes's study at Trenton. We have a long way to go before these practices become standard; nothing is said about conjugal visits or furloughs in the current *Manual of Standards of the American Correctional Association.* But the trend is clear; we can expect with some confidence that heterosexuality will receive more facilitation and encouragement in the years to come.[4]

Sykes's account of the deprivation of autonomy was accurate and sensitive. Not only did the prison authorities assume control over the minutiae of the prisoners' daily routines by imposing an endless list of needless restrictions on their activities, but everything possible was done to prevent prisoners from expressing their desires or making recommendations for changes. A prisoner who wanted to reopen his or her case or to express a grievance would be stigmatized as a "writ-writer" and usually would suffer rather serious consequences. Worse off was the yard-bird lawyer, a prisoner who assisted less educated convicts to initiate or revive litigation. To do one's own time meant to comply meticulously with both the letter and the spirit of rules that eliminated the possibility of choice and initiative. Sykes observed that the loss of autonomy created a childlike dependency on the authorities. This was the intent, and in the mega-prison that is still common. It may well be a necessity, but it does nothing positive for the convict's restoration to society.

In the two decades that followed this study, much has been done to reduce the humiliations and the regressive effects of confinement. Grievance systems are generally accepted as necessary—if not welcome—innovations. It is unusual to find one that is well administered or that has positive support from authority, but there can be little doubt that there will be improvements over the present maladroit administration.

Federal courts and some state courts have insisted on the access of prisoners to judicial process. The "hands-off" doctrine that prevailed until the late 1960s has been supplanted by vigorous judicial activism. It is fashionable to decry the role of the judge in penology. Some nostalgic critics charge that all or most of the ills of prisons can be laid to the intervention of the courts. This is a nostalgia for a halcyon prison that never was and never can be. Litigation can never make a prison a desirable place to be; it can and should scrape away the abuses that have made some prisons a disgrace to American civilization. Personal autonomy in the full sense of that phrase is rare in modern life. It will never be found in prison. Nevertheless, in some prisons the ability to choose and act is real; it is potential in many others.

The situation as to personal security is much worse than it was in the 1950s. When I was at San Quentin, about the time when Sykes was at Trenton, it was a rare man who applied for or considered himself to be in need of protective custody. Certain homosexuals who were especially vulnerable or especially active solicitors were segregated, ostensibly for their own protection but really because of the disorders to be expected if they circulated in the general population. There was also a unit for the segregation of unusually aggressive prisoners; this unit was designated an "Adjustment Center" and placed at Folsom Prison, then California's only other maximum security prison. In all, perhaps 300 prisoners were kept out of the general population in the early 1950s—out of a total of about 15,000.

In 1964, according to an article I wrote a year or so later (Conrad, 1966) there were 146 fights in California prisons that were sufficiently serious to call for disciplinary action. That was a rate of 0.62 fights per 100 prisoners in a population that was oscillating around 25,000. In 1980, the last year for which figures are available, there were 775 fights and assaults, of which 339 involved weapons, in a population of about the same size as in 1964. That works out to a rate of fights per 100 prisoners of 3.31, over 5 times the rate in 1964. (I know that these rates sound absurdly pedantic, but how else are comparisons to be made?) In 1964 there were 5 incidents that resulted in fatalities. In 1980, 14 were killed, including 1 staff member. California prisons are much more dangerous than they used to be. It is not surprising that the numbers of prisoners in protective custody of one kind or another is now far into the hundreds. Relatively few of them are so confined on account of homosexuality.

A neat summing up of the status of Sykes's five deprivations would arrive at statistically favorable conclusions. As to four of them, much progress has been made to relieve the arbitrariness and the needlessness of the pains they inflict. Prisoners are no longer so isolated, so poor, so celibate, or so restricted in permissible initiatives. Without minimizing the importance of these improvements, they lose most of their significance in prisons where sudden and unpredictable violence has to be expected as a natural part of daily living. Those who have special reason to apprehend such violence—the young, the weak, the old, the vulnerable—enjoy few of the benefits of the improvements I have described. Those who are responsible for the infliction of violence on their fellow prisoners are indifferent to these considerations. Many wear the reputations that consigned them to administrative segregation as badges of honor.

The enlightenment of the new penal leadership in easing the pains of deprivation—so far as they could—might be construed as the answer to prison reformers of Sykes's generation. In minimum security prisons the results have been benign, as might be expected. A visit to the Vienna Correctional Center in Illinois regularly leads observers to suppose that they have seen the future of the prison and that it isn't all bad; the aims of penal reform have been realized beyond the rosiest expectations. But the Illinois Department of Corrections also includes Stateville, a maximum security penitentiary in which violence and the fear of violence have been ruling concerns for many years. From the definitive study of that prison by Jacobs (1977), it is clear that it rests on a tenuous equilibrium.[5] The authority of the state is pitted against the authority of ethnic gangs based in Chicago and organized with a cohesiveness and power that the prison staff has been unable to destabilize. The freedom with which narcotics are introduced and marketed maintains the power of the gangs by creating a system of dependencies that is invulnerable to official strategies intended to disintegrate it. The repressive but reasonably safe prison of the 1940s and 1950s has been converted into a community of dread. Black prisoners who have defected from the gangs apply for protective custody, where they are prepared to remain for years, as do most of the relatively few white prisoners who are committed to Stateville.

Stateville has been more thoroughly studied than most prisons—thanks, perhaps, to the sociological traditions of the University of Chicago—but the anxieties and fears that pervade this institution are far from unique. In his recent account of the changes in prison life, Irwin (1980) has described the gangs that have assumed power in the California prisons that are comparable to those that Jacobs described in *Stateville*.[6] The great increase in prison violence in California is largely attributable to the inability of prison management to bring the gangs under control. This magnification of violence has had effects on the quality of prison life that transform the old typologies, as Irwin (1980, pp. 193-194) explains:

> The upsurge of rapacious and murderous groups has all but eliminated the right guy and drastically altered the identity of the convict. . . . Toughness has pushed out other attributes, particularly the norms of tolerance, mutual aid, and loyalty to a large number of other regulars. . . . Toughness . . . means, first, being able to take care of oneself in the prison world, where people will attack others with little or no provocation. Second, it means having the guts to take from the weak.

This theme recurs frequently in the new prison literature. Jacobs (1977, pp. 157-158) reports that

> when the gangs emerged at Stateville in 1969, they placed the old con power structure in physical and financial jeopardy. For the first time, those convicts with good jobs were not . . . protected in their dealings. Seeing strength in numbers, the gang members attempted to take what they wanted by force.

Carroll (1974, p. 69) heard, during his long immersion in studies of the "Eastern Correctional Institution," that

> prison, (in the view of the tough guy—or the "wise guy" in the local terminology), is the ultimate test of manhood. A man in prison is able to secure what he wants and protect what he has. . . . Any prisoner who does not meet these standards is not a man, "has no respect for himself," and is therefore not entitled to respect from others. Sharing such definitions, [they] work together in loose and shifting combinations and alliances to aggrandize themselves at the expense of those who prove themselves to be weak.

The attorney general's report on the riot at the Penitentiary of New Mexico at Santa Fe makes a similar point:

> The rise of the new violent cliques was closely associated . . . with inmates who "spent their career going between Cellblock 5 and [segregation] Cellblock 3." . . . These "hardcore" cliques were highly disruptive and unstable. . . . With reputations for violence as the major source of power, these Cellblock 5 inmates now had a self-interest in creating disturbances to enhance their power and reputations with other inmates. According to some interviewees, the killing of other inmates can often be attributed to a killer's desire to make a name for himself in the prison population [Bingamon, 1980].

Irwin (1980, p. 212) sums up his view of the contemporary prison as "not chaos, but a dangerous and tentative order." The February 1980 riot at Santa Fe established both the dangers and the tentative character of what order there was. My own observation of that prison and my interviews with both staff and prisoners confirm the view that there was nothing in the Santa Fe situation that could not be found at many other prisons in the United States.

In an age of professionalism and altruism, the message of Sykes has been partly heard and partly acted upon. Intentions have improved, management has learned to regard the prisoner with a new-found if grudging humanity (see Chapter 18); conditions should be much better than they were when the New Jersey State Prison at Trenton was under scrutiny. In fact, however, conditions are often much worse. It takes a strong stomach to contemplate the situation of any male offender, no matter how vicious his criminal career may have been, when he arrives at a maximum security prison and begins adjustment to the state of affairs in the prison "community" in which he will have to live for months or years or for the rest of his life. If prisoners can be tough enough, they will turn themselves into the worst kind of predators, forcing themselves on the weak and thereby protecting themselves from fellow toughs, as well as enjoying the spoils of their predation (see Chapter 4). Such people are virtually incapacitated for normal existence outside of the prison. Weaker individuals must find ways, few of them compatible with minimum human dignity, to accommodate to the tough and the wise (see Chapters 15 and 16). This is not the prison of the classic prison literature. It is not the prison about which correctional standards are written. It is not a prison in which people who do their own time, mind their own business, and keeps their noses clean can expect to survive without harm and without fear of harm. Does any offender, even the least deserving offender, deserve this kind of punishment?

III

I have described a prison in which the quality of punishment is largely determined by the prisoners. Where personal survival seems to depend not on the protection of the security staff but rather on the favor of other prisoners—in effect, the most vicious of one's fellows—the quality of punishment is no longer in the hands of the warden. At the outset of this essay, I observed that the literature on the effects of confinement does not convincingly predict the harm that is done by confinement in the traditional maximum security prison. The new prison, in which fear of each other predominates, has been described with disturbing detail, but its impact on its survivors has yet to be assessed. So far, we do not have a foundation of experience on which we can draw. Although fear has always been a feature of prison life, I do not think that it has ever been so obsessively predominant as it is now. Life in protracted fear of the closest of neighbors—a cell partner, the person in the next bunk in a dormitory, another person who cannot be avoided in the corridors—has seldom been so prominent in the experience of punishment. In allowing it to exist, the state creates a new meaning for punishment. These terrifying conditions may enhance the deterrent effect of imprisonment, and I have heard this comment made by responsible officials. But deterrence is not the only consequence of terror. The dangers in the prison of terror affect the staff as well as the prisoners. I know wardens who conveniently load their desks with paperwork and thereby avoid the dangers of the inspections they are supposed to make. The claim is credible that many guards are fearful as they go to work in the morning and relieved at the end of the day that they have survived. The extremely high turnover in custodial positions confirms this claim. The advantages of a career in penology do not outweigh the hazards in the minds of fledgling guards. For their seniors, who do not find it so easy to change careers, the advantages of assignment to a tower are compelling. Life is safer on the wall, although the opportunities to distinguish oneself by proficiency in the arts of custodial control are very infrequent.

In conditions of this kind the relations between guards and prisoners will not improve. The routines of management and control will be directed at preparations for the worst, because the worst can reasonably be expected to happen. Guards learn to think of prisoners as "animals," and prisoners have reciprocal opinions about guards. The stage is set for promotion of violence, both individual and collective (see Chapter 5).

Bad as the effects on the staff are when conditions of this kind are tolerated, it is even worse that society accepts them as natural. We live in a century when inhumanity administered by governments upon persons under total control has reached a nadir of barbarism. The worst conditions that ever prevailed in any American prison are mild compared to those that horrified the world in the Nazi Holocaust, or those that Aleksandr Solzhenitsyn has described in *The Gulag Archipelago* (1974). Consider, for example, his description of life at the north Siberian facility at Kolyma:

> The prisoners were so famished that . . . they ate the corpse of a horse which had been lying dead for more than a week and which not only stank but was covered with flies and maggots. . . . Multitudes of "goners," unable to walk by themselves, were dragged to work on sledges by other "goners" who had not become quite so weak. . . . A [thief-expediter] accompanied them, responsible for fulfillment of the plan, who kept beating them with a stave. . . . Those who did not fulfill the norm . . . were punished in this way: In the winter [the chief of the camp] ordered them to strip naked in the mine shaft, poured cold water over them, and in this state they had to run to the compound [Solzhenitsyn, 1974, pp. 126-127].

This excerpt from Solzhenitsyn's numbing recital of horrors is most easily digested as an example of the hideous brutality of the Soviet regime and peculiar to the contemporary phenomenon of totalitarianism. But comparable degradation has been too frequent in too many other cultures to allow the assumption that Kolyma is somehow peculiar to Siberia. In any country, the descent to barbarism starts in its prisons. A country that can tolerate Kolyma or Auschwitz can learn to adjust to many other social controls that are inconsistent with civilized relations between the state and the citizen, as any observer of "socialism" in its Eastern European versions must know. The conclusion made by Dostoyevsky (1962, p. 194) in the nineteenth century, after his prolonged exposure to the tsarist penal regime, is suggestive of a truth that criminal justice policymakers can ignore at the peril of the nation:

> A society which looks upon such things with an indifferent eye is already infected to the marrow. . . . The right granted to a man to inflict corporal punishment on his fellows is one of the plague-spots of our nation. It is the means of annihilating all civic spirit; it contains in germ the elements of inevitable, imminent decomposition.

Dostoyevsky's metaphorical language is impressive, but logic-ridden social scientists and their administrative colleagues may ask why this should be so. Further, is it not clear that Dostoyevsky was writing about corporal punishment administered by convicts—a practice that is countenanced in few, if any, American prisons?

The answer to this question is clear to any reader of Dostoyevsky, Solzhenitsyn, or other survivors of official terror. The product of terror is hatred. We cannot inflict harm without hating the person whom we harm in order to justify what we do. We cannot be harmed and subjected to the terror of further harm without hating those who will inflict it on us. Hatred is the element of inevitable decomposition; the hatred that germinates in prisons cannot be deflected from the community that tolerates it. Impersonality is becoming to a bureaucracy, especially a bureaucracy charged with the administration of a prison. To permit violence and the threat of violence to permeate a prison community is to assure that prisoners released will infect the streets to which they return with more hatred and more violence.

We live in an age when, for reasons no one fully understands, crime seems more vicious and criminals more numerous than ever before. Some of the crimes reported in the daily press are of a nature to revolt the most case-hardened among us. The call for severity toward offenders is certainly sincere, and it is also certain that many are quite indifferent as to the consequences. But what will be accepted as the limit of severity? If it is to be a longer term in the special new terror of the American maximum custody "Big House," we shall only prolong a condition that is already beyond the control of the state. In effect, the responsibility for settling the conditions of punishment will be shifted to the most callous and brutal convicts. For centuries that has been an acceptable way of administering punishment in Russia. Solzhenitsyn's "thief-expediters," flogging their fellows into achievement of production norms in spite of themselves, had direct ancestors in the convict-executioners who were charged with flogging their fellow convicts, as described by Dostoyevsky.

The perils of permitting brutality behind the walls have been specified by two Russian masters in especially good positions to know of what they wrote. The positive advantages of decency were eloquently outlined by Winston Churchill:

> The mood and temper of the public in regard to the treatment of crime and criminals is one of the most unfailing tests of the civilization of any country. A calm, dispassionate recognition of the rights of the accused and even of the convicted criminal against the state; a constant heart-searching of all charged with the deed of punishment; tireless efforts toward the discovery of the regenerative processes; unfailing faith that there is a treasure, if you can find it, in the heart of every man. These are the symbols which in the treatment of crime and criminals make and measure the stored-up strength of a nation and are sign and proof of the living virtue in it.[7]

IV

Contemporary discourse about prisons is divided between two themes that should overlap but usually do not. Legislators and administrators are preoccupied with policy, as they should be. For them, the questions that must be settled—and as soon as possible in the populous states—have to do with sentencing policies and laws. Which offenders must be sent to prison, and for how long? What effect will proposed changes in the sentences for particular crimes have on the need for new prisons? How many prisoners must be kept in maximum security, and how much will it cost to keep them there? These are questions for statisticians and accountants, and it is proper that they should be asked and urgent that they should be answered in terms of the realistic alternatives. Legislators and administrators must think about what they are doing; without the facts in numbers and dollars, they cannot think.

It is clear that the enormous costs of incarceration must not be frittered away on the confinement of men and women who can be controlled in any other way. The estimates submitted to Congress by the National Institute of Justice emphasize this point (Sherman & Hawkins, 1982, p. 2). According to the survey on which the National Institute's projections were based, a new maximum security cell in most jurisdictions would cost between $30,000 and $60,000 in 1978 dollars.[8] In 1977, the cost of keeping a prisoner locked up varied between $2,241 in Texas to $15,946 in New Hampshire (Sherman & Hawkins, 1981). Whatever is done in prisons should be done to and for as few prisoners as possible. Both policymakers and the general public should have a clear understanding of the huge costs that are incurred whenever a criminal is convicted and the decision is made that he or she must go to prison.

Discourse about all these numbers must go on, but it is a bloodless and odorless set of questions that it must settle. The object is to create a system in which people are the units, but the enterprise must take into account the nature of those people if it is not to make bad matters worse. This is a system that turns the people who stream into prison reception centers into person-years for the calculation of the space that will be needed. In this sort of analysis it is easy to disregard the quality of the experience to be undergone by the men and women who have been converted into data for display on a table or graph.

For the courts and for the prison reformers, the theme of discourse is the quality of the prison experience. It is no longer a question of who should go to prison and for how long, but what kind of experience should that person undergo? That question and the other qualitative questions will influence the range of prison costs, both as to construction and as to maintenance, but in presentations to a budget committee of a state legislature not much is made of the qualitative complexities. The bare statement of minimum costs is sufficiently transfixing to the ordinary budget analyst. So thoughtful a consideration of the state of penology as Sherman and Hawkins's *Imprisonment in America* (1981), written by two authors with a firm command of the data (one of whom has had extensive and successful experience in prison administration), captures none of the sound, the smell, and the sullen ambiance of the prison. The numerous tables in the invaluable *American Prisons and Jails* (Mullen & Smith, 1980) are indispensable for an understanding of the dimensions of the problem, but only those who have tramped through the cell blocks and down the corridors and across the yards can translate the numerical coefficients used to express overcrowding into the reality of life for two or three people jammed into a cell intended for one.

Sykes (1958, pp. 131-132) ended *The Society of Captives* with four general principles on the determinants of life in that society. First, the notion that prisons could be somehow eliminated could be dismissed then, as it must be dismissed now. The prison can be changed, perhaps more than is generally realized, but it cannot be destroyed. Enlightened penal policy can be based on the nature of the changes to be proposed, not on a chimerical program to abolish incarceration.

Second, Sykes saw that no amount of good will can transform an authoritarian prison into something else. The nature of the repression that is necessary for order in this community of involuntary residents does not have to be harsh, but it must be firm and efficient.

Third, much less must be expected of rehabilitative programs than the cures of criminality that penologists in the 1950s sometimes thought they could effect. The successful reform of all or most prisoners calls for the impossible. It is enough that prisoners should know that opportunities are available if they want to take advantage of them.

Fourth, and, for the purposes of this essay, the most profound of these observations was that

> whatever the influence of imprisonment on the man held captive may be, it will be a product of the patterns of social interaction which the prisoner enters into day after day, year after year, and not of the details of prison architecture, brief exhortations to reform, or sporadic public attacks on the "prison problem." . . . The extent to which the existing social system works in the direction of the prisoner's deterioration rather than his rehabilitation; the extent to which the prison can be changed; the extent to which we are willing to change it—these are the issues which confront us and not the recalcitrance of the individual inmate [Sykes, 1958, p. 132].

In the business of answering the statistical questions necessary for responsible policymaking, Sykes's simple basics are usually overlooked by those who should see to it that they are put to use. The prison of today differs in many respects from Trenton Prison in the 1950s, but Sykes's four points are still essential to the resolution of the qualitative issues that American society must settle if the prison is not to be a source of malignant infection—to revive Dostoyevsky's apt metaphor.

To put these four points into as pragmatic terms as I can, the present situation can be reduced to the following propositions: (1) The prison is a fixture in our society for the foreseeable future. (2) It is an authoritarian community. Intelligently managed, it can be a benevolent despotism at best; stupidly managed, it will belie our national claim to magnanimity, becoming either a dangerous anarchy or the worst of tyrannies. (3) The only hope for prisoners is that they can improve their prospects by participation in programs offered for their benefit. No programs, no hope. (4) Prisoners will become brutal or will deteriorate in an atmosphere of indifference and hatred. Some will deteriorate anyway, and others will routinely harm and exploit their neighbors. But some will take on the characteristics of civility in a community that places a value on civility.

V

What should a prison be like? There is no getting around the need for a system and the efficiency that the operation of a system requires. Charismatic wardens with good intuitions may achieve remarkable results while seeming to ignore the notion of a system. I prefer the installation of a system in which fairness is institutionalized, communications are as open as possible for everyone, and the world outside is welcome to help maintain as natural a social order as possible in the inescapably unnatural penal environment (see Chapter 18).

In another article, I proposed that the four essentials of a decent prison were safety, lawfulness, industriousness, and hope (Conrad, 1981). Where sufficient staff is on hand to assure personal safety, where the laws and the rules are strictly enforced, there will be fewer prisoners who serve their terms while fearing for their lives. Where everyone puts in a full day of work at jobs that are worth doing and paid accordingly, there will be less time and even less incentive to engage in the disturbances, the hostilities, and the gangsterism that infest so many of our prisons (see Chapter 4). And where everyone has some reason to hope for better things to come—or could have such a reason if he or she were willing to look for it—the prison will not only be safer, but it will also be a place in which its staff can take some pride.

There will always be some violence. Violent people come to prison and are not to be immediately chastened. There will always be some predation and corruption. Too many prisoners come from a world in which the power to intimidate and the wit to deceive are esteemed values. But violence, predation, and corruption need not have the upper hand. Where rewards and punishments are fairly distributed, community disapproval will reduce the power of the bully and the influence of the conniver (see Chapter 15). Where the quality of prison life is a matter of indifference to the management, and the mere maintenance of a system is the objective, no system will long be maintained. Tragically, the slide toward disaster will be seen as inevitable only when it is too late to do anything about it.

Prisons have changed gradually, almost imperceptibly, from year to year, but over a generation the changes have been great, and many of them have been for the worse. The principles for their governance are unchanged. The harm that prisons do can be kept to a minimum by observance of these principles. There can be some benefits to some prisoners if there is anything going on in the prison from which benefits can reasonably be expected (see Chapter 14). If there is only a system in which prisoners are interchangeable units, that system will degenerate into a pernicious anarchy in which terror imposes its own values. No criminal is so undeserving as to deserve consignment to such a condition. I have seen such prisons; they are no projections of a pleading imagination. The society that maintains them deserves what it gets.

NOTES

1. A long list of such memoirs could be assembled, but I am not charged with the listing of a bibliography. Nevertheless, three such books deserve mention here; each presents in its own way some substantiation of Sykes's theoretical position. See Parker (1970), Johnson (1975), and Sheehan (1978).

2. For an account of these programs, see Auerbach (1981).

3. I recall that in the mid-1960s I had the occasion to present a plan for conjugal visiting to the California Adult Authority—as the parole board in that state was designated. It received exceedingly short shrift; a vocal member of the board dismissed the idea as a disgusting absurdity and no other members chose to dispute him. Less than five years later conjugal visiting was a reality at San Quentin, the state's largest maximum security prison.

4. Almost certainly the permissive attitudes of prison authorities toward the circulation and display of pornographic photographs clipped from popular magazines is partly influenced by the notion that such pictures may tend to support the prisoners' allegiance to heterosexual values.

5. This remarkable book describes the social systems at this prison with authority and detail and should be read by everyone interested in the problems of a maximum security prison. The chapter on "The Penetration of the Gangs" is especially relevant to my argument.

6. Irwin's (1980) book summarizes most of the literature then available on the "contemporary" prison, making considerable reference to Carroll's *Hacks, Blacks and Cons* (1974), which is an account of the prison community in a relatively small prison in New England, and should rank with *Stateville* (Jacobs, 1977) as an authoritative study of the stresses inherent in a multiracial prison community.

7. This quotation is famous, and has been cited by many writers and speakers, but I have not been able to find when it was made or in what context except that at the time Churchill was home secretary, in 1910-1911. See Elkin (1957, p. 277).

8. If anything, these costs are too low; I know of one recently constructed prison in which the cost per cell is conservatively computed at $80,000, and the cost of confinement, per capita, will approach $25,000.

REFERENCES

Auerbach, B. Recent private industries initiatives in state prison industries. *Proceedings of the One Hundred and Eleventh Congress of Corrections*, 1981, 75-80.

Bingamon, J. *Report of the attorney general on the February 2 and 3, 1980 riot at the penitentiary of New Mexico*. Santa Fe: Office of the Attorney General, 1980.

Carroll, L. *Hacks, blacks and cons.* Prospect Heights, IL: Waveland Press, Inc., 1974 (reissued 1988).

Conrad, J. P. Violence in prison. *Annals of the American Academy of Political and Social Science*, 1966, 364, 113-119.

Conrad, J. P. Ending the drift and returning to duty. *Proceedings of the One Hundred and Eleventh Congress of Corrections*, 1981, 13-20.

Dostoyevsky, F. M. *The house of the dead.* London: Dent, 1962.

Elkin, W. A. *The English penal system.* London: Penguin, 1957.

Irwin, J. *Prisons in turmoil.* Boston: Little, Brown, 1980.

Jacobs, J. B. *Stateville: The penitentiary in mass society*. Chicago: University of Chicago Press, 1977.

Johnson, R. *Too dangerous to be at large*. New York: Quadrangle, 1975.

Merton, R. *Social theory and social structure*. New York: Free Press, 1957.

Mullen, J., & Smith, B. *American prisons and jails* (Vol. 3). Washington, DC: National Institute of Justice, 1980.

Parker, T. *The frying pan: A prison and its prisoners*. London: Hutchinson, 1970.

Sheehan, S. *A prison and a prisoner*. Boston: Houghton Mifflin, 1978.

Sherman, M., & Hawkins, G. *Imprisonment in America: Choosing the future*. Chicago: University of Chicago Press, 1981.

Solzhenitsyn, A. I. *The Gulag Archipelago* (Vol. 2). New York: Harper & Row, 1974.

Sykes, G. *The society of captives: A study of a maximum security prison*. Princeton, NJ: Princeton University Press, 1958.

About the Authors

Clemens Bartollas is a Professor of Sociology at the University of Northern Iowa.

Lee H. Bowker is the Dean of the College of Behavioral and Social Sciences at Humboldt State College.

Leo Carroll is a Professor of Sociology at the University of Rhode Island.

John P. Conrad is an author and consultant who has been affiliated with a number of universities over the years, most recently as a Fellow at Cambridge University.

James G. Fox is an Associate Professor of Criminal Justice at New York State University College at Buffalo.

Timothy J. Flanagan is an Associate Professor of Criminal Justice at the State University of New York at Albany.

John J. Gibbs is a Professor of Criminology at Indiana University of Pennsylvania.

John Hagel-Seymour is an attorney in private practice in Washington, D.C.

Robert Johnson is a Professor of Justice at The American University.

Robert B. Levinson is a Special Projects Manager with the American Correctional Association.

Daniel Lockwood is an Assistant Professor of Criminal Justice at Marist College.

Lucien X. Lombardo is an Associate Professor and Chair of the Sociology and Criminal Justice Department at Old Dominion University.

Marc Renzema is an Associate Professor of Criminology at Kutztown State College.

Dale E. Smith is a Clinical Psychologist affiliated with the Society and Justice Program at the University of Washington.

Hans Toch is a Professor of Psychology in the School of Criminal Justice at the State University of New York at Albany.

Ronald I. Weiner is a Professor of Justice at The American University.

Paul J. Wiehn is the Director of Mental Health Services at the John R. Manson Youth Institution, Connecticut Department of Corrections.